CONTESTING BODIES AND NATION IN CANADIAN HISTORY

From fur coats to nude paintings, from sports to beauty contests, the body has been central to the literal and figurative fashioning of ourselves as individuals and as a nation. In this first collection on the history of the body in Canada, an interdisciplinary group of scholars explores the multiple ways the body has served as a site of contestation in Canadian history in the nineteenth and twentieth centuries.

Showcasing a variety of methodological approaches, *Contesting Bodies and Nation in Canadian History* includes essays on many themes that engage with the larger historical relationship between the body and nation: medicine and health, fashion and consumer culture, citizenship and work, and more. The contributors reflect on the intersections of bodies with the concept of nationhood, as well as how understandings of the body are historically contingent. This volume is enriched by a critical introductory chapter on the history of bodies and the development of the body as a category of analysis.

(Studies in Gender and History)

PATRIZIA GENTILE is an associate professor in the Institute of Interdisciplinary Studies at Carleton University.

JANE NICHOLAS is an associate professor in the Department of Women's Studies at Lakehead University.

STUDIES IN GENDER AND HISTORY

General Editors: Franca Iacovetta and Karen Dubinsky

Contesting Bodies and Nation in Canadian History

EDITED BY PATRIZIA GENTILE AND
JANE NICHOLAS

UNIVERSITY OF TORONTO PRESS
Toronto Buffalo London

ISBN 978-1-4426-4559-2 (cloth)
ISBN 978-1-4426-1387-4 (paper)

♾

Library and Archives Canada Cataloguing in Publication

Contesting bodies and nation in Canadian history / edited by
Patrizia Gentile and Jane Nicholas.

(Studies in gender history)
Includes bibliographical references and index.
ISBN 978-1-4426-4559-2 (bound).   ISBN 978-1-4426-1387-4 (pbk.)

1. Human body – Social aspects – Canada – History.   2. Human body –
Canada – History.   3. Canada – Social conditions – History.   I. Gentile,
Patrizia, 1970–   II. Nicholas, Jane, 1977–   III. Series: Studies in gender
and history

GT497.C3C65 2013   391.60971   C2013-902085-3

University of Toronto Press acknowledges the financial assistance to its
publishing program of the Canada Council for the Arts and the Ontario
Arts Council.

Canada Council   Conseil des Arts
for the Arts   du Canada

ONTARIO ARTS COUNCIL
CONSEIL DES ARTS DE L'ONTARIO
50 YEARS OF ONTARIO GOVERNMENT SUPPORT OF THE ARTS
50 ANS DE SOUTIEN DU GOUVERNEMENT DE L'ONTARIO AUX ARTS

University of Toronto Press acknowledges the financial support of the
Government of Canada through the Canada Book Fund for its publishing
activities.

For Myra for her inspiration and tenacity
For Charlotte, Declan, Ethan, Ezra, George, Juliet,
and Sebastian for keeping us grounded
And in loving memory of Helen

Contents

List of Figures xi

Acknowledgments xiii

Abbreviations xv

Introduction: Contesting Bodies, Nation, and Canadian History 3
JANE NICHOLAS AND PATRIZIA GENTILE

Part One: Contested Meaning(s) of Bodies and Nations

Exploring the Writing of the History of the Body

1 Epiphany in the Archives 31
KATHRYN HARVEY

2 Following the North Star: Black Canadians, IQ Testing, and
Biopolitics in the Work of H.A. Tanser, 1939–2008 49
BARRINGTON WALKER

Defining (Canadian) Bodies: Race and Colonialism

3 Embodying Nation: Indigenous Sports in Montreal,
1860–1885 69
GILLIAN POULTER

4 The Boer War, Masculinity, and Citizenship in Canada,
1899–1902 97
AMY SHAW

Part Two: (Re)fashioning the Body

Fashion, Clothing, and Bodies

5 Packing and Unpacking: Northern Women Negotiate Fashion in
   Colonial Encounters during the Twentieth Century   117
   MYRA RUTHERDALE

6 The Domesticated Body and the Industrialized Imitation Fur Coat
   in Canada, 1919–1939   134
   GEORGE COLPITTS

Contesting Representations of the Body/Sexuality

7 An Excess of Prudery? Lilias Torrance Newton's *Nude* and the
   Censorship of Interwar Canadian Painting   155
   PANDORA SYPEREK

8 The National Ballet of Canada's Normative Bodies: Legitimizing
   and Popularizing Dance in Canada during the 1950s   180
   ALLANA C. LINDGREN

9 Gender, Spirits, and Beer: Representing Female and Male Bodies in
   Canadian Alcohol Ads, 1930s–1970s   203
   CHERYL KRASNICK WARSH AND GREG MARQUIS

Bodies in Contests

10 Nudity as Embodied Citizenship and Spectacle: Pageants at
    Canada's Nudist Clubs, 1949–1975   226
    MARY-ANN SHANTZ

11 Modelling the U.N.'s Mission in Semi-Formal Wear: Edmonton's
    Miss United Nations Pageants of the 1960s   247
    TARAH BROOKFIELD

Part Three: Regulating Bodies

Transformations, Medicalization, and the Healthy Body

12 Obesity in Children: A Medical Perception, 1920–1980   269
    WENDY MITCHINSON

13 Public Body, Private Health: *Mediscope*, the Transparent Woman, and
    Medical Authority, 1959   286
    VALERIE MINNETT

14 Trans/Forming the Citizen Body in Wartime: National and Local
    Public Discourse on Women's Bodies and "Body Work" for Women
    during the Second World War   305
    HELEN SMITH AND PAMELA WAKEWICH

Re/Producing Productive Bodies

15 "Flesh, Bone, and Blood": Working-Class Bodies and the Canadian
    Communist Press, 1922–1956   328
    ANNE FRANCES TOEWS

16 "Better Teachers, Biologically Speaking": The Authority of the
    "Marrying-Kind" of Teacher in Schools, 1945–1960   347
    KRISTINA R. LLEWELLYN

17 Contesting a Canadian Icon: Female Police Bodies and the
    Challenge to the Masculine Foundations of the Royal Canadian
    Mounted Police in the 1970s   368
    BONNIE REILLY SCHMIDT

Bibliography   387

Contributors   417

Index   423

List of Figures

3.1   William Notman, "Mr. J. Taylor, posed for Montreal Snowshoe Club composite, Montreal, 1872"   72

3.2   "The Snow Shoe Tramp," ca. 1859   74

3.3   William Notman and Henry Sandham, "St. George's Snowshoe Club at McGill Gates, Montreal, 1880"   75

3.4   "Col. Hawks and Capt. Howe, Montreal, 1867"   77

3.5   William Notman, "Mrs. Colonel Wolseley, Montreal, QC, 1868"   78

3.6   William Notman, "The Caughnawaga Lacrosse Club, 1867"   82

3.7   William Notman, "The Montreal Lacrosse Club, 1867"   83

3.8   Frontispiece, W. George Beers, *Lacrosse: The National Game of Canada* (1869)   84

3.9   Francis George Coleridge, watercolour, "How We Toboggan in Canada," 1865–66   87

3.10 John Henry Walker, drawing, "Looking from Top of Toboggan Slide," 1850–85   88

6.1   "Style Winners," by Holt, Renfrew in its 1926 *Fur Catalogue*   143

6.2   "The Out of Doors," by Holt, Renfrew in its 1926 *Fur Catalogue*   144

6.3   Calgary's Thomas Pain Furrier Ltd. Float at the Calgary Stampede, 1931   146

6.4   The early and soon-expanded R.J. Devlin Co. Ltd. in Ottawa, 1909   147

7.1   Lilias Torrance Newton, *Nude*, 1933   156

7.2   John Russell, *A Modern Fantasy*, 1927   158

7.3   Bertram Brooker, *Figures in a Landscape*, 1931   159

7.4   Edwin Holgate, *Nude in a Landscape*, ca. 1930   161

7.5   Prudence Heward, *Girl Under a Tree*, 1931   162
7.6   Dorothy Stevens, *Coloured Nude*, 1932   163
7.7   Edwin Holgate, *Interior*, 1933   164
7.8   Dorothy Stevens, *Siesta*, ca. 1934   165
8.1   Lois Smith and David Adams in *Giselle*, ca. 1953   187
8.2   Sally Brayley, Jacqueline Ivings, and Cecily Paige with Canadian Naval Cadets, 1959   190
8.3   Betty Pope, Lilian Jarvis, Angela Leigh, and Lois Smith wearing hockey sweaters, ca. 1957   194
8.4   Lilian Jarvis with Canadian Mounties on tour in Washington, 1956   196
9.1   The Industrial Worker: Institutional beer ad with masculine, working-class collective focus, 1947   206
9.2   Domestic bliss in the suburbs, *Saturday Night*, 1958   213
11.1   Miss United Nations contestants pose with costumed child, 1964   254
11.2   Sharon LaRoque, Miss United Nations contestant, at Native Music Festival, 1965   259
13.1   A physician demonstrates the diagnosis of a heart condition to *Mediscope* '59 visitors   287
13.2   The Transparent Woman on display at *Mediscope* '59   289
13.3   *Toronto Daily Star*, 10 Aug. 1961   296
14.1   American Can Company of Hamilton: Diet and nutrition ad, 1942   310
14.2   "I'M A WOMAN IN A MAN'S WORLD – BUT I'M STILL A WOMAN!" 1942   313
14.3   The Nu Fashion Beauty Salon ad offered "THE MOST VERSATILE HAIR-DO," 1943   314
14.4   Nu-Mode Dress Shoppe ad, 1943   316
14.5   July 1943 cartoon: "You've got my trousers on again!"   318
14.6   1943 cartoon: "A Genie Out of a Bottle"   319

Acknowledgments

The idea for this volume was not ours. Karen Dubinsky planted the initial seed. At the 2008 Canadian Historical Association annual meeting, she suggested that we consider editing a collection of essays on beauty contests. Since then, the project evolved to broader issues of bodies and nation of which beauty contests figure prominently. We would like to thank Karen for gently pushing us to produce this volume but most importantly, for bringing us together as a team. This has been not only an incredibly stimulating intellectual process, but also it has welded a friendship. Franca Iacovetta has proven to be a tremendous help and is always supporting colleagues in multiple ways. We thank her and promise to follow her example. We hope that the collection you hold in your hands reflects the hard work and care of a large number of people. In particular, we would like to thank our contributors for entrusting us with their essays. We are deeply grateful for all the effort and time that was put into each one. These essays demonstrate the important work being done in the history of bodies in Canada. In June 2010, we hosted a workshop at Carleton University, funded by the Social Sciences and Humanities Research Council Aid to Scholarly Workshop grant. This funding allowed the contributors and editors to spend two productive days together discussing the essays and providing invaluable feedback. We believe this workshop enabled us to produce the calibre of work you will find in this volume and would like to thank SSHRC for making it possible. The dean of the Faculty of Arts and Social Sciences at Carleton University, John Osborne, generously offered financial assistance for this endeavour, as did the dean of Social Sciences and Humanities at Lakehead University, Gillian Siddall. They are another example of established colleagues who recognize the value of supporting intellectual projects of this kind.

    We were also able to hire Fiona Mantha, a graduate student from Carleton. Fiona was indispensable to the success of this volume. She helped us with numerous tasks and did so with grace, integrity, and speed we found inspiring. They say the best compliment is imitation; we tried our best to be as productive as Fiona throughout this process! Thanks for everything, Fiona. Len Husband, our editor at University of Toronto Press, was always helpful and at the other end of the phone. We have enjoyed working with him, and he proved a wonderful guide. Many thanks to Frances Mundy for guiding the manuscript through to publication and to Kate Baltais for her excellent copyediting.

    Finally, nothing we do is possible (literally) without the support of our family members and friends. Karl Reimer and Pauline Rankin helped with editing parts of this volume. Jane would like to thank Karl and Sebastian Nicholas-Reimer for their patience and love. Patrizia thanks Pauline for being a constant source of love.

Abbreviations

ACD	Association of Canadian Distillers
ANRL	American Nudist Research Library, Kissimmeee, Florida
AO	Archives of Ontario
ARF	Addiction Research Foundation
BAC	Brewers Association of Canada
BBG	Board of Broadcast Governors
BCTF	British Columbia Teacher's Federation
BCWN	*B.C. Workers' News*
BESCO	British Empire Steel Company
BL	Bertha Lawrence Fonds
CBC	Canadian Broadcasting Corporation
CBC RA	CBC Broadcasting Centre, Radio Archives
CD	*Canadian Doctor*
CEA	City of Edmonton Archives
CEA	Canadian Education Association
CJPH	*Canadian Journal of Public Health*
CMA	Canadian Medical Association
CMAJ	*Canadian Medical Association Journal*
CNE	Canadian National Exhibition
CPC	Communist Party of Canada
CPHJ	*Canadian Public Health Journal*
CRTC	Canadian Radio Television Commission
CSA	Canadian Sunbathing Association
CT	*Canadian Tribune*
CVA	City of Vancouver Archives
DBS	Dominion Bureau of Statistics

DCD	Dance Collection Danse Archives
DEW	Distant Early Warning
ECSA	Eastern Division of the Canadian Sunbathing Association
FWDTJ	*Fort William Daily Times Journal*
HBC	Hudson's Bay Company
IPA	Labatt's India Pale Ale
LAC	Library and Archives Canada
MAAA	Montreal Amateur Athletic Association
MADD	Mothers Against Drunk Driving
MACLC	Ministerial Advisory Committee on Liquor Control
MLDA	minimum legal drinking age
MLC	Montreal Lacrosse Club
MLCC	Manitoba Liquor Control Commission
MSSC	Montreal Snow Shoe Club
NAM	*National Affairs Monthly*
NCO	non-Commissioned Officer
NWMP	North West Mounted Police
OMA	Ontario Medical Association
OSSTF	Ontario Secondary School Teachers' Federation
PA	*People's Advocate/Advocate/People/Pacific Advocate*
PHJ	*Public Health Journal*
PRIDE	Please Reduce Impaired Driving Everywhere
PT	*Pacific Tribune*
RCAF	Royal Canadian Air Force
RCMP	Royal Canadian Mounted Police
RCSWC	Royal Commission on the Status of Women in Canada
RNWMP	Royal North West Mounted Police
Smith Portfolio	Lois Smith Portfolio
SN	*Saturday Night*
TDSBA	Toronto District School Board Sesquicentennial Museum and Archives
TUTS	Theatre Under the Stars
UGGR	Underground Railroad
U.N.	United Nations
UNA	United Nations Association
UNESCO	United Nations Educational, Scientific, and Cultural Organization
UNICEF	United Nations Children's Fund
WABCO	Wartime Alcoholic Beverages Control Order

CONTESTING BODIES AND NATION IN CANADIAN HISTORY

Introduction: Contesting Bodies, Nation, and Canadian History

JANE NICHOLAS AND PATRIZIA GENTILE

The body as a signifier or metaphor of the nation has been used by twentieth-century historians to represent connections between people and the project of nation building.[1] The birth of the nation and the fathering of Confederation, for example, function as figurative language that implicitly uses the (White, female, heterosexual) body to describe the origins of the nation.[2] Such significations, however, perpetuate "the body" – uniform, whole, uncontested – as a central organizing fiction of the nation. On many levels, bodies figure nation; we aim, instead, to "refigure" both categories as contested. As Carolyn Hamilton, Verne Harris, and Graeme Reid remind us, "The word 'figure' enfolds multiple meanings – as a verb: to appear, be mentioned, represent, be a symbol of, imagine, pattern, calculate, understand, determine, consider."[3] As a noun, "figure" explicitly calls upon the body, by way of shape, performance, and motion. Together, the multiplicity of "figure" encapsulates the complicated relations of bodies and of the confluence of bodies and nation.

In re-figuring the body itself as a contested category intersecting with questions of the nation, we propose "the contested body" as a category of analysis. Renowned French body historians, Alain Corbin, Jean-Jacques Courtine, and Georges Vigarello argue that bodies are literally at the "frontier" of cultural relations since bodies are at its epicentre.[4] Thinking critically about the body as contested is an approach that foregrounds the body as a contested space and pulls in other categories of analysis to refract the means, practices, and performances in the perpetual figuring of the body. As such, this collection of essays aims to position the contested body as another category of analysis towards understanding both Canadian history and the nation. As contested spaces, bodies are constructed historically and inscribed with political, social, and cultural meanings. In turn, these meanings shape historical conceptualizations of nation, gender, race, class, age, and sexuality. Questioning definitions of the body in relation to the nation also lends itself to deeper probing of the embodiment of history. Despite some dominant conceptions of history that seem to render the body invisible, bodies are a product of, and part of, the process of history.[5] In 1995, Susan Leigh Foster suggested the idea of "choreographing history" as a way of understanding the means by which bodies produce history – at a specific moment in time and by the process of researching and writing.[6] Indeed, as scholars we also have bodies. The ways bodies embody history are profound: from the intimate – scars that bear witness to the personal histories etched into flesh – to the continuing acts of colonization in Canada, where individual bodies bear the weight of an ongoing history of violence and patriarchy by way of poverty, sexual abuse, suicide, murder, and limited access to education and health care – bodies are at once produced, marked, and shaped by history as they render new ones.[7] And writing the history of the body necessarily brings bodies into contact, even if such contact is profoundly mediated by documents. Whose bodies gain recognition in the production of history forms part of the contestation we seek to highlight, and the embodiment of history – and the recognition of that embodiment – is always figured by the politics of race, gender, sexuality, ability, social class, age, and even body size.[8]

The historical approach to "reading" the contested body opens a myriad of possibilities on how best to revisit, research, and write Canadian history – a central concern of this collection. What we hope to highlight with this volume is that the body, still often unacknowledged as a basis for community and citizenship, exists in a state of competing and fractured communities. Bodies and nations must be studied in combination in order to explore the nuances of Canadian history, including the long-standing mythology of a monolithic national community often read as White, heterosexual, and middle class, a theme challenged explicitly in this volume by Barrington Walker and Kathryn Harvey. In short, our collective vision here is twofold: the essays that follow demand not only that we rethink bodies and embodiment in Canadian history, but also the connection of bodies to the nation in all of its competing forms. As such, both bodies and nations are positioned in perpetual *contest and contestation.*

Framing the Contested Body and Nation

In her 2007 historiographical essay, Canadian historian Lisa Helps argues, "Bodies can offer new ways into seemingly old problems."[9] Helps offers an expansive list of the many treatments of the body or embodiment employed by historians such as Steven Maynard, Gary Kinsman, Mona Gleason, Karen Dubinsky, Cecilia Morgan, James Opp, Helen Lenskyj, Franca Iacovetta, Cynthia Comacchio, Wendy Mitchinson, and Mary-Ellen Kelm.[10] Few of the historical narratives cited by Helps, however, focus primarily on the body or embodiment. The current interest in intersections between bodies and topics such as rape, medicine, sexuality, disease and health, and death now leads many social historians to relabel earlier monographs and essays as historical explorations of the body. The scholars listed above, for example, with the exception of Mitchinson and Gleason, do not locate themselves necessarily in the literature called "body history." The general absence in the Canadian context of a cohesive field of body history in which the body or embodiment (representations of the body) feature as primary categories of analysis leads us to question why the body is often treated in Canadian history as incidental or in an ahistorical fashion. We hope that the essays in this collection demonstrate the significant contributions of this approach in illuminating the Canadian past and contribute to the growing international literature on the history of the body.[11] Our goal is to inspire historical analyses that consider the contested body as a fundamental category of analysis.

This collection of essays is unique in weaving together interdisciplinary approaches that discuss facets of the history of the body and nation in Canada in the nineteenth and twentieth centuries. It builds on significant scholarship developed internationally over the past twenty-five years or so, and certainly, we are not the first to undertake a project of methodological repositioning of the body or questioning the connection with nation. In her 1999 article entitled "The Body as Method? Reflections on the Place of the Body in Gender History," Kathleen Canning considers "the methodological implications of placing bodies at the heart of historical investigations."[12] Canning's own work at the time of her writing focused on citizenship and the crisis of nation in Germany after the First World War. In particular, she used the concept of embodiment as opposed to the materiality of the body to explicate ideals of citizenship and the nation. Canning stressed the methodological worth of invoking the ways in which women's bodies in the context of the writing of the Weimar constitution were often representations of specific understandings of motherhood, marital status, and wartime service.[13] Our collective project offers a close look at Canadian history where invocations of the body in the service of body history have remained more limited.

Significantly, while all of the essays here address the contested body, they do so from a wide array of theoretical and methodological positions. The contested body does not advance a shared understanding of the body and embodiment or advocate a singular approach to its study. Rather, the essays that follow are marked by theoretical and methodological differences that range from empiricism to post-structuralism, from oral history to visual culture and textual readings. The origins of body history can be traced to interdisciplinary influences and, consistent with developments in the wider field of the history of the body, this collection draws from a range of disciplines, including sociology, art history, literary criticism, and even the burgeoning subfield of animal studies. What these interdisciplinary perspectives and mixed methodologies reveal is that differences in actual bodies demand differences in theoretical and disciplinary perspectives on the body and that questions of theory and methodology are inseparable from questions about the past and attempts at its recovery.

Defining "the body" for historical study often proves a difficult task. As many of the essays in this collection reveal, "the body" is an ever-moving target. Our experience as editors of this diverse set of essays suggests to us that the body is simply a starting point for historical investigations, but that point is, in itself, often multiple and murky. An elasticity in the definition of "the body" underscores body history in general. As Bryan Turner pointed out, in 1996, the body is "at once the solid, the most elusive, illusory, concrete, metaphysical, ever present and ever distant thing – a site, an instrument, an environment, a singularity and a multiplicity."[14] Three central points suture together the essays in this collection: a particular definition of the body, an intersection with nation, and the theme of contestation. First, body history is defined by an explicit examination of the sets of discursive practices and performances interlaced with cultural texts and modes of representation. It is also about the interpretation of the material substance of bodies – the flesh, cells, blood, and bones – that are not simply neutral, pre-given, biological facts; that is, the materiality of the body is never entirely distant from the culturally and historically contingent factors that render contested interpretations. As Donna Haraway argues, facts "are rooted in specific histories, practices, languages and peoples." And historical questions about the so-called facts of the body have addressed the complicated histories of how social, moral, and cultural concerns became embodied as truths about biology and sexuality.[15] Second, in this volume, our definition of body history is complicated further by the recognition that bodies are themselves individuated and consolidated through multiple practices and performances that make them complicated territory for delineating the personal and private from the shared sets of identification that form the national body. As such, the essays that form this collection are especially interested in how body history can speak to issues of nationhood and citizenship. Third, these essays reveal some of the complicated facets of the constantly contested nature of these relationships. As Roy Porter suggested in 2001, "The history of the body must give way to histories of bodies – especially in studying women's bodies."[16] Body history ultimately questions the body itself.

Our definition is clearly indebted to the work of feminist and queer theorist Judith Butler. *Gender Trouble*, Butler's 1990 landmark work, destabilizes biological and cultural foundations of the body – routinely seen as natural, a priori, and thus without culture or history. Butler called on scholars to rethink the long-standing sex/gender, nature/culture divide, the categories of gender and sexuality that constitute the body, the nature of performance and signification of corporeality, and the body itself. She writes,

> Acts, gestures, and desire produce the effect of an internal core or substance, but produce this *on the surface* of the body, through the play of signifying absences that suggest, but never reveal, the organizing principle of identity as a cause. Such acts, gestures, enactments, generally construed, are *performative* in the sense that the essence or identity that they otherwise purport to express are *fabrications* manufactured and sustained through corporeal signs and other discursive means. That the gendered body is performative suggests that it has no ontological status apart from the various acts which constitute its reality. This also suggests that if the reality is fabricated as an interior essence, that very interiority is an effect and function of a decidedly public and social discourse, the public regulation of fantasy through the surface politics of the body, the gender border control that differentiates inner from outer, and so institutes the "integrity" of the subject.[17]

Butler's work (also used by a number of our contributors) ultimately sought to question further the epistemological foundations of the body's alleged material fixedness and its representations. As evidenced in the quotation above, Butler's work also suggests a public and political role in constituting the body, and here we build from this assertion to figure our own questions on the category of the contested body and the nation. Our collective interest in this volume as body history scholars is shaped by these questions: How might we use the contested body as an analytical category, as a question rather than an unexplored unit, to examine the surfaces, fabrications, and performances of Canadian bodies? What about the contests over "the body" in general and Canadian bodies in particular? And how do those contests function to define questions of nation, citizenship, and inclusion into the national body?

The essays presented here explore the place of bodies within a specific national framework, but also they seek to de-centre the singularity of the nation. As much as bodies are in contest in this collection, so too, is the category of nation, and what unites these essays is their focus on contestations between those categories. In proposing to destabilize the nation, our project builds on recent literature that questions the discursive formulation of Canada as a nation and its implications in regard to race, gender, and historical practice.[18] Our goal in highlighting the plurality of nation is to recognize that Canada does not exist in some stable, transhistorical form, but that it is, like bodies, constantly figured and re-figured over time and place. If the nation is an imagined space, it is only imagined unequally by those within the borders.

In this collection, the authors consider the intersections of bodies and nations, but despite the breadth of interpretations and analyses offered here, there is still much to be done. To date, the history of the body remains a fractured, interdisciplinary field in Canada, and there have been few strictly Canadian attempts to draw together the literature in special editions of journals or collected editions such as this one.[19] However, French cultural historians such as Jacques Le Goff, Georges Vigarello, Alain Corbin, and Jean-Jacques Courtine, to name only a few, have focused for decades on the body as a category of historical inquiry, publishing numerous monographs and essays comprising *l'histoire du corps*.[20] Our goal here is not to define what the limits of the field should be, or the proper method of inquiry, but to challenge existing boundaries of the scholarship by focusing on the contests in and between bodies and nations and in the conceptualization of those categories themselves.

Our use of the term *bodies* in the plural is a deliberate attempt to embrace the fractures of the field as the scholarship develops internationally and nationally with significant influence from other disciplines. We make no claim to staking out definitive territory on the body in Canada, but aim to recognize the lacunae by marking out territory within the gap rather than filling the absence entirely. As Carolyn Steedman argues, "The practice of historical inquiry and historical writing is a recognition of temporariness and impermanence."[21] We acknowledge the significant and persistent gaps in body history presented here with respect to immigration, disability, non-idealized or extraordinary bodies, transsexualism, and many other forms of bodies.[22] Further, while Harvey's essay touches on the issues of actually performing historical research, there remains an absence regarding the difficulties of archiving documents and artefacts poignant for body history.[23] How are the procedures and practices of archiving in contest with the ephemerality of the figuring of bodies? The motivation behind this collection is that these essays will spark future works that will address some existing gaps and expose others not yet even identified.

Canadian Historiographies on the Body

Mapping the historiography of the body on which the scholars in this collection build reveals a confluence of interests from varied locations, although a few specific influences, namely, second-wave feminism and the work of the late twentieth-century post-structuralist theorist Michel Foucault, loom large.[24] Indeed, grappling with the development of the history of the body at times seems like wrestling a multiheaded beast, since the literature veers off in many directions. Even without explicit citation, this volume is indebted to many of the scholars who pioneered questions about the body, including Bryan Turner, Mary Douglas, Pierre Bourdieu, Londa Schiebinger, Georges Vigarello, and Sandra Lee Bartky.

Most scholarship traces the origins of the field to the mid-1980s, when a wide-reaching "crisis" in the social sciences and humanities ushered in diverse changes and ignited contentious debates, although bodies also were of interest to historians from the 1960s onwards, even if peripherally in New Social History, especially that defined by a feminist perspective. As a contemporary field, however, the history of the body is indebted, in part, to the rise of post-structuralism and the increasing focus on representations and performativity. This is largely due to the willingness of cultural historians to cross the chasm that seems to divide historical methodology and late twentieth-century cultural theory. The history of the body or body history eventually grew into a significant subfield, even if it remains difficult to define precisely. In the Canadian context, the constellation of influences in body history (social history, women's and gender history, and post-structuralism) overlapped with the key debates in Canadian historiography of the 1990s.

When scholars in the 1970s and 1980s began to question class and gender dynamics, underscoring the fiction of a cohesive Canadian identity, debates on the fracturing of the nation resulted. By the 1990s, the most contentious debates within the Canadian historical community often pivoted around questions related to political and constitutional issues and the role of the historian in these debates. Michael Bliss argued in his now (in)famous 1992 essay that the fracturing of Canadian history was connected intimately to the perceived "withering of a sense of community in Canada" that was itself part and parcel of the wider political and constitutional crises of the moment. Moreover, Bliss lamented what he saw as concern by a new and upcoming generation of historians with "more 'private history' and less political history."[25] Jack Granatstein's short book *Who Killed Canadian History?* reiterated some of Bliss's arguments and added new ones.[26] Labour and women's historians responded to the critique, arguing the significance of their work in both adding to and, importantly, fracturing the assumptions of "the national history."[27] One repeated point in the discussion, the dismissal of the "housemaid's knee," was revealing, however, in that ridicule from some national historians seemed to point directly at working-class women's bodies, as if they were somehow trivial to the country's history.[28] Moreover, these debates affected how history and historical practice were defined, and body history, as a then-emerging field, was influenced by these debates. Our contention is that far from being "non-national" categories – gender, class, and race, in addition to sexuality, age, and health – in fact, shape and define the nation as well as ideas of what the nation is and who is reflected within its often-singular representation.[29]

Developments in medical history advanced new trajectories of historical interrogation beyond the national question. Emerging from feminist critiques of the Western medical model, the anti-psychiatry movement, and later, post-structuralism's questioning of the discourses of medicine, sexuality, governmentality, biopolitics, and the disciplining of the body, medical histories grappled with notions of disease, illness, and health, as well as competing conceptions of the body in different time periods and cultures.[30] Wendy Mitchinson's pivotal 1991 work, *The Nature of Their Bodies*, revealed how nineteenth-century women's bodies were socially constructed in opposition to men's and thought of as being in perpetual crisis. Debunking the "nature" of women's biology, Mitchinson showed how biology, culture, and gender were intimately interwoven. In her subsequent book, *Giving Birth in Canada*, Mitchinson again explored the intersection of culture, women's bodies, and medical practice. Her work documented how medical interventions into the process of pregnancy and childbirth created a culture of surveillance over and discipline of the parturient body. Importantly, Mitchinson's work on the female body never accepted women as passive victims of medicine, and in her writings, the body emerges as a site of active or passive resistance and agency. In this volume, Mitchinson continues her groundbreaking work, this time focusing on the history of childhood obesity in Canada.[31]

In 1994, Linda Nicholson argued that gender went "all the way down" to the body, which stood as an important reminder of the social and cultural constructions of biology.[32] In Canada, work on gender and the body by other scholars demonstrated the complicated relationship between the socially constructed body and greater discourses and institutions of social mediation: medicine, religion, colonialism, the law, and education. As James Opp's study, *The Lord for the Body*, aptly revealed, gender and religion were important categories in defining the nation and the body.[33] Work by Mona Gleason and Tamara Myers suggested how the bodies of boys and girls within medical, educational, and judicial institutions were sites of competing discourses and both acted upon by powerful agents and sites of agency themselves.[34] That such institutions and discourses were central to the project of nation building is also significant, especially in relation to children's bodies. As Mona Gleason argued, "Children's bodies represented an important, and largely unexplored, site upon which the sometimes competing interests of adults and children were negotiated and mediated."[35] The child body itself is a contested site where parents, medical "experts," and children themselves negotiate childhood and subjectivity.

Within the imaginary boundaries of the Canadian nation, competing, if not contradicting, conceptions of the body existed in relation to health, disease, and reproduction. Mary Ellen Kelm, Patricia Jasen, Maureen Lux, and Kristin Burnett each explore the epistemological differences that deeply affected Indigenous communities under the Canadian colonial project.[36] Bodies were the prime target of colonialism, and as Kelm argued, were culturally constructed in light of this ongoing project. In questioning the rationalization of ill health among communities in British Columbia, Kelm highlighted how different Indigenous conceptions of bodies, health, and medicine continually disrupted White, Western notions, providing a measure of agency to those communities. The collected essays in *Contact Zones* explored the ways in which women's bodies in the contact zone were an essential part of Canada's history of colonialism. By centring the focus on women's bodies, Myra Rutherdale and Katie Pickles argued that "we have revealed a new way of understanding the ways that colonial practices are carried out in day-to-day lived experiences in colonial contexts."[37] Collectively, these works set the stage for exciting new directions into body history and the fruitful analysis that "bodies" can offer in the telling of Canadian history.

Part One: Contested Meaning(s) of Bodies and Nations

The essays in this volume appear in thematic categories and are further organized into sections. The first two essays in the section "Exploring the Writing of the History of the Body" grapple with significant issues of how to research and write the history of bodies. One question at the heart of writing the history of the body is: how has the body become an object of historical research and inquiry? If the concept of the body is an invention of the twentieth century, as purported by Courtine, then this is attributable largely to the introduction of various theoretical frameworks including the introduction of psychoanalysis by Sigmund Freud to Foucault's work on post-structuralism.[38] These theorists introduced the possibility of the material as constructed and always unstable. Cultural historians who study the body draw on these theories since they allow us to focus on senses and epistemology as legitimate sites of analytical entry. The two essays in this section underline the problems and challenges with using such sites and pose possible historiographical movement towards resolving them.

Kathryn Harvey asks probing questions concerning the current shape of historical research and common historiographical narratives. Harvey uses the metaphor of suturing to question the narrative structure of Canadian history as disembodied. She argues that this narrative is disembodied since it consistently reifies colonialism and violence. In this self-reflexive essay, Harvey reaffirms the theme of materiality (also explored in Toews's essay) and subtly questions how history continuously reinscribes present-day bodies. In particular, these opening essays provide a platform for ongoing debate on body historiography and historical practice in Canada.

In his earlier work on murder trials of African-Canadian women, Barrington Walker argued that African-Canadian women's bodies were themselves a site of struggle and that competing discourses of Black masculinity inscribed themselves on the bodies of Black women.[39] For the essay in this volume, Walker draws on Foucault's notion of biopolitics to show the discursive construction of the racialized body through an exploration of the genealogy of H.A. Tanser's research on Blacks in southern Ontario in relation to the persistent, nationally held mythology around the Underground Railroad. In particular, Walker addresses how the contemporary narrative of this Canadian myth continues to exploit and erase discourses and lived experiences of Blacks in Canada. Walker explores and explodes the enduring romanticized discourse of the Underground Railroad using Tanser's ideas as they connect with biopolitics and the pseudoscience of racially driven educational psychology (namely, IQ testing) to produce a particular racialized body.

A number of essays in this volume explore how race and gender delineated hierarchical claims to citizenship. The second section, "Defining (Canadian) Bodies: Race and Colonialism," explicitly documents how racialized bodies mediated not only citizenship, but also confronted the view of the Canadian nation as implicated in a colonial project designed to institutionalize Whiteness as a gendered and racialized corporeal legacy. Discourses about the body, especially those that emphasized muscularity, manliness, and bravery as central to the survival of the nation (both in domestic and international arenas), played a part in ensuring that activities from sporting events to armed conflict reflected these constructed and contested notions on the very bodies of the men and women participating. The racialized and gendered hierarchies at the core of imperialism, colonialism, and White-settler society helped to mitigate the making of White and Christian citizens. In her work on gender, racism, commodity culture, and imperialism, Anne McClintock locates this meaning making as a ritualized practice used by European colonizers as both a fetishizing process and a way to legitimize the imperial project itself.[40] This discursive process involved showing systemically how the colonizer's body (whether in the form of a French woman, a lacrosse player, or soldier) used social and political tools such as cultural appropriation, performance, and language to materially "make" bodies "Canadian."

Gillian Poulter's essay on Victorian Montreal contributes to understanding the relationship among race, colonization, bodily performance, and clothing. Invoking Judith Butler's idea of performativity, Poulter argues that White settlers' adoption and performance of Indigenous sports, specifically, snowshoeing, lacrosse, and tobogganing, defined and provided a racialized embodiment of the Canadian nation. Poulter's work also extends much needed corporeal analysis into the history of athleticism and Canadian sport, but does so as a way of documenting how colonialists performed indigeneity – how they appropriated a colonial landscape and racialized bodies to create their own nation.[41] Deeply inscribed into the very bodies of colonizers and Indigenous peoples in Canada, we must acknowledge the colonial project as having a corporeal legacy.

Amy Shaw's chapter in this section engages with the production and performance of masculinity and femininity as well as imperialism and nation. In the early years of body history, work on gender and sexuality tended to focus on femininity and the construction of the female body in relation to what seemed to be a persistently normative male body. Shaw's essay on Canadian soldiers' bodies during the Boer War studies the connections between military manliness and the male body in the context of an imperial contest that subtly challenged the long-standing Cartesian mind/body split so integral to some nineteenth-century masculinities. Shaw reveals that exploring constructions of masculinity during the Second Anglo-Boer War can illuminate important facets of imperialism and citizenship written onto the bodies of young, Canadian soldiers.

Part Two: (Re)fashioning the Body

Consumerism has been one of the great markers of nation building and modernity. The section "Fashion, Clothing, and Bodies" aims to illustrate how consumerism and fashion are in a continuous conversation with notions of the nation and bodies as contested. Consumer culture and the rise of "mass markets" were far from homogeneous phenomena. In her book on beauty, race, and the cosmetic industry from the late nineteenth to the mid-twentieth century in the United States, Kathy Peiss reminds us that "the term 'mass market' implies both a standardized product and a standardized consumer, but in fact it conceals important difference along racial lines."[42] The mass production of goods made fashion accessible to certain sectors of Canadian society but the messages and social codes these widely available goods helped to define shaped social relations of race, gender, and class. In the period from the 1920s to the 1960s, fashion (and make-up) was synonymous with the female body; to be feminine was, by definition, to be fashionable. Women were both the consumers of fashion and its material subject. Clothing, who wore it, how they wore it, in what context, became a way to differentiate oneself based on race and class, thereby reinforcing racialized and gendered hierarchies at the centre of nation building.

Both Myra Rutherdale and George Colpitts demonstrate how mass consumption, advertising, and mass production altered bodies in a variety of ways – shaping their actual materiality as well as the way they were dressed, stylized, cared for, and of course, seen. Far from being a new area of research, scholars such as Donica Belisle, Cheryl KrasnickWarsh, and Keith Walden explore the nexus of bodies and goods in their studies.[43] Here, however, Rutherdale shows how discourses of hygiene along with fashion led to hybridization, which, in turn, reveals how colonization plays a major role in the racialization of embodiment, especially in regard to Indigenous populations. Using a number of examples, Rutherdale analyses the cultural negotiations of Indigenous bodies in relation to constructions of spaces. She focuses on the "the North" and "the South," discourses of hygiene, and how colonization shaped seemingly neutral practices of bodily care, comportment, and attire with specific racial discourses.

A number of the essays consider aspects of the culture of consumption and the connections between bodies and goods inspired by the recent cultural turn. Colpitts focuses on consumerism, gender, and class, as well as the intersection of human and animal bodies in shaping particular meanings of Canadian modernity. Colpitts argues that women's bodies not only were remade by modern practices of consumption, but also they were refashioned by animal bodies through changing practices of fur processing – what he terms "trickster transformations" of "second skins." As Colpitts shows, the impulse to consume wove together industrial changes, women's bodies, class relations, and individual consumer practices into the wider web of Canadian modernity. Like Poulter and Rutherdale, Colpitts demonstrates how consumer goods refashioned bodies with implications for the nation. In this case, fur coats suggested a rather rapid shift in Canadian women's place within the nation, but one still structured by paternalism and traditional women's roles. The fur coat also connected Canadian women in local contexts to an international sphere of fashion and design.

In his work on the Toronto Industrial Exhibition, Keith Walden analysed the multifaceted ways that bodies and goods came together in fairground displays. Illustrating how "the meaning of goods was inextricably bound to the meaning of bodies," Walden's analysis focused both on the material displays as well as how they entwined in a wider politics of looking.[44] The "Contesting Representations of the Body/Sexuality" section highlights how the visual representation of bodies played a critical part in understanding sexuality as imbued with questions of modernity, morality, and social regulation. The essays in this section showcase how bodies in ads, art, and dance are particularly vulnerable to normative prescriptions of sexuality. In these examples, the point of analytical entry is the body, not sexuality since it is the representation of the body that is the prime focus of the eliciting femininity or masculinity, morality, and heterosexuality. Transgression is not acceptable precisely because these bodies must speak to normative and national ideals of heterosexual hegemony. Various essays in this collection shed light on how bodies read and interpreted by their contemporaries marked out differences visually. This theme receives explicit attention in the multidisciplinary essays by Pandora Syperek and Allana Lindgren. In her essay on censorship and interwar Canadian nudes, art historian Syperek explains why certain paintings of nude women, but especially those by Lilias Torrance Newton, received vigilant scrutiny by Canadian moral crusaders and by some allegedly progressive members of the Canadian art community. Syperek concludes that certain paintings offended gendered codes, revealing fault lines of sexuality, nationality, and female respectability. The creation and transgression of changing gendered codes across the twentieth century is also a theme that reverberates through the essays by Lindgren and Cheryl Krasnick Warsh and Greg Marquis. A historian of dance, Lindgren offers a careful analysis of how dancers' bodies legitimized this art form in Canada after the Second World War. Embodying popular narratives of proper sexuality, gender, race, and citizenship, dancers' bodies conveyed dominant postwar ideologies that reinforced White and heterosexual Canadian-ness while attempting to make ballet part of the Canadian mainstream. As Lindgren aptly reveals, Canadians needed encouragement to consider ballet as part of the cultural landscape.

Warsh and Marquis, in their chapter on alcohol advertisements, explore how bodies and goods fit within Canadian society and culture. Canadians' relationship with alcohol has been particularly fraught, and in attempting to overcome this anxiety (and sell their product), advertisers deployed representations of bodies in particular ways. In examining a wide range of advertisements, Warsh and Marquis uncover how the gendered inscriptions of both bodies and goods inflected each other. Warsh and Marquis's essay also reflects the recent visual turn in the historiography.

Arguably, beauty pageants are one of the best examples through which to illustrate the connection between bodies and nation. The bodies of beauty contestants and the winners of the contests (whether it be Miss Donut or Miss Canada) are the sites of political and cultural inscriptions of citizenship, gender, race, and nation.[45] The essays in the section entitled "Bodies in Contests" play with the notion of contestation not only because it deals specifically with beauty contests but also because the beauty pageants in question were not major national events. Beauty contests that did not reach national or international prominence forced both the organizers and the contestants to exaggerate the reasons why the bodies in contest fit with shared ideals of citizenship and nation – indeed, why these bodies could be included in the "imaginary nation."[46] Sarah Banet-Weiser points to the impossible task of assimilating difference at the heart of beauty pageants since "despite efforts to uphold a universal standard of beauty for all women, the representation of women who have been historically excluded from this standard renders beauty itself an unstable category of experience."[47] The fact that in pageants, the bodies in contest (literally) are female bodies solidifies the artificial racial and gendered hierarchies imposed by beauty pageants.

Mary-Ann Shantz uncovers (pun intended) the history of beauty pageants at nudist resorts in postwar Canada. The nude body – both in representation and live performances – gave many Canadians an avenue to express concern over those bodies as well as related cultural, social, and political changes. From the Ontario Medical Association to the Art Gallery of Toronto to the Canadian Sunbathing Association, these diverse groups tapped into representations of female nudity for a variety of purposes. Echoing a theme similar to Helen Smith and Pamela Wakewich's notion of the body surface, Shantz argues that nudist pageants appealed to a sense of "embodied citizenship" thereby establishing nudist practices themselves as good, wholesome, and legitimate. As such, these particular pageants allowed nudists a space for moral contestation, particularly around notions of the obscene – a theme touched upon by Syperek in this volume.

By mid-twentieth century, Canadian nationalism was contested again, this time centred on the place of francophones and immigrants in the nation. Beauty contests were used extensively by municipal, provincial, and federal governments and by many different types of organizations to promote ideals of race, ethnicity, and Whiteness as the Canadian nation struggled to define its place in the international community as cohesive yet accepting of diversity. Tarah Brookfield's essay on the Miss United Nations pageant, organized in the 1960s by Edmonton's United Nations Association, reveals a particular mix of identity formation for both individuals and groups based on local, national, and international discourses. The contestants' bodies of the Miss United Nations pageant effectively solidified Canada's message as a "tolerant" home for multicultural communities and projected an image of a unified nation extolling the values of a youthful White nation to the global community. Taken together, the chapters authored by Shantz and Brookfield document the remarkable flexibility of the beauty contest format in defining beauty, the female body, and women's public roles in postwar Canada.

Part Three: Regulating Bodies

For all its "natural" and ahistorical characteristics, the modern body seems to have been an almost constant source of distress. The section "Transformations, Medicalization, and the Healthy Body" continues an established approach in body history in which notions of health and disease are used to invoke the contested state of bodies; however, this area of historical inquiry is far from exhausted. Of particular significance is how this scholarship enables historians to make clear links between the state of bodies, specifically, women's and children's bodies, and the state of the nation. In other words, healthy or diseased bodies (however these terms are defined) are often used as metaphors to invoke ideals of the nation as weak or robust, dying or thriving. The state's investment in the health of its citizens and the productive bodies that comprise the labour force has often translated into medicalized discourses that focuses on diseased bodies in whatever form they may take including obese bodies or the bodies of people living with disabilities. The result has often been an onslaught of regulations, systems of surveillance, and medical "advice" desperate to control bodies.[48]

Wendy Mitchinson investigates how fat bodies, especially those of children, garnered medical attention from Canadian doctors over the course of the twentieth century. In exploring the discourse about children's bodies, Mitchinson argues that the nation was particularly concerned and invested in the idea of a healthy body weight as children "represent a strong future for a nation; unhealthy children threaten it." Although Mitchinson reveals that, for most of the twentieth century, malnutrition was a far more pressing issue, it remained connected to obesity, which continued to spark concerns over whether or not successive generations of Canadians would be able to embrace their role as "full contributing citizens." Trying to define and establish normative categories for bodies proved to be a difficult task with respect to a host of categories, including weight, health, and sexuality. As Foucault's work reveals, power is always exercised, not held. As such, establishing normative codes for bodies meant both establishing non-normative bodies (for example, "the fat body") as well as allowing for expressions of transgression and resistance.

The themes of medicalization, discourses of health, and defining normative bodies run through a number of the essays in this volume. Valerie Minnett draws attention to a public health campaign called *Mediscope* initiated by the Ontario Medical Association that introduced viewers to the interiority of the body. Minnett examines the medical model, Lehra, and how the exhibition of her reveals the intersections among medicine, public health campaigns, education, and gender. By historicizing *Mediscope*, Minnett showcases the medical gaze and the construction of expert knowledge in Canada mediated through the mechanized transparent body of Lehra, the model of a twenty-eight-year-old German woman. Like Mitchinson's piece on the medical community and children's bodies, Minnett explains how representations of women's bodies became a central vehicle through which medical discourses formed, manipulated, and inscribed knowledge for the Canadian masses.

Continuing the theme of health, women's bodies, and the nation, Helen Smith and Pamela Wakewich use anthropologist Terence Turner's idea of "the social skin," conceptualized as a literal and metaphorical surface through and upon which culture and self are negotiated. Smith and Wakewich insist that we rethink long-standing dichotomous categories like representation/lived experience, public (society)/private (the home), and prescribed norms/subjectivity. Focusing on the body of female war plant workers in Fort William, Ontario, the authors suggest that women's "body work" reflects a deep permeability in relation to spaces (home, the local, nation) and discourses of health and family. This essay explores the connections and disjunctures in representations of the body and the actuality of embodiment.

"Re/Producing Productive Bodies" is a theme of growing scholarly interest among body scholars. The driving question for them focuses on how embodiment is a historically defined process that shapes both the discourse and materiality of flesh. Cynthia Comacchio's article, for example, on human machinery in early twentieth-century Canada reveals how machine metaphors sutured together science, medicine, public health campaigns, and workers' bodies. Industrial capitalism and metaphors of the body as a machine shaped discourses (industrial, scientific, and medical) on how the body becomes envisioned as a productive body.[49] This section examines the experience of capitalist, social, and cultural demands on bodies by tracing the struggle these bodies endure as they exert agency in a highly regulated framework.

Bodies as produced *and* productive forms a secondary theme in Smith and Wakewich's essay but this is a particularly salient theme in the chapters by Anne Frances Toews, Kristina Llewellyn, and Bonnie Reilly Schmidt. Anne Toews reminds us that discourses of the body and the processes of embodiment literally have an effect on the flesh. In her study of working-class bodies and the Canadian Communist Press, Toews writes, "It was through and to working-class bodies that the CPC delivered both its negative critique of capitalism and the positive prom- ise of socialism, demonstrating its recognition that the impulse to action – be it revolutionary or reactionary – is inseparable from the living flesh in which it is contained." Toews argues that resisting the physical impact of industrial capitalism bent on maximizing and exploiting the produc- tive bodies of workers included the detailed retelling in the Communist press of how work distorts and reshapes.

Llewellyn's chapter documents the central role that heteronormativity played in the reading of female teachers' bodies to facilitate notions of postwar democracy and citizenship. As her oral histories reveal, female teachers performed their bodies in controlled and careful ways because of the significance attached to their bodies as examples for the next gen- eration of Canadian students, underscoring an important aspect of re/ producing national bodies. Llewellyn's analysis, informed by Judith But- ler, unveils the interplay of adult and child bodies, nationalism, domestic containment, and the complicated relationship between the public and the private.

Like Llewellyn, Schmidt asks us to rethink the connections between gender and citizenship, on the one hand, and the individual body and the national one, on the other. Schmidt argues that women's bodies, metaphorically and materially, have challenged the masculine norms of the Royal Canadian Mounted Police and its place in the national narra- tive.[50] Her essay reveals how deeply ingrained constructions of sexual difference continued to shape women's lives into the 1970s.

Conclusion

The significance of this collection lies in its effort to speak to the his- torical study of bodies and nations and its documentation of the diverse manner in which historians approach such topics and interpret evi- dence related to bodies and their ongoing contestations. In proposing the contested body as an analytical category, we aim to uncover the many points and multiple ways that the body has been historically produced through complicated negotiations – sometimes obvious and sometimes subtle – but always political. In re-figuring the body and its relationship to nation, ultimately we call into question the stability of both and, in the scholarship that follows, point to ways that bodies have been con- tested, figured, and re-figured over the course of Canadian history. In her recent book on companion animals, Haraway writes, "It is a writing that I must do, because it's about a legacy, an inheritance of the flesh.

To come to accept the body's unmaking, I need to remember its becoming, I need to recognize all the members, animate and inanimate, that make up the knot of a particular life."[51] Haraway's words reflect what we collectively offer here – analyses of makings and unmakings, becomings and unbecomings, particular lives at particular moments, and a shared sense of the need to write about an inheritance – national, personal, political, and evolving. Overall, however, this collection represents what we hope is the first of more collections devoted to scholarship on the history of bodies in Canada.

Notes

1 For example, "It was a vision of Canada controlling her own destiny, retaining a free association with the mother country but standing on her own feet and embarking on a bold course of territorial and economic expansion and on the continental destiny that now lay before her." Edgar McInnis, *Canada: A Political and Social History* (Toronto: Holt, Rinehart and Winston, 1982), 361.

2 For an excellent analysis on the symbolism of women's bodies in the service of Canadian nationalism, see Christina Burr, "Gender, Sexuality, and Nationalism in J.W. Bengough's Verses and Political Cartoons," *Canadian Historical Review* 83, no. 4 (2002), 505–54.

3 Carolyn Hamilton, Verne Harris, and Graeme Reid, Introduction, in *Refiguring the Archive*, ed. Carolyn Hamilton, Verne Harris, Jane Taylor, Michele Pickover, Graeme Reid, and Razia Saleh (Dordrecht: Kluwer Academic, 2002), 7.

4 The concept of the body as frontier is explained further in the following quote: "L'originalité ultime de cette expérience est d'être à la croisée de l'enveloppe individualisée et de l'expérience sociale, de la référence subjective et de la norme collective. C'est bien parce qu'il est 'point frontière' que le corps est au Coeur de la dynamique culturelle." See A. Corbin, J.J. Courtine, and G. Vigarello, *Histoire du corps: De la Renaissance aux Lumières*, vol. 1 (Paris: Seuil, 2005), 10–11.

5 On the disembodying of history and its associated gender politic in the development of "professional" history, see Bonnie G. Smith, *The Gender of History: Men, Women and Historical Practice* (Cambridge, MA: Harvard University Press, 2000).

6 Susan Leigh Foster, "Choreographing History," in *Choreographing History*, ed. Susan Leigh Foster (Indianapolis, IN: Indiana University Press, 1995), 10–11.

7 For powerful first-person accounts of these two facets merging, see Jarvis Jay Masters, "Scars," in *The Body Reader: Essential Social and Cultural Readings*, ed. Mary Kosut and Lisa Jean Moore (New York: New York University Press, 2010), 329–31, and Emma LaRocque, "My Hometown Northern Canada South Africa," in *Making Space for Indigenous Feminism*, ed. Joyce Green (Black Point, NS: Fernwood, 2007), 216–20.

8 Recent scholarship on children's bodies and in fat studies highlights the importance of considering size. For two examples from the Canadian scholarship, see Mona Gleason, "Size Matters: Medical Experts, Educators, and the Provision of Health Services to Children in Early to Mid-Twentieth-Century English Canada," in *Healing the World's Children: Interdisciplinary Perspectives on Child Health in the Twentieth Century*, ed. Cynthia Comacchio, Janet Golden, and George Weisz (Montreal and Kingston: McGill-Queen's University Press, 2008), 176–202, and Jenny Ellison, "'Stop Postponing Your Life until You Lose Weight and Start Living Now': Vancouver's Large as Life Action Group, 1979–1985," *Journal of the Canadian Historical Association* 18, no. 1 (2007), 241–65.

9 Lisa Helps, "Body, Power, Desire: Mapping Canadian Body History," *Journal of Canadian Studies* 41, no. 1 (2007), 127.

10 Ibid.

11 The literature is far too vast to list here, but we will take this opportunity to highlight some of the international edited collections that take body history as its primary subject. See Catherine Gallagher and Thomas Laqueur, eds., *The Making of the Modern Body: Sexuality and Society in the Nineteenth Century* (Berkeley, CA: University of California Press, 1987); Jennifer Terry and Jacqueline L. Urla, eds., *Deviant Bodies: Critical Perspectives on Difference in Science and Popular Culture* (Indianapolis, IN: Indiana University Press, 1995); Tony Ballantyne and Antoinette Burton, eds., *Bodies in Contact: Rethinking Colonial Encounters in World History* (Chapel Hill, NC: Duke University Press, 2005); Alain Corbin, Jean-Jacques Courtine, and Georges Vigarello, eds., *Histoire du corps*, 3 vols. (Paris: Seuil, 2005). Many of the developments in the history of the body are indebted to feminist theory. For overviews, see Janet Price and Margrit Shildrick, eds., *Feminist Theory and the Body: A Reader* (New York: Routledge, 1999); Londa Schiebinger, *Feminism and the Body* (New York: Oxford University Press, 2000); and Judith Lorber and Lisa Jean Moore, *Gendered Bodies: Feminist Perspectives*, 2nd ed. (New York: Oxford University Press, 2010).

12 Kathleen Canning, "The Body as Method? Reflections on the Body in Gender History," *Gender and History* 11, no. 3 (1999), 499. See also the often-cited 1995 essay by Caroline Walker Bynum, "Why All the Fuss about the

Body? A Medievalist's Perspective," *Critical Inquiry* 22, no. 1 (1995), 1–33. Bynum's essay underscored persistent issues in doing body history, and it has become a must read for understanding the uses of bodies as categories of analysis.

13 Canning, "Body as Method?" 508.

14 Bryan S. Turner, *The Body and Society*, 2nd ed. (London: Sage, 1996), 43.

15 Donna Haraway, *Modest_witness@secondmillenium.femaleman_meetsoncomouse: Feminism and Technoscience* (London: Routledge, 1997), 217; Elizabeth Grosz, *Volatile Bodies: Towards a Corporeal Feminism* (Indianapolis, IN: Indiana University Press, 1994); and Anne Fausto-Sterling, *Sexing the Body: Gender Politics and the Construction of Sexuality* (New York: Basic Books, 2000).

16 Roy Porter, "The History of the Body Reconsidered," in *New Perspectives on Historical Writing*, 2nd ed., ed. Peter Burke (University Park, PA: Pennsylvania State University Press, 2001), 237.

17 Judith Butler, *Gender Trouble: Feminism and the Subversion of Identity* (New York: Routledge 1999 [1990]), 185; original emphasis. Perhaps unsurprisingly given the radical nature of her critique, the book generated an avalanche of accolades and criticisms, including one pithy comment from a sceptical critic who queried, "What about the materiality of the body, Judy?" For her response, see Judith Butler, *Bodies That Matter: On the Discursive Limits of Sex* (London: Routledge, 1993), ix. The idea of seeing discourse and materiality as mutually exclusive has also been challenged by a number of scholars who note that understanding the body as a site of continuous interpretation and construction does not render the body a fiction. See Fausto-Sterling, *Sexing the Body*, Introduction.

18 For excellent examples, see Franca Iacovetta, *Gatekeepers: Reshaping Immigrant Lives in Cold War Canada* (Toronto: Between the Lines, 2006); Daniel Coleman, *White Civility: The Literary Project of English Canada* (Toronto: University of Toronto Press, 2006); Adele Perry, "Nation, Empire and the Writing of History in Canada in English," in *Contesting Clio's Craft: New Directions and Debates in Canadian History*, ed. Christopher Dummitt and Michael Dawson (Vancouver: UBC Press, 2008), 123–40.

19 We note the important exception of the anthology by Katie Pickles and Myra Rutherdale, eds., *Contact Zones: Aboriginal and Settler Women in Canada's Colonial Past* (Vancouver: UBC Press, 2006).

20 Space restrictions prohibit us from offering an exhaustive list of French body historians but for an introduction on this extensive literature, see Jacques Le Goff and Nicolas Truong, *Une histoire du corps au Moyen-Âge* (Paris: Liana Lévi, 2003), and A. Corbin, J.J. Courtine, and G. Vigarello, eds., *Histoire du corps* (Paris: Seuil, 2005).

21 Carolyn Steedman, "*La théorie qui n'en pas une*, or Why Clio Doesn't Care," in *Feminists Revision History*, ed. Ann-Louise Shapiro (New Brunskwick, NJ: Rutgers University Press, 1994), 83.
22 For more on the immigrant body and nation, see, e.g., Alison Bashford, "Quarantine and the Imagining of the Australian Nation," *Health* 2, no. 4 (1998): 387–402. For more on freakish bodies, see, e.g., the collection edited by Rosemarie Garland Thomson, *Freakery: Cultural Spectacles of the Extraordinary Body* (New York: New York University Press, 1996), and her monograph, *Extraordinary Bodies: Figuring Physical Disability in American Culture and Literature* (New York: Columbia University Press, 1996), as well as Thomas Richard Fahy, *Freak Shows and the Modern American Imagination: Constructing the Damaged Body from Willa Cather to Truman Capote* (New York: Palgrave Macmillan, 2006). On transgenderism and transsexuality and the productive body, see Dan Irving, "Normalized Transgressions: Legitimizing the Transsexual Body as Productive," *Radical History Review*, no. 100 (Winter 2008), 38–60.
23 On archiving – in a wider and institutional sense – and the criminal body, see Allan Sekula, "The Body and the Archive," *October* 39 (Winter 1986), 3–64.
24 See Michel Foucault, *Disciple and Punish: Birth of the Prison*, trans. Alan Sheridan (New York: Vintage, 1995), for more on disciplined and docile bodies.
25 Michael Bliss, "Privatizing the Mind: The Sundering of Canadian History, the Sundering of Canada," *Journal of Canadian Studies* 26, no. 4 (1992), 5.
26 Ibid. and Jack Granatstein, *Who Killed Canadian History?* (Toronto: HarperCollins, 1998), esp. chapter 3.
27 See Gregory Kealey, "Class in English Canadian History Writing: Neither Privatizing, Nor Sundering," and Linda Kealey et al., "Teaching Canadian History in the 1990s: What 'National History' Are We Lamenting?" *Journal of Canadian Studies* 27, no. 2 (1992), 123–31.
28 Significantly, the derision of the female body highlighted the largely ahistorical nature of Bliss's and Granatstein's arguments, which sought to galvanize a particular way of envisioning and practising history. For a longer look at construction of this type of history and wider attempts to situate it as universal, see Smith, *The Gender of History*.
29 The term "non-national categories" comes from Bliss, "Privatizing the Mind," 6.
30 See, e.g., Linda Gordon, *Women's Bodies, Women's Lives* (New York: Viking, 1976), and Thomas Szasz, *The Therapeutic State: Psychiatry in the Mirror of Current Events* (New York: Prometheus, 1984).
31 The obesity epidemic routinely makes national headlines especially over the rising rate of obesity in children, and the study of obesity and fat is growing

exponentially. For more on this topic, see Peter Stearns, *Fat History: Bodies and Beauty in the Modern West* (New York: New York University Press, 1997); Jana Evans Braziel and Kathleen LeBesco, eds., *Bodies Out of Bounds: Fatness and Transgression* (Berkeley, CA: University of California Press, 2001); Ester Rothblum and Sondra Solovay, eds., *Fat Studies Reader* (New York: New York University Press, 2009; and Mitchinson, this volume). For an important treatment of diet, weight control, and class with some Canadian references, see Keith Walden, "The Road to Fat City: An Interpretation of the Development of Weight Consciousness in Western Society," *Historical Reflections* 12, no. 3 (1985), 331–73.

32 Linda Nicholson, "Interpreting Gender," *Signs* 20 (1994), 83. See also Joan Scott, "Gender: A Useful Category of Historical Analysis," *American Historical Review* 91, no. 5 (1986), 1053–75. For some excellent examples, see Londa Schiebinger, *The Mind Has No Sex? Women in the Origins of Modern Science* (Cambridge, MA: Harvard University Press, 1991); Thomas Laqueur, *Making Sex: Body and Gender from the Greeks to Freud* (Cambridge, MA: Harvard University Press, 1992); Emily Martin, *The Woman in the Body: A Cultural Analysis of Reproduction* (Boston, MA: Beacon Press, 2001); Fausto-Sterling, *Sexing the Body*.

33 James Opp, *The Lord for the Body: Religion. Medicine, and Protestant Faith Healing in Canada, 1880–1930* (Montreal and Kingston: McGill-Queen's University Press, 2005).

34 Mona Gleason, "Lost Voices, Lost Bodies? Doctors and the Embodiment of Children and Youth in English Canada from 1900 to 1940," in *Lost Kids: Vulnerable Children and Youth in Twentieth-Century Canada and the United States*, ed. Mona Gleason, Tamara Myers, Leslie Paris, and Veronica Strong-Boag (Vancouver: UBC Press, 2009); Mona Gleason, "Disciplining the Student Body: Schooling and the Construction of Canadian Children's Bodies, 1930 to 1960," *History of Education Quarterly* 41, no. 2 (2001), 189–215; Tamara Myers, "Embodying Delinquency: Boys' Bodies, Sexuality, and Juvenile Justice History in Early-Twentieth-Century Quebec," *Journal of the History of Sexuality* 14, no. 4 (2005), 383–414; Tamara Myers, *Caught: Montreal's Modern Girls and the Law, 1869–1945* (Toronto: University of Toronto Press, 2006). For further work on the body and the judicial system but in regard to adult bodies and the death penalty, see Carolyn Strange, "The Undercurrents of Penal Culture: Punishment of the Body in Mid-Twentieth-Century Canada," *Law and History Review* 19, no. 2 (2001), 343–85.

35 Mona Gleason, "Embodied Negotiations: Children's Bodies and Historical Change in Canada, 1930 to 1960," *Journal of Canadian Studies* 34, no. 1 (1999), 112–38.

36 Mary Ellen Kelm, *Colonizing Bodies: Aboriginal Health and Healing in British Columbia, 1900–1950* (Vancouver: UBC Press, 1998); Patricia Jasen, "Race, Culture and the Colonization of Childbirth in Northern Canada," *Social History of Medicine* 10, no. 3 (1997), 383–400; Maureen Lux, *Medicine That Walks: Disease, Medicine, and Canadian Plains Native People, 1880–1940* (Toronto: University of Toronto Press, 2001); and Kristin Burnett, *Taking Medicine: Women's Healing Work and Contact in Southern Alberta, 1880–1930* (Vancouver: UBC Press, 2010). For another important treatment on bodies and the imperial project, see Anne McClintock, *Imperial Leather: Race, Gender, and Sexuality in the Colonial Contest* (New York: Routledge, 1995).

37 Pickles and Rutherdale, Introduction, in *Contact Zones*, 3.

38 Jean-Jacques Courtine, Introduction, in *Histoire du corps: Le mutations du regard*, vol. 3, 7.

39 Barrington Walker, "Killing the Black Female Body: Black Womanhood, Black Patriarchy, and Spousal Murder in Two Ontario Criminal Trials, 1892–1894," in *Sisters or Strangers? Immigrant, Ethnic, and Racialized Women in Canadian History*, ed., Marlene Epp, Franca Iacovetta, and Frances Swyripa (Toronto: University of Toronto Press, 2004), 90.

40 McClintock, *Imperial Leather*, 26.

41 On bodies and sport in Canada, see Chapter 5 of Colin D. Howell's *Blood, Sweat and Cheers: Sport and the Making of Modern Canada* (Toronto: University of Toronto Press, 2001).

42 See Kathy Peiss, *Hope in a Jar: The Making of America's Beauty Culture* (New York: Metropolitan Books, 1998), 203. On the production of beautiful and normative female bodies in twentieth-century America, see also Joan Jacobs Brumberg, *The Body Project: An Intimate History of American Girls* (New York: Vintage, 1998.)

43 See Donica Belisle, *Retail Nation: Department Stores and the Making of Modern Canada* (Vancouver: UBC Press, 2011); Cheryl Krasnick Warsh, "Smoke and Mirrors: Gender Representation in North American Tobacco and Alcohol Advertisement before 1950," *Histoire sociale/Social History* 31, no. 62 (1998), 183–222; Keith Walden "Speaking Modern: Language, Culture, and Hegemony in Grocery Window Displays, 1887–1920," *Canadian Historical Review* 70, no. 3 (Sept. 1989), 285–310.

44 Keith Walden, *Becoming Modern in Toronto: The Industrial Exhibition and the Shaping of a Late Victorian Culture* (Toronto: University of Toronto Press, 1997), 121.

45 For an example of Miss America, see Sarah Banet-Weiser, *The Most Beautiful Girl in the World* (Berkeley, CA: University of California Press, 1999). For Canada, see Patrizia Gentile, "Queen of the Maple Leaf: Beauty Contests in

Twentieth-Century Canada," doctoral dissertation, Queen's University, 2006, and Jane Nicholas, "Gendering the Jubilee: Gender and Modernity in the Diamond Jubilee of Confederation Celebrations, 1927," *Canadian Historical Review* 90, no. 2 (2009), 247–74.

46 See Benedict Anderson, *Imagined Communities: Reflections on the Origin and Spread of Nationalism* (New York: Verso, 1991).

47 Banet-Weiser, *Most Beautiful Girl in the World*, 9.

48 For more, see Cynthia Commachio, *Nations Are Built of Babies* (Montreal and Kingston: McGill-Queen's University Press, 1993).

49 Cynthia Comacchio, "Mechanomorphosis: Science, Management, and 'Human Machinery' in Industrial Canada, 1900-45," *Labour/Le Travail* 41 (Spring 1998), 38–9.

50 Michael Dawson focuses on the RCMP, nation building, and masculinity in late nineteenth- and early twentieth-century Canada in his book, *The Mountie: From Dime Novel to Disney* (Toronto: Between the Lines, 1998).

51 Donna Haraway, *When Species Meet* (Minneapolis, MN: University of Minnesota Press, 2008), 162. We note that Haraway's argument here is in regard to the life, body, and passing of her father.

PART ONE

Contested Meaning(s) of Bodies and Nations

1 Epiphany in the Archives

KATHRYN HARVEY

The Artist's role is to demolish the deceptive image of history as an abstraction (as an ideological and/or statistical, administrative picture in which death becomes invisible) by bearing witness to the body.

– Shoshana Felman[1]

In the mid-1990s, I was a doctoral student in history at McGill University. Part of the requirements for attaining what is referred to in academic parlance as a "terminal degree" involved spending many hours warming the seat of one of the cane chairs in the McCord Museum's library while my white-gloved hands busied themselves pulling file folders from banker's boxes. Fingering documents became my raison d'être as I attempted to gather "evidence" for my dissertation on the museum's founder, David Ross McCord.

After about a year of this kind of activity, it was assumed I was ready to move on. I had read through most of McCord's personal papers and those pertaining to his collection, dutifully taken notes, transcribed hundreds of pages of text, and accumulated piles of photocopies, all in preparation for the next stage. If it hadn't been for an offhand invitation from the curator of the museum's First Nations collection, I likely would have left the archives of the McCord Museum with my ignorance intact as to what the true vocation of a historian really is. Diligently sifting through the personal papers of a dead man left me believing that I had accomplished what my graduate school education had prepared me to be: a historian of the abstract and the disembodied.

My reluctance to visit the museum's reserves had been wholly unconscious. It never occurred to me that viewing the objects McCord had taken such pains to collect would tell me anything more than the textual record had already revealed about the man and his vision of Canadian history. I had no background in First Nations history and knew even less about material culture, Indigenous or otherwise. I was an academic historian not a museologist, was the excuse I made to myself. But my day of reckoning came the afternoon I took the freight elevator down two stories to the basement of the museum to see firsthand the things McCord had coveted as a collector.

Entering the windowless room, I was treated to a spectacle that filled me with wonder. Wrapped in white conservation paper and stored in metallic drawers that shared more than a passing resemblance to a morgue, the objects I viewed possessed a numinous quality that even their surroundings failed to extinguish. The museum may have consigned these objects to the dead but they still bristled with knowledge about past rituals, pastimes, and a world-view that continues to inspire despite being driven underground by the forces of Canadian colonialism.[2] I marvelled at the richness of the natural materials and the skill that had gone into crafting the bead, quillwork, and trade silver by Iroquois, Abenaki, and Mi'kmaq artists. The fact that some of these objects had been produced for the nineteenth-century tourist market made them no less "authentic."[3] I couldn't help but contrast the beauty of these pieces with the generic mass-produced goods that pass for souvenirs today.

The act of looking at these objects was a sensual experience, transforming my knowledge in ways that written descriptions could not. The objects were thick with information about the people, cultures, and environments that had created them. They also spoke volumes about their owner. Seeing first-hand what David McCord had coveted, what he had paid a family fortune to obtain, tipped me off to an underlying truth about how history is made – one that my education had not only failed to provide, but had actively denied. That is, that history is made through *bodies*, both alive and dead. From that moment on, my challenge as a historian would be to bring a somatic awareness to David Ross McCord and his collecting and museum-making activities. What this might mean for the writing of Canadian history took me longer to comprehend.

As distinct from the current online collecting and trading of objects, collecting in McCord's time was a physical activity, one that engaged the senses and the faculty of memory. Without an understanding of McCord's somatic presence – his passions, his desires, his memories, and preoccupations of an interior life – his collection was bereft of meaning. "The human drama is first and foremost a somatic one," writes Morris

Berman. "How is it, then, that things such as emotions, or more generally the life of the body, gets left out of academic history?"[4] How indeed!

How we are educated to think about the past, I would argue, is partially responsible. Bodies exist in historical narratives, but too often only to be counted. Western intellectual traditions since the Renaissance have been predicated on the idea that the head is sovereign over the heart. In this context, the role of history is to impose order on the endless processes associated with animate bodies and their unreason.[5]

When history as a discipline entered universities, towards the end of the nineteenth century, professional historians looked to the sciences for a methodology that would distinguish their work from that of the amateur whose romantic narrative style had come to define history writing in the Victorian period.[6] By applying the procedures of the natural scientist – observing, accumulating, and verifying facts in a detached manner – historians hoped to accrue to their discipline some of the authority and influence enjoyed by the sciences. To represent the past "as it really was" became the maxim associated with German historicist Leopold von Ranke and his new "scientific" approach to writing history.[7]

The historical method that evolved from history's encounter with nineteenth-century science placed a high value on physical detachment. Historians were encouraged to make their observations from an "objective" distance. What constituted the surface of things became their entirety; the underlying assumption being that only what is visible exists. What literally disappeared from the historian's view was that vast domain of human experience that takes place in relation to the body.

What history writing gained from this development was more than offset by the losses. But what got squeezed out, to quote archivists Joan Schwartz and Terry Cook, was, "the story-telling, the ghostly and psychic, the spiritual and the feminine (and of course all 'amateur' women practitioners), in favour of men (exclusively) pursuing a 'scientific' and 'professional' history."[8] As a consequence, history became about its principle subject: men and their relationship to power. National governments, diplomacy, and war were what constituted *The World in Action*.[9] Human subjects were perceived as statistical abstractions: votes to be counted, census figures to be parsed, and the bottom line for measuring the consequences of war (which, of course, was accounted for by the euphemism "collateral damage").

Writing about an individual life invites an intimate approach. How could I hope to understand the workings of McCord's interior life – be a witness to expressions of love, envy, compassion, wonder, rage, and sadness – if I adopted the objectifying gaze of empirical science to the exclusion of all else? These emotional states are events of the interior life. "Interior events are not seen in an exterior or objective manner," writes the philosopher Ken Wilber, "they are seen by introspection and interpretation."[10] When I came across a heavily annotated letter by McCord, with passages boldly underlined in jet black ink, or saw a photograph of the interior of his drawing room filled with objects, unless I was merely content with describing the contents of this letter or that drawing room, I had to enter into a dialogue with their owner to understand their meaning. David McCord is not an object that I can stare at, dispassionately, across the divide of time. Like myself, he is a subject who once loved, suffered the pain of loss, experienced joy and pangs of hunger, laughed and cried, felt disappointment – in short, every state identified with the human condition. Science has provided us with a highly effective method for discerning "truth," but it is with art that we make meaning.

It is an unusual relationship, this connection I have forged with the dead. By necessity, it is a one-sided link based on written records and objects from the McCord Museum, but a relationship nonetheless. My authority as a professional historian rests on my ability to accurately translate these sources into a "truthful" portrait of my subject and his times. This endeavour frequently overwhelms the poet in me. I wish to restore a complexity to the man's life in defiance of the simple dichotomies created by nineteenth-century historical discourse which values fact over fiction, history over memory, reason over feeling, bodies of knowledge over human bodies, and sight over touch. Poetry, however, evokes, speaks in the language of metaphor, and relies on allusion to make its point.[11] "Poetry in its making and reception [is] bound up with the somatic, with memory as well as the sense experience, and with the overdetermination of symbols," writes poet and cultural theorist Susan Stewart.[12] As a form of expression, poetry is much more adept at capturing the nuances of self-concept. To write about an individual life calls for an approach and a language that corresponds to the immense human scale of the project – tools for romancing the self.

The conceptual tools that I had honed at McGill's history department were forged from the tailings of an intellectual tradition that endorsed a mechanistic world-view. Under this paradigm, humans and nature are likened to a clock, one that may be taken apart, examined, and classified, all the while eschewing the whole for its parts. Applied to history writing, this paradigm accounts for the invention of periodization, a concept central to the historiographical process.[13] Periodization allows for the breaking up of time into discrete blocks, arranged along a continuum that moves from the past to the present. But as efficient as periodization may have been to the modern historiographical project, it also erased something primal to our understanding of memory and how it works.

My epiphany in the archives, my epistemological meltdown as it were, had been triggered by a heart-opening event: sharing what McCord had loved. Finding a sense of attachment to McCord was one thing but that alone would probably not have been enough to awaken me to this other perspective. It was the objects themselves: the porcupine quill portfolio, the moose hair armband, and even the human scalp I was not meant to see. They all evinced a quality that is difficult to put into words but in their presence I felt awe. It would take me many years and a completed Ph.D. to understand what these remnants of an Earth-bound divinity had aroused in me. But what these objects pointed to at the time was another epistemological path, another way of doing history that did not engage with the dualisms that prevailed in European modernist approaches to history making but were rooted instead in the body sensual.[14]

How do I account for the depth of my reaction, a reaction that would call into question the very tools of my trade? Having been given no instruction on how to make meaning from this impromptu display, my imagination filled the void, and I undertook what French philosopher Gaston Bachelard describes, in *The Poetics of Space*, as creating my own poetics of representation: "The poetic image is not subject to an inner thrust. It is not an echo of the past. On the contrary: through the brilliance of an image, the distant past resounds with echoes, and it is hard to know at what depth these echoes will reverberate and die away. Because of its novelty and its action, the poetic image has an entity and a dynamism of its own."[15] In Bachelard's view of poetry, one's response to poetic images is not informed by "archetype lying dormant in the depths of the subconscious," nor is it subject to causation, something most historians would have difficulty understanding.[16] "The image, in its simplicity, has no need of scholarship. It is the property of a naïve consciousness."[17]

My naïve consciousness told me these objects were alive when everything about their *academic* context told me they should be dead. The people who had created them, the world they had inhabited, and the person who had collected them were long gone. Yet, something tangible lived on. Indeed, the idea of bodies and objects "frozen" in time through the act of collecting and preserving in a museum is a central fiction of historicist approaches. People are encouraged to believe that museums are meant to "take us back" in time through the visual experience of viewing objects that have been removed from both time and place. The "museum effect" of isolating the objects from all other associations, and using them to represent events and peoples from another time and place, had not rendered them historical – the intended effect – but instead spoke to me of the ongoing power of an Earth-bound divinity. In this instance, my memory was not uniquely centred on the past, but was also encapsulating the present, and the future.

How we remember is far from universal. Diana Drake Wilson makes this point in her fascinating article "Realizing Memory, Transforming History," when she writes, "For many American Indians, even those who do not speak an indigenous language, remembering is understood as not only the passive recall or representation of events gone by, but also a creative action instantiating the present and prefiguring the future."[18] Her main point is not that American Indians may remember differently than other kinds of Americans, "such sweeping generalizations will always break down when looking at specific instances of memory use,"[19] but that, when comparing the two types of remembering, "memory, so necessary for the so-called higher cognitive practices, is also a potentially subversive mode of knowing because it so obviously uses as its medium not only the representational tools of words and images, but also all the senses, the body itself, to remember."[20] Museums may have instructed us to remember in specific ways with specific ends in mind but, as my experience suggests, they were not always successful in completing the picture.

A century before, David Ross McCord had been confronted with a similar choice regarding his collection. Did he adhere to the path that his history education had prepared him for and create a legacy for the Canadian public that honoured First Nations objects while at the same time ignoring the individuals and the cultures that had produced them? Or was he truly the "handmaiden" of Canada, as he claimed to be, helping birth a distinctly Canadian culture that did not elevate one religion or language or cultural group over another. John Ralston Saul, in *A Fair Country*, accuses the mythmakers of the late nineteenth century of "writing out Canada's past and writing in the glory of the British Empire."[21] Did he have McCord in mind?

When I began frequenting the McCord Museum in the 1990s, academic history and history museums were already going their separate ways. During the course of the twentieth century, the originating bonds that had brought museums and academia together in a shared pursuit of research and teaching began to dissolve. In the social sciences and the humanities, especially, the methods of knowledge creation that had

come to dominate eschewed the artefact and the specimen, in defer-
ence to the text.[22] A tension was inherent in their differing modes of
representation. Objects told a static story, whereas the written narrative
seemed more suited to capturing the dynamic sequence of events considered the staple of historical writing.[23] But despite their differences,
the modern museum and modern historiography had common anteced-
ents. The rapid proliferation of museums in the nineteenth century was
also closely tied to the emergence of new disciplines (history included)
and their modes of expression (history = the past).[24] Both had been
birthed in the shadow of the nation state at the end of the eighteenth
century, and both had been enlisted in its cause.

Tony Bennett, in his discipline-defining article, "The Exhibitionary
Complex," describes how museums and historical narrative came to play
pivotal roles in the creation of new techniques for maintaining and extending the powers of the nation state. Much subtler than the ancien
régime's penal practices, "the Exhibitionary Complex" was an attempt to
educate citizens, especially working-class citizens, in a set of "object lessons" displayed in museums on how to comport themselves in this new
sociopolitical reality: "They sought to allow the people, en masse rather
than individually, to know rather than be known, to become the subjects
rather than the objects of knowledge. Yet, ideally, they sought also to allow the people to know and thence to regulate themselves; to become,
in seeing themselves from the side of power, both the subjects and the
objects of knowledge, knowing power and what power knows."[25] As Benedict Anderson reminds us, one of the central fictions of the nation state
is the belief in "horizontal comradeship" regardless of how much real
inequality exists within a country.[26] The liberal democratic model that
evolved in Western Europe and was exported to White-settler states such
as Canada, not only required that people be governable but that they
agree to be governed.

The role of the museum was to make power/knowledge visible through
the arrangement of bodies and their objects. The contributions of history, natural history, and ethnography were to create new forms of representation and classification that allowed for the telling of the national
story as the progressive development of peoples, states, and civilizations
through time: "The recent past was historicized as the newly emerging
nation-states sought to preserve and memorialize their own formation as
a part of that process of 'nationing' their populations that was essential
to their further development."[27] But as Bennett points out, in the context of late nineteenth-century imperialism, what was central to the

ideological fashioning of the "exhibitionary complex was the dualistic mindset which defined representations of Western culture in relation to those who found themselves outside the specific geo-political and cultural parameters of the Western nation states. The narrative logic of these ethno-historically determined exhibitions required the presence of the 'primitive' other against which the 'civilized' was then defined."[28]

Envisioning Canada's Past?

When David Ross McCord was fashioning his own national narrative of colonial conquest, Canada had a ribbon-thin population of less than five million stretched along the border with the United States. Recently independent from Britain, the largest empire in the world, and neighbour to the United States, a country that would soon surpass Britain in industrial strength and influence, Canada's future as a separate nation was far from guaranteed. Men like McCord believed that Canada's survival was best served by promoting an imperial federation with the British Empire.[29] If Canada was to exercise any power within this arrangement, the country needed to strengthen independence by cultivating its own brand of nationalism. A vision of Canada's past was seen as central to any project of creating a Canadian identity. With this in mind, McCord went about devising a museum that would showcase the story of Canada's origins: "Canada is beginning to take her place as a nation and assume responsibilities, but she must be taught," wrote McCord in 1919.[30] It was McCord's intention to create a history of Canada that would unify its citizens and inspire them in a shared project of nation building.

McCord's own personal history in no small way helped account for his lifelong preoccupation with national unity. His father, John Samuel, had been the commander of the Montreal militia during the Rebellions of 1837–38. This position made him a key player in the defeat of the Patriot forces, an event that seriously undermined French-Canadian influence in the Canadas and would take a couple of generations to repair. A strong Canadian identity built on a shared knowledge of Canada's past was McCord's antidote against these threats to the country's survival.[31]

It was the South Kensington Museum, where he likely visited in 1877, that provided McCord with his model. Founded in 1857, London's South Kensington Museum, later the Victoria and Albert Museum, was one of a new breed of public institutions. Considered the most up-to-date with regards to museological practices because of its free admissions policy and late evening opening hours, the South Kensington combined education and popular entertainment as a means to increasing the general standards of education among skilled labourers and artisans.

Henry Cole, the first director, paid lip service to the idea of the museum as "a school-room for everyone," but the main priority remained the promotion of good design among producers and consumers. Key to this process was the use of non-Western objects as examples of excellence in design. The acquisition of objects from Britain's colonial possessions also made it a kind of "three-dimensional imperial archive," writes Tim Barringer, which "enshrined a uniquely modern world-view, that of Victorian imperialism."[32]

McCord, too, saw his museum as a part of the larger British imperial project. In the introduction to the history of the McCord National Museum, he described the museum as "illustrating British Empire History but specializing in Canadiana." In 1919, following McGill's acceptance of his collection, he wrote, "I am putting into the Museum my family china and mahogany except what little Mrs. McCord and I shall require in what must now be the short period we can expect to remain on Earth. I do this in order to give an example to others. I want to see a Canadian South Kensington. We are far behind England and also far behind the United States."[33] Inspired by South Kensington's ambitious mandate, McCord, too, envisioned the creation of a school "of the useful and ornamental arts based on types of native industry, such as the manufacture of wall paper, works in metal of all kinds, and ceramic work – domestic and ornamental."[34] Central to South Kensington's project was the use of non-Western objects as examples of good design, and in this McCord concurred. Although he had none of the "imperial spoils," the Indigenous objects that dominated McCord's collection served a similar purpose. An anti-modernist at heart, McCord turned to hand-made Indigenous crafts as symbols of a pre-industrial world, of whose loss he lamented.[35]

"When there is no vision the people will perish," were the first words that greeted visitors to the McCord National Museum.[36] The same motto was posted at the entrance to the McCord family home and appeared on the letterhead used by David McCord on all of his museum correspondence. This fear of extinction spelled out in his motto is a motif that ran through both his private and public life. It spoke to David McCord's fear of the dissolution of his young country under the fragmenting forces of French-Canadian nationalism, regionalism, and American cultural and economic domination. The words also gave voice to a more private fear of destruction posed by a family history of alcohol abuse, impotence, and premature death.

Knowledge of Canada's past was McCord's bulwark against threats to both Canada's and his own existence. Integral to that history was the story of the McCord family, their arrival in Quebec following the British victory on the Plains of Abraham, and their subsequent rise to social prominence in the first decades of the nineteenth century. In McCord's version of Canadian history, family and personal myth were conflated with that of nation. The McCord Museum acted as David McCord's theatre of memory, where fragments of his life story were reassembled to create a narrative of national origins and personal redemption.

In McCord's choice of museum motto, "When there is no vision, the people will perish," vision was invested with the divine power to extend the limits of corporal existence. When read as "with vision the people will not perish," historical vision, the ability to look inward and uncover a treasure store of memories, provided the only real protection humans had against the ravages inflicted on flesh by the passage of time. McCord did not have the power to resurrect his family whole from the dead, but he could enliven their memory by preserving the images and objects that recalled them to mind.

The museum was McCord's world in miniature. The narrative he assembled in the old Joseph House owned by McGill University was mapped out in eight rooms and arranged along thematic lines. It began with "Our Aboriginals," followed by the French regime and a room containing relics of items that had belonged to generals Wolfe and Montcalm. At the centre of the house, on the ground floor, was the McCord family room. Upstairs, the room names provided apt descriptions: the Spiritual Pioneers, the American Revolution, the War of 1812–14, Old Quebec, Quebec Province, Old Montreal, Artists, Generals and Poets, McGill University. National museums in this period were established to teach citizens the appropriate chronologies that memorialized the formation of nation states.[37] At the McCord National Museum, the Canadian narrative of nation building was overlaid with the story of McCord and his family. The rough chronology that emerged from the placement of the thematic rooms gave shape to a foundational family story that began with the Conquest – "Our Aboriginals" and the "French regime" were bracketed as the past – and ended with McGill University, David Ross McCord's Alma Mater and sponsor of his museum project. Within the rooms themselves, the displays followed ethnographic conventions not historical ones with objects of a similar nature being grouped together.

In beginning with "Our Aboriginals," McCord was emphasizing the romantic nature of his vision. Ruins of all sorts held a special fascination for nineteenth-century Romantics whether they took the form of geographical ruins or those created by the human hand. "The romantic sensibility," writes Patricia Jasen, "especially when infused with nationalism, encouraged an appreciation of those scenes in which landscape and history, especially in the form of ruins and graveyards, were blended together."[38] Scenes of age, decay, and desolation were particularly popular, and this extended to include images of peoples and their culture like the Highland Scots and the North American Indians, to name two groups threatened with extinction. Romantic remembering was often prefigured by a sense of loss. Raphael Samuels has described romantic memory as being "built on time's ruins."[39]

The Colonial Past on Display

By the time McCord began collecting, at the end of the nineteenth century, Canada's First Nations were considered a spent political force. Unlike the French-English conflict that continued to simmer close to the surface, Indigenous peoples were a diminishing presence that could easily be reconstrued as an already absent one. First Nations culture, in this period, acted as a kind of tabula rasa minus ruins on which McCord and others projected their vision for Canada. Revealing of this attitude was the absence of any sign of First Nations in the exhibition room devoted to Canada's Spiritual Pioneers, located on the second floor just above "Our Aboriginals." On display were family mementos from the Anglican Church, and artefacts representing other Protestant dominations, in addition to a rich selection of paraphernalia associated with Roman Catholic ritual and the Church, but not a trace of any mention of First Nations spirituality. Here, as elsewhere in his exhibit, McCord was silent on First Nations contributions to Canada when they pointed to an ongoing relationship. By placing Indigenous peoples in the nation's prehistory, McCord was contributing to the erasure of Indigenous people in the present.

It is not exactly clear when collecting objects made by Indigenous peoples became his singular passion. At the end of the 1880s, McCord's law practice had taken him to Indian reserves in Ontario and Quebec. It was through this work that he came into contact with the Indian agents who would act as his middlemen in procuring objects. In 1890, he was given the name Rononshonni by the Six Nations Council at Brantford, Ontario, in recognition, it appears, of his legal services.[40] Twenty-six years after the ceremony he wrote, "Years ago at a Council of the Six Nations at Brantford this name [Rononshonni] was conferred upon me. There was something most prophetic in it which now impresses me as I near the end of my earthly term ... I always thought it meant a member of the Iroquois Confederacy ... but it was much more in fact and [in] the light of my life-work ... this National Museum – and the part the Indian section of it plays – I do not know what the Council saw in me – but the name means *a builder.*"[41]

McCord was quick to claim "Indian" status especially, one suspects, when it furthered his ends as a collector. "I have the honour of being an Indian Chief, and I have brought out amazing loyalty from *my* brethren in order to show the 'pale-faces' what we once were when we were the owners of the forest and prairie."[42] With an audacity that can be barely imagined today, McCord's claim to Indian status not only added to his own personal mythology, but it enhanced his collecting authority by allowing him to straddle the line between past and present, Savage and Noble, them and us.

At the time when McCord was collecting, the goal of Canadian government policy with regards to First Nations was complete assimilation into the majority White-settler population.[43] Having outlived their political and economic usefulness, "Denied any history of their own, it was the fate of 'primitive peoples' to be dropped out of the bottom of human history in order that they might serve, representationally, as its support."[44] The belief that Indigenous peoples' history had run its course and that they were on the edge of extinction helped drive the rush of ethnographic collecting which helped empty Indigenous communities of their cultural wealth while filling the reserves of museums such as the McCord.[45]

Conclusion

What would Canadian historiography look like today if David Ross McCord had taken another path, one that had not hewed so closely to his historical education? Modern historiography in the nineteenth century coincided with the development of the museum and the nation state. In a case of history being used to provide justification for what went before, history writing in this context lent itself to telling the story of the "progressive" evolution of government from its absolutist origins to the various styles of self-government practised by Western democracies after the French Revolution. Embedded in these narratives was the belief that Western nations and the White-settler colonies that they spawned were the finest expression of a civilization that had been millennia in the making. The idea that social progress was both inevitable and ongoing was a Victorian invention. Up until the 1970s, Canadian history displayed a similar prejudice. English-Canadian historians (French-Canadian historians adopted a separate narrative) told the story of Canada's progressive movement from colony to nation.[46] As Carl Berger writes, "History was looked upon as an indispensable index of a maturing nationality."[47]

In the Canadian meta-narrative, little attention has been paid to the suffering caused to First Nations people by the constitutional arrangements that culminated in the passage of the British North America Act. Confederation is still portrayed in our national histories as a benign constitutional process that created no victims. We pride ourselves in having achieved nationhood without following the American and French models of violent revolution. But one only has to look to the desperate social and economic conditions that prevail on most reserves today, the painful legacy of the residential school system, and the disproportionate numbers of the Indigenous in prison, to see the scope of the destruction wrought by Canada's nation-building practices. The cultural genocide visited on Indigenous cultures by European colonization in this country is a secret we keep from ourselves. "The disaster ruins everything," writes Maurice Blanchot, "all the while leaving everything intact. It does not touch anyone in particular; 'I' am not threatened by it, but spared, left aside. It is in this way I am threatened. It is in this way that the disaster threatens in me that which is exterior to me – an other than I who passively became another."[48]

The meta-narrative of Canadian nation building, which celebrated the nation as the measure of social, economic, and political progress, acknowledged no gaps. It was a history that claimed to represent all Canadians. Social history, which arose in reaction to this totalizing narrative, strove to create a new history by integrating the stories of the groups who had been left out: the working class, women, the poor, racial and cultural minorities, and even First Nations. What social historians underestimated, however, was the legitimizing power of the nation-building narrative, to which they were still a party. They assumed that by filling in the gaps with histories of the marginalized, truth would be restored to the historical record.

However, we need these gaps. To draw attention to them and to contemplate what these gaps represent is the task of the historical witness.[49] Sewing up these gaps, or ruptures, in the historical record may bring comfort and narrative completion, but by doing so prematurely, we risk not heeding what they have to say. "There is a crack in everything. That's how the light gets in," sings Leonard Cohen.[50] The term *to suture* comes from the Sanskrit *sutra*. In Sanskrit literature, sutras are maxims; general truths that are drawn from experience. What general truth can I formulate about the writing of Canadian history after having witnessed the gaps in McCord's historical operation?

Bodies, like histories, have gaps. After having sat with David Ross McCord and his collection for a decade, the gap, the gaping wound, the places where traumatic memory had congealed, pointed to a historical practice that systematically rendered First Nations people invisible. One of the marks of the colonized is that they don't get to speak for themselves. In McCord's museum, he used First Nations objects but he never acknowledged the artists, their memories, and their stories. Stories give voice to the body. In nineteenth-century Canada, Indigenous bodies were in serious trouble, but without a voice in their history, the impact of colonization on these bodies was never acknowledged.

The disembodied way David Ross McCord went about making history has reverberated through the generations and throughout the country. Collecting is a destructive, fetishistic act. It severs the art from the maker. By neglecting to attribute authorship to any of the Native objects he owned, and by disregarding the stories of those who created them, McCord was free to attach his own meanings. Collections arise out of the desire to appropriate. "[They] are made through a species of colonialist," writes Susan Pearce.[51] The appropriation of another's objects, identity, and authorship is a form of theft. McCord took from an Aboriginal culture that was under attack to create a vision of Canada that had no place for First Nations unless they were among the heroic dead. He profited from the cultural genocide that was being perpetrated on Canada's Aboriginal population just as Canada was sacrificing its First Nations to a narrower definition of nation that only had room for the English and French. The eventual triumph of McCord's vision for a history museum and the Canadian nation-building project that was celebrated within its walls, masked much suffering, both personal and collective. There was a cost to what David Ross McCord did. But, in the disembodied narratives of Canadian nation building, there have been few places to register that suffering.

What sutures can we apply to the Canadian narrative?

Notes

I would like to offer my thanks to Joy Parr for sharing her unpublished article, "Our Bodies and Our *Histories* of Technology and the Environment," with me.

Her example offered great encouragement. This essay would not have been possible without the joint efforts of the editors of this collection Pat Gentile and Jane Nicholas who brought us together, and whose close readings heightened this body's awareness of new possibilities and new directions for this text. At an earlier time conversations with Alice Nash helped shape my thoughts on this subject, as did Brian Deer's knowledge of Wampum, and much more. A special thanks is due to Leila Marshy for her encouragement and formidable editing skills.

1 Shoshana Felman and Dori Laub, *Testimony: Crises of Witnessing in Literature, Psychoanalysis and Theory* (London: Routledge, 1992), 108.

2 See *Royal Commission on Aboriginal Peoples: People to People, Nation to Nation* (Ottawa: Royal Commission, 1996).

3 Ruth Phillips, "Re-placing Objects: Historical Practices for the Second Museum Age," *Canadian Historical Association* 86, no. 1 (2005), 91–2.

4 Morris Berman, *Coming to Our Senses: Body and Spirit in the Hidden History of the West* (New York: Bantam, 1989), 108.

5 George Woodcock, *The Monk and His Message: Undermining the Myth of History* (Vancouver: Douglas and McIntyre, 1992), 13.

6 According to Carl Berger, the ideal of Rankean history gained an unchallenged ascendancy in the United States in the last decades of the nineteenth century. In Canada, the scientific method was slower to take root, in part because fewer Canadians had studied in Germany with Ranke. George Wrong, who was appointed chair of history at the University of Toronto in 1895, was rather reserved in his support of the new scientific approach, while his counterpart at Queen's University, the empiricist Adam Shortt, wholeheartedly welcomed the development. See Carl Berger, *The Writing of Canadian History* (Toronto: University of Toronto Press, 1986), 1–31. Also see Donald Wright, *The Professionalization of History in English Canada* (Toronto: University of Toronto Press, 2005).

7 See Peter Novick, *That Noble Dream: The "Objectivity Question" and the American Historical Profession* (Chicago, IL: University of Chicago Press, 1988), 21–31, where he discusses the contribution of German historian Leopold von Ranke to the making of the American historical profession. Ranke's famous dictum, the past "*wie es eigentlich gewesen*" was understood by the Americans to mean "as it really was" or "as it actually was." In fact, the word *eigentlich* had an ambiguity it no longer has; it also meant "essentially," which is the way Ranke used it since his historical project was to penetrate to the "essence" of things.

8 Joan Schwartz and Terry Cook, "Archives, Records, and Power: The Making of Modern Memory," *Archival Science* 2, nos. 1–2 (2002), 16–17.

9 *The World in Action* refers to a series of Second World War propaganda films created by the National Film Board to boost morale and highlight the Allied war effort. See the Canadian Film Encyclopedia Film Reference Library, available online at http://www.filmreferencelibrary.ca/index.asp?layid=44& csid1=628&navid=46.

10 Ken Wilber, *The Marriage of Sense and Soul* (New York: Random House, 1998), 117.

11 Deena Metzger, *Writing for Your Life* (New York: Random House, 1992), 11.

12 Interview with Susan Stewart by Jon Thompson, *FreeVerse*, 2003, 2.

13 See E.H. Carr, *What Is History?* (Harmondsworth: University of Cambridge Press and Penguin, 1961), 60–1, and R.G. Collingwood, *The Idea of History* (London: Oxford University Press, 1956 [1946]), 327–8.

14 See Shawn Wilson, *Research Is Ceremony* (Halifax: Fernwood, 2008), and Eva Marie Garroutte, *Real Indians: Identity and the Survival of Native America* (Berkeley, CA: University of California Press 2003), 101–12.

15 Gaston Bachelard, *The Poetics of Space* (Boston, MA: Beacon Press, 1969), xvi.

16 Patrick Houlihan, "Poetic Image," in *Exhibiting Cultures: The Poetics and Politics of Museum Display*, ed. Ivan Karp and Steven D. Lavine (Washington, DC: Smithsonian Books, 1990), 207.

17 Bachelard, *Poetics of Space*, xviii.

18 Diana Drake Wilson, "Realizing Memory, Transforming History," in *Museums and Memory*, ed. Susan Crane (Stanford, CA: Stanford University Press, 2000), 116.

19 Ibid.

20 Ibid., 117.

21 John Ralston Saul, *A Fair Country: Telling the Truths about Canada* (Toronto: Viking Canada, 2008), 12.

22 At the McCord Museum this process was initiated in the 1980s during an ambitious rebuilding and renovation project that culminated in the museum reopening in 1992. At this time, McGill University remained the owner of the objects of the museum but the museum itself became an independent institution.

23 Edward P. Alexander, *Museums in Motion* (Nashville, TN: Rowman and Littlefield, 1979), 93–4.

24 Tony Bennett, "The Exhibitionary Complex," in *Culture/Power/History: A Reader in Contemporary Social Theory*, ed. Nicholas B. Dirks et al. (Princeton, NJ: Princeton University Press, 1994), 123.

25 Ibid., 126.

26 Benedict Anderson, *Imagined Communities* (London: Verso, 1991 [1983]), 7.

27 Ibid., 141.

28 Sunera Thobani, *Exalted Subjects: Studies in the Making of Race and Nation in Canada* (Toronto: University of Toronto Press, 2007), 5.

29 Carl Berger, *The Sense of Power: Studies in the Ideas of Canadian Imperialism, 1867–1914* (Toronto: University of Toronto Press, 1970).

30 MCFP, file #5324, DRM to Miss Horden and Miss Broughton, 13 Feb. 1919.

31 MCFP, file #2048, Museum correspondence, DRM to C.F. Crandal, editor, *Montreal Star*, 24 April 1920.

32 Tim Barringer, "The South Kensington Museum and the Colonial Project," in *Colonialism and the Object: Empire, Material Culture and the Museum*, ed. Tim Barringer and Tom Flynn (London: Routledge, 1998), 11.

33 MCFP, file #2055, "Museum Correspondence," DRM to Mrs. W.C. Hodgson, Regent of the Daughters of the Empire, 15 Sept. 1919.

34 MCFP, file #2055, "Museum Correspondence," DRM to unknown recipient, Feb. 1920.

35 Donald Wright, "W.D. Lighthall and David Ross McCord: Antimodernism and English-Canadian Imperialism, 1880s–1918," *Journal of Canadian Studies* 32, no. 2 (1997), 135.

36 Proverbs 13:18, Bible, King James Version (Cleveland: World Publishing Company, no date).

37 Alexander, *Museums in Motion*, 86.

38 Patricia Jasen, *Wild Things: Nature, Culture, and Tourism in Ontario, 1790–1914* (Toronto: University of Toronto Press, 1995), 10.

39 Raphael Samuel, *Theatres of Memory* (London: Verso, 1994), ix.

40 Moira McCaffrey, "Rononshonni – the Builder: McCord's Collection of Ethnographic Objects," in *The McCord Family: A Passionate Vision*, ed. Pamela Miller et al. (Montreal and Kingston: McGill-Queen's University Press, 1992), 103.

41 MCFP file #1998, "Community Club Activities," 13 Sept. 1916; original emphasis.

42 Library and Archives Canada (LAC), Vol. 105, MG 26 H, Reel C4336, Borden papers, DRM to Robert Borden and to Dean Adams, Ph.D., D.Sc. FGSA, acting Principal of McGill University, 22 Aug. 1919; original emphasis.

43 For more about Canadian government policy, see J.R. Miller, *Skyscrapers Hide the Heavens: A History of Indian-White Relations in Canada* (Toronto: University of Toronto Press, 2000), 254–82.

44 Bennett, "The Exhibitionary Complex," 143.

45 McCaffrey, "Rononshonni – the Builder," 103–15.

46 Ronald Rudin, *Making History in Twentieth-Century Quebec* (Toronto: University of Toronto Press, 1997).

47 Berger, *Sense of Power*, 2.

48 Maurice Blanchot, *The Writing of the Disaster* (Lincoln, NE: University of Nebraska Press, 1995), 1.

49 I wish to thank Shauna Beharry for drawing my attention to the word "suture" and how it might apply in this context.

50 Leonard Cohen, "Anthem," *More Best of Leonard Cohen*, Columbia, 1997.

51 Susan Pearce, *Collecting in Contemporary Practice* (London: Sage, 1998), 169.

2 Following the North Star: Black Canadians, IQ Testing, and Biopolitics in the Work of H.A. Tanser, 1939–2008

BARRINGTON WALKER

The writer takes this opportunity to thank the teachers who have helped him in his present investigation, and also his friends in Kent County, both white and coloured, who have supplied him with material or information. Thanks are due to Professor F.W. Landon, for allowing the writer access to his valuable collection of original documents in connection with Negro Settlements in Canada.

– H.A. Tanser

The Underground Railroad has always played a key role in shaping English Canadians' sense of their history. Kent County, Ontario, was an important destination for U.S. fugitive slaves from the 1820s until the outbreak of the American Civil War. Harry Ambrose Tanser, the superintendent of schools for Chatham in Kent County in the 1930s was also taken by this legacy of the Underground Railroad (UGRR). Like others, for him the proud history of the Underground Railroad era was tangible evidence of national progress – British colonial civilization and benevolence towards the less fortunate – all of which were part of the literary, sociocultural, and historical project that one scholar has called White civility.[1]

This chapter shows how a slim book authored by Tanser complicates our understanding of the legend of the UGRR. Tanser drew on a particular historical understanding of the Underground Railroad – particularly the idea of Canada West as a "haven" – to substantiate scientific racism.[2] Similar to Kathryn Harvey's piece in this collection, I grapple with the complexities of writing the body into Canadian historiography. My chapter, too, will broach the socially constituted and contested nature of scientific discourse and the racialized body in Canadian history themes that are echoed in the offerings of Minnet, Poulter, and Rutherdale. But, most importantly, this chapter explores two major themes. First, it traces one neglected trajectory of the romantic narrative of the Underground Railroad that has been almost completely ignored by historians: Tanser's production of racialized bodies through his linking this narrative to early twentieth-century scientific racism, educational psychology, and biopolitics. Second, this chapter shows how Tanser's ideas continue to influence racial thought, both inside and outside of academic circles.

Race, Intelligence Testing, and Biopolitics in North America

The emergence of the science of "race" and "IQ" was essentially the product of two epistemological fictions forged together with devastating consequences for those racialized as non-European and non-White. There is a rich interdisciplinary literature – too extensive to do justice to in this brief piece – that has debunked the idea of "race" as a biological reality. The case for an empirical and objective unified measurement of innate intelligence is equally specious.[3] And yet, scientists housed in some of Europe's most august centres of learning forged a symbiotic relationship between the science of "race" and "intelligence" testing in pre- and post-Darwinian Europe and throughout its imperial spheres, both near its metropoles and in its far-flung colonies.

Stephen J. Gould traces the trajectory of the science of "race" to the late eighteenth and early twentieth centuries. During this era, Europe's privileging of its own cultures, religion, and bodily aesthetics over the "others" they encountered during the nascent days of imperialism were, over time, increasingly supported by biological science.[4] In the eighteenth- and nineteenth-century United States, says Gould, intellectuals "did not doubt the propriety of racial ranking." Blacks were deemed inferior to all, Whites the very opposite, and Indians were slotted above the former and below the latter.[5] It is out of this cultural and intellectual milieu that sciences such as polygenicism (a belief in the multiple origins of man and a rejection of the idea of humanity's common roots) and craniology (the measuring of skulls) began to emerge.

By the mid-nineteenth century, craniology was largely discredited. But out of its "ashes" emerged the hereditary theory of intelligence. Alfred Binnet, a Sorbonne psychologist, abandoned craniology, finding it an unreliable way to measure intelligence. Proponents of this science simply had too little success correlating intelligence to skull size to consistently affirm their preconceptions of European intellectual superiority.[6] Binnet eventually switched from the primarily physiological approach of his predecessors to a psychological one.

Binnet turned his attention to finding a way to quantify intelligence. The result of his efforts, the Binnet Scale, was designed as a metric for the myriad psychological processes to which he assigned various "mental ages" and from which he determined one's intelligence and assigned a single score.[7] Binnet's scale was later further refined by German psychologist W. Stern who took the mental ages determined by the Binnet Scale and divided them by chronological ages, thus creating the intelligence quotient, the value commonly referred to as "IQ."[8] This empirical expression of a single quotient to represent intelligence was the beginning of the realization of Binnet's concerns about the uses to which his insights would be used. Binnet rejected the idea that his intelligence scale was a measure of "inborn intelligence," and he "greatly feared that his practical device, if reified as an entity, could be perverted as an indelible label, rather than a guide for identifying children who needed help."[9] But, to Binnet's dismay, this is precisely what happened.

North American psychologists subsequently geared Binnet's work towards the ends he feared most: a hereditary based, numerically expressed, and linear scale of intelligence.[10] Soon the science of intelligence testing and the "proof" of a hereditary basis for intelligence would become popularized and mass marketed by psychologist Lewis M. Terman's Stanford-Binnet tests. These tests became ubiquitous in the nation's public schools. R.M. Yerkes, a Harvard psychologist devised similar tests for the U.S. Army, where he administered them to almost two million enlistees in 1917.[11] During this era, psychiatrists made the link between low IQ, "feeble-mindedness," criminality, prostitution, and alcoholism. Of course, the IQ debate also had "racial" dimensions. Newly arrived immigrants from Eastern and Southern Europe and Blacks were, not surprisingly, found to have disproportionately high numbers of morons and the feeble-minded among them. These sorts of observations fuelled the eugenicists' call for tight controls on immigration.[12]

This U.S. hereditarian theory of intelligence was swiftly perhaps seamlessly adopted by the Canadian state, and it profoundly shaped public policy in areas such as public health, immigration, and education. It is precisely this mode of governmentality, the state's growing concern with both the biological aspects of and metrics for managing and measuring its populations, for which Michel Foucault coined the term "biopolitics." Foucault traces the emergence of biopolitics to the mid-eighteenth century, an age that gave birth to a new mode of governance, a new technology that was

> addressed to a multiplicity of men, not to the extent that they are nothing more than their individual bodies, but to the extent that they form, on the contrary, a global mass that is affected by overall processes characteristic of birth, death, production, illness and so on. So after the first seizure of power over the body in an individualizing mode, we have a second seizure of power that is not as individualizing but, if you like, massifying, that is directed not as man-as-body but as man as species ... what I would call a "biopolitics" of the human race.[13]

IQ testing in Canada thus became one of the "massifying" manifestations of biopolitics' mode of power. Public health officials, for example, obsessively tried to identify and institutionalize the "mentally feeble," and as a testament to their success the Immigration Act of 1910 listed the feeble-minded among its undesirable classes.[14] Not surprisingly, intelligence testing provided much of the intellectual heft behind these developments in public and social policy in Canada. Indeed, Canadians had a crucial role to play in the history of IQ testing; this was not a body of expertise we passively received from the United States. It was developed by experts on both sides of the border, working hand in glove. Angus McLaren notes that Canadian psychiatrist Carl C. Birgham, an employee of the Ontario Military Hospitals Commission, received three experts who were sent by the U.S. government to observe how the Canadian military screened its recruits. One of the U.S. experts who Birgham trained was Robert Mearns Yerkes who, in turn, brought Birgham to the United States to work on tests for the American military alongside other U.S. experts in the field.[15]

Peter Sandiford, a University of Toronto academic and an advocate of IQ testing in the schools, was one of the foremost proponents of hereditary intelligence. He conducted studies of the Chinese and Japanese in British Columbia and "Southern Ontario Indians" over the course of his career. He was faculty member at the University of Toronto in the Faculty of Education when H.A. Tanser conducted his study.[16] Sandiford was one of the founders of the Educational Psychology movement and the author of an influential book published in 1940 entitled *Foundations of Educational Psychology: Nature's Gifts to Man*. Sandiford's work also appeared in the *Canadian Journal of Mental Hygiene*. Sandiford's ideas clearly had a profound influence on Tanser. While the precise ways in which Kent

County's educational policy was shaped by Tanser's work falls outside the purview of this study, what is clear is that for the purposes of his research Tanser subjected his captive Black students to a battery of IQ tests that were to inform the basis of his study on the relationship between race and IQ. Tanser administered a series of what he called "achievement tests" to "all Negroes present at the time of testing in grades IV to VIII" in seven schools.[17] But before Tanser turned to his science to explain the differences between his students, he turned to history.

Tanser's Underground Railroad

Born in 1897, H.A. Tanser rose to become the superintendent of schools in Chatham during which time he wrote on the subject of race and IQ in his 1939 book (a revised Education thesis for the University of Toronto), a slim volume entitled *The Settlement of Negroes in Kent County, Ontario and the Mental Capacity of Their Descendants.* Tanser's work had two primary objectives. First, to "give some account of the history" of Kent County's Blacks and, second, to "examine the mental capacity of [a] reasonably large group of Canadian Negroes."[18] Tanser's position as the superintendent of schools provided him with privileged access to the scholastic records of the students who were in his charge. Tanser's book was organized according to a fairly standard social science formula: investigation, methods, data analysis, and significance of the results. Tanser's work was also deeply shaped by his understanding of the Black experience in Canada. His understanding of this history was, in turn, marshalled to support a scientific inquiry into the intelligence of Chatham's Black community.

It is not surprising that Tanser's depiction of Black Canadian history in the era of the Underground Railroad was closely aligned with the views of Fred Landon who offered him extensive use of his library. Born in London, Ontario, in 1880, Landon went on to have a career as a journalist and academic, and he was the first full-time librarian appointed to Huron College. Landon, a White scholar of Black Canadian history, was, for his time, quite sympathetic to (mainstream and middle-class) Black civil rights activism, as evidenced by his seat on the executive board of the Canadian League for the Advancement of Coloured People in the 1920s. Landon – with perhaps the exception of Justice William Renwick Riddell – was the most prominent writer on the subject of Blacks on Ontario, and his work explored various topics in Black Underground Railroad history including Black communities (including all Black settlements), abolitionism and abolitionists (mostly White but a few Black), religion, and high-profile legal cases involving fugitive slaves.[19]

Landon's approach to the history of Blacks in Canada – and by extension Tanser's – was, in essence, a celebration of the freedoms that Blacks enjoyed under the British flag in contrast to the conditions they suffered in the United States. In fairness, both recognized that Blacks suffered various forms of societal prejudice in Canada West but the considerable weight of their analysis and interpretation emphasized the idea that Canada was a nineteenth-century Canaan for fugitive slaves.

Roughly the first half of Tanser's book painted the historical backdrop for his empirical research. History was vitally important for Tanser's work. Tanser himself had dabbled in Black-Canadian history, having previously written a short and rather romantic piece on the story of fugitive slave Josiah Henson.[20] In the context of his work on race and IQ, however, history took on added significance. Previous U.S.-based studies on race and IQ had always been bedevilled by the question of whether the achievement gaps suffered by Black children, and Blacks in general, were a consequence of their innate nature or the effects of racial prejudice. For Tanser, Kent County's Blacks, a population who lived under the protections of British North America, solved this dilemma.

Tanser argued that the Blacks in Kent County, Ontario, had benefited from "conditions of freedom for a much longer period," had been the targets of "less pronounced colour prejudices," and had enjoyed, overall, "better social, cultural, economic and educational advantages" than Blacks in the Southern United States.[21] Tanser argued that Blacks in Canada were the beneficiaries of more favourable "environmental conditions." To support his claim, Tanser mobilized many of the clichéd arguments that animated many of the rhetorical excesses of the abolitionist movement: "Every coloured man, as is well known, the moment he sets his feet on the Canadian soil, is forever free and not only free but he is on a level in regard to every political and social advantage, with the white man. He can vote for members of Parliament and for magistrates and in every other popular election."[22]

The image of the fugitive slave touching his feet on free Canadian soil is a stock image of the abolitionist movement and its direct historiographical progeny, the turn of the century Underground Railroad historical scholarship (and, as noted earlier, its rather strange re-emergence in the early twenty-first century). But for Tanser, this image was no cliché. On the contrary, its ubiquity and its currency was evidence of its truthfulness. A lengthy quote from Josiah Henson underscored the author's point. Henson described the scene whereupon he crossed the border and his joy upon having touched British-Canadian soil: "my first impulse was to throw myself upon the ground and giving way to the riotous exultation of my feelings, to execute sundry antics which excited the astonishment of those who were looking on."[23] Henson continued, "A gentleman of the neighborhood, Colonel Warren, who happened to be present, thought I was in a fit, and as he inquired what was the matter with the poor fellow, I jumped up and told him – I was free! 'O,' said he, with a hearty laugh, 'Is that it? I never knew freedom made a man roll in the sand before.'"[24]

The image of the fugitive slave throwing himself on British soil or kneeling while kissing it was a common image in contemporary anti-slavery literature. The tactility of the Black body meeting free British soil was a fixture of this genre. It was meant to illustrate the dramatic transformation that occurred in the lives of Blacks while under the British flag. And yet, the very tactility that shot through these sorts of scenes was, ironically, evocative of the embodied experiences of slavery: the coffle, the slave pen, the rough-hewn planks of the slave ship's hull pressed against Black flesh, gang labour, and the lash. The physicality of Blacks' joy after slavery was, in other words, authentic precisely because of its alignment with the physicality of slavery. These overtly physical displays, these "heart-rending scenes," in Tanser's words, were clear and poignant examples of a much wider trend, two general principles: "(1) the misery and sufferings of the Negroes in the United States and (2) the freedom and happiness of Negroes in Canada."[25]

The next two historical chapters in Tanser's work sought to flesh out these principles by examining two areas of Black-Canadian life in nineteenth-century Ontario: the early Negro settlements and, most crucially for Tanser's purposes, the history of Blacks in Ontario's schools. The first, chapter 2, sketched the history of Blacks in Kent County, Ontario; its history as a terminus of the Underground Railroad; its pivotal role of John Brown's 1858 Chatham Convention in fomenting support – both logistical and moral – for Harper's Ferry; and its "Negro Settlements" at Dawn and Buxton. Not surprisingly (and rather redundantly), Tanser argued that all of these features of Chatham's UGRR history were evidence that Ontario was a much more favourable environment than the Southern United States. When slaves crossed the border, in short, they left "misery" behind to embrace "happiness."[26]

Next, Tanser delved into the history of Chatham's schools. The history of racially segregated schooling in Chatham posed a bit of a challenge for Tanser's rather rosy picture of Black life in UGRR-era Chatham. Subsequent literature on the history of Blacks in Canada West's schools has quite decisively shown us that the school system was one of the areas where Blacks faced very pronounced racial exclusion. Blacks felt this exclusion acutely precisely because they saw education as one of the central routes to achieving full equality.[27] Even Landon's early twentieth-century library provided compelling evidence of the exclusion of Blacks from the schools. To his credit, Tanser acknowledged what the historical evidence baldly told him, there was "undoubtedly a manifestation of prejudice against the education of Negroes in the common schools in many places; and the records indicate that Kent County was not free from such prejudices."[28] The evidence of pervasive legally supported customary discrimination (rather than strictly legal discrimination) against Blacks in the common schools – a singular manifestation of Canada's broader liberal racial order – nonetheless, did not dissuade Tanser from reiterating his central thesis on Black life in the UGRR era: "even in the days before the Negroes were allowed to attend the common public schools, their educational opportunities compared favourably with those of whites."[29] We know, in fact, that the history of all Black schools in Canada West was one of limited victories in the face of constant struggle and overwhelming odds. Black separate schools during this era, although they were run with pluck and guile by charismatic figures, were – with a few exceptions – definitely not equal to their White counterparts.[30] But for Tanser, these Black separate schools were a success story. He pointed to figures such as Henson, co-founder of the Dawn Institute, as evidence that some Blacks accepted the reality of these prejudices and successfully asked for their own coloured schools. These schools, with the support of "ardent friends of the Negro," argued Tanser, were quite successful. So, what then accounted for the continued lack of success among Chatham's Black populace in the 1930s, and in particular, those flailing – and failing – Black students who were under Tanser's watchful eyes?

"A Positive Correlation between Intelligence and White Blood": Producing Racialized Bodies

The answer lay in the correlation between race and intelligence among Tanser's students. At the centre of Tanser's methodology was his biopolitical project: his production of a hierarchy of bodies based on "racial" criteria. These criteria were ostensibly calibrated on the non-visible racial register of blood admixture, but in reality, they were overdetermined by what one theorist (in a slightly different context) has cheekily called an "ocular obsession" with somatic markers of racial difference, or, put a another way, race as essentially a colour-code scheme.[31]

A total of 732 students in Chatham's non-segregated Central School were the subjects of Tanser's study: 188 were Negroes, and 554 were Whites.[32] Among his Negro students, Tanser made further distinctions that were not at all dissimilar to the kinds that North American slave owners had made in an earlier era: "full blooded negroes" (101 students), "three quarter bloods" (42 students), "half bloods" (27 students), and "quarter bloods" (18 students).[33] Tanser further classified the students according to how frequently they attended classes, and their distribution according to age and grade with an eye towards determining what he called their degree of "over-ageness." He found that Black students fell short of Whites in both instances. They missed considerably more days of school, and they had lower levels of age-appropriate grade placement than their White counterparts.[34] Tanser did not seriously consider possible social, economic, or even cultural explanations for these disparities (see below). He presented a perfunctory and impressionistic consideration of these factors rather than an assessment based on hard data. First, he opined that the economic status of urban Whites in his study was "considerably higher" than urban Blacks, and second, rural students from both groups tended to work on the land which they owned in many cases. His brief consideration of these key contextual factors is somewhat surprising given the careful attention he gave – albeit considerably biased – to the role of historical factors in shaping the lives of Chatham's Blacks.

These ill-contextualized data on Black-White attendance records coupled with those on age-appropriate grade placement were Tanser's first step in producing a hierarchy of race and scholastic achievement in Chatham's schools and the broader community. IQ testing was the next and most substantive aspect of his study. His students were given two well-known IQ tests: The National Intelligence Test and various Pinter "non-language" and "primary mental aptitude" tests. The National Intelligence Test was a product of the popularization – the mass marketing – of the Sandiford-Binnet test authors' claim to measure natural and innate intelligence.[35] The Pinter tests consisted of a series of mental exercises that did not depend on the students' proficiency with language. These were particularly useful for Tanser because, he argued, "the Negro child generally does not speak the language well and consistently and may be handicapped in intelligence tests which involve a precise discrimination of the meaning of the terms."[36] The Pinter tests, then, allowed Tanser to address Negro students' alleged linguistic deficiencies as they were comprised of "imitations, picture completions, reversed drawings, etc." Tanser was confident in the accuracy of the Pinter series for testing the intelligence of his Black students because it had been used to test Aboriginal students in Canada and Blacks in the United States.[37]

What were the results of Tanser's tests? Both the National Intelligence Test and the Pinter tests yielded similar results. In the instance of the first the "central tendency" (or mean and median) of White students' intelligence quotient measures was greater than that of his Negro students by a "wide margin," approximately 14.17 points.[38] Tanser also measured the difference in IQ scores between "Negro Full-Bloods" and "Mixed Bloods." He began his discussion of these groups by problemetizing the very notion of such distinctions (but not, notably, the very category of race itself): "It will be readily understood that an experimenter is faced with no small difficulty in attempting to locate subjects who may by classified as of pure racial stock. In other words, by what criteria are we to distinguish the full-bloods from the hybrids?"[39] He acknowledged the work of ethnographic scholars like Herskovits and Hooton who rejected "colour of skin, hair and eyes, thickness of lips, the nasal breadth, prognathism, interpupillary distance, texture of hair, etc." as a "poor criterion of the degree of Negro blood." This dilemma, argued Tanser, would be addressed by relying on the expert testimony of his teaching staff and "local informants," although, he admitted, he could "not pretend to guarantee the absolute correctness of the classification." What Tanser found (rather predictably given his biases) is that the median IQ of the Quarter-bloods was highest, second were the Half-bloods, and lastly the Full-bloods who, Tanser noted, were "almost 9 points below the Quarter-bloods."[40]

The results for the Pinter tests mirrored the findings for the National Intelligence Test. Whites, Tanser found, outperformed Black students by a "wide margin." The Pinter tests were slightly different from the National Intelligence Test in that Pinter's tests arranged what he called "mental indices" from 0 to 100, 50 being the norm mental index. The White median was 56.52, and the Negro median was 46.4. In terms of more conventional IQ measurements, this meant that the White median IQ was 109.87, while the Negro median IQ was 96.02.[41]

Tanser then proceeded to parse his data even further to more dramatically demonstrate the chasm between White and Negro intellectual achievement. And this, Tanser found, was most pronounced in the upper middle and upper ranges for each group: "It is seen ... that the range of the middle half of the Negroes lies between 52.63 and 39.64, while that of the Whites is between 64.65 and 48.01. The evidence points, therefore, to a conclusion that on the Pinter Non-Language the Negroes as a group are a little below normal intelligence."[42]

Tanser concluded, in short, that there was "a positive correlation between intelligence and White blood."[43] The question remains: is Tanser's study significant? Is it an embarrassing aberration, or has its impact resonated more deeply among various scholarly communities? Is Tanser's work still cited and considered relevant today?

Engaging Tanser

Historians have tended to deal with Tanser's book in one of two ways. They have either cursorily noted that his work on race and IQ reflected the "conventional wisdom of the 1930s," a hereditary conception of race that was – or so the conventional wisdom goes – in its last days. Or, they have selectively chosen to engage with the strictly historical chapters in Tanser's work while quite deliberately avoiding discussions of the later chapters. Canada's leading role in crafting the hereditarian science of race is not a comfortable topic. And, while it has largely been treated both analytically and quite literally as a footnote by Canadian historians, Tanser's work has been the subject of past and continued debate and reflection outside of academic history circles.

Some of the earliest reviews of Tanser's work were quite sympathetic to his major findings (lower IQ scores among Blacks), but yet distinctly uncomfortable with his portrayal of Canada as a haven for Blacks. They were sceptical of the categorical nature of Tanser's claims and (not entirely surprisingly as they were U.S. scholars) mildly affronted by his negative depiction of the racial status of Blacks in the Southern United States as a means to highlight the superiority of the Canadian racial climate. In 1942, one reviewer, while opining that "without a doubt a very credible study has been completed," nonetheless argued, "[the] historical background of Kent County Negroes is no doubt quite authentic, yet this reader must admit that it appears more to have been used to dramatize the early Negro's status in Canada and his fortunes, than as a valid basis for comparing the Canadian Negro and the Southern Negro in the United States."[44] While the reviewer agreed that Black Canadians benefited from legal equality and more freedom to mingle with Whites socially, he questioned the overall accuracy of the historical picture painted by

Tanser. He cited African-American historian Charles H. Wesley's study of Canada's Blacks in Chapter VII of *The Negro in the Americas*. Wesley's major findings are worth citing at length:

> The Negro people in Canada form an unnoticed and powerless minority. Scattered through the towns and living in isolated districts the masses seem to be existing on unsatisfactory economic and social standards. Their children look forward to coming to the United States where wider opportunities seem to be offered for their abilities, or to remaining without these advantages in a limited community. There is no doubt that prejudice and discrimination are subtle and deep rooted in Canada, but racial friction has not broken into the open. Without laws and without active pressure, Canada has prevented an advance of its Negro population on any similar scale with the Negro population in the United States ... With all the disabilities to which he is heir on this continent, the most satisfactory progress, and the best status of the Negro group as a whole is found in the United States rather than Canada.[45]

Over time, reviewers combined their distrust of the historical accuracy of Tanser's account of Blacks' lives in the UGRR era (or the historical orientation of the first part of his analysis) with a more pointed critique of his conclusions. Tanser's biased historical account led to suspicions about the trustworthiness of his major findings. It is also true that the political climate in North America was beginning to shift under Tanser's little book. It was becoming marked by increased civil rights activism among African Americans, most dramatically in the U.S. South. A number of psychologists began to eye hereditarian conceptions of race and intelligence with increasing suspicion if not yet outright derision. One reviewer writing in 1957 signalled this shift when he wrote, "As I write, the gravest domestic crisis since the Civil War is being played out in the states of Arkansas and Virginia."[46] This reviewer was concerned with Tanser's considerable influence on a widely read textbook of the era entitled *Racial Differences in Intelligence* and criticized the authors' claims that Tanser's work offered socioeconomically comparable White and Black populations. Not only was this untrue, the reviewer suggested, but it failed to take into account "the interpretation of empirically discovered differences in intelligence between whites and Negroes is a function of the degree of compatibility of the two populations in terms of geographic distribution, language, education, socioeconomic status, motivation and a host of other factors." And this is precisely where the reviewer found

Tanser's work lacking. It is almost impossible," he wrote, "to find sizable groups of Negro and white children who have equally good schooling, [or] equally good educational opportunities (these requirements are not met in our Northern states, nor even in Kent County)."[47]

By the 1960s, heriditarians were in full retreat. Otto Klineberg, one of Tanser's best-known critics, penned a piece in *American Psychologist* in 1963 entitled "Negro-White Differences in Intelligence Test Perform-ance: A New Look at an Old Problem." Klineberg's rebuttal of Tanser's work was powerful because not only had Klineberg emerged as one of the most widely known critics of the hereditarian theory of intelligence, but also he had a somewhat personal take on Tanser's argument and conclusions. Klineberg was born in Canada, where he spent the first twenty-five years of his life. Klineberg argued against the idea of what he called "native differences" in intelligence between Black and White children. He argued, "As children get older … differences in test per-formance appear. Surely this is to be expected on the basis of the cumu-lative effect of an inferior environment."[48] Klineberg was also sceptical of Tanser's depiction of the social and cultural environment for Blacks in Canada and his insistence that Blacks in Canada lived under conditions of formal legal and relative social equality. Klineberg did not doubt that Negroes in Canada were "reasonably well off," but he compared their situation to Blacks in the northeastern United States (a not unreason-able comparison) and doubted emphatically that "they lived under con-ditions of complete equality, or that the social environment was free of prejudice." Klineberg admitted he did not have any knowledge of Kent County but wondered "whether this particular Canadian community can be so exceptional."[49] The same year, Mollie Smart wrote "Confirming Klineberg's Suspicion" in *American Psychologist*. Whereas Klineberg could claim no intimate knowledge of Kent County, Smart had no such prob-lem, as she was "probably the only member of the APA who was born and grew up in Kent County." She shared her pointed and poignant experiences growing up in Kent County with the APA's readers. Smart had attended school in Chatham in the 1920s and 1930s and, hence, had witnessed the treatment and conditions of the city's Blacks first-hand:

> The Negroes lived in the East End, and in a few spots on the outskirts of town. Nearly all of their houses were small wood buildings, often lacking in paint and tending towards dilapidation. The theatres had a policy of seating Negroes in certain areas. The all Negro school had been abandoned by my day. My Negro classmates were usually poorly clothed and badly groomed.

Negroes held the low status jobs. They were servants, garbage collectors, and odd-job men. People called them "Nigger" more often than "Negro." I did not know until I grew up that a Negro could be a doctor, lawyer, teacher, member of Parliament, or even a clerk in a store. The only Negro boy of my acquaintance who went to college became an MD and went to a larger city to practice. It was often said that ambitious Negroes should go to Detroit where they would have opportunities for advancement.[50]

Unlike her contemporaries, Smart, a consummate environmentalist, did not bother to comment on Tanser's findings on race and IQ. Her highly privileged and personal (although ironically at times stereotypical) rebuke of Tanser's portrayal of Black life in Kent County surely, in her mind, was sufficient to debunk his scientific work. The link between faulty history and faulty science was clear; the dismantling of the former was by implication the dismantling of the latter. Surely, Smart thought that hers would be the final word on the matter, that confirming the suspicions of a giant like Klineberg would have signalled the end of Tanser's book and, more broadly, the triumph of environmentalism over the fallacy of theories of race and hereditary intelligence and the destruction of one of the most cherished myths Canadians hold about their racial past? This was not to be the case.

Conclusion: Tanser's Legacy

Smart's critique did not signal the death-knell for the hereditarian view of race and IQ. In 1969, Arthur Jenson, an educational psychologist at the University of California, published an incendiary article in the *Harvard Educational Review* entitled "How Much Can We Boost IQ and Scholastic Achievement?" Jenson's well-known position was, simply put, that innate intelligence had a much more profound role in determining educational achievement and, by extension, intelligence than environment.[51] His work has met fierce opposition but its lasting effect on the field of educational psychology is indisputable, with Jensonism reaching its crescendo with the publication of the much debated, celebrated, and maligned book *The Bell Curve* in 1994, by Richard Herrnstein and Charles Murray.[52]

There is no smoking gun that leads from Tanser to Jensen, so in that regard it is difficult to make any claims about the effect of Tanser's work on the popular culture. Not even Phillipe Rushton, Canada's best-known proponent of Jensonism, who both collaborated with and wrote in honour of Jenson, cited Tanser's work (at least I have yet to find any evidence of such among Rushton's vast number of publications).[53]

But while Tanser's book is not as well known as the work of later figures like Jenson and Rushton, it was singularly important in two ways. First, it was remarkable because it is evidence of a little known and underexplored trajectory of early twentieth-century work on Blacks in the era of the Underground Railroad. And, for a time, the historicity of Black-Canadian life became a key point of debate among mainstream educational psychologists. For that relatively brief moment in time, in fact, it seems to have occupied a more central place in this field than it did in the Canadian history profession. Tanser's work and the debate it sparked is evidence that a liberal culture of race and scientific racism are not mutually exclusive; they are more aligned than we would like to think.

This chapter has attempted to show the complex career of Tanser's book. It represents two poles of the articulation of Blackness in the dominant imagination in nineteenth- and twentieth-century Canada. The first is Black Canadians as the beneficiaries of White beneficence and national (if not imperial) favour. The archetypal trope of this image of Blackness is the fugitive slave stepping onto free soil under the British flag, the lion's paw. Their presence in Canada was evidence of the superiority of White civilization in British North America. The late nineteenth century witnessed the end of the Underground Railroad era, the hardening of racial attitudes, and the ascendance of scientific racism. Blacks increasingly became regarded as unwelcome guests, an intractable social problem with an intractable biological root. This is the second articulation of Blackness that emerges in Tanser's work. What is unusual about Tanser's book is that it provides a rare window on how the two images became linked in his mind and in his work.

Tanser's work is one that has been incredibly yet quietly influential. It is cited in dozens of sources in the extensive literature on educational psychology including a 1980s study of schooling in India. The most convincing evidence of its enduring legacy in these circles is that it is prominently cited in Richard Lynn's 2008 publication *The Global Bell Curve: Race, IQ, and Inequality Worldwide*. Far from being consigned to the dustbin of history, these sorts of arguments have taken on new vigour. Here the discourse of race and IQ has been developed to a predictable and devastating conclusion: the poorer and less developed areas of the world are poorer not because of histories of colonialism nor the historic transfers of wealth from these former colonies to Europe but because of the low IQ scores of their people.[54] References to Tanser's book also appear in a few unexpected places. Tanser's work was cited in a 1959 U.S. Senate Sub-committee on Constitutional Rights, and it was debated in the *Alabama Lawyer*, the state organ of the Alabama Law Association in 1962.[55] In the twenty-first century, it has also achieved renewed significance in the far right and White nationalist movement blogosphere. The strange career of Tanser's strange little book continues.

Notes

I would like to thank David Austin and Tamari Kitossa and David Sealy for offering their encouragement and for knowingly and unknowingly helping me work through some of the key issues in this piece through our various conversations. This chapter is dedicated in loving memory of David Sealy.

1 Daniel Coleman, *White Civility: The White Literary Project of English Canada* (Toronto: University of Toronto Press, 2006). Coleman's impressive study excavates the literary project of White Civility in four sites, or as he puts it "four ubiquitous allegorical figures: The Loyalist brother, the enterprising Scottish orphan, the Muscular Christian, and the maturing colonial son." There is some – but nonetheless relatively scant – attention paid to Blacks in this book. The glaring and rather surprising omission is the role that fugitive slaves played in discourses of White Civility during the era of the Underground Railroad and its aftermath.

2 Two examples of precisely this sort of romantic post-revisionist lens for the history of the Underground Railroad – particularly life at the end of its northern terminus – are Karolyn Smardz Frost, *I've Got a Home in Glory Land: A Lost Tale of the Underground Railroad* (Toronto: Thomas Allen, 2007) and the even more recent *Ontario's African-Canadian Heritage: Collected Writings by Fred Landon, 1918–1967*, ed. Karolyn Smardz Frost et al. (Toronto: Dundurn, 2009). To its credit, the former text avoids the mistake of portraying the Underground Railroad and its Canadian termini as the product of the initiative and energy of White philanthropists and rightly celebrates the efforts of people of African descent who shaped the movement. Both texts, nonetheless, fail to adequately deal with the reality of White supremacy and class and gender inequalities that profoundly affected the lives of Blacks once they arrived in Canada West. These works make two fatal errors. First, they err in universalizing the experiences of a highly successful petty Black bourgeoisie while ignoring the far more representative struggles of those Black men and women who toiled at the margins of the capitalist wage economy alongside the White working class with little more to leverage

than what they had during the days of slavery: their bodies. Second, writers like Smardz Frost, firmly ensconced in the Whiggish tradition of history, also err in that they fail to see beyond the fiction that formal legal equality under the British flag was a proxy for social and economic equality. Indeed, they fail to see that this sort of racial liberal order often perpetuated such inequalities through strategies of legal colour-blinding, and its inability and unwillingness to address racial and class inequalities in the context of a rights regime that could not even acknowledge their existence, thereby reinscribing them.

3 Ashley Montagu, Introduction, in *Race and I.Q.: Expanded Edition*, ed. Ashley Montagu (New York: Oxford University Press, 1999), 2–3.

4 Stephen J. Gould, *The Mismeasure of Man* (New York: W.W. Norton, 1981), 31.

5 Ibid.

6 An excellent discussion of this history can be found in Constance Backhouse, *Colour Coded: A Legal History of Racism in Canada, 1900–1950* (Toronto: Osgoode Society for Canadian Legal History, 1999), 5–6.

7 Gould, *Mismeasure of Man*, 145.

8 Ibid.

9 Ibid., 151–2.

10 Ibid., 158–9.

11 Ibid., 194.

12 Ibid., 168.

13 Michel Foucault, *Society Must Be Defended: Lectures at the College de France 1975–1976* (New York: Picador, 1997), 242–3.

14 Angus McLaren, *Our Own Master Race: Eugenics in Canada, 1885–1945* (Toronto: McClelland and Stewart, 1990), 41, 58–9.

15 Ibid., 61.

16 Ibid. See also Jennifer Stephen, *Pick One Intelligent Girl: Employability, Domesticity, and the Gendering of Canada's Welfare State* (Toronto: University of Toronto Press, 2007), 68–73, and Timothy J. Stanley, *Contesting White Supremacy: School Segregation, Anti-Racism, and the Making of Chinese Canadians* (Vancouver: UBC Press, 2011), 91.

17 H.A. Tanser, *The Settlement of Negroes in Kent County, Ontario, and a Study of the Mental Capacity of Their Descendants* (Westport, CT: Negro Universities Press, 1970), 139.

18 Ibid., 15.

19 Smardz Frost et al., *Ontario's African Canadian Heritage*, 27–33.

20 H.A. Tanser, "Josiah Henson: The Moses of His People," *Journal of Negro Education* 12, no. 4 (1943), 630–2.

21 Ibid.

22 Fred Landon, Ontario Historical Society Papers and Records, vol. XXII, as cited in ibid.

23 Ibid., 17, as quoted in Josiah Henson, *The Life of Josiah Henson: Formerly a Slave: Now an Inhabitant of Canada as Narrated by Himself* (Boston: A.D. Phelps, 1849).

24 Ibid.

25 Ibid., 20.

26 Ibid., 30.

27 See, e.g., Donald G. Simpson, *Under the North Star: Black Communities in Upper Canada* (Toronto: Africa New World Press, 2005); Jason Silverman, *Unwelcome Guests: Canada West's Response to America Fugitive Slaves, 1800–1865* (Milwood, NY: Associated Faculty Press, 1985); Kristen McLaren, "We Had No Desire to Be Set Apart": Forced Segregation of Black Students in Canada West Public Schools and Myths of British Egalitarianism," in *The History of Immigration and Racism in Canada: Essential Readings*, ed. Barrington Walker (Toronto: Canadian Scholars' Press, 2008), 69–81.

28 Tanser, *Settlement of Negroes in Kent County*, 47.

29 Ibid., 55.

30 See Afua P. Cooper, "Black Women and Work in Nineteenth-Century Canada West: Black Woman Teacher Mary Bibb," in *We're Rooted Here and They Can't Pull Us Up: Essays in African Canadian Women's History*, ed. Peggy Bristow (Toronto: University of Toronto Press, 1994), 150–2. Robin Winks, *The Blacks in Canada: A History* (Montreal and Kingston: McGill-Queen's University Press, 1997), 371.

31 Ann Laura Stoler, "Racial Histories and Their Regimes of Truth," in *Race Critical Theories: Text and Context*, ed. Philomena Essed and David Theo Goldberg (Malden, MA: Blackwell, 2002), 369–70.

32 Tanser, *Settlement of Negroes*, 72.

33 Ibid., 72, 96.

34 Ibid., 78–88.

35 Tanser, *Settlement of Negroes*, 174–8.

36 Ibid., 90.

37 Ibid.

38 Ibid., 98.

39 Ibid., 103.

40 Ibid., 105.

41 Ibid., 117.

42 Ibid., 118.

43 Ibid., 131.

44 Ellis O. Knox, "Review of 'The Settlement of Negroes in Kent County, Ontario, and a Study of the Mental Capacity of Their Descendants,' by H.A. Tanser," *Journal of Negro Education* 11, no. 2 (1942), 194.

45 Charles H. Wesley, *The Negro in the Americas* (Cambridge, MA: Harvard University Press, 1940), cited in ibid.

46 Lawrence Plotkin, "Racial Differences in Intelligence," *American Psychologist* 14, no. 8 (1957), 527. The reviewer was presumably referring to the battle over school desegregation that was taking place in Little Rock, Arkansas, most notably President Eisenhower's decision to order federal troops to enforce this policy there. This story has been recounted in numerous surveys of twentieth-century U.S. history. See, e.g., Darlene Clark Hine et al., eds., *The African-American Odyssey: Combined Volume, Special Edition*, 4th ed. (Upper Saddle River, NJ: Pearson Education/Prentice-Hall, 2010), 548. The reference to Virginia is less clear, but it probably refers to a similar confrontation between the state and the federal government that was taking place in that state on race and the schools question during that year. See www.vahistorical .org/civilrights/massiveresistacne.htm, accessed 15 July 2010.

47 Plotkin, "Racial Differences in Intelligence," 527.

48 Otto Klineberg, "Negro-White Differences in Intelligence Test Performance: A New Look at an Old Problem," *American Psychologist* 18, no. 9 (1963), 200.

49 Ibid.

50 Mollie Smart, "Confirming Klineberg's Suspicion," *American Psychologist* 18, no. 9 (1963), 621.

51 Arthur Jenson, "How Much Can We Boost IQ and Scholastic Achievement?" *Harvard Educational Review* 39 (1969), 1–123.

52 Richard Herrnstein and Charles Murray, *The Bell Curve: Intelligence and Class Structure in American Life* (New York: Free Press, 1994).

53 See J. Phillipe Rushton, "Race Differences in *g* and the 'Jenson Effect,'" in *The Scientific Study of General Intelligence: Tribute to Arthur R. Jenson*, ed. Helmuth Nyborg (Boston, MA: Pergamon, 2003), 147–63, and J. Phillipe Rushton and Arthur R. Jenson, "Thirty Years of Research on Race Difference and Cognitive Ability," *Psychology, Public Policy and Law* 11, no. 2 (2005), 235–94.

54 Richard Lynn, *The Global Bell Curve: Race, IQ, and Inequality Worldwide* (Augusta, GA: Washington Summit Publishers, 2008), 118, 339.

55 See *The Alabama Lawyer: Official State Bar of Alabama*, vol. 23 (Alabama: The Bar, 1962), 369; United States Congress, *Civil Rights, 1959: Hearings Before the Subcommittee on Constitutional Rights of the Committee on the Judiciary, United States Senate, Eighty-sixty Congress, First Session, on S. 435 [and Other] Proposals*

to Secure, Protect, and Strengthen Civil Rights of Persons Under the Constitution and Laws of the United States, United States. Congress. Committee on the Judiciary. Subcommittee on Constitutional Rights, vols. 1–2 (Washington: U.S. Printing Office, 1959), 950; Ashole Dumodor Rangari, *Indian Caste System and Education* (Ann Arbor, MI: Deep Publications/University of Michigan Press, 1984), 273.

3 Embodying Nation: Indigenous Sports in Montreal, 1860–1885

GILLIAN POULTER

In the summer of 1860, a meeting was held in St. Lawrence Hall in Toronto to resolve a difficulty that had arisen in connection with preparations for the upcoming visit of Albert Edward, the Prince of Wales. The group of notable gentlemen who had organized the meeting averred that "His Royal Highness ... should be able to say, on his return to his native land, that he had seen Canadians. This he could do if the people turned out in one uniform mass, without banners to distinguish those who were born in Canada from those who were not."[1] However, the problem was that Torontonians were *not* planning to "turn out in a body." Instead, members of the St. George, St. Andrew, St. Patrick, and other national societies were planning to march under their respective banners. Consequently, the meeting had been called to encourage "Native Canadians" to "walk in the same procession in a separate body to show that we are Canadians."[2] As Mr. J.H. Morris explained, this was not just a problem of being noticed by the royal visitor: "At present when a Canadian visited the neighbouring States, he was simply recognized as an Englishman, Scotchman or Irishman from Canada; while, on the other hand, when he visited the Mother Country, he was acknowledged only in the light of an American. This was not as it ought to be, and in his opinion, Canadians should have a nationality of their own, and be known to the world as Canadians. (Cheers.)"[3]

Two days later, he commented further in a letter to the editor of the *Daily Globe*: "We have too long been known as colonists, and called by that name, and consequently I am not surprised at Mr. Jarvis stating 'that a colonist is not received with the same attention in England as a Yankee.' The Yankee has nationality, the Colonist none."

This incident demonstrates the growing desire of some colonists in the Canadas for their own nationality. This was not just a matter of distinguishing themselves from their French-speaking neighbours. To create a new national identity, they had to distinguish themselves from several others as well, including British, Americans, and Indigenous peoples. The incident also suggests that a sense of national identity is not just summoned into being through intellectual or political fiat, but is (perhaps even more importantly) corporeal. As postmodern scholarship has so convincingly revealed, identities are multiple and need to be examined from a variety of viewpoints. Benedict Anderson famously argued that nations are imagined, and I have argued elsewhere that they must also be envisaged.[4] Here I would like to bring together some of the same evidence in order to put the focus more particularly on ways in which national identity is embodied. As Judith Butler points out, identities have no essential or natural existence, but are something we put on or perform. She argues that it is the repeated embodiment and performance of identity for an audience that constitutes who we are.[5] If these performances are convincing representations of national character they will be recognized and accepted as legitimate, and others will emulate them. When Canadian bodies can be picked out in a crowd, colonists will have made the transition to national status.

In 1860, Torontonians solved their dilemma by urging "Native Canadians" to pin the emblem of the maple leaf on their chests, and local entrepreneurs rushed to satisfy the demand.[6] National identity was assumed to be unproblematically White and male; no consideration at all was given to women, First Nations, or African Canadians as national subjects. In the following decades, colonists in Montreal took a slightly more sophisticated approach.[7] There, national identity was not signified superficially with a badge but manifested in the male body. It, too, was conceived as exclusively White, but at times it was extended in strictly limited ways to women. Members of Montreal snowshoe, lacrosse, and toboggan clubs developed activities that displayed physical and behavioural characteristics that became recognized and naturalized as "Canadian." Through these, Canadian bodies were represented as robust masculine figures that delighted in physical activity in the rugged outdoors and espoused British ideals of order, hierarchy, and fair play. This "new nationality" called for by politicians such as Thomas D'Arcy McGee and intellectuals like Robert Grant Haliburton proved to be hybrid.[8] It was imbued, on the one hand, with British values and liberal ideology, but at the same time, it created a distinctively Canadian "look" through appropriating and transforming Indigenous clothing and tools, and engaging in indigenizing cultural activities. They were *Indigenous* in that they were activities appropriated from Indigenous peoples (French Canadians and First Nations) rather than being imported from the Metropole. They were *indigenizing* in that participation in the sports involved repeated and stylized interaction with the natural environment. In effect, dressing and performing as a Native made you native, and this corporeal manifestation of Canadian identity became widely recognized at home and abroad through the activities of the snowshoe, lacrosse, and tobogganing clubs. Snowshoeing, in particular, provided participants with the opportunity to become conversant with and physically comfortable in the colonial landscape, and was thus a way colonists could feel themselves to be Indigenous.

Snowshoeing

The first club devoted to Indigenous rather than imported sports emerged in the 1840s with the creation of the Montreal Snow Shoe Club (MSSC). Early French colonists had quickly recognized the benefits of travelling by snowshoe, and snowshoes became indispensible in the fur trade. By the time MSSC members were taking to the slopes of Mount Royal for their weekly evening tramp, or gathering at the McGill Gates for their longer trips into the countryside on Saturdays, accounts and illustrations of snowshoeing had begun to make it familiar abroad as a characteristically Canadian activity, well suited to the snowy northern climate.[9] The new sport proved popular with the urban middle classes in the second half of the nineteenth century, and dozens of snowshoe clubs were formed in Montreal and other towns and cities.[10]

Club tramps were organized along quasi-military lines, and members were expected to wear an outfit that generally consisted of a white blanket coat tied with a long sash, leggings, moccasins, and tasseled tuque. By the mid-1870s, each club had its own distinguishing colours. Mr. J. Taylor posed for his portrait in the Notman Photographic Studio in 1872 wearing the uniform of the MSSC: a white coat with red and blue stripes and epaulets, a red sash, and a blue tuque (see Figure 3.1). In putting on this uniform, snowshoe club members dressed up as composite Natives: moccasins and leggings were Aboriginal, the woven sash was a French-Canadian *ceinture fléchée*, the tuque was a French liberty cap, and the blanket coat resembled typical *habitant* winter clothing cut from the blanket cloth associated with the North West fur trade.[11] Their cloth-

Figure 3.1 William Notman, "Mr. J. Taylor, posed for Montreal Snowshoe Club composite, Montreal, 1872." Posing stands help Mr. Taylor keep still for the long exposure required to take this picture in the photographer's studio. In the final composite, the posing stands were cropped out and Mr. Taylor is shown holding an oil torch aloft in a snowy outdoor setting. McCord Museum I-71173.1.

ing and activities, therefore, harkened back to the history of the French Regime and the "olden days" of the fur trade, and by substituting their bodies for those of the "real" Indigenes, members became the new Canadian Native.[12]

This new image of a Canadian enjoyed high visibility in the city because of the snowshoers' frequent presence on the streets, and also because accounts of their activities were well publicized and circulated in a variety of media. Their weekly tramps and occasional steeplechases and races were regularly reported in city newspapers, as were the benefit concerts they organized. These were popular events at which members sang club songs such as "The Snow Shoe Tramp" and presented re-enactments of their tramps and activities (see Figure 3.2).[13] In their snowshoe outfits, they were considered a novel and picturesque sight that constituted a distinctively Canadian "look" that was photographed extensively. It was memorialized frequently in composite club portraits for which members posed individually in the photographer's studio. These portraits were then assembled en masse against appropriately painted backgrounds.[14] An example can be seen in Figure 3.3, where members of the St. George's Snow Shoe Club are gathered at the "McGill gates" for a week-night tramp over Mount Royal. As Alan Trachtenberg observes, in a group portrait, the subjects have double identities as individuals and as members of a group.[15] In the snowshoe club composites, everyone is given his individual due, but together the members make up the corporeal body of the snowshoe club whose masculinity is emphasized by the exclusion of women. The corporeality of members is also emphasized since the composites portray members as active bodies, not the disembodied heads so common for group portraits at the time. The composites were widely circulated at international exhibitions; consequently, the image of distinctively dressed Canadians engaged in vigorous winter sports received international recognition, reinforcing and updating an already existing visual image.[16] Thus, snowshoeing became a national identifier representing Canada, Canadians, and Canadian-ness.

This identity was further disseminated abroad in souvenir portraits taken for visitors. A Montreal *Gazette* advertisement for the Notman Studio, dated 10 April 1867, indicates that Indigenous winter activities and costume had become *the* national signifier:

Portraits in Winter Costume
This style is very effective, and has the additional advantage of affording to

THE SNOW SHOE TRAMP

Up! Up! The morn is beaming,
Through the forest breaks the Sun,
Rouse ye Sleepers, time for dreaming
When our daily journey's done.
Bind the snow shoes,
Fast with thongs too,
See that all is right and sure.
All is bliss to, naught's amiss to
A brave North Western voyageur, oh ...

Chorus:
Tramp, tramp on snow shoes tramping,
All the day we marching go,
Till at night by fire's encamping,
We find couches on the snow.

On, on let men find pleasure
In the city, dark and drear.
Life is freedom, life's a treasure,
As we all enjoy it here.
Ha, ha, ha, ha, ha, ha, ha, ha,
see the novice down once more;
Hear him shout then, pull him out then,
Many a fall he's had before, oh ...

Chorus:

Figure 3.2 "The Snow Shoe Tramp," ca. 1859. Music by Harold Palmer, words by Alfred Bailey, first performed by the Aurora Snow Shoe Club of Montreal. It became one of the most popular songs sung on tramps and at snowshoe concerts.

Figure 3.3 William Notman and Henry Sandham, "St. George's Snowshoe Club at McGill Gates, Montreal, 1880." This is one of many composite club portraits produced by the Notman Studios. The artists attempted to solve the problem of composing a picture with so many figures by separating them into several groups. Note the skill with which the photographer and painter have handled scale and lighting in the composition of the figures. McCord Museum M2000.38.90.

friends at a distance an excellent idea of our Canadian winters, and of the following Canadian sports and out-door amusements:

Snow-Shoeing
Tobogganing
Sleighing

To create this style, customers could choose from a selection of props and settings provided by the photographer, including blanket coats, snowshoes, and sleds. Between 1860 and 1900, the Notman Studio took more than 450 photographs of sitters wearing blanket coats, and even during summer months, customers chose to be portrayed against a winter backdrop.[17] A portrait of Captain Hawks and Captain Howe, military officers stationed in Montreal, suggests that an outdoor setting, a sash, and snowshoes were enough to signify the scene as "Canadian" (see Figure 3.4). This was true for female sitters, too. Although women were never included in competitive races or tramps, they were at times invited to "stroll" on snowshoes, and in Figure 3.5 Louise Erskine Wolseley, the wife of the senior British military officer stationed in Canada, is portrayed in the female version of the snowshoe outfit. A political cartoon in *Grip*, a satirical magazine published in Toronto, indicated how well established the connection between snowshoeing and the nation was by the 1880s. It showed Miss Canada, dressed in a blanket coat, sash, and tuque in dialogue with American Brother Jonathan.[18] A *Punch* cartoon published in England in 1883 depicting Lord Lansdowne, the new governor general, dressed "in his new Canadian costume" also recognized the snowshoe outfit as distinctively Canadian.[19]

Some snowshoe club members were content to just wear the costume and take a carriage to social events, but these "driving members" were criticized for being too soft and not living up to the desired level of manliness. "Bona fide" snowshoers did not just look the part; they strove to act it, too.[20] Club records and newspaper reports show that members valued stamina, pluck, and athletic prowess and celebrated difficult weather conditions or strenuous routes. On one expedition, "five men' ran fourteen straight miles," and the route of another took them "over hill and dale, fence and wall, occasionally through the bush, here a gully had to be jumped, there a steep descent made, requiring all one's agility to avert a tumble."[21] Terrain such as this was an important backdrop against which to display their physicality. In the nineteenth century, Canada was popularly believed to be a snowy northern wilderness, a land of

Figure 3.4 "Col. Hawks and Capt. Howe, Montreal, 1867." Notman was known for his realistic special effects. Here real boughs were set up against a painted background and fox fur and salt were used to create the effect of snow. McCord Museum I-24948

Figure 3.5 William Notman, "Mrs. Colonel Wolseley, Montreal, QC, 1868." McCord Museum I-30221.1.

vast, impenetrable forests and rugged landscapes, with a bracing climate that bred healthy, hardy, and physically vigorous "Men of the North," as opposed to the febrile health and effeminate bodies of southern peoples.[22] Thus, Mount Royal and the countryside the snowshoers tramped through was what cultural geographers have called a "fabricated" national landscape, in which snowshoers could believe themselves to be authentic Natives and be recognized as such by others.[23] The vigour of the activity trained and transformed their bodies, and their endurance on long tramps in bad weather demonstrated their manliness. They combined the Indigenous "bush masculinity" of voyageurs, *coureurs de bois*, and First Nations with imported "gentry masculinity," which valued personal honour, class, duty, and sportsmanship.[24] Reaching "The Pines" at the summit of Mount Royal symbolized their conquest of "the mountain" (in reality, it was little more than a large hill) and put them in a commanding position – visually and strategically in possession of the city, its environs, and its peoples. Crossing rural fields, whose fences were lost under snow, they could imagine themselves to be pioneers in a virgin landscape, exploring and claiming the land.

The significance of the physicality of snowshoeing should not be underestimated. Paul Connerton has persuasively argued that physical performance plays an essential role in the construction of social memory. As an activity that became habitual through repetition, snowshoeing constituted what he calls a "mnemonics of the body."[25] The physical repetition constructed cognitive knowledge and memory of the "proper" characteristics of the White, male Canadian body. As the words to "The Snow Shoe Tramp" make clear, the tramps were cultural performances in which members envisioned themselves as "brave Nor'Western voyageurs" – members of a fur brigade of earlier times, struggling manfully through deep snows in "Indian" file. The meal and sociability they enjoyed at their destination mirrored the homosociability of the annual rendezvous in the *pays d'en haut* or the legendary dinners of the Beaver Club.[26] Wearing Indigenous clothing and performing Indigenous activities, snowshoe club members literally stepped into the shoes of the "real" Canadian Natives, both Aboriginal and French. Thus, organized club snowshoeing was not just a way to get exercise; it functioned to usurp and erase the Aboriginal and French-Canadian histories of snowshoeing, rendering them instead part of the British history of Canada. Moreover, acting out these myths of origin dressed in "Indigenous" clothing caused the performers to feel themselves part of that history on a conscious, cognitive level, and through bodily knowledge this feeling became a matter of belief, a sensation of physical rootedness in the land. Since all the snowshoe clubs organized similar activities, espoused like values, celebrated with each other at annual races and dinners, and read about each others' exploits in the newspaper, members had a common set of interests and a common culture, and they were readily able to imagine themselves as a larger, national body that shared the interests of snowshoers in other cities and towns across the Dominion. Furthermore, many snowshoers also belonged to lacrosse clubs, so this common identity was also disseminated in the summer season through the game of lacrosse.

Lacrosse

Lacrosse was another Indigenous rather than imported sport, and became popular as both a participatory and a spectator sport. There are reports of games between Native teams and Montrealers from the 1840s onward, with the Montreal Lacrosse Club (MLC) being formed in 1856. It rapidly grew in popularity when a Montreal dentist and enthusiastic sportsman, Dr. W. George Beers, founded the National Lacrosse Association in September 1867 and published *Lacrosse: The National Game of Canada* (1867), which set out rules of play and gave explicit instructions on technique, strategy, training, and practice. His efforts were so successful that by 1884 an estimated twenty thousand players were registered in clubs from coast to coast, and championship games were attracting large crowds of five thousand or more spectators.[27] It was a lively, aggressive, and competitive game that was exciting to watch and to play. As can be seen from the title of his book, Beers enthusiastically promoted the game as a national signifier, and like snowshoeing, it was another means by which a putative national identity could be repeatedly embodied and displayed to an audience. It also functioned as a colonialist strategy that subordinated and replaced Aboriginal peoples by usurping another of their most distinctive activities.

In accordance with the tenets of "muscular Christianity," prevalent in the English public schools and popularized by books such as *Tom Brown's Schooldays* by Thomas Hughes (1857), Beers and his peers believed that vigorous team sports played in a gentlemanly manner would promote manliness, morality, health, and patriotism. Skills and discipline learned on the sports field would be transferred to the world outside to improve and morally uplift society. But this could only be achieved if the "primitive" aspects of the Aboriginal game of *baggataway* were "civilized" through the imposition of rules and regulations. To show this had been done, the White players would have to disport themselves differently from their Native counterparts. Analysis of Beers's rules and contemporary visual images of the players reveal that the bodies and actions of White players were distinguished and privileged through a series of visual and physical oppositions: White teams wore distinctive club uniforms, they played "scientifically" rather than "innately," they made "improvements" in positioning, and they regulated the amount of physical contact and violence tolerated. These changes, in effect, invented the new sport of lacrosse and justified the claim that it was "our" game, as well as "taming" the game and forcing Native players to play according to White standards.[28] Tours abroad publicized the game and further constructed Canadians as lovers of outdoor sports.

Portraits of teams from Caughnawaga (present-day Kahnawake; see Figure 3.6) and the MLC (see Figure 3.7) were made at the Notman Studio, possibly on the same day. Comparison reveals significant differences in representation between the two. The Native players wore no uniform, whereas the MLC players were dressed identically.[29] The MLC players were arranged in banked rows creating a tight diamond shape, with the captain between the flags at the top. These were the Caxton flags, awarded only to championship winners, and hence, a clue to the high status of the team. In contrast, the Caughnawaga team was arranged asymmetrically with their captain at the back, but not placed in the same dominant position as his opponent, and with no indication of the team's status. The differences in clothing and composition reveal the values and qualities attached to each group because symmetry requires forethought; iconologically, it represents hierarchy and order. By comparison, asymmetrical compositions appear to be unpremeditated, with no concern for rank or hierarchy. The purposeful dress and arrangement of the White team contrasts with the apparently indolent pose and random clothing of the Native players, solidifying a representational strategy that confirmed already existing prejudices and stereotypes about Native peoples. The composition of the lacrosse sticks is also suggestive. In the Caughnawaga portrait, they form a diamond, whereas in the MLC portrait they merely echo the composition of the men's bodies, thus suggesting that the photographer saw the subject of the Caughnawaga portrait as being the game rather than the players. Native bodies are thus diminished and subordinated in contrast to the robust masculine bodies of the White players.

As with snowshoeing, it was not only how they looked but also how they played that differentiated White from Native players. A series of in-

Figure 3.6 William Notman, "The Caughnawaga Lacrosse Club, 1867." McCord Museum I-29099.1.

structional photographs showing the correct stance and handling of the crosse was published as the frontispiece of Beers's book (see Figure 3.8). Even though White teams rarely beat Native teams at this time, in the photos it is White players who are presented as the experts, and hence, lacrosse is represented as a White "Canadian" game. Although Native players were admired for their individual skills and physical capacities, they were still considered inferior to White players since these were said to be innate abilities unrelated to the intellect and will. According to this way of thinking, Whites were better players than Natives because Whites had to train and practise to achieve the skills and the physical condition that Natives enjoyed innately. Beers criticized the individualistic style of Native players, where running rather than passing the ball was the key.

Figure 3.7 William Notman, "The Montreal Lacrosse Club, 1867." McCord Museum I-29210.

Figure 3.8 Frontispiece, W. George Beers, *Lacrosse: The National Game of Canada* (Montreal: Dawson Bros., 1869). Eric R. Dennis Collection, Special Collections, Vaughan Memorial Library, Acadia University.

He advocated "scientific" play, which meant that White players were assigned to certain field positions, each position with its own particular responsibilities. The deployment of White teams on the field, therefore, looked somewhat different from that of Native teams. Newspaper reports frequently remarked that Native players tended to knot or bunch up at the goals, whereas White players remained more spread out, playing their positions in a more disciplined way. As one reporter commented, "The 'playing together' of the Montreal men is one more indication that science and skill, opposed to strength and endurance without either of the former attributes is, in nine cases out of ten, certain of success."[30] Substituting the "improved" body of the colonist for the "inferior" body of the Native created a new Canadian national body, and this new "Canadian" style of play embodied in exercise relationships and values held in other spheres of life. Individual achievement and self-improvement were encouraged, but they had to be balanced by the need to work together in harmony for the good of the group.

The amount of rough play allowed and how the body could be used were also regulated. Beers did not want to prevent "hard running" or the "occasional honest shoulder encounters," but he deplored "slashing and swiping and wounding *by crosses*."[31] The rules also outlawed spiked shoes, tripping, holding, pushing, and fighting, and the ideal "gentlemanly" player avoided all of these. The *Montreal Family Herald* of 31 October 1874 agreed, opining, "Strength of character consists of two things, power of will and power of self-restraint."[32] Using muscle developed through scientific training was admired, but cutting a player's feet out from under him with equipment was considered undisciplined and unsporting. In combination with newspaper reporters' general disapproval of rough play, Beers's rules and the frontispiece illustrations were didactic, publicizing acceptable and unacceptable behaviours. Illustration number 10, for instance, is a model for the legitimate use of force: opposing players are in a shoulder-to-shoulder struggle, but without infringing the rules. The discipline to control one's body mentally and physically was a metaphor for social and economic independence, and this liberal ideal of gentlemanly behaviour was a way that the middle classes, at least in theory, could physically distinguish themselves from their social subordinates.

Even so, there was a good deal of violence among players and spectators, and it was not restricted to games that pitted Natives against Whites: over a quarter of the games played between the senior White clubs had disputes, violence, and even rioting.[33] From newspaper reports, it appears that this was particularly the case when White teams played the Montreal Shamrocks, an Irish Catholic team whose players and fans were mostly working class. These class and religious differences led to tremendous interteam rivalries manifested by physically violent and acrimonious matches. Lacrosse was, therefore, an arena in which competing groups struggled to control "definitions of the legitimate body and the legitimate use of the body."[34] It also allowed a display of manliness that was, theoretically at least, disciplined and gentlemanly but much more exciting to watch than British games such as cricket.

As a fervent nationalist, Beers was eager to have lacrosse recognized as "the Canadian game," and White and Native teams toured England on several occasions, playing in front of Queen Victoria and travelling to the Paris World's Fair in 1866.[35] These tours were well received, and additional visits to Australia and New Zealand ensured that lacrosse became Canada's imperial sport, recognized as Canadian throughout the British Empire.[36] Canadian teams were also received enthusiastically in northern U.S. cities, so much so that American teams were formed. The success of Montrealers in distinguishing Canadians through sport can be judged by an article in the *Acadian Recorder* [Halifax] of 18 July 1874 headed "Canadian Nerve and Muscle." The report reads: "It is no new thing – the men of these Provinces taking vigorously to athletic experiences and sports. Unlike the people southward of them, it has always seemed to come natural to them."[37] The writer stated what had been constructed as "natural" and "obvious": Canadians have always been a northern people, innately predisposed to excel at sports, unlike their American neighbours to the south. Visitors from abroad, therefore, found it to be a matter of curiosity and note, but no big surprise, when Canadians young and old, male and female, participated in the activities of the Montreal winter carnivals. In fact, visitors tried out some of the Canadian sports themselves, with tobogganing being particularly popular.

Tobogganing

By the 1880s, snowshoeing and lacrosse and the White men who played them had been recognized at home and abroad as Canadian. The series of winter carnivals held in Montreal in that decade cemented that identity and gave visitors from abroad and other parts of Canada the chance to learn and try out for themselves what it felt like to be Canadian. While snowshoeing and lacrosse needed some practice and skill, tobogganing

Figure 3.9 Francis George Coleridge, watercolour, *How We Toboggan in Canada*, 1865–66. Public hills could get very crowded, especially on weekends when hundreds of tobogganers might come out. Sleds were steered from behind, either with a short stick or by trailing one leg, and tumbles were common, as can be seen here. Library and Archives Canada C-102538.

was a more accessible activity, enjoyed by women, children, and even the elderly. This made it ideal to share with visitors as a distinctively Canadian activity.[38]

The toboggan, or sled, was a means of transporting goods over the snow adopted from Native peoples by French and British colonists. It became a favourite winter amusement and until the latter part of the nineteenth century was a free-for-all pastime, full of thrills and spills, as can be seen in Figure 3.9. Like lacrosse, however, it was "tamed" by being organized into a middle-class club activity carried out in specific locations and subjected to British-style order, discipline, and technological "improvement." Toboggan clubs (many of them offshoots of snowshoe or lacrosse clubs) emerged in Montreal in the late 1870s. Instead of al-

Figure 3.10 John Henry Walker, drawing, *Looking from Top of Toboggan Slide*, 1850–85. Toboggan club members can be seen climbing up the stairs at each side of one of the club slides, and then taking their turn going down one of the several ice chutes. McCord Museum M991X.5.799.

lowing tobogganers free rein on the streets and hills, the clubs built slides composed of a series of ice chutes separated by low ice walls, often with a wooden extension at the top to give a steeper drop. Some clubs built a stairway beside the slide to make the ascent easier and more efficient.[39] Tobogganers could then take their turn at flying down the hill in a safer and much more orderly fashion, and those on the return trip would not impede the sleighs coming down (see Figure 3.10). The drop was steep and long, providing a physical experience that would have been relatively unique at that time. Ed Ruthven, writing for *The Week* (Toronto) found it "more than merely exhilarating. A quarter of a mile in fourteen seconds, the first part of the journey down a hill the descent of which is like falling off a roof of a four-storey house, is calculated to quicken the pulse to a point which 'exhilaration' is not sufficiently strong to do justice to. Yes, tobogganing is becoming an institution and a hair-raising, breath-catching, glorious institution it is."[40]

Dressed in a feminine version of the snowshoe club outfit, women were a frequent sight on the Montreal toboggan slopes, whereas they had been restricted to the role of spectator or occasional guest for lacrosse and snowshoeing. This was because organized sports in general in the nineteenth century were a means by which male gender roles were defined, enacted, and displayed. The scientific discourse that constructed women as frail and physically incapacitated had kept them on the sidelines, and their exclusion had served to heighten the players' masculinity.[41] However, by the 1880s, attitudes towards women's participation in physical activities were changing, and respectable female behaviour in public included a measure of active participation. To be sure, tobogganing was a leisure activity rather than an organized sport proper, and it was assumed that their "delicate" presence on the toboggan slopes required the provision of a warm clubroom in which to sip tea or spiced wine and adjust their clothing.[42] Nevertheless, tobogganing did extend to women the experience of embodying national identity.

The *New York Sun* reporter could easily recognize Canadian girls. He commented on their natural beauty, praising their bright red cheeks and flashing eyes as the product of healthy outdoor exercise rather than reliance on cosmetics, as seen among their American counterparts.[43] Souvenir booklets for the 1880s winter carnivals frequently referred to the healthy, rosy cheeks of young Canadian girls, whose "faces are ruddy from exercise, and eyes are flashing with healthful excitement." The writer went on to enthuse: "A Canadian belle in white blanket suit, gaily trimmed, and with pale blue tuque jauntily set upon her head, stepping springingly along with mocassined feet is a sight worth going to Canada to see."[44] The pluck and courage of Canadian girls was also often remarked on: "Nothing astonishes our winter visitors more than the indifference to danger, and the genuine delight in hard, rough pleasure shown by our Canadian girls," claimed one souvenir booklet.[45] Canadian ladies displayed much more confidence on the slopes than American women: "There is something of a national relish in their demeanour ... with the Americans, however, it is different. They peep down the shoot with tremulous emotion."[46] Evidently, the stereotype of Canadians as healthy, vigorous lovers of the outdoors could overcome the disadvantages of gender for nationalistic reasons, and national identity could be extended to include women, once it had been secured for men.

Visitors arrived in Montreal to attend the winter carnivals from all over Canada, Europe, and the United States in response to extensive advertising. In 1885, as many as fifty thousand watched displays of snowshoeing, toured the Ice Palace, lined the streets for the tandem parade, and enjoyed parties, fireworks displays, and toboggan rides.[47] At the carnival events, they learned to recognize organized winter sports as distinctively Canadian. However, the identity on display was exclusively middle class. Carnival events were held during working hours, and they were well beyond the means of most working people. Women could participate in prescribed ways, but that was true only for women of the middle classes. There was room, too, for French-Canadian participation, but not if it displayed a rival ethnic or religious identity, as was evident in competing French and English tandem and snowshoe parades during the 1885 carnival week.[48] Nevertheless, the carnivals were instrumental in promoting Canadian identity. Visitors' admiration for Canadian sports, and the evident ease with which they could pick out the Canadians in the crowd, showed that by the 1880s colonial bodies had been transformed into national ones.

Conclusion

Torontonian "Native Canadians" identified themselves with a maple leaf emblem, but in the following decades male and, to a strictly limited extent, female members of the middle classes in Montreal embodied their national identity, giving colonists the "Canuck" identity they had lacked. Lacrosse, snowshoeing, and tobogganing became widely recognized as Canadian national sports because they were Indigenous and sufficiently different from British and American sports to distinguish the players as Canadian. By training and clothing the male body in specific ways, and by performing in the distinctive Canadian environment, British colonists indigenized themselves, becoming "Native Canadians." Rules and regulations erased the "primitive" associations of these Indigenous activities and were held up as evidence of the progressive, ordered, and "civilized" nature of Canadian society. Repeated participation in or viewing of the players and sports, as well as repeated exposure to representations of these performances in the form of visual images and textual re-presentations published in the daily and periodical press, cemented this distinctive identity.

The vast number of portraits of men in various sporting guises produced by the Notman Studio is a clue that masculinity, physical ability, and the body itself were crucial to colonists' identification of themselves as Canadian. The role of performance and the agency of the audience in the construction of meaning must also be considered. A performance is a reciprocal act of showing and observing, with each party observing itself as well.[49] Repetition of the performance/observation renders it habitual and, thus, characteristic. Members of the sports clubs and their audiences identified the performers as people like themselves acting as Canadians, which signalled to them how to act Canadian. In embodying national identity, their bodies became both pedagogical objects and performative subjects.

British colonists in Montreal found a physical identity that would signify them as Canadian, but it was not an identity they would extend to all members of society. Women, Natives, and "foreigners" could not qualify for sport club membership, and in any case, they would lack the shared values or resources necessary to participate. Nor did organized sport encourage social unity. Native players were increasingly excluded, and when French-Canadian Montrealers took up sports in larger numbers in the 1890s, they did so in part to contest English domination, not to be assimilated.[50] Working-class men used the forms of middle-class sports and fraternal organizations, but they put them to their own purposes and created their own class identities.[51] Despite ethnic and class differences, however, the national identity created by middle-class clubs was not totally unappealing to other social groups. Physical prowess, stamina, and virile masculinity were qualities valued by all classes, as were asymmetrical gender and racial hierarchies. Thus, identities of race and gender could override class positions and produce a common national identity in the body of the Canadian sportsman – aspects of which persist to the present day in Canada's identification with vigorous winter sports.

Notes

1 *Daily Globe* [Toronto], 22 Aug. 1860, 2. The organizers included many well-known Torontonians, such as Hon. W.B. Robinson, J.H. Morris, Col. R.L. Denison, Dr. Egerson Ryerson, and W.H. Boulton.

2 Ibid., 23 Aug. 1860, 2.

3 Ibid., 22 Aug. 1860, 2.

4 Benedict Anderson, *Imagined Communities: Reflections on the Origin and Spread of Nationalism* (London: Verso, 1991 [1983]). In putting the focus on the body for this collection, I have revisited some of my earlier articles and

revised some portions of text, which appear here with the permission of the publishers. These publications are *Becoming Native in a Foreign Land: Sport, Visual Culture, and Identity in Montreal, 1840–1885* (Vancouver: UBC Press, 2009); "'Eminently Canadian': Indigenous Sports and Canadian Identity in Victorian Montreal," in *Hidden in Plain Sight: Contributions of Aboriginal Peoples to Canadian Identity and Culture*, ed. David R. Newhouse, Cora J. Voyageur, and Dan Beavon (Toronto: University of Toronto Press, 2005), 352–75; "Montreal and Its Environs: Imagining a National Landscape, c. 1867–1885," *Journal of Canadian Studies* 38, no. 3 (2004), 69–100; and "Snowshoeing and Lacrosse: Canada's Nineteenth-Century 'National Games,'" *Culture, Sport, Society* 6, nos. 2–3 (2003), 293–320, reprinted in *Ethnicity, Sport, Identity: Struggles for Status*, ed. J.A. Mangan and Andrew Ritchie (London: Frank Cass, 2004), 293–320.

5 Judith Butler, "Performative Arts and Gender Constitution: An Essay in Phenomenology and Feminist Theory," in *Performing Feminisms: Feminist Critical Theory and Theatre*, ed. Sue-Ellen Case (Baltimore, MD: Johns Hopkins University Press, 1990), 277n9.

6 Ian Radforth, *Royal Spectacle: The 1860 Visit of the Prince of Wales to Canada and the United States* (Toronto: University of Toronto Press, 2004), 278.

7 As the largest and most diverse city with four main ethnic groups (French, English, Scottish, and Irish), two language blocks, two major religious denominations, and two nearby Native reserves, cultural and political tensions were particularly prevalent in Montreal.

8 Nationalist/imperialist debates are examined by Carl Berger, *The Sense of Power: Studies in the Ideas of Canadian Imperialism, 1867–1914* (Toronto: University of Toronto Press, 1970).

9 Paintings by early Quebec artists and sketches by visiting British military topographical artists often featured Native peoples and snowshoes. For examples, see *Painting in Quebec, 1820–1850*, ed. Mario Béland (Quebec City: Musée du Québec, 1992).

10 Members of the MSSC in the early years included professionals and businessmen whose circumstances ranged from comfortable to wealthy. As sports clubs proliferated, membership widened to encompass men from the lower ranks: bookkeepers, clerks, and other salaried employees who lacked their independence but shared, or aspired to, their status and values. The term "middle classes" is used here to refer to this heterogeneous group. In the mid-1880s, there were approximately twenty-five snowshoe clubs in Montreal alone, and the MSSC had 1,100 active members. Don Morrow, "The Knights of the Snowshoe: A Study of the Evolution of Sport in Nineteenth-Century Montreal," *Journal of Sport History* 15, no. 1 (1988), 5,

37; and Alan Metcalfe, "The Evolution of Organized Physical Recreation in Montreal, 1840–1895," *Histoire sociale/Social History* 11 (May 1978): 149.

11 The blanket coat is examined in more detail by Eileen Stack, "Very Picturesque and Very Canadian: The Blanket Coat and Anglo-Canadian Identity in the Second Half of the Nineteenth Century," in *Fashion: A Canadian Perspective*, ed. Alexandra Palmer (Toronto: University of Toronto Press, 2004), 17–40.

12 Thus also creating a new "narrative of nation." Homi K. Bhabha, "Introduction: Narrating the Nation," in *Nation and Narration*, ed. Homi K. Bhabha (London: Routledge, 1990), 1–7. George Colpitts, this volume, and Myra Rutherdale, this volume, contend that clothing is invested with meanings, and I would argue that here is another illustration of that point.

13 A recording has been made by Mary Lou Fallis, *Primadonna on a Moose*, CD (Burlington, ON: Opening Day Recordings, 1997).

14 Stanley G. Triggs, *The Composite Photographs of William Notman* (Montreal: McCord Museum, 1994), 21–5.

15 Alan Trachtenberg, "The Group Portrait," in *Multiple Exposure: The Group Portrait in Photography*, ed. Leslie Tonkonow and Alan Trachtenberg, exhibition catalogue (New York: Independent Curators, 1995), 11–23.

16 Notman regularly won prizes for his photographs at international expositions such as the 1867 Paris Universal Exposition and the 1876 Philadelphia Centennial Exhibition. See *The World of William Notman: The Nineteenth Century through a Master Lens*, ed. Robert Hall, Gordon Dodds, and Stanley Triggs (Toronto: McClelland and Stewart, 1993), 42–7.

17 Eileen Stack, "The Significance of the Blanket Coat to Anglo-Canadian Identity," paper presented to at the 25th Annual Symposium of the Costume Society of America, Santa Fe, New Mexico, 22–5 May 1999, 5.

18 William Bengough, "The True State of Her Feelings," *Grip*, 19 Jan. 1889.

19 "Lord Lansdowne, in His New Canadian Costume Adapted to Remaining for Some Time Out in the Cold," *Punch*, 2 June 1883, 262. Lord Lansdowne's appointment to Canada was considered political exile because he had broken with Gladstone over Irish policy. R.H. Hubbard, *Rideau Hall: An Illustrated History of Government House, Ottawa* (Ottawa: Queen's Printer, 1967), 72.

20 "The Snowshoe Parade," *Gazette* [Montreal], 24 Jan. 1885, 5.

21 Newspaper clipping, Montreal Amateur Athletic Association (MAAA) Scrapook 1, 93; "The Torchlight Procession," Jan. 1873, Scrapbook 1, 4. The records of the MSSC are contained in the MAAA archives deposited at Library and Archives Canada, MG 28 I-351, which include four scrapbooks of newspaper clippings and memorabilia.

22 This image was employed by Robert Grant Haliburton, *The Men of the North and Their Place in History: A Lecture Delivered before the Montreal Literary Club, March 31st, 1869* (Montreal: John Lovell, 1869). The dominance of the northern image is discussed by Sherrill Grace, *Canada and the Idea of North* (Montreal and Kingston: McGill-Queen's University Press, 2001).

23 Brian S. Osborne, "'Grounding' National Mythologies: The Case of Canada," in *Espace et culture*, ed. Serge Courville and Normand Séguin (Sainte Foy, QC: Presses de l'Université Laval, 1995), 265–7.

24 Kevin B. Wamsley makes this contrast in "The Public Importance of Men and the Importance of Public Men: Sport and Masculinities in 19th Century Canada," in *Sport and Gender in Canada*, ed. Philip White and Kevin Young (New York: Oxford University Press, 1999), 26.

25 Paul Connerton, *How Societies Remember* (Cambridge: Cambridge University Press, 1989), 74.

26 Carolyn Podruchny, "Festivals, Fortitude, and Fraternalism: Fur Trade Masculinity and the Beaver Club, 1785–1827," in *New Faces of the Fur Trade: Selected Papers of the Seventh North American Fur Trade Conference, Halifax, Nova Scotia, 1995*, ed. Jo-Anne Fiske, Susan Sleeper-Smith, and William Wicken (East Lansing, MI: Michigan State University Press, 1998), 31–52.

27 T. George Vellathottam and Kevin G. Jones, "Highlights in the Development of Canadian Lacrosse to 1931," *Canadian Journal of History of Sport and Physical Education* 5, no. 2 (1974), 40. See also Alan Metcalfe, *Canada Learns to Play: The Emergence of Organized Sport, 1807–1914* (Toronto: McClelland and Stewart, 1987), 185.

28 Bonnie Reilly Schmidt, this volume, also illustrates the crucial role of representation in the process of marginalization and exclusion.

29 Montreal *Gazette*, 4 July 1867. Paul Connerton discusses the significance of uniforms in his *How Societies Remember* (Cambridge: Cambridge University Press, 1989), 7–11; Nathan Joseph, *Uniforms and Nonuniforms: Communication through Clothing* (New York: Greenwood, 1986).

30 MAAA, Scrapbook 1, 115.

31 Beers, *Lacrosse*, 54, 53; original emphasis.

32 Cited by Jennifer Susan Marotta, "'Rejoicing that You Are a Subject of Her Gracious Queen Victoria': Race and Respectability within the Pages of *The Family Herald and Weekly Star*, 1873–1890," paper presented at the Annual Conference of the Canadian Historical Association, Université de Laval, Quebec City, 15–27 May 2001, 5.

33 An estimated 28 per cent of these games manifested violence; see Metcalfe, *Canada Learns*, 193.

34 Pierre Bourdieu, "Sport and Social Class," *Social Science Information* 17

(1978), 826, cited by John W. Loy, David L. Andrews, and Robert E. Rinehart, "The Body in Culture and Sport," *Sport Science Review* 2, no. 1 (1993),
79.

35 Johnny Beauvais, *Kahnawake: A Mohawk Look at Canada and Adventures of Big
John Canadian, 1840–1919* ([Montreal]: n.p., 1985), 57, 44.

36 David Brown, "Canadian Imperialism and Sporting Exchanges: The Nineteenth-Century Cultural Experience of Cricket and Lacrosse," *Canadian
Journal of History of Sport* 18, no. 1 (1987), 60.

37 MAAA Scrapbook 1, 116.

38 I follow contemporary usage in calling tourists "visitors," especially since
many were lodged in private homes owing to insufficient hotel accommoda-
tion.

39 Thanks to one of the anonymous readers for the suggestion that these
wooden slopes may have been inspired by the timber chutes built by loggers
and famously tried out by the Prince of Wales during his visit in 1860.

40 Ed Ruthven, *The Week* [Toronto], 7 Feb. 1884, 158.

41 Patricia Vertinsky, *The Eternally Wounded Woman: Women, Doctors and Exercise
in the Late Nineteenth Century* (Manchester, UK: Manchester University Press,
1990); Carroll Smith-Rosenberg and Charles Rosenberg, "The Female Animal: Medical and Biological Views of Women and Their Role in Nineteenth-
Century America," in *From "Fair Sex" to Feminism: Sport and the Socialization of
Women in the Industrial and Post-Industrial Eras*, ed. J.A. Mangan and Roberta
J. Park (London: Frank Cass, 1987), 13–37.

42 Agnes Macdonald, "On a Tobogan," *Murray's Magazine* [London] 3 (Jan.–
June 1888), 78.

43 Montreal *Gazette*, 27 Jan. 1883.

44 Samuel Edward Dawson, *Montreal Winter Carnival, February 4th to 9th, 1884*.
Supplement to Dawson's handbook for the City of Montreal ([Montreal]:
Montreal Gazette Printing, [1884]), 4.

45 Written by none other than W. George Beers, *Over the Snow, or The Montreal
Carnival* (Montreal: W. Drysdale and J. Tho. Robinson, 1883), 40.

46 *Montreal Daily Star*, 6 Feb. 1884.

47 The organization and events of the winter carnivals are examined in detail
in Sylvie Dufresne, "Le Carnaval d'hiver de Montreal (1883–1889)," M.A.
thesis, Université du Québec à Montréal, 1980.

48 This claim is explored in depth in my *Becoming Native*, 186–204.

49 Tom F. Driver, *The Magic of Ritual: Our Need for Liberating Rites That Transform
Our Lives and Our Communities* (San Francisco, CA: Harper, 1991), 80–1.

50 Donald Guay, *La Conquête du sport: Le sport et la société québecoise au XiXe siècle*
(Montreal: Lanctot, 1997), chapter 5, concludes that before 1880 French

Canadians were generally either uninterested in participating in organized sports, rejected them because they were dominated by anglophones, or were respectful of the Catholic Church's disapproval of organized sports as being morally dubious and subversive.

51 This argument is made by Carl William Stempel, "Towards a Historical Sociology of Sport in the United States: 1825–1875," doctoral dissertation, University of Oregon, 1992, 75, and Barbara Pinto, "'Ain't Misbehavin': The Montreal Shamrock Lacrosse Club Fans, 1868–1884,'" in *Proceedings of the North American Society for Sport History* (Banff, AB: 1990), 92.

4 The Boer War, Masculinity, and Citizenship in Canada, 1899–1902

AMY SHAW

In 1899, Britain declared war on the South African republics of the Transvaal and the Orange Free State. Canada followed Britain into the conflict. Having its beginning in the chauvinistic close of Victoria's reign, and its completion, after numerous unforeseen disasters, in a more uncertain world, the Boer War, symbolically as well as chronologically, linked the nineteenth with the twentieth century. The Canadian response to the war acted in a similar way, with early evocations of imperial loyalty shifting to the more nationalist sentiments later expressed in Wilfrid Laurier's evocation of the twentieth as "Canada's century." An examination of the way the Canadian men who volunteered to fight in the Boer War were presented and described, especially in newspapers at the time, reveals an interesting focus on their physical bodies. These men served as representatives of prescriptive manliness to Canadians reading about their exploits, and as foils for the images of the Boers against whom they were fighting. Canada's citizen-soldiers were described in ways that not only presented them as recognizable physical types, but also, in discussing their motives for enlisting and behaviour overseas, presented a model of appropriate manly purpose and conduct. An examination of these responses to Canadian soldiers in the Anglo-Boer War reveals important insights not only about the colonial relationship, but also, and more particularly, about national concerns relating to the perceived responsibilities of Canadian citizenship and the constructions of idealized masculinity, especially in wartime.

Canada's relationship with imperialism was complex and has been understudied. While a colony of Britain, the country sometimes presented itself as the heir of the British Empire and, in sending soldiers to South Africa was behaving, arguably, in an imperialist way. Although a self-evidently international ideology, imperialism was also understood in a very personal, individual way; the bodies of British subjects read as evidence of their superiority. This focus coexisted, often quite comfortably, with a nationalism based in notions of robust "northern" superiority.[1]

To discover how imperialism was understood, on a personal level, in the context of the later nineteenth century, it is necessary to examine the way constructions of gender, and its intersections with ethnicity and social class have shaped, and been shaped by, imperialism. Constructions of masculinity were an integral part of imperialist discourse. Kirsten Hoganson's study of how gendered ideology in the United States shaped the Spanish American War calls on historians to use gender as lens through which to investigate other brands and facets of imperialism. An examination of the various ways that constructions of colonial masculinity, especially ideals of manliness, were articulated, is essential to understanding Canada at the turn of the twentieth century. This essay takes a step in that direction.[2]

Rationale for War

The Second Anglo-Boer War (known in South Africa as Vryheidsoorloeë, or the War of Freedom) lasted from 1899 to 1902, much longer than anyone expected. It is generally divided into three phases. The first, a period of heavy British losses, culminated in "Black Week" in December 1899. The second was a period of reorganization and reinforcement ending with the capture of Bloemfontein and Pretoria – the capitals of the Orange Free State and South African Republic. Everyone assumed this would mean the end of the war. There were, however, another two years of bitter guerrilla warfare, during which British frustration with the "bitter enders" led to Lord Roberts's scorched earth campaign and the novelty of the concentration camp.[3]

When the South African republics declared war on Britain, in October 1899, there was considerable pressure in the Dominion to send a tangible demonstration of support to the mother country. Some of the pressure came from Britain and British representatives in Canada. Colonial Secretary Joseph Chamberlain, for whom imperial unity was key, especially the fostering of closer relations between Britain and the settler colonies, wanted an enthusiastic colonial initiative. Neither the War Office nor Chamberlain believed that colonial troops would actually be needed. What the Colonial Office wanted was a clear, symbolic, and official colonial demonstration of support.[4]

More cynical thinkers pointed to the gold deposits in the Boer territories; nevertheless, the avowed purpose for the declaration of war were the grievances of the Uitlanders. These were the mainly British non-Boers who had emigrated to the Transvaal upon the discovery of gold in the Witwatersrand in 1886. Participant John Hays Hammond offers a typical contemporary interpretation of the conditions they faced. He argued that the Uitlanders were being denied elementary rights. They faced limitations in terms of franchise, high taxes, and education in Taal rather than English. Furthermore, justice was said to be unequally administered, the courts corrupt, and the Uitlanders denied a free press and right of public meeting. Britain, according to this argument, had a duty to redress the wrong to its subjects. Not to respond strongly to the Uitlanders' petition for redress would not only be unethical, it could weaken the support of the other self-governing colonies, which were watching to see whether their own interests would be protected.[5]

Demands for a tangible expression of support also came from ordinary Canadians within the country. The popular rhetoric of the time framed this as a moral imperative. Newspaper articles emphasized the interpretation that Boer leader Paul Kruger's denial of the franchise to the Uitlanders made peaceful change impossible, and that his subsequent ultimatum and invasion of the Cape Colony compelled Britain to protect its colony. Colonial support for Britain's declaration of war stemmed from the fact that "a liberty common to all the colonies has been threatened, a new grown pride in the Empire was struck at, a feeling of manly aversion to further dependence was touched, an inherent but sometimes dormant love for the Mother Land was aroused."[6] In September 1899, the Toronto *Globe* printed an extract from a letter sent by Canadians resident in the Transvaal. It asserted that "the Uitlanders are justly entitled to these rights ... as British subjects and white men."[7] Because of the limitations on the franchise in Canada, where voting was limited to male British subjects, excluding not only women but Aboriginal, Japanese, and Chinese Canadians as well, the motivations for war were themselves explicitly gendered and racialized.

Although popular, and loud, support for the war was not a universal Canadian response. As in Britain, there were voices in Canada who viewed the war as motivated more clearly by the gold in the Transvaal than by the need to redress the wrongs done to British subjects there. This perception was most visible among Québécois, many of whom found themselves identifying more with the religious, rural Boers, surrounded by expansionist English, than with the rest of the British Empire. Prime Minister Wilfrid Laurier, and several of his cabinet members, were also against participation, worrying about the precedent such assistance might set for future imperial conflicts. In 1977, C.P. Stacey observed, "Never since 1899 has the outbreak of a war found the national government so deeply and gravely divided."[8]

Laurier attempted to defuse the arguments of those who had an alternate perception of the country's duty with an agreement to send a small contingent of volunteers. He stressed, perhaps futilely, that this delegation was intended to set no precedent. Laurier's address to the first contingent as they prepared to board the *Sardinian* on 30 October 1899 emphasized the nobility of their task: "The cause for which you men of Canada are going to fight is the cause of justice, the cause of humanity, of civil rights and religious liberty. This is not a war of conquest ... The object is not to crush out the Dutch population, but to establish in that land ... British sovereign law, to assure to all men an equal share of liberty."[9] Over the next three years, more than seven thousand Canadians served overseas.[10] These soldiers carried a heavy symbolic weight.

"Fine Strapping Fellows"

The physical bodies of the volunteers were a singular focus in the discourse about the war. Victorian commentators were engaged in an ongoing debate about the meaning of the body, corporeality, and gender ideals. Throughout the Empire the bodies of the soldiers who fought in the Boer War represented idealized late-Victorian masculinity: a devotion to duty, British civilization, and a muscular Christianity. This is interesting partly because the focus on physical hardiness and increasing primacy of loyalty to the group over individuality was a shift from earlier understandings of ideal manliness promoted by such writers as Thomas Carlyle, which had equated manliness with intellectual energy, moral purpose, and independence.[11] The ramifications of this new understanding of masculinity were one of the root causes for the focus on the physically athletic bodies of the Canadian contingent in the Boer War.

Newspapers and government rhetoric presented Canadian soldiers in the Boer War as a recognizable physical type. They were described as "the representatives of ideal Canadian manhood," the "pick of the nation's sinew and brain." The men were depicted poetically as "Lords of the Northland," and "pure as the air of the sunlit North." Civilian enthusiasts viewed the Canadian contingent as composed of "fine, strapping fellows, broad-shouldered, clean-limbed and blue-eyed."[12] This tendency to describe the Canadian contingent as having a distinctive physical appearance and healthy, youthful, sense of adventure continued in some of the descriptions of the arrival of the First Canadian Contingent at Cape Town. Carman Miller observes that "the Canadian Press never tired of repeating the Cape Town papers' glowing reports of the Canadians as 'the finest body of men that has yet come here, except Her Majesty's Guards. They have, as a rule, a light, springy, devil-may-care sort of swagger.'"[13] The discourse surrounding the volunteers seems a good indication of how the country saw itself – hardy, northern, and youthful. The soldiers were presented as the embodiment of country's idealized self-image.

Sometimes the focus was on the impressive physical characteristics of one's particular regiment or battalion. In his memoir, *The Royal Canadians in South Africa, 1899–1902*, Alexander Stearns McCormick is proud of the qualities, in terms of social class and appearance, of his colleagues, describing them as "the finest class of men, well educated, of good families, who left good business positions, professions or universities. Among them fifty officers, I one of them, who resigned commissions in other regiments in order to enlist. Physique exceptional; fifty per cent being six feet or more, few less than five feet nine."[14]

Because this was Canada's first overseas fighting experience, there was a clear sense that the soldiers were being presented, representing Canada, to the world, and especially Britain. Their physical appearance was evidence of Canada's national qualities. That commentators were seeing at least a degree of what they wanted to see is evident in the experience of A.E. Hilder. He was a member of the Second Contingent Royal Dragoons, who, like the other Canadian units, was represented as among the country's physical elite. One history notes "the remarkable physique of the Dragoons. Rigorous physical examination eliminated all but the fittest, one even being rejected because he had a chipped tooth." However, because of bad eyesight in his right eye, Hilder had been turned down in his application to enlist in England's Second Life Guards just before he emigrated to Canada and enlisted, and after the war was turned down, again in England, in his application to join the Rhodesian Mounted Police. Clearly, physical standards were not so high as vaunted.[15]

The importance of corporeal representations of national characteristics means that the Boers were described in a similarly physical way. Proponents of the war justified Canadian participation by publicizing the South Africans' "backwardness" and poor treatment of the Natives. A 1900 history of South Africa, by J. Castell Hopkins and Murat Halstead, focused on the reasons for the war with Britain, and saw them mainly in Boer ignorance and stubbornness. Part of the reason for this was their long isolation. Hopkins and Halstead cite Olive Schreiner, who found that even their "degraded" language revealed their dullness and stagnation. Hopkins and Halstead point out, "The vocabulary of the Taal has shrunk to a few hundred words, which have been shorn of almost all their inflections and otherwise clipped ... so sparse is the vocabulary and so broken are its forms that it is impossible in the Taal to express a subtle emotion, an abstract conception, or a wide generalization."[16]

This sense of degradation, contrasted with British civilization, was often expressed in physical descriptions: "Physically and mentally ... the Dutch farmer is much the same everywhere in South Africa – tall, raw-boned, awkward in manner, slow of speech, fond of hunting whenever and wherever possible, accustomed to the open air, lazy as regards work, but active in pursuits involving personal pleasure."[17] The presentation of the slow and heavy Boers is in marked contrast to the active and attractive Canadians.

Descriptions of Boer women emphasized their physical lassitude and unattractiveness, as well as the sexual inequality of their society: "The women of the republics are very ignorant, and as mentally feeble as might be expected from their surroundings and history. Physically, stoutness is the end aim of female ambition, and to weigh two, or even three hundred pounds is the greatest pride of the Dutch women of the veldt. They are invariably treated as the inferior sex, and even eat apart from the men."[18]

Presenting the women as physically large served to emasculate the Boer men. As well, at a time when societies with greater gender differentiation were perceived to be more civilized, this description of the Afrikaner woman as different from the ideal, delicate "angel of the house" added support to the social Darwinist interpretation of the inevitable and proper demise of less civilized societies before superior British-Canadian culture.

Although their cruelty to the "Kaffirs" was another constant theme in explanations for the necessity of the war, the Boers were also described as like them. According to Hopkins and Halstead, "His covered wagon was to him what the wigwam has been to the savage of the American continent, while his skill in shooting held a similar place to that of the bow and arrow in Indian economy." Sometimes, the description of Boer boorishness went further; one missionary compared Boers to beasts, when writing, "They are subject to alterations of lethargic idleness and fierceness of courage which characterize many wild animals."[19] These characterizations meant that the British implicitly had a right to the land because the Boers, like Natives, were "less civilized" and were not using it to its full extent.[20] Fighting in South Africa was presented as something like a frontier war: "Added to the quality of native cunning in warfare is an alertness of movement derived from long and hereditary skill in hunting wild animals and living constantly on horseback; as well as in fighting continuously a wily and ambush making native foe. As with the Kaffir himself, laziness disappears when the game of the Boer is on the horizon, and it matters not whether the quarry be animal or human."[21] Images of Boer lethargy and backwardness needed to be reconciled with their surprising success against Britain in the early years of the war.

Northern Bodies

The emphasis on the body stemmed partly from the way that imperialism had become connected to popular ideas about social Darwinism and race. In keeping with this philosophy, imperial rivalries were part of an inevitable historical process of natural selection according to "survival of the fittest."[22] Many of the racial explanations for empire were explicitly tied to gender. One verse in "Song of the Saxon," a poem calling on those of British racial stock to take on their "white man's duty," goes:

Then hail to the Saxon, hail!
And honour the work he's done;
Bless Saxon heart and Saxon brain,
Whose every deed is the whole world's gain,
Saxon and manhood are one.[23]

Some Canadians, because of their "racial" and political connections to Britain, understood themselves to be representatives of the highest expression of evolution. These racial characteristics were reinforced by geography and climate. As discussed by Carl Berger, Canada understood itself to be a "northern" country, with clear concomitant virtues.[24] These imaginings were expressed in the portrayals of the Boer farmer. Canon Knox, in his *Sketches and Studies in South Africa*, explained:

He did not carve his farm out of some primeval forest, build a permanent home for his family on his own land, or cultivate the soil with the strenuous labour of his hands. During the century in which his racial type was developing the Dutch settler moved from point to point with his cattle in accordance with the season and the pastures and lived an almost nomadic life ... Hence the accentuation of his intellectual narrowness by continued isolation and the strengthening of his physical frame at the expense of mental power.[25]

The way that the pioneer experiences of Canadians had shaped them – this being a significant element in Canadian physical, mental, and spiritual superiority – was contrasted with how the Boers had been formed in and by South Africa. Canada was a northern country, and the myth of the northern race, a hardy race created by a stern and demanding climate, had been used to express Canadian nationalism and pride since Confederation. It became more prominent, however, by the turn of the century, and the ideal physical and behavioural characteristics associated with the country were imagined into the soldiers in the Anglo-Boer War. One Canadian newspaper hailed the beginning of war in South Africa with the headline "Civilization Advances."[26]

This interpretation of Canadian qualities affected understandings of imperialism. Despite its transatlantic affiliations, the Canadian imperialist movement had its own character. Advocates saw imperialism as a highway to a larger world. For some, Canada's bracing geographical and climatic superiority meant that it had a future role as Britain's heir in the Empire. British newspapers often supported this perspective during the war. The *London Telegraph* linked colonial aptitude to environment, writing, "The free life in foreign lands has developed ... these qualities in the colonial soldier: Ready, alert, self-reliant, keen of his eyes, quick of his hands, resourceful and alive in every faculty, he has shown the supreme fighting stuff. In 'the colonies in khaki,' a new era of Empire will be visibly embodied."[27] This aspect of imperialist ideology was particularly heady and helped shape Canadian response to the war in South Africa.

Underlining these ideas of the superiority of aspects of British and Canadian culture was a sense of insecurity. The growing imperial fervour of the end of the nineteenth century was linked to worries about Britain's ability to maintain its position. Part of this was due to anxieties about the potentially degenerate tendencies in increased urbanization and industrialization. Industrial changes meant that many men were now working the kinds of white-collar jobs that challenged their manliness. These anxieties amplified the martial strains inherent in imperialism. War had an increased appeal because of its perceived abilities to counter the feminizing softness of civilization.[28]

Further research needs to be done into the expressed motives of the Canadians who volunteered for service in the Boer War; however, some information can be gleaned from looking at the social make-up of soldiers who enlisted. Jack Granatstein and David Bercuson have shown that "just over seven in ten had been born in Canada, with one-quarter coming from Britain. Overwhelmingly, the regiment's officers and men were English-speaking. Most were city-dwellers, only 5 per cent coming from rural areas; and roughly equal numbers, just over 35 per cent in both cases, came from white-collar and blue-collar employment." Further, Carman Miller states, "One volunteer in four had been employed in sales and clerical occupations ... [even] though this category represented only 2.9 per cent of Canada's male workers over fourteen years of age."[29] The information about the primarily urban character of the soldiers conforms to studies about imperialism's appeal to lower- and middle-class workers in clerical occupations, and it is also notable in how it challenges the frontier cowboy image of Canadian soldiers in the Boer War.

Connected to the worries about modern degeneracy were anxieties raised by the notion of a crisis in masculinity stemming partly from the threat posed by agitation for wider social, economic, and political roles for women.[30] This, however, needs to be coupled with awareness of shifts in the social underpinnings of masculinity in the same period. Popular support for imperialism provides important context here. British social historians have drawn attention to the degree to which "the empire served to underpin beleaguered masculinities at home."[31] It is worth exploring if similar motivations shaped Canadian responses.

The focus on their physical appearance, and the characteristics of the ideal Canadian body, show that imperialism was tied to a certain type of masculine behaviour and identity. Part of the reason for the great support for the warriors as they were sent off was the martial tendencies inherent in imperialism. In *War in South Africa*, Birch describes a parade of the volunteers in Saint John, including the assurance that the soldiers "would acquit themselves like men."[32] He was drawing on well-articulated ideas of appropriate masculine behaviour. Military drills, demonstrations, and patriotic exercises had become part of the English-Canadian school curriculum. Many had read Rudyard Kipling, G.A. Henty, H. Rider Haggard, as well as *Chums* and *Boys' Own Paper*. They were familiar with their stories of manly adventure, endurance, and heroism.[33] There was a broad shift over the Victorian era from the earnest, expressive manliness of the Evangelicals to the hearty, stiff-upper-lip variant in the era of Baden-Powell. John Tosh submits, "While manliness can in theory be defined as a mingling of the ethical and the physiological, a great deal of the literature of the day left the overwhelming impression that masculine identification resided in the life of the mind (heavily overlain by conscious) rather than the body. This was certainly no longer the case by the end of the nineteenth century, when there was a growing tension between the moral and physical criteria of manliness."[34] Historian Jonathan Rutherford indicates that the greater focus on physical strength came about partly as a result of "the rising popularity of imperialism and the influence of social Darwinism."[35] This new understanding of masculinity as one of the root causes for the focus on the physically athletic bodies of the Canadian contingent in the Boer War.

The focus on certain characteristics of the Canadian soldiers was not limited to the war's outbreak, and it developed over the course of the war. It is especially apparent in the way their participation in the early victory at Paardeberg was described. To contextualize this battle, the Boer War had begun badly for the British. In what the press called "Black Week," from 10 to 17 December 1899, their army suffered a series of humiliating defeats by the Boer republics. Canadians reached Cape Town in late November 1899, and by mid-February 1900, they were ready for action. The Canadians experienced their first important overseas battle as part of the move to retake the town of Kimberly in the Paardeberg sector. On 26 February, the Canadians relieved an English battalion in a line of trenches located some six hundred metres from the Boer positions. They were ordered to advance. As they did so, they were seriously battered. Four of the six companies fell back, the other two hung on to their new positions. After several days, their opponents, under General Cronje, surrendered to the Canadians. The Canadians were congratulated for this feat, which assumed mythic proportions.[36]

Paardeberg was psychologically important for the British. It was, finally, the first significant British victory of the war. It was also Canada's first overseas victory. The day of the victory became "Majuba Day," because the Boer defeat took place on the nineteenth anniversary of a British disaster at Majuba Hill during the first South African War. It seemed fitting that the disaster at Majuba had been avenged by Canadians, revealing imperial unity and the Dominion's coming of age. Much of the credit for Cronje's surrender fell to the Canadians. Roberts, the British General, spoke to the battalion, and praised their spirit and gallantry, tributes he had incorporated into his dispatch to the British government earlier in the day. "Canadian," he asserted, "now stands for bravery, dash and courage."[37]

The Battle of Paardeberg became a key aspect of Canada's imagination of the characteristics of its soldiers in the war. The various reiterations of the battle described "mostly beardless youths" who "fought like veterans" and "jumped like race horses." They were "wonders" and had made "a charge which will live in history." The rhetoric was appealing enough that the soldiers involved repeated the story of how the ablest general in the Boer army surrendered to them. They recounted how Boer prisoners had remarked: "You are not men, you are devils. We can stand the shooting of the average British soldiers but your Canadians are regular fire eaters and know no fear ... It's easily seen now what nation is going to rule the world."[38] Especially in the retelling, it was clearly Canadian national characteristics that won the battle. According to one version, simply the knowledge that the Canadians were in the trenches had filled the Boers with fear and forced them to surrender.[39]

The discourse concerning the soldiers overseas focused on their active, decisive, adventurous qualities, contrasted with the lazy Boers. Another aspect of this was the language of their coming of age. The soldiers took on an important role as representatives of the oldest colony country's coming of age and ascent into adulthood. Although there was, apparently, no substance to the claim of a *Times* reporter that it was "the insistence of Canada" that "broke down Roberts's reluctance," and persuaded him to send "the men of the oldest colony ... in the small hours of Tuesday morning to redeem the blot on the name of the mother country,"[40] this is one example of the representations of the soldiers, and through them Canada, as taking on the responsibilities of adulthood through participation in the Boer War. According to one spokesman, Canadians "did not rejoice [after the Battle of Paardeberg] because Cronje was defeated but because their sons had become men in the eyes of the world."[41] It was a coming of age on both an individual and a national basis. Many Canadians expressed confidence that from the victory of Paardeberg would spring a new patriotism based on national unity and purpose.

The ascent into national manhood was welcome not just because of the sense of admiration Canadians believed they were earning internationally, but because of the maturity they felt it would bring to the British Empire and to the Dominion at home. Imperialists in Canada were galvanized by Paardeberg, which they hailed as an eloquent rebuke to "little Englandism," and the clear beginnings of a new era of imperial cooperation. If the representation of Canadian physical prowess expressed colonial unity, it was also used as a foil to criticize British failures. James Wood argues, "At the height of the war, the trend of opinion in the British press held colonial soldiers in the highest regard, often contrasting their performance in South Africa to that of the British regulars."[42] The victory at Paardeberg demonstrated the solidarity of the Empire. The emphasis on imperial unity was clear in one romantic version of the battle, which claimed "that few of this gallant Company of Great Britain's defenders could speak English."[43]

With such victories holding pride of place in the discourse of the time and national memory of the war, other bodies are notable by their absence. During the last two years of the South African War, the British responded to the Boer commandos' successful guerrilla warfare with farm burnings and the removal of their inhabitants to concentration camps. This led to a strong outcry in Britain but, while Canadians participated, there is remarkably little comment on this in the Canadian press. Here, though, are other bodies. The death rate in the concentration camps was despicable, over twenty-six thousand, most of them women and children, died.[44] Also curious by their relative absence are the various Native groups in South Africa.

Reports of the soldiers who returned to Canada from South Africa emphasized the beneficial effects of fighting. An account of the return of one company to Halifax described "the war-tried sons of Canada ... with faces browned and straightened back, with shoulders square and heads held high, down they came, the heroes of the Empire."[45] Seasoned by war, they were presented as stronger for it. This was obviously not the case for everyone. The letters home speak of frequent short or absent rations and undrinkable water. McCormack's memoir gives a sense of the effect of campaigning on their appearance: "Our men were dirty, lousy, unwashed, unshaved, uniforms ragged, boots sometimes falling apart when the ground was rocky. Except when in garrison ninety per cent of the British grew beards; water was too scarce for shaving." Pension claims also offer a corrective to the war as an individually strengthening venture.[46]

The dead body, an inescapable aspect of war, is more problematic. Two hundred and twenty-four men died, more of diseases than killed in actual combat. In the narratives of the soldiers returning hardier, stronger, more noble, death is not wholly ignored, but it is a distant, romanticized presence. J.C.M. Duncan's, poem "Our Dead" is typical:

> Our sons have been put to the stern proof of death,
> Their loyal love. What, mother, would'st thou more?
> Facing the fury of war's deadly breath,

They fell as bravely as their sires of yore.
With fearless steps they sought the fronting tide;
With fearless front they faced the common foe;
Like veterans they stood, like veterans, died.
And not in vain did their brave life-stream flow.[47]

That they have risked and seen death is part of what has tempered these soldiers, but in a poetic rather than a visceral sense. The dead body is the least real of all the bodies in this war.

Along with the physical bodies of the soldier, the distinctive clothing worn by the soldiers became representations of Canadian nation building. For example, during the Boer War, almost all Canadian units that served in South Africa wore Stetson hats. Their adoption for use by Canadian units in South Africa was probably due to the fact that many members of Canada's second contingent were former members of the North-West Mounted Police (NWMP). Stetsons had been worn unofficially by members of the NWMP since 1895, an increasing number of whom preferred it to the standard-issue white pith helmet. The Stetson hats and Strathcona boots linked Canadian soldiers in the South African War to the NWMP, a force whose own highly gendered mythology has been a key aspect of Canada's self-imagining, more recent manifestations of which Bonnie Reilly Schmidt examines in this volume.

Conclusion

The Canadian volunteer for participation in the Boer War was a robust, adventurous frontiersman, physically pure, and cheerfully careless of the danger that his devotion to a duty to protect the British Empire imposed. The audience for these images was a public that wanted to be assured that it was Canada's bracing climate and geography, along with its British racial heritage, that produced such fine specimens of manliness. Together, the soldiers' bodies and the representations of those they fought suggest an internal struggle in Canadians' self-image as they sent their soldiers off to war in Africa. On the one hand, they were good citizens of the British Empire, inculcated with the Victorian values of duty and valour. On the other hand, these materialities suggested a growing distinction from the mother country, thus beginning the construction of a unique Canadian masculinity and citizenship.

The Second Anglo-Boer War was seen by many Canadians as an opportunity to showcase British imperial righteousness and unity, as well as the distinctive national strengths of the young Dominion. Much of this debate was inscribed upon the physical bodies of those who volunteered for the war. Exploring prescriptive manliness helps understand the lived experience of imperialism more fully. Examining how the soldiers were represented, and what this might mean about normative manliness and the qualities and behaviour of ideal citizens, offers useful insight into the society of the day, and of Canadians' relationship to imperialism at the turn of the twentieth century.

Notes

1 For an early study of the intersections between imperialism and Canadian nationalism, see Carl Berger, *The Sense of Power: Studies in the Ideas of Canadian Imperialism, 1867–1914* (Toronto: University of Toronto Press, 1970). In "Canada's 'Nationalistic' Imperialists," *Journal of Canadian Studies* 5, no. 3 (1970), 44–9, Douglas Cole challenges this, arguing that "Imperialism was not a Canadian phenomenon; it was a Britannic movement." More recent work by Phillip Buckner is also important. See his edited collections: *Canada and the British Empire* (Oxford: Oxford University Press, 2008), and with R. Douglas Francis, *Canada and the British World: Culture, Migration, and Identity* (Vancouver: UBC Press, 2006).

2 Kristin L. Hoganson, *Fighting for American Manhood: How Gender Politics Provoked the Spanish-American and Philippine-American Wars* (New Haven, CT: Yale University Press, 1998). For discussion of gender and imperialism, see Anne McClintock, *Imperial Leather: Race, Gender and Sexuality in the Colonial Contest* (New York: Routledge, 1995), and *Gender and Empire*, ed. Philippa Levine (Oxford: Oxford University Press, 2004). Gender's relation to the particularly Canadian experience of imperialism is understudied. See Katie Pickles, *Female Imperialism and National Identity* (Manchester: Manchester University Press, 2002).

3 The standard text on Canada in the South African War is Carman Miller, *Painting the Map Red: Canada and the South African War, 1899–1902* (Montreal and Kingston: McGill-Queen's University Press, 1993). See also J.L. Granatstein and David Bercuson, *War and Peacekeeping: From South Africa to the Gulf – Canada's Limited Wars* (Toronto: Key Porter Books, 1991), 47.

4 Robert Page shows that the principle of imperial unity, especially in the beginning, was more important to Chamberlain than actual fighting men. He writes, "I am sorry and a good deal disappointed at Laurier's decision with regard to the contingent. We do not intend to accept any offer of volunteers. We do not want the men and the whole point of the offer would be

lost unless it were endorsed by the Colony and applied to an organized body of the Colonial Forces." Robert Page, *Imperialism and Canada, 1895–1903* (Toronto: Holt, Rinehart, and Winston, 1972), 11.

5 Hammond's justifications (he was a principal conspirator in the plot that led to the Jameson Raid) are included in *The Anglo-Boer War: Why Was It Fought? Who Was Responsible?* ed. Theodore C. Caldwell (Boston: D.C. Heath, 1965). See also J.A. Hobson, *The War in South Africa: Its Causes and Effects* (New York: H. Fertig, 1969 [1900]). For a specifically Canadian view, see Miller, *Painting the Map Red.* According to Norman Penlington, the settlement of the Alaska boundary dispute was also an important factor in the decision to send Canadian troops. See Norman Penlington, *Canada and Imperialism, 1896–1899* (Toronto: University of Toronto Press, 1965), 240–1.

6 *London Telegraph,* n.d., quoted in *Canadian Military Gazette* 15, no. 13 (1900), 10.

7 *Globe,* "Canadians Glad," 13 Sept. 1899, 2.

8 C.P. Stacey, *Canada and the Age of Conflict, 1867–1921* (Toronto: Macmillan, 1977), 61. Desmond Morton has argued, "Service in South Africa was a precedent for Canada's role in two world wars and Korea." See his *A Military History of Canada: From Champlain to Kosovo* (Toronto: McClelland and Stewart, 1999 [1985]), 118.

9 Cited in Page, *Imperialism and Canada,* 13.

10 Including men taking over the Halifax Garrison to free British soldiers for service in South Africa, unofficial units such as that raised independently by Lord Strathcona, and the later sending of the South African Constabulary, 8,372 men were enlisted in the cause of the Boer War. See Granatstein and Bercuson, *War and Peacekeeping,* 82.

11 Carlyle's influential *On Heroes, Hero-Worship, and the Heroic in History,* for example, lauds the qualities of sincerity, inner strength, and wisdom, and cites Shakespeare, Goethe, and Dante as examples of such ideal masculine heroes. Thomas Carlyle, *On Heroes, Hero-Worship and the Heroic in History* (Lincoln, NE: University of Nebraska Press, 1966 [1869]). Herbert Sussman examines Victorian masculinity as advocated by Robert Browning, William Pater, and the pre-Raphaelites, among others, as "the behavioral state of rigorously controlled and disciplined manliness achieved ... through arduous public and private ritual." See Herbert Sussman *Victorian Masculinities: Manhood and Masculine Poetics in Early Victorian Literature and Art* (Cambridge: Cambridge University Press, 1995), 13.

12 S.M. Brown, *With the Royal Canadians* (Toronto: Publishers' Syndicate, 1900), 6; T.G. Marquis, *Canada's Sons on Kopje and Veldt* (Toronto: n.p.,

1900), 71; J. Douglas Borthwick, *Poems and Songs of the South Africa War* (Montreal: n.p., 1901), 125.

13 Public Archives of British Columbia, "British Columbia Scrapbook," quoted in Miller, *Painting the Map Red*, 76.

14 Alexander Stearns McCormick, *The Royal Canadians in South Africa, 1899–1902* [n.d., n.p.]. John Cranfield and Kris Inwood have used Boer War enlistment records in their study of the trends in height and weight (and thereby physical well-being) of Canadians during the nineteenth century. Acknowledging the minimum height requirements, especially for mounted regiments, and the middle-class origins of many volunteers, which would have also meant a rather taller sample group than the population at large, they show average heights at between 67.5 and 68.6 inches. John Cranfield and Kris Inwood, "The Great Transformation: A Long-Run Perspective on Physical Well-Being in Canada," *Economics and Human Biology* 5 (2007), 204–28.

15 See A.G. Morris ed., *A Canadian Mounted Rifleman at War, 1899–1902: The Reminiscences of A.E. Hilder* (Cape Town: Van Riebeeck Society), xv–xvii, and H. Robertson, "The Royal Canadian Dragoons and the Anglo-Boer War, 1900," M.A. thesis, University of Ottawa 1902.

16 Olive Schreiner in Basil Worsfold, *The Story of South Africa* (n.p.), 1898, quoted in J. Castell Hopkins and Murat Halstead, *South Africa and the Boer-British War: Comprising A History of South Africa and Its People, Including the War of 1899 and 1900* (Toronto: John C. Winston and Co, 1900), 31. This is similar to the sense of the public performance of "Canadianess" that Gillian Poulter shows in her discussion, this volume, of sporting activities in Montreal.

17 Hopkins and Halstead, *South Africa and the Boer-British War*, 167.

18 Ibid., 174.

19 Ibid., 259.

20 For discussion of how Europeans often justified appropriation of their land with the argument that Natives were not exploiting it sufficiently, see William Cronon, *Changes in the Land: Indians, Colonists, and the Ecology of New England* (New York: Hill and Wang, 1983); John C. Weaver, *The Great Land Rush and the Making of the Modern World, 1650–1900* (Montreal and Kingston: McGill-Queen's University Press, 2003).

21 Hopkins and Halstead, *South Africa and the Boer-British War*, 168. There is evidence that the South Africans used similar criteria to assess their opponents in the war. Sandra Swart notes the importance of having a beard to understandings of Boer manliness, whereas the archetypical British soldier was clean-shaven. Sandra Swart, "A Boer and His Gun and His Wife Are Three

Things Always Together: Republican Masculinity and the 1914 Rebellion," *Journal of Southern African Studies* 24, no. 4 (1998), 737–51.

22 Adele Perry, *On the Edge of Empire: Gender, Race, and the Making of British Columbia, 1849–1871* (Toronto: University of Toronto Press, 2001).

23 Marvin Dana, "Song of the Saxon," *Onward*, 16 Feb. 1900, cited in Gordon L. Heath, *A War with a Silver Lining: Canadian Protestant Churches and the South African War, 1899–1902* (Montreal and Kingston: McGill-Queen's University Press, 2009), 74.

24 Carl Berger, "The True North Strong and Free," in *Nationalism in Canada*, ed. Peter Russell (Toronto: McGraw-Hill, 1966), 3–26.

25 Canon W.J. Knox Little, *Sketches and Studies in South Africa* (London: Isbister and Co., 1899).

26 *Empire* [Toronto], 21 Feb. 1898, cited in Miller, *Painting the Map Red*, 18.

27 Quoted in Annie Mellish, *Our Boys under Fire* (Charlottetown: n.p., 1900), 30. See also Montreal *Star*, 11 May 1900.

28 See Cynthia Comacchio, "Mechanomorphosis: Science, Management, and 'Human Machinery' in Industrial Canada, 1900-45," *Labour/Le Travail* 41 (Spring 1998), 35–67, and Elaine Showalter, *Sexual Anarchy: Gender and Culture at the Fin de Siècle* (New York: Viking, 1991).

29 Miller, *Painting the Maple Red*, 59. See also Carman Miller, "A Preliminary Analysis of the Socio-Economic Composition of Canada's South Africa War Contingents," *Histoire sociale/Social History* (Nov. 1975), 219–37.

30 This perceived crisis in masculinity has been more broadly studied in its British and American than Canadian manifestations. See J.A. Mangan and James Walvin, eds., *Manliness and Morality: Middle-Class Masculinity in Britain and America, 1800–1940* (Manchester: Manchester University Press, 1987); Michael Roper and John Tosh, eds., *Manful Assertions: Masculinities in Britain since 1800* (London: Routledge, 1991); John Tosh, "What Should Historians Do with Masculinity? Reflections on Nineteenth-Century Britain," *History Workshop*, no. 38 (1994), 179–202; Arnaldo Testi. "The Gender of Reform Politics: Theodore Roosevelt and the Culture of Masculinity," *Journal of American History* 81, no. 4 (1995), 1509–33; Gail Bederman, *Manliness and Civilization: A Cultural History of Gender and Race in the United States, 1880–1917* (Chicago, IL: University of Chicago Press, 1995). See also Mark Moss, *Manliness and Militarism: Educating Young Boys in Ontario for War* (Don Mills, ON: Oxford University Press, 2001).

31 Tosh, "What Should Historians Do with Masculinity?" 194. See also Ronald Hyam, *Empire and Sexuality* (Manchester: Manchester University Press, 1991).

32 James H. Birch, *The Complete History of the War in South Africa: Containing an*

Authentic Account of the Entire Struggle Between the British and the Boers including the causes of the conflict; vivid descriptions of the fierce battles; superb heroism and daring deeds; narratives of personal adventures; life in camp, field and hospital, etc., etc.,; together with the wonderful story of the Transvaal, the Orange Free State; Natal and Cape Colony; the Kaffirs and Zulus; richest gold and diamond mines in the world, etc., etc (St. John, NB: R.A.H. Morrow, 1902, 369. Quoted in Miller, *Painting the Map Red,* 105.

33 For discussion of the connection between popular literature and the character of imperialism and manliness, see Moss, *Manliness and Militarism.*

34 Tosh, "What Should Historians Do with Masculinity?" 179–202.

35 Jonathan Rutherford, *Forever England: Reflections on Race, Masculinity and Empire* (London: Lawrence and Wishart, 1997), 14.

36 Canadian participation in the battle of Paardeberg is discussed in Miller, *Painting the Map Red,* 86–112.

37 Brown, *With the Royal Canadians,* 6; Marquis, *Canada's Sons on Kopje and Veldt,* 71; Borthwick, *Poems and Songs of the South Africa War,* 125.

38 *Montreal Star* 9 May 1900.

39 Quoted in Miller, *Painting the Map Red,* 109–12. See also Russell C. Hubley, *"G" Company, or Every-Day Life of the R.C.R. Being a Descriptive Account of the Typical Events in the Life of the First Canadian Contingent in South Africa by the Late Russell C. Hubley* (Montreal: Witness Printing House, 1901), 106; Mellish, *Our Boys under Fire,* 33–5.

40 Mellish, *Our Boys under Fire,* 34; Miller, *Painting the Map Red,* 109.

41 Norman Patterson, "The War and Canada," *Canadian Magazine* (July 1902), 204.

42 James Wood, *Militia Myths: Ideas of the Canadian Citizen Soldier, 1896–1921* (Vancouver: UBC Press, 2010), 213.

43 Miller, *Painting the Map Red,* 112.

44 http://www.icon.co.za/~dup42/abw.htm.

45 "Canada's Sons," *Montreal Star,* 12 June 1901, 1

46 McCormick, *Royal Canadians in South Africa,* 4. The pension records are at Library and Archives Canada (LAC), RG 24, Vol. 5910, files HQ 49-1-2.

47 J.C.M. Duncan, "Our Dead," in *Poems and Songs,* 140. For an unromantic discussion of men's bodies and war, see Joanna Bourke, *Dismembering the Male: Men's Bodies, Britain and the Great War* (Chicago, IL: University of Chicago Press, 1996).

PART TWO

(Re)fashioning the Body

5 Packing and Unpacking: Northern Women Negotiate Fashion in Colonial Encounters during the Twentieth Century

MYRA RUTHERDALE

In June 1960, the Toronto newspaper *Style* featured an article that proclaimed "Inuvik, Near Arctic Ocean, Holds First Fashion Show." Fashion journalist, Marilyn McLean described how the community members of Inuvik, the new seat of government administration only fifty miles south of the Arctic Ocean, had mobilized for their first ever fashion show. "Models wear mukluks," the headline declared. McLean went on to say, "The clothes worn by the shy teen-agers – Eskimo, Indian and a few whites – were gay cotton shirtwaists, blouses, bouffant skirts, and slim jims. The native girls showed a strong preference for bright colours. A popular combination was a red blouse and colonial blue skirt."[1] The author of the piece concluded that "comment on the show was favourable and the school plans to have similar shows to teach the girls poise." The shy teenagers were the same girls who had sewn the clothes in their home economics class at the federal school.

With a similar focus on young Aboriginal children, an article had appeared in the Toronto *Globe and Mail* the previous summer. This piece featured a young schoolteacher, Mary Ellis, from Alliston, Ontario, who was in her first year of teaching at Frobisher Bay in the Eastern Arctic. Ellis was described as a loving teacher, trying to overcome the challenges of life in the Arctic, including what she understood as a rather liberal attitude towards school. When the question of student attire and appearance was raised the journalist reported, "Eskimo children like 'southern' clothing and their idea of a fine time is to dress up in cowboy clothes. On very cold days – it sometimes goes to 50 below – they wear typical Eskimo clothing to school, sealskin, or cloth parkas and 'Kamiks' or mukluks as they're usually known. But generally they wear dresses, or jeans and tartan shirts."[2]

The observation about cowboy clothes, or western-styled clothing was one that was reiterated by other newcomers who visited during the 1950s and 1960s and sometimes even earlier.[3] Sheila Burnford, author of the travel narrative, *One Woman's Arctic*, visited Igloolik in the late 1960s and was struck by the difference between children in that community and those of Pond Inlet, a community only three hundred miles away: "The people seemed more sophisticated in keeping, most of them wearing store-bought clothes; the teenagers – a delightful friendly lot, not a bit shy, and far more outgoing than their Pond contemporaries – were dressed for the most part in western fashion, cowboy hats and Levis and all spoke surprisingly colloquial English."[4]

Newcomers to Inuit communities such as Igloolik and to mixed-race Inuit/Inuvialuit/White communities such as Inuvik were compelled to write about the attire of northern Aboriginal people. In this essay, I try to tease out why there was such intense scrutiny and commentary on clothing and bodily hygiene. External bodily appearance including hygiene, comportment, attire, and fashion have attracted scholarly attention because they tell us much about perceptions of social class, race, ethnicity, gender, time, and place.[5] As Susan Bordo has reminded us, the body can be read as a cultural text upon which trends are acted out and desires are expressed: "Not chiefly through ideology, but through the organization and regulation of the time, space and movements of our daily lives, our bodies are trained, shaped, and impressed with the stamp of prevailing historical forms of selfhood, desire, masculinity, femininity."[6] Decisions about how the body is clothed, decorated, and cared for are not incidental, and often they reveal how individuals wish to construct their cultural and social identity. As such, this essay argues that clothing became invested with meanings that were not just neutral in the dynamic relations between Natives and newcomers. Clothing became a matter for negotiation, for trade, and later, symbolized Aboriginal people's access, or lack thereof to the northern cash economy. Clothing and descriptions of bodily hygiene were invested with racialized discourse. Newcomers frequently referred to traditional northern clothing as "Eskimo clothing" or used terms like "white man's clothing" to dichotomize race through attire. In that sense clothing assumed explicitly racialized meanings, and was a visible marker of cultural change.[7] Clothing and hygiene were often targeted by outsiders or newcomers to northern Aboriginal communities to distinguish in their minds the success of colonization. The body became a text on which transformation was marked. At the same time, northern Canada is a significant location for a study such as this since the evidence suggests a hybridized use of clothing as a marker of colonial change and adaptation, by both newcomers and the permanent population. That is, Euro-Canadians used northern "Aboriginal" clothing, and northerners adapted southern clothing in complex ways. Similar to Gillian Poulter's nineteenth-century sporting men, in northern Canada, too, clothing and identity became conflated and experimental.

This essay draws from the written records of missionaries, nurses, doctors, and other professional sojourners who travelled to and worked in northern Canada from the early twentieth century through to the 1960s. As well, oral interviews with northern Aboriginal people are examined here in order to gain an understanding of how changes in style and fashion were viewed from the perspective of local community members. Before I look at examples of how newcomers discussed Aboriginal clothing choices, it is first necessary to understand how the newcomers themselves dressed and how they viewed their place in the northern fashion hierarchy.

Newcomers: Fashion and Respectability

As in other colonial settings, newcomers in early twentieth-century Dawson, Yukon, were especially aware of class differentiation. They participated in rituals associated with maintaining their newly acquired status. According to Charlene Porsild, Dawson residents quickly moved to distinguish themselves as belonging to the "upper crust" or "inner circle," by holding "at homes" or joining mission societies and fraternal associations. Part of this anxiety may be attributed to what Barbara Kelcey argues was a desire for respectability. According to her, when women set out for the Klondike in the late 1890s, they were very much aware of the need to appear to be proper: "Women's Klondike outfits reflected nineteenth-century expectations of women, so consequently what to wear to the Klondike presented a dilemma for women who saw the need to be comfortably, yet fashionably and respectably dressed. This quandry was complicated by representations in newspapers and periodical accounts that depicted women on their way to the Yukon dressed in calf-length garments or trousers, reflecting that journalists saw female stampeders as unconventional, and perhaps lending some credence to the already developing myth that female gold rushers were all women of easy virtue."[8] Respectability was key. So interested were Dawson women to "keep up appearances" that they made it a priority to order "the 'latest' fashions from Toronto, New York, and Paris for the many society functions they attended in Dawson."[9] Attire was associated with status, and they wanted to be sure to distinguish themselves.

This does not seem to have been the case for missionary women in the north. They were not quite as concerned with how they dressed. In some cases, the practical realities of mission life were responsible for their relationship to clothing. Susan Bowen, a schoolteacher from Ireland, and later a missionary in Dawson, recalled just how practical she had to be during the gold rush: "One Easter ... I wanted a new hat, and the milliner brought out one at $100. I said: 'Too dear!' In turn she brought one at $50, another at $25, and finally a common little sailor hat you could buy outside for 50 cents, 'very cheap at $15.' I said: 'The hat I have is only seven years old. I will wear it.'"[10]

Bowen was most certainly not to be outwitted by the milliner and her inflated prices, no matter how much she may have wanted a new hat. Not only did missionary women enjoy their freedom from current styles, but they also did not feel compelled to shop. From her perspective in Pangnirtung, in the early 1930s, nurse Prue Hockin claimed that she did not miss shopping: "It doesn't look much like Xmas but I guess it is because there are no Xmas shop windows. It is sort of a relief not to have to shop."[11] Another woman boasted about her freedom from changing tastes in fashion: "One doesn't have to worry about fashions up here."[12]

Although the above statements reflect a certain practicality achieved once non-Native women had arrived in the north, this same common sense approach was not always demonstrated when women were preparing for their northern sojourns. For example, Mena Orford recalled some difficulty in convincing her mother that she did not require an extensive fancy wardrobe. According to Orford, who moved to Panuk, on Baffin Island, in 1936, she had to dissuade her mother from purchasing for her a blue velvet dinner dress. Orford's mother was also not keen on her son-in-law, who was unable to make much of a living from his medical profession in the late 1930s. To make their new posting at Panuk sound more promising, her daughter not only described the house they would arrive in, but also the "two servants" that came along with it. This impressed her mother, and as Orford wrote, "I wouldn't have minded the deception so much if she hadn't insisted on buying me clothes to fit the position. Her final effort had been a blue velvet dinner dress. I'd protested this on the grounds of having nowhere to have it cleaned. She'd got really sharp with me. Try not to be ridiculous, Mary ... Baffin Island is the third largest island in the world – there will certainly be a dry cleaning establishment in one of the larger centres."[13]

The question of what to pack for northern work and travel also troubled Dorothy Knight, a nurse at Lake Harbour, in the late 1950s. Although she could not be described as impractical in her approach to her patients, she was certainly unsure of what to expect, at least when she was packing her bags. Her biographer noted that after her arrival and once she started to arrange her clothing she wondered what she had been thinking: "She glanced quickly inside the wardrobe at the clothes Oola had unpacked. They already seemed hopelessly inappropriate. She had stopped wearing the short muskrat jacket as soon as she acquired the parka. And would she ever wear that midnight-blue silk party dress with the starched crinoline underskirt? Or the green gabardine suit? Or the three pairs of high-heeled shoes?"[14]

Knight's and Orford's mother's enthusiasm would be somewhat quashed by the reality of their lives in the north. There were social occasions and opportunities to dress formally, but both of these women quickly adopted a more practical approach. In fact, while women were relieved to be free of shopping or liberated from the most recent everyday fashions and expectations, they were keenly aware that winter necessitated a new, more practical manner of dress, indeed, an entire new wardrobe.

Cultural Contact and Preparing Clothing

Missionaries and nurses alike turned to Aboriginal women for help to prepare their winter attire. Similar to the Aboriginal women in George Colpitts's essay in this collection, northern Aboriginal women also did the work of preparing and maintaining bodies for northern climes. Carolyn Soper, a nurse who accompanied her husband of the Department of the Interior to Lake Harbour, in the early 1930s, recalled many years later how she and her family had their winter clothing supplied by Neve, an Inuk woman. Neve's husband was hired to interpret for the Sopers, and it soon became apparent that Neve could be very helpful to the Soper family:

> It fell to Neve's lot to make our Arctic clothing. Caribou skins were used for winter: duffle cloth for summer; and our waterproof boots or *kamiks* were made of sealskin. No patterns were used. She studiously looked us over for size and then went to work. In what seemed to me a remarkably short time, she returned with our duffle parkas and pairs of sealskin boots for the three of us. Without doubt the hardest part of all was preparing the skins and

subsequently keeping all our boots in condition. The work does not end with removing the hair, drying the skin and making the *kamiks*. Each time they are worn and become damp or wet the skin drys very hard and must be softened before the boots can be worn again. The only method of softening them effectively is by chewing and this is done by the women.[15]

Carolyn Soper's description of her encounter with Neve and the preparation of winter clothing is representative of a common narrative in the writing of Euro-Canadian women who sojourned in the north. In the early 1950s, another nurse, Donalda McKillop Copeland, wrote about how one local woman came to measure her daughter for a suit of winter clothing: "In the fashioning of parkas and boots, Nana's mother, Enukpowyuk, was an excellent seamstress. So with Kitty I sent the request to her to make an outdoor outfit for Patsy. From the trading post I bought one of the caribou hides that had been brought in for sale to the Eskimos. Enukpowyuk arrived to measure our little daughter, and within three days we had a complete set of caribou clothing ready for her."[16]

In each of the above portrayals, Inuit women were represented as wise women, women who were very capable in the traditional art of sewing for the purposes of clothing preparation. Many newcomers commented with undo surprise that they did not even have to measure their customers when sewing either winter clothing or boots.[17] Dr. Gareth Howerd, who practised in the 1950s as a doctor along Canada's Dew Line of military radar stations, noted that both the Inuit spousal partners who worked as the interpreter and the maid at the nursing station had "abandoned Eskimo styles." Tikivik, the husband, "no longer combed his hair in a fringe like other Eskimo men, and usually he wore an open-neck shirt," while his wife, Martha, "was clean and efficient around the nursing station," but Howerd commented, "I never became used to seeing this Eskimo woman dressed in tartan slacks and blouse, and ironing away like a southern housewife on a Monday afternoon." He was saddled with other expectations about Inuit women. However, like other newcomers, he also needed northern clothing, and as he recalled, "Martha made a parka for me and it was interesting to see her work without a pattern. She took a few measurements and then cut out the garment from a single piece of skin."[18]

This was not always the custom, though. In fact, Inuit women had often relied on patterns sketched out on animal skins. Sarah Amakallak Haulli described how she prepared the skins: "After it is ready to be patterned the skin will be marked with bite marks having first been *suqqaaqtaq* [measured with a piece of sinew thread]. In addition, they will use their hands to make some of the measurements. This is commonly referred to as *isaatktaqtuq*, which is to stretch the hand and use the number of lengths for the measurement."[19]

Another woman, Sarah Ulayuruluk, recalled how she used her *ulu* to engrave the skins she was preparing to cut and sew. She, too, remembered how her mother measured everything by hand. The measurements were extremely accurate, and if the hand was too large then fingers would be used: "If a span shorter than this needed to be added, she used other measurements such as the length of her thumb, or a finger, or the bones between the joints in the finger."[20] Patterns were actually made in the skins before the sewing was done.

There appeared to be some confusion over how outsiders viewed women's capabilities. Commonly, Inuit women were described as amazingly fast with their work and brilliant seamstresses. This characteristic lends credence to anthropologist Hugh Brody's observation that Inuit peoples were almost always depicted by newcomers at dichotomized extremes as either simple-minded, stone-aged anachronisms or wise, environmentally adapted, practical geniuses. When it came to dressing their own children, the former trope most often prevailed. Infant clothing prompted constant criticism from newcomers in northern communities, especially women. Southerners wrote endlessly about their perception that Inuit women did not dress their infants in warm clothing, despite the excessively cold winters. They wondered if the high rates of pneumonia and respiratory problems might be attributed to this apparent lack of clothing.

Dressing Babies and Colonial Conflict

In 1928 Minnie Hackett, an Anglican missionary/nurse stationed at Aklavik, chose to compare Dene and Inuvialuit infant fashion as follows:

> When the babies are born I visit the mothers, and see that they are getting the right care, and show the mother how to dress the baby – advice which is neglected as they prefer their own way. The Indians put a flannelette shirt or dress (I don't know what they call it) on the baby, and wrap several squares of the same material around it, in a moss bag, which is laced in front with moose-hide strings. It is a good method in this country as the baby keeps warm, but I want to teach them to use the barracoats, and by persevering I hope to succeed – after several years. The Eskimos do not use

a moss bag; the baby has just one flannelette shirt and is placed inside the mother's dress on her back and a belt around the waist saves the baby from falling through.[21]

Less frustrated with Dene mothers than with the Inuvialuit women, Hackett nonetheless wanted to introduce the babies to "barracoats."

In her memoir, *Journey North,* Mena Orford recalled her first encounter with a naked Inuk baby. In September 1936, she and her family arrived at Panuk, on Baffin Island, where her husband was assigned by Ottawa to work as the regional medical officer. Orford recollected her first apparently tension-filled moments as she met both the local European/Canadian inhabitants, as well as many of the Inuit who gathered to greet the ship: "The formalities over, the women crowded round Penny and Zanne who stood woodenly, mystified as dark hands stroked. 'They've never seen blonde children before,' McKay beamed at the little side show. 'In fact they've never seen a white child before.' 'Are there no other children here?' I burst out. McKay's face lost its benign expression, and he turned his deep-set eyes on me and stared down. My face reddened under his scrutiny."

To demonstrate his annoyance at Mena, McKay grabbed an infant from one mother's hood. Orford gazed at the baby in absolute shock: "Except for the miniature fur bonnet on his head, the baby was stark naked."[22] To break the tension, the new Medical Officer, as Orford put it, quickly "covered the nakedness with his hand and joked: 'Well! I see they have no diaper problem up here.'"[23]

Like Orford, Donalda Copeland, a nurse at Southhampton Island in the early 1950s, revealed her concern for the condition of Inuit infant attire. Her housekeeper, Kitty, was late for work one day, and, when she finally showed up Copeland noticed that she was especially enamoured: "In a moment she revealed the reason for her joy. She lifted the hood of her loose kooletah to show me. Snuggled down within the warm enclosure was Okalik and Eyakak's new-born daughter, deep in slumber. And she was now stark naked. I stifled an exclamation of shock and dismay."[24]

Kitty announced that this little infant had just been adopted by herself and her husband, and instead of ruining Kitty's surprise, Copeland told her how lovely the baby was, only after proceeding to "hunt out warm clothing for the babe – shirt, diaper, sweater, bonnet and blanket."[25] Even though the baby girl was in a "warm enclosure" in the kooletah, Copeland still expressed her sense of "shock" when she saw her naked. Naked infants frequently attracted the critical gaze of newcomers.

But, these little babies were not necessarily considered to be naked by the Inuk women who carried them. They were often wrapped in caribou fawn skins. What was described as naked to one woman may not have been understood as wholly unclothed to another. And, all items of clothing had specific cultural meanings. According to Rosie Iqallijuq, Inuit hats were gender-based, with girls wearing traditional head coverings that were "sharply curved at the nape," for instance, and boys' were "funnel shaped in the narrow edging."[26] Not only were they cozy in their mothers' packs, but the Inuit had their own way of cleaning their animal skin diapers. Lucy Tupik described what can only be considered an efficient diapering system used by northern mothers:

> When we were going to put the baby in the [amauti], we would cut a piece of fur taken from the neck of the caribou. Then we would shape it round and put it in place inside the [amauti]. When the baby wet, the piece of fur was removed, wrung out and put into the porch of the [iglu] to freeze. It was then beaten with a stick to remove the urine that had frozen. Afterwards it was placed on the shelf near the *quiliq* to dry, then used again. The same was done for the overnight diaper, except the piece of caribou fur was longer.[27]

These diapers seemed to have gone unnoticed by outsiders. But, newcomers did recognize that Aboriginal mothers were competent at the moss diapering system. Amy Wilson, who worked as a nurse along the Alaska Highway in the late 1940s, for example, commented on the practicality and success of the muskeg moss diapers. In one particular instance, Wilson noted that moss had been gathered, washed, and dried by a mother before the baby's birth, and she concluded, "One seldom sees a baby with sore buttocks if muskeg moss has been used as a diaper."[28]

Diapers and infant attire were not the only bodily objects that northern newcomers throughout the twentieth century felt compelled to discuss or attempt to reform. Many bodily parts caught their attention, but the bodies of children were under particularly close surveillance. Under the tutelage of Gareth Howerd, then working as a medical doctor on the DEW line, a young boy, Elijah, was introduced to a toothbrush and tooth paste: "During his stay Elijah and I became good friends, and I tried to teach him hygiene. He was anxious to learn, and I showed him how to use a toothbrush. When he left for home I gave him a new toothbrush and some tooth paste and told him to use them every day." When Howerd next visited Elijah in his village, he asked that Elijah should show him his teeth, just to make sure he was doing his job: "He smiled widely and showed me them. They were not as white as they had been when he left Frobisher, but I had to admit they looked pretty healthy."[29]

This narrative is less dramatic than others which involved children and lessons taught by newcomers about Western-based hygiene. Stories of more violent and invasive intrusion into bodily practices are part of the, at times, tragic Native/newcomer legacy. One example of this kind of interference is offered by Martha Flaherty. She was the grand-daughter of the film maker Robert Flaherty and a qualified nurse, originally from Inukjuak in northern Quebec. Flaherty wrote about her experience as a young Inuk woman, with a southern doctor and nurse on board the ship the *C.D. Howe*, a much-used northern vessel, as her family was being forced by the federal government to relocate from Inukjuak to Grise Fiord. While growing up, she had been taught that White people were friendly, but this was hardly confirmed in her early contact with them. She recounted, "For as long as I can remember, Inuit believed that the white people were very helpful. Because these sayings were driven into my soft mind, I really believed we were going to get some help. Instead I went through hell with doctors and nurses. Not to name any of them, they wore white clothes, carried needles, stethoscopes, tongue depressors, cotton balls and scissors. Of course, that is not to mention what they smelled like. That is scary enough for any kid. It is the scissors, I remember the most. With needles and other equipment, I wasn't going to lose anything. But with scissors I found out they wanted something from me. They wanted my hair – to give me a brush cut."[30]

Indeed, it is clear that Flaherty had memorized much about how the bodies of medical workers were identifiable with the "white clothes" and various paraphernalia. Again, identity became infused with clothing. Martha Flaherty went on to say that while on board the *C.D. Howe*, a doctor had witnessed an Inuk mother looking for lice in her child's hair. He summarily decided that all the children on board should have their heads shaved, boy or girl, regardless of the feelings of the parents. Flaherty ran away and managed to elude capture. This is a familiar story, told time and time again, when Aboriginal adults remembered their first encounters with nurses or doctors in the north. The cases around hygienic bodily practices are somewhat different, since they often were portrayed as much more invasive than the introduction of Western-styled clothing and the degree of preferential choice involved in purchasing cotton clothing.

Newcomers, nevertheless, expressed ambiguity. They admired the fine needlework, or the moss diapers, and yet, they could be critical of "naked" babies or other traditional ways. Nurses and missionaries doled out second-hand clothing from local church bails for infant apparel, and they helped sew dresses for young women who worked around mission houses or nursing stations. They boasted about those who dressed in White man's clothing with a certain amount of surprise and delight. For example, one of Donalda McKillop Copeland's new acquaintances at Coral Harbour, an Inuk man, Harry Gibbons, liked to dress quite formally. On one of his visits to the dispensary, Copeland was rather stupefied by his outfit: "At my invitation, the visitor took off his caribou parka, and I was again amazed. He was wearing a clean white shirt with a bow tie, above grey flannel trousers and seal skin boots. With his elegant accent and dress, he was a fantastic contrast to the type of native we had thus far encountered."[31]

Copeland responded with admiration to Gibbons, finding him to be a "contrast to the type of native" she had thus far met. She appreciated his "elegant" clothing and was "amazed" by his appearance.

Fashion and Cultural Hybridity

Southerners frequently pointed out the desire of northern Aboriginal people to participate in Western culture. Country and western music, transistor radios, and record players were the rage among the more "modern"-looking Inuit men in the 1950s. Nurse Dorothy Knight said of one local Lake Harbour resident, "Georgie wore a black leather jacket over his checkered shirt; his eyes always hidden behind dark glasses."[32] His style reflected the fact that he chose to wear store-bought clothing over more traditional attire. But, at the same time, while there was admiration for adopting "white man's clothes" there was concern expressed for these choices. Some observers wondered whether supplying Aboriginal people with new modern clothing was actually in their best interests.

By the late 1950s, Margery Hinds, a schoolteacher at Port Harrison, found herself in a conversation about women's attire with Inuk elder and artist Johnny Inukpuk. He was amused by the way Hinds dressed, and commented that her attire reminded him of the way that Inuit women once appeared. "Our women used to dress something like that," Inukpuk remarked, "only their clothes were made of caribou skin. There were lots more caribou here then than there are now. But, after the missionaries came, they taught our women to cover up their trousers with skirts. Then, after a time, they didn't wear trousers any more, only bloomers that they buy at the store."[33] Hinds concluded that if she wore the "print dresses over fleece-lined bloomers," then in style elsewhere, she would "freeze in such clothing."[34]

The implication that missionaries suggested the transition in clothing is not entirely surprising. Along with their goal of conversion to Christianity, they often wanted to transform cultural tastes and social behaviours, and they were particularly proud to feature Aboriginals in Western clothing as part of the evidence of their progress. This suggested that the body had been, through a complex and historical process of redressing, at least somewhat colonized. Increased contact with other northern sojourners played a key part in this prolonged set of transitions. The inappropriateness of light cotton clothing had obviously struck other Aboriginal people, including one grandmother who failed to be impressed exclaiming in reference to her new jacket shipped from the south: "How useless, the wind goes right through this."[35]

The cotton that became increasingly available was often seen mixed with traditional clothing to ensure a combination of recent style and warmth. A description of such blending was included in a biographical sketch of a young Inuk woman "Lucy of Povungnetuk," delivered by Malvina Bolus, then editor of the *Beaver*. Bolus wrote about Lucy's chores, and she was especially cognizant of her clothing:

> She was wearing a scarlet short sleeved sweater over a long sleeved brown sweater; she put on her blue cardigan and satin windbreaker. She adjusted her bright plastic barrettes in her gleaming hair – worn shoulder length and home-permed, though many of her friends still wore braids looped across the back of their heads – tied on a silk kerchief and wrapped a tartan wool shawl around herself. The rest of her costume was a print skirt worn over grey slacks, two pairs of duffle socks – one pair long and embroidered on the turned-down-top, and skin boots shorter than the usual knee length were topped with white fur.
>
> In some of her attire and hair fashion choices, Lucy stood out. Her barrettes and hair were more modern than that of the other girls, and her boots too appeared to be different from what others wore. They were not like the "local *kumiks*" and had been a gift from the wife of the manager of the Hudson's Bay store in the community.[36]

The clerks in Hudson's Bay Company stores actively stocked bolts of cotton and other Westernized clothing for trade. Euro-Canadian women such as Mena Orford ordered clothing from southern catalogues for her housemaid so that she would appear in the latest "cotton house-dresses" which, according to her husband, looked more like "Madam Butterfly" than modern fashion.[37]

Cultural contact and interventionist state policies also involved northerners' relocation to southern locales for Westernized medical treatment, and this, too, is reflected in shifting histories of the dressed body. Because of high rates of tuberculosis, especially in the 1950s, many Inuit were evacuated to southern sanitaria. Leah Idlout d'Argencourt, a writer and interpreter, remembered how as a child she was taken on board the *C.D. Howe* and shipped to a sanitarium in Quebec City. Upon her arrival, she and the other passengers were greeted by curious bystanders. Idlout d'Argencourt was struck by how the women were dressed: "The women especially looked so funny in their fancy hats, with fox pelts draped over their shoulders – pelts that the Inuit could have put to much better use as fur trim for parka hoods. And the high-heeled shoes that looked impossible to stand up on; they made my heels feel tired just looking at them."[38] Of course, the children who were sent to the south for treatment would be somewhat surprised at what they saw upon arrival. But, on their return, the impact of their southern experiences was quite visible as well. In one case, Sheownarlook, a young woman who had been in southern Canada for four years, caused a perceptible stir upon her return to Coral Harbour: "During her four years' absence, Sheownarlook had become something of a woman of the world. Her jet black hair was cropped short and curled, her cheeks were smeared with face powder and rouge and on her lips was a bright red colouring which contrasted oddly with her sallow skin."[39]

Here, Donalda McKillop Copeland constructs an image of a returning woman who looked significantly different from what she had expected: "a woman of the world." Copeland saw her as "modern," and, of course in so exclaiming, she portrayed the other community women as outdated. She went on to say that this woman's "tundra sisters, with their long plaits of hair and their faces quite untouched by beauty aids, cast covert glances at the newcomer" and stroked her "black curls and patted her cosmeticized cheeks."[40] This is very interesting because it suggests the extent to which the northern women's bodies were now also targets of consumer products. Consumerism certainly had begun to reach a hand into northern communities.

Conclusion

The extent to which clothing and often hygiene featured in newcomer narratives suggests a number of interpretative possibilities. As for northern sojourners who felt a sense of freedom from commoditization, their experiences mirror those for whom going north became what many observers have seen as a way to escape the constraints of southern life and to seek instead what they constructed through their experiences and memoirs as a quintessentially "northern adventure." While they enjoyed their freedom, they also engaged in a program of reform to re-dress Inuit babies, young children, and adults as well. At the same time, many newcomers from the south started to reform their own dress and recognize the value of northern clothes.

By the time of the Arctic fashion show in 1960, southerners were dressing in northern clothes and northerners in southern clothes, suggesting a "hybridized" fashion consciousness. Certainly, the evidence points to ways in which cultural contact was "embodied" contact. Clothes were a marker of cultural difference, but clothes also became a matter for negotiation, desire, display, and even, in some cases, artistic representation as portrayed in the painting and sculpture of many Inuit women artists.

Notes

I would like to acknowledge Jane Nicholas and Patrizia Gentile for their kindness and their efforts at bringing together this collection. Thanks also for their editorial skills and thanks to Robert Rutherdale for his support and terrific ability at proofreading.

1 Marilyn McLean, "Inuvik, Near Arctic Ocean, Holds First Fashion Show," *Style* [Toronto], 29 June 1960.
2 "Means 'To Teach with Love': Eskimo Children Don't HAVE to Go to School. If Classes Are Dull, Pupils Get Up and Walk Out," *Globe and Mail*, 1 June 1959.
3 The reference to cowboys or cowboy culture was not entirely new. See, e.g., an article taken from notes originally written in 1936: R.N. Hourde "Sophisticated Eskimos," *Beaver* 283, no. 2 (1952), 36. In describing the Western "Eskimo," Hourde observed, "It is rare that an Eskimo family is without a household phonograph. A new set of records is bought for it each year; and strangely enough Kentucky Hill Billy tunes are favourites. Cowboy laments rate a close second."
4 Sheila Burnford, *One Woman's Arctic* (Toronto: McClelland and Stewart, 1973).
5 In Canada, Alexandra Palmer has done much to elucidate some of the con-

tours of fashion history. See *Couture and Commerce: The Transatlantic Fashion Trade in the 1950s* (Vancouver: UBC Press, 2001). See also Alexandra Palmer, ed., *Fashion: A Canadian Perspective* (Toronto: University of Toronto Press, 2004). Attention to body history has been a bit sparse, and the best studies tend to focus on either medical history or the conflation of race, colonization, and the body. See, e.g., Wendy Mitchinson, *The Nature of Their Bodies: Women and Their Doctors in Victorian Canada* (Toronto: University of Toronto Press, 1991); Mona Gleason, "Lost Voices, Lost Bodies? Doctors and the Embodiment of Children and Youth in English Canada from 1900 to 1940," in *Lost Kids: Vulnerable Children and Youth in Twentieth-Century Canada and the United States*, ed. Mona Gleason, Tamara Myers, Leslie Paris, and Veronica Strong-Boag (Vancouver: UBC Press, 2009), 136–53; Mona Gleason, "Size Matters: Medical Experts, Educators, and the Provision of Health Services to Children in Early to Mid-Twentieth-Century English Canada," in *Healing the World's Children: Interdisciplinary Perspectives on Child Health in the Twentieth Century*, ed. Cynthia Comacchio, Janet Golden, and George Weisz (Montreal and Kingston: McGill-Queen's University Press, 2008), 176–202; Mary-Ellen Kelm, *Colonizing Bodies: Aboriginal Health and Healing in British Columbia, 1900–1950* (Vancouver: UBC Press, 1998); Katie Pickles and Myra Rutherdale, eds., *Contact Zones: Aboriginal and Settler Women in Canada's Colonial Past* (Vancouver: UBC Press, 2005). Sport history has also critically approached the topic of embodiment, and some successful examples include Bruce Kidd, "In Defense of Tom Longboat," *Canadian Journal of the History of Sport* 14, no. 1 (1983), 34–63; Don Morrow, "Sweetheart Sport, Barbara Ann Scott and the Post–World War II Image of the Female Athlete," *CJHS* 18, no. 1 (1987), 36–54; Mary Louise Adams, "To Be an Ordinary Hero: Male Figure Skaters and the Ideology of Gender," online at http://www.plover.com/rainbowice/mla1.html.

6 Susan Bordo, "The Body and the Reproduction of Femininity," in *Writing on the Body: Female Embodiment and Feminist Theory*, ed. Kate Conboy et al. (New York: Columbia University Press, 1997), 91.

7 For a fascinating comparative piece, see Nicholette Prince, "Influence of the Hudson's Bay Company on Carrier and Coast Salish Dress, 1830–1850," *Material History Review* 38 (Fall 1993), 15–26.

8 Barbara E. Kelcey, "What to Wear to the Klondike: Outfitting Women for the Gold Rush," *Material History Review* 37 (Spring 1993), 20.

9 Charlene Porsild, *Gamblers and Dreamers: Women, Men and Community in the Klondike* (Vancouver: UBC Press, 1999), 197.

10 W.E. Elliott, "Clergy Widow Recalls Early Days in the Yukon," *Canadian Churchman*, June 1960, 9. This article was written by Yukon resident Flo

Whyard and published under her father's name. A similar rendition of the story appeared in Yukon Diocesan Board, *Five Pioneer Women of the Anglican Church of the Yukon* (Whitehorse: Yukon Diocesan Board Women's Auxiliary, 1964), 3.

11 Glenbow Museum, M4745, files 24 and 25, E.P. Hockin correspondence files, 8 Dec. 1931.

12 General Synod Archives of the Anglican Church of Canada, Butler Papers, Letter from Adelaide Butler to Dollie Butler, 27 April 1935.

13 Mena Orford, *Journey North* (Toronto: McClelland and Stewart, 1957), 23.

14 Betty Lee, *Lutiapik: The Story of a Young Woman's Year of Isolation and Survival in the Arctic* (Toronto: McClelland and Stewart, 1975), 50.

15 Carolyn K. Soper, "A Nurse Goes To Baffin Land," *Beaver* 295 (Winter 1964), 33.

16 Donalda McKillop Copeland, as told to Eugenie Louise Myers, *Remember, Nurse* (Toronto: Ryerson Press, 1960).

17 A good example of this is offered by Malvina Bolus in her description of a young seamstress who was making a parka: "Lucy never used a pattern to cut them out; she could judge by eye how the size would work out and the peculiar way of cutting was long familiar." Malvina Bolus, "Lucy of Povungnetuk," *Beaver* 290, no. 1 (1959), 22.

18 Gareth Howerd, *DEW Line Doctor* (London: Robert Hale, 1960), 76 –7.

19 John Bennett and Susan Rowley, *Uqalurait: An Oral History of Nunavut* (Montreal and Kingston: McGill-Queen's University Press, 2004), 322.

20 Bennett and Rowley, *Uqalurait*, 322.

21 General Synod Archives of the Anglican Church of Canada, Minnie Hackett, "Extracts of Interest from Letters Written by Miss Hackett, of Aklavik Hospital," *Living Message*, April 1928, 135.

22 Orford, *Journey North*, 15.

23 Ibid.

24 Copeland, *Remember, Nurse*, 150.

25 Ibid., 151.

26 Bennett and Rowley, *Uqalurait*, 331.

27 Ibid.

28 Amy Wilson, *No Man Stands Alone* (Sidney: Gray's Publishing, 1965), 49.

29 Howerd, *DEW Line Doctor*, 91.

30 Martha Flaherty, "I Fought to Keep My Hair," in *Northern Voices: Inuit Writing in English*, ed. Penny Petrone (Toronto: University of Toronto, 1988), 274.

31 Copeland, *Remember, Nurse*, 35–6.

32 Lee, *Lutiapik*.

33 Margery Hinds, *School House in the Arctic* (London: Geoffrey Bles, 1957), 146.

34 Ibid., 147.

35 Penny Petrone, ed., *Northern Voices: Inuit Writing in English* (Toronto: University of Toronto Press, 1988), 237. See also Myra Rutherdale, "'She Was a Ragged Little Thing': Missionaries, Embodiment, and Refashioning Aboriginal Womanhood in Northern Canada," in Pickles and Rutherdale, *Contact Zones*, 228–45.

36 Bolus, "Lucy of Povungnetuk," 22. Other articles in the *Beaver* acknowledged this blend of traditions. One article highlighted a woman looking outside of her house with a caption that read, "The girl of Ikaluit, (sic) dressed like any southerner, looks out on a White Man's world," and in the same article another photograph caption read, "This Eskimo shopping in the HBC store shows in her outfit the mingling of north and south." Len Peterson, "Frobisher Bay – Halfway to Somewhere," *Beaver* 289, no. 3 (1958), 51, 53. A fascinating and critical synopsis of some of these northern articles is provided by Joan Sangster, "The Beaver as Ideology: Constructing Images of Inuit and Native Life in Post–World War II Canada," *Anthropologica* 49, no. 2 (2007), 191–209.

37 Orford, *Journey North*, 131.

38 Leah Idlout d'Argencourt, "C.D. Howe," in Petrone, *Northern Voices*, 232.

39 Copeland, *Remember, Nurse*, 221.

40 Ibid.

6 The Domesticated Body and the Industrialized Imitation Fur Coat in Canada, 1919–1939

GEORGE COLPITTS

After the First World War, the fur coat clothed the Canadian woman's body and became a means by which women negotiated their place in a society grappling with modernity. Worn by greater proportions of women, even year-round,[1] the fur coat can add to understandings of the body's history in Canada,[2] particularly since "Milady's fur" came to have a myriad of meanings in the context of rapidly expanding urban growth, industrial capitalism, gender relations, and labour unrest of the 1920s and 1930s. As women within new class-oriented and consumerist societies entered employment or took advantage of more liberal sensibilities around sexual and social relations, they often turned to this consumer product as a means to either challenge social ordering or reaffirm it.[3]

Within the industrialized world, the story of the fur coat in Canada is a fascinating, but complex, subject of study. In the interwar years, Canadian furriers produced an astounding 1.3 million fur coats for women and an equally expansive stock of fur for women's fashion accessories and clothing trim.[4] The abundant supply of furs in Canada and the proliferation of medium- and small-sized retail manufacturers – or furriers – considerably cheapened and widened the accessibility of the Canadian-made coat to consumers.[5] But, explaining the appeal of the fur coat up and down social and economic classes and deciphering meanings in the "magic of display" in fur is not easy.[6] Communications specialist Chantal Nadeau argues that long-standing associations existed between women, sexuality, and fur in Canada, "the fur coat [serving] as a natural extension of female skin."[7] The work of philosopher Alphonso Lingis suggests that the interwar resurgence in fur fashion constituted another instance of women – and men in other circumstances – using animal parts, scents, textures, and furs to make the human body and its sexuality simply more alluring.[8] It is Susan David Berstein's work in gender and English studies, however, that provides an analytical jumping-off point for the present essay. Fur likely found value in societies well entrenched in Darwinian thought by the 1920s: women alerted to the principles of sexual selection had already turned to "vestimentary excess" and donned peacock feathers, fish scales, wasp wings, and other animal parts to set themselves apart.[9] Following this reasoning, the fur garment was, in many ways, the *ultimate* selection identifier, from the higher class and impossibly expensive chinchilla to the working-class rabbit. This chapter builds on that premise, but makes the observation that complicating this coded identification were trickster transformations offered by modern and industrial processes. In short, the rabbit might be recreated by "the alchemy of the furrier" into "Hudson seal" and other imitations. By 1946, *Chatelaine* magazine, suggesting Canada was a thoroughly "fur-conscious nation,"[10] might have added that it was one deeply divided by women consolidating their status or crossing social boundaries with these "second skins" – many of them the transmutated and industrialized fur coat.

The Fur Coat and Canadian Modernity

Consumer historians have explained female buying behaviour in the early twentieth century by examining the rising purchasing power within the middle classes or their reaction to retail giants. Consumerism might well have pushed Canadians into modernity while, concurrently, it confronted female buyers with a new and more powerful form of paternalism. Their reaction to capitalized and metropolitan retailing power was never simple, however. Retail activities were usually contested even in the modern era, and consumerist behaviours were "complex blends of refusal and acceptance."[11]

Modernity, as an ongoing theme in the history of the body in Canada, and well explored in this volume's chapters in their discussions of class, gender, and race, is central to the story of the fur coat as it developed into a mass consumer item.[12] Given the sexualization of the woman's body, which affirmed new values, the emergence of radical "flapper" design, and celebrity fashion branding idealizing specific body types, coats in the 1920s captured the emerging "modern" economic and social place of women, especially in North America.[13] In the years immediately after the First World War, dressers bred the functional bulk of fur coats out of fashion lines. Innovative processing, piling, shearing, and dyeing allowed animal pelts to be used more commonly as full-length coats with fur outside rather than more practically inside. Concurrently, the Edwardian corseted fur coat with costly tapering was completely lost in the second decade to Paul Poirot's "Empire figure" with long, straight lines and far cheaper seamstress demands, a look that endured for half a century and beyond during the *belle epoch* of the female fur coat.[14] But it was the technical, industrial, and chemical innovations of the early decades of the century that allowed for the widespread adoption and democratization of the fur coat. New technology and industrialized processes that previously overwhelmed millinery and dressmaking establishments in Canada now transformed the manufacture of fur goods.[15] The results were dramatic. Prices dropped on fur garments, and a startling new range of fur products became available. In 1921, Holt, Renfrew and Co., already well established as one of Canada's largest furriers, made mention of "present uncertain price conditions," where female consumers could now snag better coats at lower prices, or better prices on formerly very expensive models.[16]

Fur, perhaps since the Middle Ages considered a luxury product and sometimes subject to sumptuary restrictions, continued to serve as a status identifier in the modern age. Fur coats provided the well-born (and often viewed as *well-bred*) woman a means to distinguish herself within the ranks. A fine (or shorthaired) fur came to represent, quite literally, the elite woman's body itself, when journalists in society columns simply referred to them as "Mrs. Silver Fox," "Mrs. Russian Sable," and "Mrs. Beaver," and so on.[17] Print media set aside those individuals who could afford these "evening furs," whose lives were nocturnal, rather than organized in labour-filled daylight – the starlets, wives of notables, the cultured, and the classy individualists, or simply, the truly rich.[18] By "transforming Darwin's natural law of evolution into contemporary dress,"[19] these women displayed their power, wealth, and procreative attractiveness in sables and chinchillas – furs which, because of the larger demand for them in these years, commanded their highest prices ever.

However, the cheapening of other furs and the availability of "mock" varieties offered a new means for women of all ranks to emulate their betters and even challenge hardening class distinctions. These industrialized furs, hard to distinguish from their real counterparts, could be purchased as a coat or even trim with small wages and salaries.[20] Furs of this sort could do more than transform a lower-class working woman into a "princess"; they could announce and nuance her sexual and physical attributes in the social tumult of the times. In 1921, one coat ad pointed out that there "was just one thing that can change a plain girl into a pretty girl and a pretty girl into a beautiful one, and a beautiful one into a goddess – and that one thing is a fur coat." The wearer, it was claimed, became "Hebe [the goddess of Spring] or Venus [of love or beauty] or better still Diana [the powerful goddess of the hunt]."[21]

All the same, moral authorities and capitalist-backed retailers and manufacturers were not distant from the "look" that women were appropriating. Whatever its availability to larger numbers of women, the Empire figure coat served much like a body-length curtain. It hid as much as it revealed. Moreover, its style was almost slavishly adhered to in design, creating uniformity in which individuality and specific body features of a woman were lost. The straight lines demanded height and slimness which, almost from the beginning of its widespread adoption, pressured wearers to strive for a single body type, a norm reinforced by newspaper advertisements and retail catalogues. The garment that exacted tall and thin dimensions from all wearers came bundled with dietary demands and pointed criticisms of different and, especially, larger, body types. "Her friends chuckle behind her back when she put on excess weight," whispers Bovril's 1929 ad of the fur-clad woman who had bulged beyond her coat's requisite classic lines.[22] As significantly, mass advertising of the new fur "look" showed women almost invariably immobile. The models in catalogue and newspaper advertisements struck largely ornamental poses – which contradicted the new roles for females in workplaces and sport in popular culture.[23] Although female aviators, skiers, and skaters donned fur to express their own newfound liberty in the age, print ads continued to depict the Canadian female as passive, as the recipient of a reader's, and presumably, a male's gaze. In no small way, women posing in fur were transfixed almost as completely as the trapped furbearing animals now attached to their bodies.

It is also apparent that the same fur that promised to liberate women beyond their class and social boundaries was frequently the basis of power contests in sexual relations. The female body, wrapped in these garments, can be located in numerous literary pieces and newspaper reports of the femme fatale and, conversely, the fallen woman. The fur coat became central to popular interwar nude fetishism, in which men found fantasy in sexual subjugation and sadomasochistic relations with women, as suggested in the many studio photographs produced in the interwar years of naked models wearing nothing but opened fur coats.[24] Although such "libidinal exchanges" abounded in novels and photographs since Leopold von Sacher Masoch's *Venus in Furs* (1870), the interwar proliferation of the materials is worthy of note.[25] Certainly, the widespread use of fur, especially among women, was hardly a neutral adoption of a mere clothing accessory. Fur lent itself to either the woman's power over the man, as Masoch's aloof "Venus" had enjoyed, or created a backlash against her, where fur implicated the wearer in a fantasy of animal mastery, and male dominance over Nature, the woman, herself. It might not be simply coincidental that in the period when many women were wearing fur that libidinous associations with it and slang terminology around female genitalia – the course and vulgar term "beaver" being one – emerged in the English lexicon by 1921, and found popularization in the crude limericks of *Immortalia* (1927) and the works of James Joyce by 1939.[26]

Industrialized Fur – Domesticated Bodies

Just how the fur coat came to express such a multitude of meanings – affirming class and sexual lines among some wearers, and challenging them among others – is directly related to revolutionary changes in its treatment and processing. As a young Harold Innis observed, in his overview of the fur-manufacturing industry in the 1920s, the late nineteenth century saw breakthroughs in dyeing, heavily capitalized mechanical factory methods, and communications revolutions that allowed metropolitan fashion centres to make fur a central and rapidly changing fashion commodity. Furbearers with specific felts found new popularity and fetched high prices on the market.[27] New mechanized dressing and chemical dyeing techniques replaced labour-intensive ones; and new uses for fur and its greater pliability in the hands of designers allowed prices to rise on a broad array of furbearing animals, even those that had formerly offered almost valueless trim materials. The disreputable muskrat fetched unprecedented prices when, by the interwar years, this very small fur could be dressed en masse in enormous mechanical tumbling and beating machines – processing thousands at a time, rather than singly by hand.

Muskrat benefited from ever more impressive chemical dyeing, based on new aniline dyes derived from coal tar. As a result, the quite respectable – and cheap – muskrat coat was born; with more intensive treatment, muskrat could be chemically reincarnated into imitation fur ("French Beaver" or "Hudson Seal"). Cheap furbearers found all sorts of dramatic rebirth: lamb through intensive piling, dyeing, and shearing could look a lot like beaver (hence, the popular "Beaver Lamb" or "Thibetine," offered in Eaton's catalogues and popular among low-end clientele: $39.75

delivered, in 1934). Rabbit was dyed dark and reborn as "Sable Beaver" or stained brown as "Imperial Mink."[28]

The new mass market created with such changes can be seen in the fur coats offered by Eaton's and Sears. Both establishments had evolved into the largest merchandisers in Canada by the First World War.[29] Eaton's Fur Department, organizing early in the interwar period to capitalize on the growing demands for fur goods, helped develop the store's offerings so typical of the Edwardian period,[30] into those formalized in window displays after the war. These now highlighted the modern and comparatively cheap fur coat available. Merchandise included truly high-end fine furbearers – classical mink, beaver, lynx, and others. But, also offered were newer, industrialized furs that imitated more valuable animals, in effect, reaching while separating out lower-income purchasers who could partake in "mental consumption" in the process.[31] This differentiation is best seen in Eaton's Montreal and Toronto stores, where expensive furs found display on mannequins in annual "shows." After 1924, when the store began using live models and launched fall fur fashion shows,[32] it sought to underline its adherence to Paris fashion dictates and reinforced them in window displays in Montreal, Edmonton, and Winnipeg. Montreal's storefront in the late 1920s, therefore, was "inspired" by Paris's Madam Paquin, who by then dominated emerging styles.[33] Vogue and other leading houses overshadowed the 1930s. The window showing the "Aristocrats of the Autumn Collections: Peltries fit for a Princess," in the Edmonton store's grand opening in 1935,[34] or Helena Rubinstein's "Nightfall Blue" ensembles in the same period,[35] showed fur garments that were clearly higher-end in terms of consumption, and suggestive of the power of haute-couture. Eaton's mass-market catalogues,[36] and newspaper ad runs,[37] meanwhile, catered to lower-income brackets and offered imitations of the same styles, promising the same quality but now using "trade name" furs which provided to middle- and even lower-class consumers coats made up of fur that, chemically and mechanically treated, looked a lot like far more valuable furry pedigrees – sometimes hard even to an experienced eye to tell apart. From expensive to affordable, then, Eaton's and other retailers captured their various classes of buyers by using industrial processes that, in effect, allowed lesser-offs to emulate their betters on terms set by metropolitan designers.

But, just as capital and industry were gaining greater control over women's choices and their very bodies through fashion dictates, the same possibilities in production and industrialized treatments allowed many consumers to buck emulation and simply masquerade as something they were not. By 1923, the New York International Fur Exposition addressed the widespread problematic "misnaming" of furs. Numerous "unscrupulous" dealers were peddling cheap wares for expensive, and in the hands of retailers or inexperienced department store clerks, wrapping women in faux varieties.[38] Not all women were by any means victims in all this. In an age when industrial processes could create stunningly convincing fake mink and ermine from rabbits and domestic dog pelts, many women could now emulate without having the name, social status, or money to back up the image of their bodies. Fur, then, was a deceptive and potentially subversive commodity, at least insofar as a capitalizing fur garment industry was concerned.

Dominion, provincial and, in the United States, federal laws soon attempted to limit, unsuccessfully, such abuse.[39] In 1923, no fewer than seventy-four common aliases were on the market, either being sold in good faith or through chicanery to unsuspecting buyers. Offenders included the "Adelaide chinchilla," really the Australian opossum, the "Alaska bear" (a darkly dyed raccoon), and the skunk posing as "black martin." Fixative dyes and mechanical treatments had now transformed the once humble rabbit into no less than twenty-four known false identities. Bedevilling any of the "power" of the metropolitan fashion centre further, at least in the department stores, was the difficulty in catching such imposters. As an American commentator charged, it did not help that fur departments were usually run by mere "graduates of the ribbon counter" transferred into fur sections as retailers expanded into the market. Many department store retailers lacked specialists who knew fake and phoney furs from the real thing, something that "requires years of training and experience, and even an expert may be fooled sometimes."[40] Cyril Rosenberg concurred. The authority on fur cutting in the era admitted to the wide ranges of dyeing techniques, the periodically fashionable "pointing" of furs, and the attentiveness needed, even within the industry, to sort out "imitation" from genuine fine fur.[41]

Negotiating the Woman's Body in Fur – Canada's Retail-Manufacturers

In Canada, many women negotiated what was on their body beyond the shadow of such official, capitalist, and industrial power. They joined in a close relationship, one might say in collusion, with a retail-manufacturer. These small enterprises proliferated across Canada in most urban settings. By 1927, there were 244 of them in operation, mostly in Ontario and Quebec, and ranging in size from the small (such as L.M. Benson

Ltd. on Toronto's Yonge Street) to the large (such as the nine companies in Quebec employing over fifty people each).[42] Americans indeed often lamented that their money-spending wives could find a Canadian furrier – always with a fake French accent it seemed – offering cheap coats in any hotel in large centres like Montreal. But such furriers in large centres and even rural settings among travelling seamstresses were hardly just imposers and counterfeiters. The consumer and producer meeting in small furrier shops blurred lines between genuine and fine varieties and mock cheap lines. Undoubtedly, confusion occurred inside their doors. Although department stores were required by law to advertise trade names next to real names in printed catalogues, and they followed suit in newspaper ads, many small furriers enjoyed being under the radar of such regulation. The result was a free-for-all in a local market, largely negotiated by female buyers and furriers themselves, who, in turn, applied or rejected elements of metropolitan design. In Trois Rivières, one furrier used metropolitan-designed stock illustrations in advertisements to impart a metropolitan "look" to its enterprises which functioned, largely, with copied and innovated designs. Ovide Richelieu and his sons, purchasing their furs in the St. Maurice Valley were, typically for the time, both wholesaling and retailing in the industry (in their English advertisements claiming that "if if is fur we have it").[43] The company's coats were hand-made and designed according to the well-established retail-manufacturer's knowledge of furs and "la beauté de models."[44] The shop had its own looks. It also offered "Mouton de Perce," or Persian lamb, and quite possibly its infamous false friend, the dyed and curled hair of the domestic dog, as well as the French Seal (or the lowly rabbit). It is hard to say exactly what was being offered at the Royaume de la Mode, whose advertisements had their genesis in metropolitan ad books but whose wares were locally derived and inspired.

Very rarely did these small enterprises simply offer mere copies of French styles, anyway. The mail-order retailing Quebec giant, Paquet, well exemplified the Canadian retailer-wholesaler in furs.[45] Its massive fur-dressing factory (or *mégisserie*) opening in 1907 in lower town Quebec, at Point-aux-lievres, was easily the largest in Canada. The famous "Paquet Seal" (transformed muskrat) was sold by smaller furriers in cities such as Ottawa.[46] Despite the company's shift into ever larger orders of scale, its storefronts and advertising retained a strong degree of localism and, tied to that, a claim that it directly responded to demands by women consumers, rich or not, who could enjoy a service "from the trapper to you, without intermediaries."[47]

Fur retail-manufacturers thrived on abundant, local supplies, and now a range of dyed and industrialized fur to offer distinctively Canadian looks, or, simply what the individual wanted to look like. By 1927, at least six capitalized dressers, offering fur dyeing, were operating in Canada; retailers, however, could just as easily ship their furs for dressing by specialist dyers in Chicago and London. Most retained complete control over cutting and seamstressing. Holt, Renfrew and Co. Ltd., one of the largest by 1925, had a string of stores and two prominent fur goods establishments in Quebec and Montreal. The company enjoyed the royal seal as the furrier of the British Crown, a distinction frequently publicized in its advertisements.[48] The company reached its high-end clientele with fur catalogues that stressed the new active lifestyles and prominence of women in the public sphere (see Figures 6.1 and 6.2). But, even by the mid-1920s, when metropolitan designs were making a greater presence in the market, the company stressed that autonomy, flair, and identity stayed in-house, where women could consult and choose for themselves what to put on their bodies. In 1925, its line included "Paris-inspired" models.[49] But, the company, arguing that "no longer is the Fur Coat a luxury from the standpoint of cost," and offering the comparatively cheap $95 "fine Chapal Electric Seal" (or muskrat), with matching collar and cuffs, promised that it "follows closely, *yet conservatively*, the style edicts of Paris, even to its lovely lining."[50] Other advertisements maintained the distinction that Paris houses might have inspired but the company's Montreal designers and the female purchaser had the last word: "Styles [were] brought fresh from Paris by our own Designers."[51] Indeed, as the company followed the booming demand for fox, by the end of the 1920s supplied cheaply from Canada's hundreds of new fox fur farms, it offered "custom-made coats" for clients who could select their own furs and coats, these "to be made to her own design or to any of the designs we shall be pleased to submit."[52] The tension between local and metropolitan will, between copies and originality, was evident in other respects when the store promised in 1924 "strict adherence to the season's approved mode, yet every individual garment seems to be possessed of some charm all its own – a something that can never be copied, and which therefore achieves true exclusiveness."[53] By the 1930s, the company still arbitrated New York and Paris designs for its female customers. It had "chosen and adapted [designs] which we believe will be most appealing to Canadian women."[54]

Holt, Renfrew was not really innovative in this message. Smaller furriers, who garnered the loyalty and trust of their female clientele, saw

Holt Renfrew

STYLE WINNERS

At the football game or the hockey-match—day in and day out—the girl who loves sports clothes will revel in the beauty of these style winners. They are designed especially to emphasize the charm of her vivacious personality.

Silver Muskrat

The girl at the game above is wearing a Holt, Renfrew Silver Muskrat Coat—youthful, sportive and trimmed with soft, glistening Brown Fox, equally pleasing for Street wear and smart occasions.
No. 2713   Price $325.00

Plum Shade Susliki

A novel fur from Russia which achieves a richness and a lustre that is unique. This delightful Fox trimmed model is Sports Coat, Street Coat, or Dressy Wrap at your pleasure, and always to your delight.
No 2714   Price $295.00

Page Ten

Figure 6.1 "Style Winners," by Holt, Renfrew in its 1926 *Fur Catalogue.* Photographs courtesy of Holt, Renfrew & Co. Ltd.

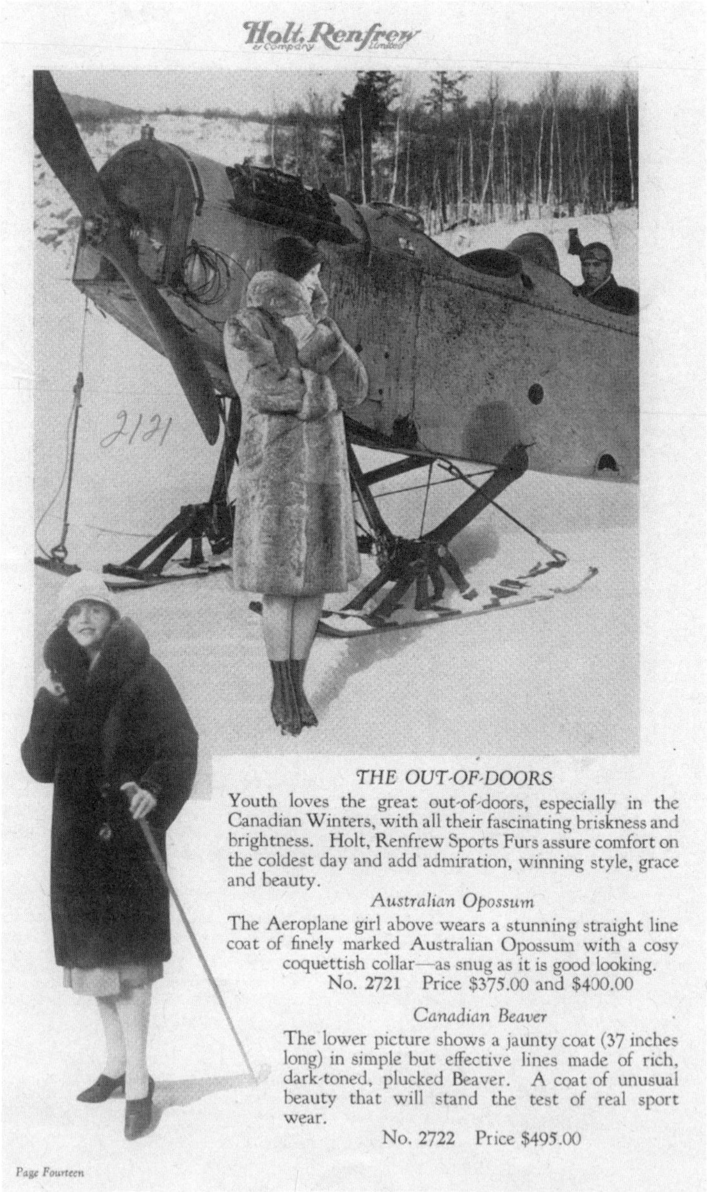

Figure 6.2 "The Out of Doors," by Holt, Renfrew in its 1926 *Fur Catalogue.* Photographs courtesy of Holt, Renfrew & Co. Ltd.

their role as adapting their wares to fashion and innovating upon them, such as in the case of the Eastern Canada Fur Company in Ottawa, offering "Trimmings to suit every individual taste ... Every garment speaks for itself as to quality."[55]

In the fragmented organization of its various players, the fur industry had really little means of coordinating or controlling as a whole the expanding supply of furs, their various dyeing and mechanical transformations, or even sales in the interwar years.[56] The industry, often depicted in euphoric terms of high modernism and early twentieth-century large-scale capitalism, in fact, continued to be largely artisanal and locally based, especially in the interwar years.[57] Quebec and Ontario, which had the largest numbers of furriers, were typically small, almost artisanal shops, producing the majority of coats and trim apparel. The typical establishment numbered fewer than ten employees.[58] These small-scale furriers purchased raw product and sent it off-site for dressing. Then, in-house, employees cut and seamstressed coats.[59] These practices formed the business of the Brock Fur Company in Saskatoon, whose in-house coats were made with the promise of "full value for your money, whatever garments you may buy."[60]

Thomas Pain, one of Calgary's furriers, prospered, at least in these years, within a close relationship between customers and manufacturers: seamstresses made coats in the back of the store, using a leather sewing machine for the purpose purchased in the 1920s. The company's founder remembered buying furs "from Indian trappers," and its Calgary Stampede float in 1931 emphasized that its coats were delivered direct, "from trapper to wearer."[61] Tellingly, the parade float had the working-class seamstresses who *made* the "high class" coats modelling them in the back. If such a potential social transformation was missed in the choice of *who* wore the coats on the float, the raw pelts and furs hanging on the float's peripheries likely reinforced that very idea (see Figure 6.3).

While many of these shops designed and manufactured coats, they continued to modify them for customers to keep pace with changing fashion, to resize them, or to repair them – no small consideration since cheaper, industrialized fur generally was more fragile than genuine fine furs.[62] At such time, the customer could also keep up with the nuanced changes to collars and cuffs imposed by fashion centres. But, in such shops, fur coat manufacture was never fully dependent on Parisian designers – and could not be.[63] Most furriers continued to see it as a point of honour to acquire designs from a couturier but add value in their own innovations, continuing to rely on cutters and dressers in-house to make

Figure 6.3 Calgary's Thomas Pain Furrier Ltd. Float at the Calgary Stampede, 1931. The head cutter is standing at the front of the float; the four women wearing fur coats are the company's seamstresses (the float won first prize that year): The owner remembered that in these years "Furs were bought from Indian trappers ... and were made in the back of the store." Glenbow Archives NA-3919–1, Pain Furrier Ltd. Fond.

up the coats themselves. A great deal of interpretation, negotiation on the cutting floor, and arbitrage between a furrier and a female consumer, and her body, took place. Most certainly, a woman had in mind what she wanted or did not want in a coat being made or altered, very often, specifically around her desires (see Figure 6.4).

In such circumstances, the fur coat consumer enjoyed considerable autonomy. Even Eaton's had to downplay any determinism of Paris, New York, and London. By 1947, the scripted commentary for its fur fashion show stressed its fur department's arbitrating of, not tutelage to, these

Figure 6.4 The early and soon-expanded R.J. Devlin Co. Ltd. in Ottawa, 1909, a typical retail-manufacturer that custom made women's coats on the spot. Library and Archives Canada, PA-042573.

centres' power. Its premier lines were, after all, supplied by the Canadian furrier, Poslun, of the well-established Irving Poslun family, which the company stressed, *had created fashion* for Canadian women for three generations. These coats were made "with an eye to Paris and a vigilant look to New York, the Poslun's brothers have evolved fashions which are essentially Canadian in feeling."[64]

In such a context, the local autonomy of even a department store's fur department, or a furrier's own hired "couturier" continued to negotiate fashion for the needs and wants of women, whatever metropolitan centres dictated. When R.J. Devlin, a prominent and independent furrier in Ottawa, replaced its departing Ladies Fur Department head, Miss Nora Daly, it therefore announced the arrival of Mr. Percy G. Stott, former manager of Holt, Renfrew's fur departments in Montreal and Toronto by highlighting the advantages offered to Stott: "large handsome new fur showrooms filled with a huge stock of fine furs, the fur workrooms, broad, bright and airy, where a staff of skilled workers greater in number than most wholesale factories produce the garments on which the Devlin Company bases its reputation" and "the enormous supply of unmanufactured peltries" in its stock.[65]

Its autonomy made the fare at Alexandor's in Montreal attractive to women. In 1925, the store offered, among its very pricey genuine fine furs of squirrel and chinchilla, serving as trim for garments, coats made up mainly of trade name furs: Hudson Seal (plucked and dyed muskrat), Chapal Seal, Persian Lamb, Hudson Bay Sable, White Coney and Kolinsky Coney (both imitation rabbits), and mole (likely sheared and dyed muskrat).[66] The same held true in Montreal's large furrier, Cummings & Cummings, which insisted that "the manufacturer was the place where you should buy furs."[67] But the same autonomy was found in smaller-capital fur houses – like Bleau & Rousseau, on King Street East, Montreal, offering fur coat manufacture and repair to its small-number clientele,[68] independent furriers like Montreal's Charles Desjardins & Cie,[69] or even home-visiting seamstresses, the *couturières à domicile*, purchasing and mutating designer patterns themselves.

The Fur Coat on the Canadian Female Body

In an era of hardening economic distinctions between the working, middle, and upper ranks, furs whether fake or real, imitative or genuine, were grabbed up in a haste of self-representation and definition. When the *Ottawa Citizen* spoke of changing women's status in the 1920s, central to the "social structure of the nation," and referred to the franchise and the "march of civilization," it turned to fashion to measure the change to women's "business, professional, athletic, and civil service" since Confederation. One measure, the comparatively few fur coats worn by women at the time of the nation's birth and their high cost, suggested the democratization and proliferation of fur among the newly enfranchised woman.[70] By the same token, fur still firmly anchored women in convention and traditional, maternal roles. The paper's society pages, it is worth noting, almost always reported on honeymooning couples leaving for their destinations with the new bride wearing "a lapin fur coat," or one bride frocked "in deep green under a brown seal coat" for their nuptial confirmation.[71]

The fur coat, like the fur industry producing it, could not be harnessed well to metropolitan power, centralized control, or even much regulation – economic or social. Fakes, imitations, and recreated furs passed in complex undercurrents of consumer tastes, demands, and emulative behaviours. In the 1920s, a single furbearer such as fox could now lend numerous genuine colour phases to the market, and with dyeing and industrial treatments, appear in numerous false forms, so that *Le Bien Public*, with some caution, pointed out the great opportunity to choose between a "yellow plebeian to the aristocratic silver" in a time of new, lower prices.[72] All the same, the report counselled care in such a market, as unscrupulous dealers abounded. Indeed, in such a context, women up and down class gradients, within and outside social norms and traditional constraints, commanded and informed the expansion of the market itself. The fur garment defies simple generalizations about consumer behaviour or designer control. In a discussion of the female body as a contested terrain, this aspect of clothing was hardly dominated by industrialized capitalism. Beyond this consumer item, many more questions can be asked of production, marketing, and purchasing in the retail world helping form the underpinnings of modern Canadian society, and the woman's transformed presence, and body, within it.

Notes

1 Cyril J. Rosenberg, *Furs and Furriery* (London: Sir Isaac Pitman and Sons, 1927), 21, and Jean Patou, "Fur Becomes Accepted Fabric," *Pittsburg Press*, 31 Oct. 1929. On the "Summer Fur," *Evening Independent*, 6 Aug. 1923.

2 This study follows a material approach adopted by Joan Sangster who, for different purposes, studied the fur coat after the Second World War. Joan

Sangster, "Making a Fur Coat: Women, the Labouring Body, and Working-Class History," *International Review of Social History* 52 (2007), 241–70.

3 R. Turner Wilcox, *The Mode in Furs: The History of Furred Costume of the World from the Earliest Times to the Present* (New York: Charles Scribner's Sons, 1951), 155.

4 Computed from annual reports of "Fur Goods and Fur Dressing Industries," Dominion Bureau of Statistics (hereafter DBS Reports), 1921–1939 (Ottawa: Ministry of Trade and Commerce). I have used an average figure for 1923 production, the only year without statistics.

5 "Tourists – buy a fur coat before you leave Canada," ad by A.J. Alexandor Furs, "Canada is the land of fine furs. Nowhere else in the world are they so beautiful or so reasonably priced," *Ottawa Citizen*, 5 July 1928. Roy K. Moulton, "Moulton Says this Is Not a Land of Milk and Honey," *Milwaukee Sentinel*, 27 Aug. 1926. See also Roe Fulkerson, "Imogene and Andrew," *Miami News*, 22 Oct. 1929. The DBS Reports offered few statistics on the undoubtedly pricier fur coat imports into Canada. However, it well documented the numbers of cheap fur coats produced in the interwar years: 1924 (40,610) to 1928 (78,037); the Depression years affected production, but by 1936, they more than recovered (90,602) and steadily climbed to 123,273 in 1939. In this time, the overall average value of a fur coat went from $168 to $173 and $92 to $93 each respectively.

6 Elizabeth Ewing, *Fur in Dress* (London: B.T. Batsford, 1981), 128, and Gary Cross's expression, quoted in Sangster, "Making a Fur Coat," 242.

7 Chantal Nadeau, *Fur Nation: From the Beaver to Brigitte Bardot* (London: Routledge, 2001), 15.

8 Alphonso Lingis, "Animal Body, Inhuman Face," in *Zoontologies: The Question of the Animal*, ed. Cary Wolfe (Minneapolis, MN: University of Minnesota Press, 2003), 174.

9 Susan David Bernstein, "Designs after Nature: Evolutionary Fashions, Animals, and Gender," in *Victorian Animal Dreams: Representations of Animals in Victorian Literature and Culture*, ed., Deborah Morse and Martin Danahay (Burlington, VT: Ashgate, 2007), 65–80.

10 *Saturday Night*, 23 Feb. 1946, 30.

11 Quoted and discussed by Mary Lynn Stewart, *Dressing Modern Frenchwomen: Marketing Haute Couture, 1919–1939* (Baltimore, MD: Johns Hopkins University Press, 2008), xv, 227–30; Julia V. Emberley, *Venus and Furs: The Cultural Politics of Fur* (London: I.B. Tauris, 1998); Keith Walden, *Becoming Modern in Toronto: The Industrial Exhibition and the Shaping of a Late Victorian Culture* (Toronto: University of Toronto Press, 1997), 334–6.

12 See, e.g., Myra Rutherdale, this volume.

13 Kenneth A. Yellis, "Prosperity's Child: Some Thoughts on the Flapper," *American Quarterly* 21 (1969), 44–64; David Desser, *Hollywood Goes Shopping* (Minneapolis, MN: University of Minnesota Press, 2000); John C. Spurlock, *New and Improved: The Transformation of American Women's Emotional Culture* (New York: New York University Press, 1998).

14 Wilcox, *Mode in Furs*, 156, and Ewing, *Fur in Dress*, 120–1.

15 See Christina Bates, "Shop and Factory: The Ontario Millinery Trade in Transition, 1870–1930," in *Fashion: A Canadian Identity*, ed. Alexandra Palmer (Toronto: University of Toronto Press, 2004), 113.

16 See "The Proof of Holt Renfrew Fur Values," Montreal *Gazette*, 22 Jan. 1921.

17 See the wealthy wearers referenced in "Fur Gathering Presents Cruel Feature, Claim," *Southeast Missourian*, 15 Jan. 1925.

18 "Finest Sable Coat Cost Buyer $60,000," *New York Times*, 1 Nov. 1921, 19.

19 Bernstein, "Designs after Nature," 70.

20 "Women Regard Fur Coat as Wardrobe Necessity: Modern Methods Have Put Fur Garments within Price Range of Women of All Classes – Many Less Expensive Pelts Desirable," *Hartford Courant*, 7 Nov. 1937, and "The Business Woman and Her Fur Coat," Montreal *Gazette*, 12 Sept. 1925.

21 "Furs Make Any Woman a Diana: Marvelous Display of Skin Garments at Sage-Allen & Co. Store," *Hartford Courant*, 6 Nov. 1921, 18.

22 "Keep Your Youthful Figure," *Chatelaine* (Nov. 1929), 66, and "Keep Your Youthful Figure," *Chatelaine* (Oct. 1929), 70.

23 See "$500,000 in Furs Displayed," *New York Times*, 14 Feb. 1922. The story, discussing the opulent fine furs at a Quebec sale, also cited "Sport furs of opossum, beaver and raccoon … displayed by living models driving in husky dog teams and toboggans."

24 Nude fetishism and the phenomenon of the nude "Venus" in furs is recounted in Emberley, *Venus and Furs*, 73–102. Or, the Richard Merkin Collection studio photo shown in *Delta of Venus, Little Birds: Erotica by Anaïs Nin* (New York: Quality Paperbacks, 1993). "What are you going to wear under your fur coat, this winter? Male scoffers needn't retort 'Very little,'" *Chicago Tribune*, 24 Nov. 1929.

25 On these exchanges, see Nadeau, *Fur Nation*, 15–16.

26 "Beaver *noun*," *The Oxford Dictionary of Modern Slang*, ed. Johy Ayto and John Simpson; also, "Beaver," *Oxford English Dictionary*, 2nd ed., 1989.

27 Harold Innis, *The Fur-Trade of Canada* (Toronto: University of Toronto Library, 1927), 140–1.

28 See "Breeding of Fur Rabbits," *Evening Independent*, 31 May 1929.

29 Donica Belisle, "Negotiating Paternalism: Women and Canada's Largest Department Stores, 1890–1960," *Journal of Women's History* 19, no. 1 (2007),

59–60; Cynthia Wright, "'Feminine Trifles of Vast Importance': Writing Gender into the History of Consumption," *Gender Conflicts: New Essays in Women's History*, ed. Franca Iacovetta and Mariana Valverde (Toronto: University of Toronto Press, 1992), 229–35.

30 See Archives of Ontario (hereafter AO), Eaton's Fonds, Window, Eaton's Winnipeg, 1910, F229-308-0-1188.

31 Wright, "'Feminine Trifles of Vast Importance,'" 232.

32 AO, F229-162-0-1026; "Ideas for Article on History of Fashion Shows and Models at Eaton's."

33 AO, "Window," Montreal, ca. 1928, F-229-308-0-1193.

34 AO, "Window," Edmonton, 1935, F-229-308-0-1196.

35 AO, "Window," ca. 1930s, F-229-308-0-1194.

36 In Quebec, the French-language editions highlighted, as in its 1928–29 Catalogue, the $47.50, with an opossum tinted as mink, or platinum fox, 5. "Eatonia" and "Braemore" were labels promoted in many of the interwar years. The most common: "coney" (rabbit), opossum dyed to various colour imitations or natural, Black Alaska Sable (skunk), raccoon, and cheap brown fox. Its cheaper-end coats of Electric Seal (sheared and dyed hare) and Alaska Sable (skunk) came in various fur grades at different prices. See AO, Eaton's Microfilmed Catalogue collection.

37 AO, F-229-91, Ad Books, Toronto, 1926–1927, appearing in the *Toronto Mail* and *Toronto Star*, RG 30, vols. V2989, D357372. Newspaper advertisements like that of 17 Oct. 1931, in the *Toronto Globe*, pitched "Hudson Seal Coats Have a New Style Importance," lauding the virtues of these dyed Rice Lake muskrats.

38 Frank G. Ashbrook, "Trade Names in the Fur Industry," *Journal of Mammalogy* 4, no. 4 (1923), 216–17.

39 Innis, *The Fur-Trade of Canada*, see notes on regulations in 115n1.

40 Ashbrook, "Trade Names," 220.

41 Rosenburg, *Furs and Furriery*, 331, 348.

42 See Table 11 and "List of Fur Goods Establishments," *Dominion Bureau of Statistics Report on the Fur Goods and Fur Dressing Industries in Canada 1927* (Ottawa: Ministry of Trade and Commerce, 1929).

43 Business card, *St. Maurice Valley Chronicle*, 4 Oct. 1945.

44 *Le Bien Public* (newspaper, Mauricie, Quebec), 14 Oct. 1920.

45 Alyne LeBel, "Une vitrine populaire: Les Grands magasins Paquet," *Cap-Aux-Diamants* 4, no. 2 (1988), 45–8.

46 "The Upstairs Fur Shop," *Ottawa Citizen*, 7 Nov. 1928.

47 Zephirin Paquet, *Sa famille, sa vie, son oeuvre* (Quebec City: n.p., 1927), 203–4.

48 *Canadian Jewish Chronicle*, 24 Sept. 1919.

49 Montreal *Gazette*, 25 Sept. 1926.

50 Ibid.; emphasis added.

51 Montreal *Gazette*, 16 Oct. 1926.

52 "Holt-Renfrew Fine Furs," Montreal *Gazette*, 24 Nov. 1928.

53 "Exclusive Note in Autumn Modes," Montreal *Gazette*, 13 Sept.1924.

54 "Special Preview Showing of New Fall Models," Montreal *Gazette*, 6 Sept. 1933.

55 "The Upstairs Fur Shop," *Ottawa Citizen*, 7 Nov. 1928.

56 Victor R. Fuchs, *The Economics of the Fur Industry* (New York: Columbia University Press, 1957), 5–7, 17.

57 Innis overemphasized this "modernizing" "industry" in his little-known *The Fur-Trade of Canada* (1927), not to be confused with his 1930 classic, *The Fur Trade in Canada*. H.A. Innis, *The Fur-Trade of Canada* (Toronto: University of Toronto Library, 1927). So did DBS Reports, reporting statistics on the evident capitalization, greater application of electrical motorization (in rated horsepower), and larger employment in factory enterprises. See *DBS Report, 1921–22*, 2. See my "Conservation, Science, and Canada's Fur Farming industry, 1913–1945," *Histoire sociale/Social History* 30, no. 59 (1997), 77–108.

58 Table 10, "Classification of Establishments According to Number of Employees, 1925," *DBS Report, 1925*, 8.

59 G. Howard D. Simpson, Thesis, "The Sales Organization of the Fur Trade," Box 4, Commerce Undergraduate Theses, University of Toronto Archives, 1925.

60 Glenbow Archives, "Brock Fur Company," Catalogue, Saskatoon, 1928–29.

61 Glenbow Archives, Thomas Pain Furrier Ltd., M1501; with photograph, NA-3919-1.

62 See durability chart in Innis, *The Fur-Trade of Canada*, 116–17.

63 Ewing, *Fur in Dress*, 135.

64 Fashion show commentary, Eaton's, 15 to 19 Sept. 1947, with "Overture to Fashion," printed for the occasion and Poslun advertisements. AO Fashion Files, F-229-162-0-1026.

65 "Comes to Devlin's," *Ottawa Citizen*, 20 June 1927.

66 *Montreal Gazette*, 13 Feb. 1925.

67 "La fabrique est l'endroit ou acheter les fourrures." "Cummings & Cummings," Advertisement, *La Patrie*, 4 March 1926.

68 "Fourrures de qualité: CONFECTION ET REPARATIONS," *Le Devoir*, 31 Jan. 1925.

69 "Nos Grands Rabais de Février," *Le Devoir*, 3 Feb. 1925.

70 "Women in the Confederation Period," *Ottawa Citizen*, 28 June 1927.

71 "Social and Personal," *Ottawa Citizen*, 13 Jan. 1936. "Social and Personal," Montreal *Gazette*, 19 Jan. 1932, and 26 Feb. 1938.

72 *Le Bien Public*, 20 Aug. 1936.

7 An Excess of Prudery? Lilias Torrance Newton's *Nude* and the Censorship of Interwar Canadian Painting

PANDORA SYPEREK

Sentimental figures, ones that seem symbolical or of purely academic study can be accepted. Naked women are also wholesome if they have the great outdoors as a canopy. But be once disarming and natural and simply paint a model naked in a studio, let the figure be not veiled in a wistful aurora, or let her be not poised alone in a wilderness of rocks and distant forests, but be standing solid and flesh-ly, like a Renoir maid-servant, and then taboo – you are out and in the basement.

– Donald Buchanan[1]

As artists we must be free to paint and exhibit what we see and feel. Here we are not free. We are confronted with all kinds of obstacles, imposed by an excess of prudery.

– Louis Muhlstock[2]

When Lilias Torrance Newton submitted her large oil painting *Nude* (see Figure 7.1) to the 1933 Canadian Group of Painters exhibition at the Art Gallery of Toronto,[3] figurative painting was enjoying a newfound popu-larity in eastern Canada.[4] Following the dominance of landscape paint-ing ushered in by the Group of Seven in the 1910s and 1920s, portraits, social themes, and nudes became common in Toronto and Montreal exhibitions in the 1930s. Yet, although the exhibiting group initially ac-cepted Newton's submission, the gallery board pulled the canvas from exhibition at the last minute. Writing in the progressive magazine the *Canadian Forum*, art critic Donald Buchanan explained, "They called the model a naked lady, not a nude, you see, for she wore green slippers."[5]

Subsequent accounts of *Nude*'s disqualification have reiterated this rationale, since the shoes "disrupt the concept of an idealized female

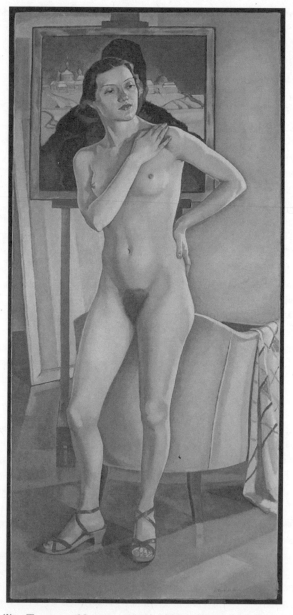

Figure 7.1 Lilias Torrance Newton, *Nude*, 1933. Oil on canvas, 203.2 × 91.5 cm. Private Collection. Courtesy of A.K. Prakash.

beauty existing outside of time" that traditionally defines the nude genre.[6] Other features equally upset this classical timelessness: au courant finger-waved short hair, heavy make-up, and pink nail polish firmly situate the model in the contemporary 1930s. Even the distinctive face resists generalization, while the toned physique marks the current fashion for tanning and exercise. Esther Trépanier points out that along with the superficial details signifying "the new aesthetic criteria embodied by the garçonne, the 'it girl' and the Art Deco élégante," the body in Nude reflects the changing ideals of feminine beauty between the wars.[7] Furthermore, the figure's fully rendered pubic hair blatantly transgresses the ideal hairless female body of Western art, while the confrontational, standing pose departs from the traditional passive, reclining nude. Anna Hudson infers that the body and pose belong to a dancer; the model hence confidently "performed her body" in a manner uncomfortably redolent of burlesque.[8] A framed painting curiously obscured behind the model's head and such domestic details as the plush armchair nonchalantly draped with a garment – likely the model's discarded robe – impart an intimacy in the artist's studio setting which might have contributed to the painting's perceived impropriety.

The censure was not unique, however. In 1927, a public furore erupted over the display of John Russell's reclining nude A Modern Fantasy (see Figure 7.2) at the Canadian National Exhibition (CNE). Four years later, in an incident much like that affecting Newton, despite selection by jury for the Ontario Society of Artists 1931 spring exhibition at the Art Gallery of Toronto, Bertram Brooker's Figures in a Landscape (see Figure 7.3) was subsequently withdrawn and stricken from the catalogue before the show's opening.

These well-documented scandals over the nude have resulted in an image of interwar Canada as deeply repressive. Writing after the Second World War, artist Louis Muhlstock blamed artistic constraint on "an excess of prudery." Art historians have routinely echoed this sentiment, attributing censorship and continuing neglect of the nude to a restrictive Canadian society. As Michèle Grandbois remarks, "The effects of our legendary prudishness linger still."[9] Yet, this explanation fails to account for the fact that the interwar period witnessed a proliferation of the nude genre in Canada. Grandbois notes that "over one hundred and fifty exhibitions presented in Canada between 1918 and 1939 each included at least one nude."[10] An investigation into the social and artistic contexts within which this paradox manifested itself will reveal that the causes for scandal were far more complex than mere prudery. It becomes evident

Figure 7.2 John Russell, *A Modern Fantasy*, 1927. Oil on canvas, 224 × 250 cm. Private collection.

that the failure of Newton's painting, among others, to conform to established standards transgressed not only allegedly conservative notions of decency, but also gendered codes of the nude as a site of Canadian modernism.

"More Humanly Canadian"

The profile of the Canadian art world underwent dramatic changes in the 1930s. In 1933, the national stronghold of the Group of Seven, with its near exclusive attention to the Ontario wilderness, dissolved

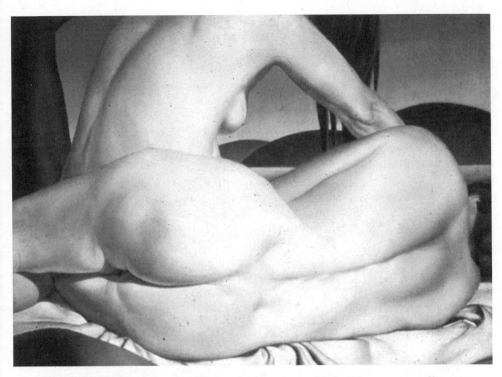

Figure 7.3 Bertram Brooker, *Figures in a Landscape*, 1931. Oil on canvas, dimensions and whereabouts unknown.

into the larger and more geographically widespread Canadian Group of Painters, which included several figure painters. Critic Augustus Bridle pronounced the need for this new organization to represent a "more humanly Canadian" art.[11] Accompanying the rise of figure painting was rhetoric promoting images of people as a more direct alternative to the dominant landscape painting. In one particularly resonant instance, painter Paraskeva Clark commanded artists to "Come Out from Behind the Pre-Cambrian Shield" – referring directly to the Group of Seven's unpeopled northern landscapes – and to refocus their energies on "the people and their struggles."[12] The onset of the Great Depression and increasing social unrest had sparked the desire for a human element in art; to the largely left-leaning art community, figuration appeared consistent with a democratic ideal.[13] Buchanan wrote, "No graphic art can genuinely flourish unless figure painters become as favoured individuals as landscape artists."[14]

In addition to embodying a sense of the Canadian people, the movement towards figurative painting – coupled with increased formal concerns – was equally thought to align modernism in Canada with an international avant-garde. Before his run-in with censorship, Brooker predicted that the emphasis on figure and form would "inevitably bear a closer relationship to the modern movement in other countries."[15] Since the nude – specifically, the female nude – was a locus of innovation in European modernism, it was deemed a necessary and previously deficient genre with which Canadian art could assert its national and international significance as well as modernist ambitions. Artists belonging to the Canadian Group of Painters and the Ontario Society of Artists eagerly took up the subject, exhibiting regularly in Toronto's two primary venues, the Canadian National Exhibition and the Art Gallery of Toronto.[16]

Against this backdrop, why did some nudes come under fire? To properly address this question, it is important to establish what kinds of nudes by Canadian artists *were* on display in Toronto at this time.[17] Like Lilias Torrance Newton's, the vast majority featured women: "the nude," as is ubiquitous in modern art, tacitly indicated the undressed female form. Outdoor scenes were favoured, marking a natural transition from the Group of Seven landscape towards figuration, while adhering to the Western tradition of the female nude in nature pervasive since the Renaissance. Edwin Holgate's female nudes set against the Quebec wilderness most clearly exemplified this tendency and have come to embody the quintessential Canadian nude. However, when Holgate exhibited two nudes (see Figure 7.4) at the Art Gallery of Toronto in 1930, the reception was mixed. The gallery reportedly received complaints for a year following the exhibit, and Holgate recalled that the paintings had "brought some irate letters from some very right-minded Methodist fathers in Toronto."[18] Nevertheless, they proved a success with critics, who applauded Holgate's choice of setting. Bridle wrote, "Holgate sets a new fashion in nudes – away from French decadence to the Laurentians for a background; splendidly painted nudes, without cosmetics."[19] The Art Gallery of Toronto and the National Gallery promptly purchased the paintings.

The following year, also at the Art Gallery of Toronto, Prudence Heward, Newton's fellow member of the Montreal-based Beaver Hall exhibiting group, showed a large reclining nude to glowing reviews. While patently referencing the tradition of the landscape nude, Heward's *Girl*

Figure 7.4 Edwin Holgate, *Nude in a Landscape*, ca. 1930. Oil on canvas, 73.7 × 92.3 cm. Photo © National Gallery of Canada.

Under a Tree (see Figure 7.5) diverges from Holgate's harmonious pastoral compositions. The tense and highly detailed physicality of the model conflicts with the flattened, generalized park setting and distant cityscape backdrop. Although painter John Lyman balked at this discord, dismissing the painting as "Bouguereau nude against Cézanne background," other critics praised *Girl Under a Tree* as "assertive," and Group of Seven member A.Y. Jackson declared it "one of the finest nudes ever painted in Canada."[20] Even so, Brian Foss notes that compared with the grand praise Holgate's nudes elicited, Heward's painting "was given a polite but reserved reception," perhaps due to its tensions.[21]

Images of Black female nudes in tropical landscapes were a popular alternative to the White, domestic variety. Dorothy Stevens's *Coloured*

Figure 7.5 Prudence Heward, *Girl Under a Tree*, 1931. Oil on canvas, 122.5 × 193.7 cm. Art Gallery of Hamilton.

Nude (see Figure 7.6) was so well received after its inclusion in a 1932 Royal Canadian Academy exhibition that the Art Gallery of Toronto purchased it the following year (the same year the gallery removed Newton's canvas). Despite the painting's palpable eroticism, Charmaine Nelson suggests that the figure's Blackness enabled the full-frontal nudity and coyly sensuous pose to evoke praise rather than censure. Racist attitudes generated a separate standard of acceptability where the Black model was concerned.[22] The *contrapposto* stance was in keeping with the classical tradition, while the jungle backdrop emphasized the model's otherness. Whereas White women set against idyllic Canadian backdrops instilled wholesome nationalism in the nude, Black women in tropical surrounds catered to exotic fantasy.

Although landscape nudes typify Canadian figure painting at this time, nudes set in interiors were also commonly exhibited. Holgate's *Interior* (see Figure 7.7), which pictures a woman grooming herself, is particu-

Figure 7.6 Dorothy Stevens, *Coloured Nude*, 1932. Oil on canvas, 86.4 × 76.2 cm. Art Gallery of Ontario. Purchase 1933. © Estate.

larly notable as it was not only included in the 1933 Canadian Group of Painters show from which Newton's *Nude* was omitted, but it was even re-produced in the catalogue's frontispiece, subsequently to be purchased by the Art Gallery of Toronto. As with the studio setting of *Nude*, the background is familiar and detailed, although associations with popular Impressionist boudoir scenes suggest how *Interior* could have been read-

Figure 7.7 Edwin Holgate, *Interior*, 1933. Oil on canvas, 76.2 × 63.5 cm. Art Gallery of Ontario. Purchase 1933. © Estate

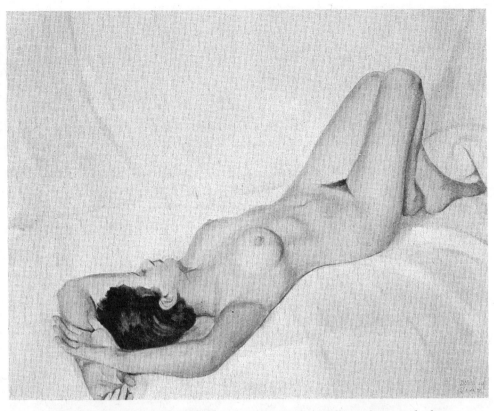

Figure 7.8 Dorothy Stevens, *Siesta*, ca. 1934. Medium, dimensions, and where-abouts unknown. Photo reproduced from Ontario Society of Artists, *Annual Exhibition of the Ontario Society of Artists*, exh. cat., Art Gallery of Toronto, 1934. © Estate.

ily accepted. The theme invokes the modern European tradition, while the rustic wooden furniture and heavy cookware Canadianize the scene. Unlike the self-aware, confident model Newton portrays, the woman in Holgate's painting glances downward, unaware, and unassuming.

Likewise, in Stevens's *Siesta* (see Figure 7.8), the undressed model lying obliquely on a bed with arms crossed overhead eludes confrontation, rendering the viewer's gaze voyeuristic and detached. The work was included in the 1934 Ontario Society of Artists exhibition at the Art Gallery of Toronto, mere months after Newton's canvas was rejected.

Both Holgate's and Stevens's nudes, although removed from an outdoor setting, retain a "natural" context in the seeming inconspicuousness of their nudity. Like the lake and the countryside, the bed and the boudoir appear appropriate contexts for undress, and the models' apparent obliviousness complements this innocence.

Prudery, Prurience, or a Repressive Hypothesis?

These examples demonstrate that "the nude" is not a singular category, nor a natural, a priori artistic subject, but is polysemous and historically contingent.[23] Apart from sidestepping the evidence that nudes were commonly exhibited in interwar Toronto, insistence that reaction against the nude resulted from widespread repression precludes analysis into the highly specific criteria for accepting certain images. Furthermore, the continued idea that progress in Canadian art suffered from "an excess of prudery" sustains belief in the proverbial time lag of Canadian modernism, the notion that Canada has always been one step behind the broader art world. Despite the perceived conservativeness of interwar Canadian painting compared with international developments, artists of the nude ironically emerge as social and artistic progressives working against the repressive forces of a backward society. Although a "wall of apathy"[24] may well have confronted display and study of the nude in Canadian art history, the conflation of its breach with artistic liberation neglects complex assumptions regarding gender, sexuality, and progress.

This problematic link between the nude and modernist progress resonates with Michel Foucault's thesis in *The History of Sexuality*, that popular notions of sexual repression in the modern era mark a misreading of what, in fact, constitutes a discursive explosion in the arena of sexuality.[25] The sheer abundance of nudes exhibited during the interwar period contradicts the prevailing "repressive hypothesis" writers have propagated up to the present day.[26] Martin Myrone relates Foucault's theory to the Victorian nude, which in spite of its allegedly restrictive context experienced vast proliferation. He argues that though typically characterized as insipid vehicle for the sublimation of repressed sexuality, the academic nude of late nineteenth-century British art actually generated desire with its erotically charged "aesthetic of frozen possession."[27] Instead of a challenge or exception to Canadian interwar puritanism, the increase in nudes at this time may well represent a mounting discourse on sexuality and, like the Victorian nude, can be understood as imaging the very language of desire.

Artists and critics both reproachful and defensive can equally be understood as having actively produced the surrounding sexual discourse. In his retaliatory essay, "Nudes and Prudes," Brooker critiqued the exploitative press coverage of his own encounter with censorship: "Knowing only too well, that a puritanical public delights in the discussion of those things which it considers illicit, these papers make a great show of frowning upon anything which smacks of pornography. This policy provides an excuse for reporters and critics to smell out the faintest aroma of irregularity, which they pursue with gusto."[28]

Brooker derides one report's gratuitous use of the words "nudes" and "naked."[29] In the same spirit, Buchanan shrewdly noted, "Prudery thus has its complement in prurience."[30]

Meanwhile, the most vocal defenders of the nude in interwar Canada implicitly portrayed themselves as sexually liberated. Although Brooker insists that the nude is not necessarily linked to sex, he proposes that art provides an exemplary source for "acquainting children with the organs and functions of the body in an atmosphere of candour and beauty" – in essence, high-culture sex education.[31] Rather than merely popularizing a category of art, the rise of the nude in interwar Canada was and remains a symbol of truth in sexuality, and ultimately freedom from repression. What gets glossed over is that by and large this subversive progress is achieved only on gendered grounds: through the acts of portraying and looking at undressed female bodies in representation, visual pleasure and enlightened knowledge are conflated.[32]

"Naked-Woman Pictures"

Investigation into the well-publicized scandals over the female nude that preceded Newton's censorship reveals their complexity. Although other works in the 1927 CNE were also subject to criticism, the most prolific and extended controversy concerned John Russell's *A Modern Fantasy*.[33] The large illusionistic painting featured a young woman reclining naked on a bed, surrounded by sumptuous pillows, drapery, flowers in vases, and china figurines. Writers have cited the profusion of responding angry letters to newspapers as epitomizing the puritanism of the period. Foss quotes one of the most vitriolic, which condemns "the display of naked-woman pictures," depicting "lounging, lolling, frenzied, freak postured, naked females," as "unwholesome, unnecessary, and unwanted."[34]

Such vehemence is not, however, entirely typical of the public reaction, given that while dozens of letters and articles were in protest, a

nearly equal number defended Russell's nude against such denuncia-
tion. "As to my mind it is the most beautiful picture that has ever come
to Canada and we as Canadians should feel greatly honored at having
such a wonderful work of art grace the walls of our gallery," wrote one
respondent.[35] Others scoffed at the "evil-minded few," "newspaper mor-
alists," and "busybodies" who would actively seek lewdness in the nude,
citing such adages as "*honi soit qui mal y pense*" (shame upon one who
thinks evil of it).[36] Like Brooker's derision of the excessive utterance of
"nudes" and "naked," such letters reprove opponents' prurient pleasure
in their scorn of the nude.

The *succès de scandale* surrounding *A Modern Fantasy* bore out in the tremendous increase in visitors to the CNE gallery, with ticket sales almost
tripling those of the previous year.[37] Some demonized the long line-ups
for the show as exemplifying the corruptive capacity of Russell's painting: "The story passed from mouth to mouth and the answer appeared
in the long queues of cigaret-smoking [sic] youths and giggling girls who
stood in line daily to see paintings which to most of them must have
been merely pictures."[38] But the gallery challenged this notion: "We are
getting a good class of people in the gallery, not just the seekers after
a cheap sensation or a thrill. Our sales of the art catalogues are much
greater than ever before. Casual callers who are looking for nudes do not
as a rule buy catalogues. The art lovers do."[39]

Beyond a debate between puritans and progressives, these statements
point to another conflict, between those educated in art and those who
are not, between true "art lovers" and visitors unable to discern master-
pieces from "mere pictures." Letters to the editor on both sides invoked
this dichotomy. Some suggested that the scandal demonstrated a need
for better art education, since "the propriety of the nude in art depends
largely on the mental attitudes and degree of education of the observer,"
while others felt that the proven inability of some to assume the necessary sophistication required that the gallery cater to these "ordinary
folks," who in the nude "can only see the unclothed human body."[40]

This rhetoric resonates with Kenneth Clark's influential but problematic dialectic between the nude and the naked. According to Clark,
the nude is the body "clothed in art," while the naked eludes aesthetic
transformation.[41] Of course, this subtle distinction tends to be lost on
those not trained to see it. Many visitors to the CNE expressed resent-
ment at the privilege afforded *A Modern Fantasy* on account of its artistic
pretext. One asked, "Is there an artistic law for the rich and another
for the poor?" and added astutely, "I am certain that if a showman on

the Midway featured three or four of the naked woman pictures now in the Exhibition Art Gallery, his show would be censored."[42] Conversely, Russell's supporters questioned how the nude could trigger such outrage considering the immodesty of current women's fashions, including knee-revealing skirts, skimpy bathing costumes, and make-up.[43] These concerns resonate with some of the potentially uncomfortable aspects of Newton's painting: those with the education to recognize the aesthetic transcendence of the nude in art still expressed disapproval of "real" women's apparently escalating indecency.

While the controversy over *A Modern Fantasy* that played out in Toronto newspapers was heated and multifaceted, the artistic community never came to Russell's defence. This was partly due to Russell's derision of the city's art scene, including the Group of Seven, the Royal Canadian Academy, and the Art Gallery of Toronto, which he labelled petty and provincial.[44] Russell distinguished himself as "decidedly European."[45] Prior to 1927, he had spent a couple of decades in Paris, which he believed was evident in his work. His sentimental academicism was far removed from the coarse Post-Impressionism and consciously Canadian themes prevalent among the national school. Several years after the CNE scandal, the Hamilton, Ontario-born painter still represented a pariah to Canadian art. Group of Seven member Arthur Lismer lambasted Russell's Parisian bohemianism as disqualifying him from matters of national importance in painting: "Russell has been living the life of a studio artist in Paris so long that it has got into his blood and he is acting like a St. Simeon on his pedestal, and hurling invectives at a northern breed of people who have no trace of the Latin attitude towards art."[46] Brooker and Buchanan both mentioned Russell's cause célèbre in their denunciations of Toronto parochialism, but treated the incident as if self-orchestrated by Russell, denouncing his subsequent exhibition of nudes as "a showman's trick of the first magnitude" and shameless "bootlegging of the nude."[47]

Circumstances surrounding the removal of Brooker's *Figures in a Landscape* from the 1931 Ontario Society of Artists exhibition at the Art Gallery of Toronto were altogether different. There was no motivating public outcry; the censorious forces were purely institutional. The painting's dismounting was abrupt and scarcely justified, and media reports were conflicted, although it appeared that the work had been listed and illustrated in the exhibition catalogue before being "scratched out."[48] The gallery's explanation was lack of space, according to one source.[49] Another claimed that Lismer, who was head of the educational department, had instigated the painting's removal, "because, in his opinion, the presence of the picture might be detrimental to children who might view it."[50] Overall, there was consensus that the gallery's educational programming and young visitors were at the source of the painting's unsuitability for hanging.

This justification does not, however, explain what made the painting stand out as inappropriate in comparison with others shown contemporaneously in Canada, in Toronto, and even in the same gallery. Why Brooker's landscape nude was deemed unfit for public consumption by the very gallery that exhibited Holgate's and Heward's versions of the theme is not obvious. *Figures in a Landscape* features the same monumentality of form that made Holgate's nudes resonate with critics as reflective of the Canadian scenery, and a similarly careful level of detail as in Heward's *Girl Under a Tree*. Yet, the models dominate the image, leaving only sufficient space to indicate their natural setting. Abruptly cropped, without legs or heads, the main subject becomes the models' naked flesh. One commentator speculated that it was deemed unacceptable, "because little enough of the heads were shown as to make the work practically a study of torsos" – in other words, an incomplete painting lacking the proper context to be "clothed in art."[51]

Nude and the National Discourse

As with Newton's *Nude*, art professionals – in both cases, officials at the Art Gallery of Toronto – determined the ineligibility of *Figures in a Landscape*. Although these institutional decisions may be symptomatic of paternalistic concern for their audiences or fear of public reaction, it is inaccurate to directly attribute them to the puritanical public, especially when that public never even had a chance to see the two famously censored paintings. This is likely why so many have turned to the Russell scandal to illustrate Canadian prudishness, since *A Modern Fantasy* sparked a veritable uproar. And yet, by the early 1930s, objections by members of the public to subsequent exhibitions of nudes by Russell were negligible. The debate had significantly shifted into the art world, as one between the established nationalist concerns and home-grown earnestness of the Group of Seven and the European bohemianism or "French decadence" represented by Russell. The circumscription of the nude was then primarily an enterprise of an elite art world rather than a prudish – or prurient – general public.

Like Brooker's canvas, Newton's nude ostensibly conforms to the ideals propagated within the national cultural discourse, albeit in different ways. *Figures in a Landscape* upholds the popular trope of the figure's union with the Canadian countryside, what Hudson has termed the "civilized landscape."[52] In the 1933 catalogue, from which Newton's *Nude* was stricken, the Canadian Group of Painters proclaimed its mandate "to encourage and foster the growth of Art in Canada, which has a national character, not necessarily of time and place, but also expressive of its philosophy, and a wide appreciation of the right of Canadian artists to find beauty and character in all things."[53] *Nude* appeals to this combined ideal of formalism and humanism that defined artistic modernism in Canada.[54] Employing a deliberate formal composition of geometric patterns repeated in intersecting shadows on the floor, the furniture's rigid lines, the checked drapery, the shoes' crisscrossing straps, and the model's peculiar arm position, the painting simultaneously conveys a strong message on the importance of the arts to society.

The nude is not a nude, but as Buchanan points out, "a naked lady," or specifically, an artist's model, apparent in both the studio setting, and the recognizability of the woman, which revealed her Russian origin. The model's identity was integral to the work as it connected the figure with the painting behind, a portrait of the Russian composer Andre Illiashenko, which Newton had exhibited a year prior with the Royal Canadian Academy. The inclusion of Illiashenko's portrait in *Nude* – identifiable by the fur coat and hat, onion domes, and wintry background – suggests an attempt to draw links between various art forms, genres, creative productivity, and social democracy. Newton's choice of model, if indeed a dancer as suggested by her body and pose, further emphasizes these connections.

According to Buchanan, however, even members of the Canadian Group of Painters jury, which had originally accepted the painting, took exception: "Why, they asked, had the artist dared to paint a Russian! Were not Canadians good enough!"[55] Although the sentiment appears anti-communist or xenophobic, socialist sympathies clearly ran strong in the 1930s Toronto art community, and as demonstrated, exoticism was a popular feature in the female nude at this time. But the difference of Newton's model is one of nationality, not race. Her otherness is not mollified by tropes of timelessness and nature, which artists commonly used in their construction of the wholesome White nude as well as the exotic Black nude, but is, in fact, vital to the social message of the image. While the worker as individual personified a democratic ideal, the artist's model was too deeply embroiled in artistic tradition to acceptably bridge this gap. As an individual, the woman in *Nude* defies both classical ide-alization and modernist abstraction. Newton, Canada's "leading portrait painter,"[56] first and foremost paints her model's likeness.

A Lack of Containment

The model in *Nude* becomes an unstable nucleus around which a se-ries of transgressions emerges. Contemporary styling and an identifiable individual in the painting break down the division between nude and naked, as recognized by Buchanan and theorized by Clark. Newton's treatment of the figure marks an overlap of genres between the nude and the portrait, further underscored by the example of the painter's typical subject matter in the background. The model's own identity evades easy classification, since as a "White Russian" she is uncomfortably same yet other to the painting's intended audience. Furthermore, through the figure's simultaneous role as signifying object and self-possessed subject, the image attempts to unite artistic tradition and progressive politics. The painting, in effect, marks a collapse of the contemporary terms on which the nude was predicated.

In a twist on Clark's exegesis contrasting the nude's aestheticism to the naked's profanity, Lynda Nead writes, "One of the principal goals of the female nude has been the containment and regulation of the female sexual body." The "hermetically sealed" female form distinguishes art from obscenity, which is marked by a lack of such containment.[57] But is the obscene's definitive failure to contain necessarily erotic? Concerning Newton's nude among others, writers have automatically assumed that its transgression was of a sexual nature. Within a Foucauldian model of sexual constructivism, this link becomes tenuous, especially since *Nude* evades many conventional erotic signifiers. Unlike Heward's *Girl Under a Tree*, Stevens's *Siesta*, or Russell's *Modern Fantasy*, the model is not splayed languorously for the viewer's consumption, but instead stands thought-fully with conviction, as if paused momentarily: this is hardly the "fro-zen possession" Myrone locates in the Victorian nude. Although Newton "breaks the seal" of the idealized female body by picturing pubic hair and realistic details, the result may be more alarming for its want of eroti-cism than for its excess.

The studio context equally presents a lack of demarcation between art and life; the imaginary sanctified space of the nude and the prag-matic mise en scène of the artist merge in *Nude*. What this setting in-vokes may have been more disturbing: the artist herself. Marcia Pointon writes, "The subjectivities of artists, of makers of images, are interpolated in readings – whether consciously or unconsciously – by readers whose other, different, but in some ways complementary, subjectivities are brought into play by this process."[58] Members of the gallery board undoubtedly would have considered Newton's persona in their evaluation of her painting. It was not taboo for a woman to paint the female nude: works of that genre by Heward and Stevens enjoyed much success and helped to establish those artists' reputations. Newton, however, was renowned for her portraiture, painting many notable Canadians and eventually Queen Elizabeth II.[59] One will consider the extent to which Russell's bohemian-tinged persona tainted his work in the eyes of the art world, or Brooker's self-styled modernism may have menaced gallery officials. Newton exhibited no such audacity, but on the contrary, was praised for her amenable nature as for her accomplished talent. One writer described her as "a slip of a girl," elaborating, "She was gentle of voice and manner, with not a suggestion of the smart sophistication which the world calls 'Bohemian.'"[60] One can imagine the shock *Nude* must have delivered to its viewers' expectations.

As well as a departure from her typical oeuvre, Newton's painting differed substantially from nudes by other contemporary female artists. Subscribing to conventions of the nude, such as pastoral settings and reclining poses, Heward and Stevens maintained distance between the model and viewer through contrived postures and averted gazes, meanwhile avoiding direct association with the artist. Newton, on the other hand, not only negates the viewer's distance through the model's confrontational stance, but moreover, she effectively inserts herself into the image by way of the model's context. The artist's self-insertion, whether through literal rendering or subtler inclusion of possessions and other signifiers, is common in the modern nude, marrying the self-consciousness of modernism with the liberating potential of the unclothed figure. The message is one not only of progress but also of mastery. In contrast to the artist's assertive subjectivity, the female body in art is comparable to a blank canvas, a raw material the artist transforms and elevates to the aesthetic realm. Nead writes, "Within critical language woman is figured as the resistant, unnamable 'otherness' of paper/canvas, the sign of absolute non-signification. The female nude within patriarchy thus signifies that the woman/surface has come under the government of male style."[61] Nead points to the traditionally gendered confines of production of the female nude, as a passive and feminized object created and consumed under the masculine gaze. But what happens when this dichotomous relationship collapses under the mastery, the impression of meaning in the nude, by a female artist?

In *Nude*, the identity of the female artist is not demurely elided, but on the contrary, made explicit by Newton. While confusing the gendered stipulations of artistic genius, the gesture is also potentially problematic for the sheer proximity between female artist and female model. To the jury and board members, the painting would have immediately resonated as set in the portraitist's studio. Some may have even been aware that the model was, in fact, Newton's student, who had exchanged modelling hours for a drawing by the senior artist.[62] The alarming image of two women together likely contributed to the censorship of Brooker's painting. Although not explicitly pictured in *Nude*, the subversiveness of this relationship may indeed be stronger, as it denies regulation by the male artist's gaze. The result is a transgenderism of the image, manifest not only in the stylish androgyny of the model's appearance, but also in the author's staged role in the painting as virile creator. Carol Duncan says that the female gaze can pollute pornography;[63] the same can be said for high art. Brooker and Russell went on to produce and exhibit many more nudes with little debate following the controversies over their work, while after the Art Gallery of Toronto fiasco, Newton retreated to portraiture and her former image as a respected woman painter.

Conclusion

Remaining in this analysis is the one aspect of the image that has traditionally been its point of entry: the green shoes. Apart from disrupting the timeless serenity of the nude, the model's footwear may function on a subconscious level as a sexual signifier. According to psychoanalytic readings of the nude, the omission of the female genitals dispels castration anxiety with the ideal hairless, sexless female body onto which male fantasies can be projected without complication.[64] Other phallic stand-ins displace the erotic urge, for example, shoes, a particularly potent fetish symbol. In addition to *Nude*'s high-heeled, strappy wedges, the fur of Illiashenko's hat and coat, which appears to cloak the model's shoulders, presents another common object of displacement. Yet, the image redundantly combines these symbols with the model's fully revealed pubic hair, lack made visible. This excess may render the fetishes effete in dispelling sexual terror, leaving only a disturbing overload of sensuous imagery. In this respect, the painting functions similarly to Russell's *Fantasy*, which provoked outrage at its surplus of knick-knacks displayed alongside the exposed model. Newton simultaneously pictures male fantasy while negating it, contributing to the painting's overall lack of containment, to use Nead's term.[65]

The potential threat of the image not only impinges on the individual viewing experience within the confines of the art exhibition, but also it responds to broader discursive tendencies and social realities, the most pressing of these being the contemporary status of women. By the 1920s, the suffrage movement had won the right for women to vote in provincial elections across Canada.[66] Only in 1929 did women gain legal definition as "persons," thanks to the campaigning of social activists; in the process, women gained the right to be appointed to the Senate.[67] With women's dramatically altering roles and rights came an inevitable backlash; increasing social unrest and political turmoil elicited widespread discomfort with shifting gender roles. This expanded historical context might shed light on a couple of the specificities of the model in *Nude* that remain troubling. First, her Russian identity suggests a new social status for women, who were rapidly gaining equality in the workplace and other areas of society under the communist regime in Russia. This intimidating otherness is further enhanced by the model's body, which is almost androgynous in its developed musculature and angular features. Second, the contemporary details that form some of the image's most jarring aspects – fashionable styling and adornments – reinforce the model's contemporaneity and mobility as a "new woman." She comes to embody the unease with a mounting consumer culture and the transforming social roles its technologies entail.

By positioning her model in the interstice between art and life, Newton opened up yet another area in which women's place had by and large maintained the status quo: the artistic nude. Contemporary styling and real-world props, including footwear that enable the model to virtually walk out of the painting, along with self-proclaimed female authorship, endowed in *Nude* a perilous resonance with the audacity of women's liberation. Since the risky permeation – uncontainability – of Newton's *Nude* could not fully be voiced within the contemporary discursive confines, it was and has remained effectively displaced onto a pair of green shoes.

Notes

1 Donald Buchanan, "Naked Ladies," *Canadian Forum* 15, no.175 (1935), 273.
2 Louis Muhlstock, "An Excess of Prudery," *Canadian Art* 5, no. 2 (1947–48), 78.
3 Now the Art Gallery of Ontario.

4 Also known as *Nude in a Studio* or *Standing Nude*. The date of this incident has been cited variously as 1933, 1934, and 1935. In April 1935, Donald Buchanan referred to the incident as having occurred "last year," but the 1934 Canadian Group of Painters exhibition was held in Montreal, so the exhibition in question must have been that of late 1933.

5 Buchanan, "Naked Ladies," 273.

6 Barbara Meadowcroft, *Painting Friends: The Beaver Hall Women Painters* (Montreal: Vehicule, 1999), 129.

7 Esther Trépanier, "A Consideration of the Nude and Artistic Modernity in Canada," in Michèle Grandbois et al., *The Nude in Modern Canadian Art, 1920–1950*, exh. cat. (Quebec City: Musée national des beaux-arts du Québec, 2009), 142.

8 Anna Hudson, "Disarming Conventions of Nudity in Canadian Art," in Grandbois et al., *The Nude*, 105–6.

9 Grandbois et al., *The Nude*, 12.

10 Grandbois et al., "The Challenge of the Nude," in ibid., 44.

11 Augustus Bridle, "New 'Group' of Painters Challenged to Be Human," *Toronto Star*, 4 Nov. 1933, 6.

12 Paraskeva Clark, as told to G. Campbell McInnes, "Come Out from Behind the Pre-Cambrian Shield," *New Frontier* 1, no. 12 (1937), 16.

13 Anna Hudson, "Art and Social Progress: The Toronto Community of Painters, 1933–1950," doctoral dissertation, University of Toronto, 1997, 110.

14 Buchanan, "Naked Ladies," 273.

15 Bertram Brooker, "The Seven Arts," *Ottawa Citizen*, 19 April 1930.

16 My focus is on the English-Canadian debate over the nude in Toronto exhibitions, since the majority of scandals took place in this city. For a broader analysis of social attitudes towards nudes on exhibition across Canada, see Grandbois et al., *The Nude*, and Jerrold Morris, *The Nude in Canadian Painting* (Toronto: New Press, 1972).

17 Attitudes towards non-Canadian artists' representation and exhibition of the nude were distinct and require separate analysis. See Sybille Pantazzi, "Foreign Art at the Canadian National Exhibition, 1905–1938," *National Gallery of Canada Bulletin* 22 (1973), 21–41.

18 See Bertram Brooker, "Nudes and Prudes" (1931), in *Documents in Canadian Art*, ed. Douglas Featherling (Peterborough: Broadview, 1987), 411, and Edwin Holgate, letter to Eric Brown (Director, National Gallery of Canada), 9 Jan. 1936, NGC Archives, quoted in Brian Foss, "Living Landscape," *Edwin Holgate*, exh. cat., ed. Rosalind Pepall and Brian Foss (Montreal: Montreal Museum of Fine Arts, 2005), 48. Natalie Luckyj writes that these nudes were, in fact, removed from the exhibition, although no evidence supports this

claim. See Natalie Luckyj, *Expressions of Will: The Art of Prudence Heward* exh. cat. (Kingston, ON: Agnes Etherington Art Centre, 1986), 63.

19 Augustus Bridle, "All Space Is Occupied for Art Gallery's Opening," *Toronto Star*, 3 April 1930, 25.

20 John Lyman, "Journal," vol. 2, entry for 28 Apr. 1932, quoted in Foss, "Living Landscape," 51; E.W.H. *Ottawa Morning Citizen*, 29 Dec. 1931, quoted in Luckyj, *Expressions of Will*, 63; A.Y. Jackson, "Paintings by Prudence Heward Placed on Exhibition in Montreal," *Montreal Star*, 27 April 1932.

21 Foss, "Living Landscape," 52. The distinctiveness of *Girl Under a Tree* has elicited comparisons to Newton's *Nude* by feminist art historians, who believe that the defiant personae of the female models in both paintings signify the artists' diverging sensibilities from their male counterparts. See Luckyj, *Expressions of Will*, 61–3. Heward's traditional reclining pose and pastoral setting likely evaded the hostility that Newton's painting faced.

22 Charmaine Nelson, "Coloured Nude: Fetishization, Disguise, Dichotomy," M.A. thesis, Concordia University, 1995, 34–6.

23 See Nicholas Mirzoeff, *Bodyscape: Art, Modernity and the Ideal Figure* (London: Routledge, 1995), 3.

24 Grandbois et al., *The Nude*, 14.

25 Michel Foucault, *The History of Sexuality*, vol. 1, *An Introduction* (1978), trans. Robert Hurley (New York: Vintage, 1990), 17.

26 For example, Foss writes, "Nudes were not common subjects in Canadian exhibitions between the wars." Foss, "Living Landscapes," 46.

27 Martin Myrone, "Prudery, Pornography and the Victorian Nude (Or, What Do We Think the Butler Saw?)," *Exposed: The Victorian Nude*, exh. cat., ed. Alison Smith (London: Tate Britain, 2000), 361.

28 Brooker, "Nudes and Prudes," 69.

29 Ibid.

30 Buchanan, "Naked Ladies," 274.

31 Brooker, "Nudes and Prudes," 74. This contradiction is reflected in Mary-Ann Shantz's analysis of postwar nudist beauty pageants, which were simultaneously sexualized and promoted as non-sexual and wholesome. See Mary-Ann Shantz, this volume.

32 For a detailed evaluation of this phenomenon within scientific knowledge, see Valerie Minnett, this volume.

33 For a detailed analysis of the controversy over nudes in the 1927 CNE, see Jane Nicholas, "'A Figure of a Nude Woman': Art, Popular Culture, and Modernity at the Canadian National Exhibition, 1927," *Histoire sociale/Social History* 41, no. 82 (2008), 313–44.

34 A Father, "Those Pictures of the Nude at the Exhibition Art Gallery: One

Father's Protest," *Toronto Telegram*, 27 Aug. 1927, quoted in Foss, "Living Landscape," 47.

35 A Lover of Real Art, "Inconsistency," *Toronto Star*, 13 Sept. 1927.

36 "Gene" LaVerne Devore, "Art and the Critic," *Toronto Globe*, 14 Sept. 1927; "Dashes Off Opinion Just before Visiting Art Gallery," *Toronto Telegram*, 30 Aug. 1927.

37 "158,888 Filed Past the Nude Pictures," *Toronto Star*, 12 Sept. 1927.

38 "An Exhibition Mistake," *Toronto Globe*, 9 Sept. 1927.

39 "Box Office Rush at 'Ex' Art Gallery Not due to Nude Art, Says Official," *Toronto Star*, 3 Sept. 1927.

40 Hugh McKanday, "'Art Lover' a Misnomer," *Toronto Star*, 2 Sept. 1927; Art Lover, "Those Pictures at the Fair," *Toronto Star*, 29 Aug. 1927. Also see Characterologist, "Human Nature," *Toronto Globe*, 22 Sept. 1927.

41 Kenneth Clark, *The Nude: A Study in Ideal Form* (Harmondsworth: Penguin, 1960), 14. For a thorough critique of Clark's mind-body dualism and its gendered implications, as well as his distinction between art and pornography, see Lynda Nead, *The Female Nude: Art, Obscenity and Sexuality* (London: Routledge, 1992), 12–27.

42 A Father, "Those Pictures of the Nude." Some have suggested that the proximity of the CNE gallery to the midway threatened the artistic justification of the nudity in Russell's and others' paintings. See Nicholas, "'A Figure of a Nude Woman,'" 326–30, and Hudson, "Disarming Conventions of Nudity," 88.

43 J.W. Jones, "Fashions and Art," *Toronto Globe*, 22 Sept. 1927; One Who Risked an Eye and Not Ashamed, "Thought It Beautiful," *Toronto Star*, 16 Sept. 1927; Burgess Robertson, "Toronto's Provincialism," *Toronto Globe*, 15 Sept. 1927.

44 "'Art Getting Nowhere,' Charges John Russell," *Toronto Star*, 1 Oct. 1927.

45 John Russell, quoted in "False Standards Grow a Toronto Artist Finds," *Toronto Star*, 7 Sept. 1927.

46 Arthur Lismer, untitled, *Toronto Telegram*, 18 Nov. 1933.

47 Buchanan, "Naked Ladies," 274; Brooker, "Nudes and Prudes," 68.

48 Augustus Bridle, "Brooker's Nude was Crated by Decision of Majority," *Toronto Star*, 14 March 1931.

49 "Nude Painting Sent to Cellar as Artists' Exhibition Opens Creating First-Rate Mystery," *Mail and Empire*, 7 March 1931.

50 "'Nudes in Landscape' Causes Art Dispute," *Toronto Star*, 7 March 1931. The author conceded that gallery officials and some members of the Ontario Society of Artists committee denied this allegation.

51 "Painting Removed from Ontario Show," Montreal *Gazette*, 9 March 1931, quoted in Foss, "Living Landscapes," 47.

52 Hudson, "Art and Social Progress," 58.

53 Canadian Group of Painters, Foreword, *Canadian Group of Painters*, exh. cat. (Toronto: Art Gallery of Toronto, 1933), 3.

54 See Hudson, "Art and Social Progress," and Charles Hill, *Canadian Painting in the 1930s*, exh. cat., (Ottawa: National Gallery of Canada, 1975).

55 Buchanan, "Naked Ladies," 273.

56 Carl Weiselberger, "New Vision in an Old Art," *Ottawa Citizen*, 19 Nov. 1951.

57 Nead, *The Female Nude*, 8.

58 Marcia Pointon, *Naked Authority: The Body in Western Painting, 1830–1908* (Cambridge: Cambridge University Press, 1990), 1.

59 "Portraits of Queen and Duke by Canadian Artist to Hang in Government House," *Globe and Mail*, 4 Oct. 1957.

60 "A Gracious Artist," *Saturday Night*, 31 May 1930.

61 Nead, *The Female Nude*, 57.

62 Charles Hill, "Interview with Lilias Torrance Newton," 11 Sept 1973, transcription of interview, NGC Archives, 5.

63 Carol Duncan, "MoMA's Hot Mamas," in *The Expanding Discourse: Feminism and Art History*, ed. Norma Broude and Mary D. Gerrard (New York: Westview, 1992), 355.

64 See Nead, *The Female Nude*, 18, and Nelson, "Coloured Nude," 101. On castration anxiety, see Sigmund Freud, "The Sexual Aberrations" (1905), in *On Sexuality: Three Essays on the Theory of Sexuality and Other Works*, ed. Àngela Richards, trans. James Strachey (London: Penguin, 1991), 67.

65 Contemporary analyses of the painting's censorship, such as Buchanan's equation of "naked lady" status with the fact of the green slippers, point towards increasing familiarity with psychoanalytic theory among intellectual circles. However, these links were never explicitly made, again suggesting the extent to which the controversy was a matter of institutional regulation.

66 1940 in Quebec.

67 Anne White, "The *Persons* Case, 1929: A Legal Definition of Women as Persons," in *Framing Our Past: Canadian Women's History in the Twentieth Century*, ed. Sharon Anne Cook, Lorna R. McLean, and Kate O'Rourke (Montreal and Kingston: McGill-Queen's University Press, 2001), 216.

8 The National Ballet of Canada's Normative Bodies: Legitimizing and Popularizing Dance in Canada during the 1950s

ALLANA C. LINDGREN

As an art form that uses corporeality as its main mode of communication, dance provides an opportunity to study how attitudes towards subjectivity and social norms have been reinscribed or challenged through performers' bodies. Indeed, the issue of embodiment has been of interest to dance historians since the late twentieth century, although Canadian case studies have received relatively little attention.[1] This chapter adds to the scholarly conversation by examining how normalcy was defined and conveyed through the bodies of the National Ballet of Canada's dancers during the 1950s. Specifically, this chapter argues that the newly formed troupe led by Celia Franca, the founding artistic director, can be viewed as legitimizing and popularizing ballet by using the bodies of dancers as pliable conduits for a variety of narratives that equated the Company with mainstream culture and promoted theatrical dance as an unthreatening art form in support of dominant ideologies.

Bodies have been regularly co-opted as marketing tools by advertisers who use corporeality to equate their products with shifting definitions of socially acceptable lifestyles.[2] According to sociologist Alexandra Howson, the potency of using bodies in advertising lies in convincing people that they see themselves in the context of the product being sold by aligning themselves with the values that are simultaneously communicated.[3] Dance research usually does not focus on the publicity strategies of dance companies or consider how dancers can function as marketing tools, but by examining the National Ballet within this context, it is possible to see the bodies of the Company's dancers as publicity tools that helped to align the National Ballet with dominant cultural narratives, particularly related to gender roles and national identities.

The National Ballet had reason to promote itself and ballet as "normal" because the art form was not widely accepted in Canada during the 1950s. Granted, the range of attitudes towards ballet in Canada at the time included boosters like the *Globe and Mail*'s Herbert Whittaker, who promoted Toronto as a "top ballet town" and wrote encouraging reviews of the National Ballet, beginning with the Company's first official performance at Eaton Auditorium on 12 November 1951. However, not everyone was so enthusiastic.[4] At the other end of the spectrum of responses was reticence and consternation over the perceived corrupting influence of dancing bodies. In 1950, for instance, the Ballets de Paris was stopped from performing Roland Petit's *Carmen* in Quebec City because the choreography was deemed too provocative. When the CBC began broadcasting in Montreal in 1952, the censors in Quebec were particularly concerned about the costumes of male performers. As historian Iro Valaskakis Tembeck writes, "On a few occasions, male dancers were required to don an extra pair of tights to hide unsightly male bulges."[5]

Similar reticence about corporeal propriety could also be found in the federal government and English Canada. Prime Minister Louis St. Laurent allegedly hesitated to support the proposed Royal Commission on National Development in the Arts, Letters and Sciences (more commonly known as the Massey Commission). According to J.W. Pickersgill, the head of the Prime Minister's Office at the time, St. Laurent was initially not predisposed to provide aid to the arts, and particularly, he did not want his government to be perceived as "subsidizing ballet dancing."[6] Although St. Laurent's specific concerns about ballet are unknown, the resulting Commission Report articulated moral trepidation about dance: "Ballet has been a late-comer among the arts in Canada ... still somewhat self-consciously, with other English-speaking people, we are beginning to discern the fallacy in the ancient maxim, 'no sober man ever dances,' on which our attitude toward the dance has for so long been based."[7]

To consider how Franca, her dancers, and their supporters worked to overcome these challenges, this essay surveys a register of embodied identities, beginning with gender. The media's interest in the personal lives of the National Ballet's dancers as well as the Company's various off-stage attempts to legitimize and popularize ballet in Canada has resulted in a cache of publicity materials and press clippings that invite historians to look beyond choreography to investigate how dancers' bodies were used to equate ballet with gendered norms for both men and women.

In addition to gender issues, the National Ballet distributed images of its dancers that associated ballet with popular Canadian physical activities, including hockey, as if to suggest that ballet was also quintessentially Canadian. Other images used by the Company showed the dancers engaged in cultural diplomacy events that portrayed the dancers as patriotic Canadian citizens.

It should be noted that all of these "normative bodies" were "official" bodies as the primary sources accessed for this article were largely created for public consumption and therefore do not address identities performed behind the closed doors of the studio or backstage. Instead, they reveal how the Company ostensibly wished to be viewed and how journalists, as surrogate audience members, responded.

White Bodies

Before examining how traditional narratives of gender and nation helped to advertise that the National Ballet was aligned with mainstream values, it is important to remember that historians must often look beneath stated intentions, in order to uncover how normative values are less overtly projected. To do so, a brief discussion of racialized assumptions is particularly helpful. Underpinning the narratives of embodied heterosexuality and nationalism evident in the National Ballet's public image during the Company's first decade was the unspoken and perhaps unwitting assertion of Whiteness as the social norm. In his influential study of Whiteness, Richard Dyer argues, "As long as race is something only applied to non-white peoples, as long as white people are not racially seen and named, they/we function as a human norm. Other people are raced, we are just people."[8] In this light, the absence of any significant racial diversity in the Company provides an opportunity to consider how "Whiteness" was the unacknowledged image of Canadian citizenry.

It is true that the dancers in the company were overwhelmingly of European heritage, but the Company was not uniformly White. Robert Ito, a Canadian-born dancer of Japanese descent, who later became an actor known for his role as Sam Fujiyama on the television program *Quincy, M.E.*, was a charter member of the National Ballet. As a corps member, it is not surprising that Ito's performances were not frequently mentioned in the press. (The most coverage Ito seems to have garnered was in a newspaper story that mentions he broke his arm during a performance.)[9] When his name did appear, however, reviewers did not remark on his race.[10] This lack of commentary is curious and perhaps indicative of progressive attitudes within the arts communities and the press in Canada and parts of the United States. It also might signal that ballet is a meritocracy: skin colour cannot obscure or trump talent and technical ability. Whatever the case for the lack of commentary, to her credit, Franca appears to have been colour-blind in her hiring practices.

Franca's progressiveness aside, the question of why there were not more non-White dancers in the Company remains. The ability of non-White families to pay for ballet lessons and/or the limits of White audience liberalism are perhaps two factors contributing to the racial reinscription of ballet as a European art form on stage and, thus, in the Company's publicity materials as well. As a result, the images of the mostly White dancers performing a European art form for audiences who were also largely White implicitly reinforced the hegemony of White definitions of "normalcy." In other words, White bodies performing a European-originated dance style subtly conveyed an ideal that validated the hegemony of the racial status quo in Canada. In publicity photograph after publicity photograph, and in press story after press story, the clearly assumed naturalness of White skin was, no doubt, evident to those Canadians whose complexions excluded them from the dominant social narrative. In short, the absence of racial diversity in the Company's publicity materials and the media's human interest stories appear to have unwittingly reinscribed the tandem views that "high" art really meant art created by and for White people, and that Canadian culture more generally was the exclusive purview of White Canadians.

Choreographed Gender Roles

While ballet was implicitly and uncomplicatedly presented as a "White" art form, the National Ballet's relationship to gender was more publicly vexed. One of the most common negative stereotypes about ballet was that its ranks were populated by homosexual men.[11] Certainly, in Canada during the 1950s, the few men who took ballet lessons and pursued careers in dance were often sexually suspect and socially ostracized. As one Canadian reviewer wrote, in 1957, "The status of the male dancer in the public domain is not generally an agreeable one. He may be thought of as sissy, effeminate or worse. Most parents, especially fathers, do not look on ballet as a proud calling for their sons."[12]

Even seemingly humorous attempts by the media to encourage women to bring their wary husbands to the National Ballet's performances were often couched in homophobic (and sexist) language: "Do you happen to have a husband who holds the view that ballet is strictly for pantywaists and wrist-slappers and who is frightened of being seen within a block of a performance? ... The thing to take them to, girls, is *Les Sylphides*. If the fellow can't get enjoyment from *Les Sylphides* with its charming music and its pretty girls in those short skirts, then he just naturally has no feeling no how and you'd better keep him at home and buy him vitamin pills."[13]

There were gay men in the National Ballet from its inception (it is unclear if any of the women were lesbians), and the Company provided a safe place for them to live openly. According to Grant Strate, a charter member of the National Ballet, within the protected enclave of the Company, he and his partner, Earl Kraul, who also was a dancer in the National Ballet, did not have to hide their relationship. Moreover, while Kraul's family was very accepting of the couple and Strate's family was obliquely supportive (although Strate's homosexuality was never discussed openly), outside of the studio and their extended families, they were careful to conceal the truth.[14]

Although homosexuality was accepted within the Company, the early years of the National Ballet are noteworthy for the gay bodies that were obscured or rendered absent by sublimating them into the larger discourse of heterosexuality. As if to allay the moral anxiety of homophobic audiences and to deny the reality of the gay men who were Company members, the National Ballet worked to convince its audiences that ballet was comfortably heterosexual. As a result, although the bodies of men who were gay appeared on stage, they were projected as heterosexual by the choreographic narratives and male-female partnering. Throughout his career, for example, Kraul performed the leading male roles, including the Groom in *Antic Spring*, James in *La Sylphide*, Romeo in *Romeo and Juliet*, and various princes in ballets at the core of the Imperial Russian canon such as *Swan Lake* and *The Nutcracker*. In other words, to be a successful male ballet dancer meant reinscribing heterosexuality as the social norm.[15]

The private lives of heterosexual male dancers and their supposed adherence to traditional family values were repeatedly emphasized in the press. One of the Company's principal male dancers, David Adams, for instance, became the poster boy for ballet heterosexuality. Originally from Winnipeg, Adams performed with the Winnipeg Ballet before leaving Canada in 1946 to join the Sadler's Wells Theatre Ballet. He later also danced with the Metropolitan Ballet in England where he first met Franca who was also a dancer in the company. He returned to Canada in 1948. When Franca arrived in Canada, she invited Adams and his wife,

Lois Smith, to join the newly formed National Ballet as principal dancers. This Canadian-born couple became the Company's first ballet stars, endearing themselves to their fans and the press with their home-grown talent.

Verbal imagery reifying stereotypical heterosexual masculine bodies was particularly emphasized in the press when discussing Adams. One narrative circulated by Adams was that ballet could turn the bodies of sickly boys into the physiques of sturdy men. Perhaps unintentionally evoking the Charles Atlas "I was a ninety-seven pound weakling" ads that were ubiquitous in comic books during the 1950s, Adams was fond of telling reporters that he had been a spindly child unable to absorb vitamin C. He claimed that he had almost died several times.[16] The only thing that changed his health, he insisted, were his ballet classes, which had given him physical strength and, as one reporter noted, turned him into a "handsome" and "husky six-footer."[17]

The language critics frequently used to describe Adams framed the Canadian dancer's physicality in terms of desirable and stereotypical masculinity. In addition to "handsome" and "husky," the National Ballet star was deemed to embody "manliness" and "virility." He was not just manly, however. His was a "manly charm" and "natural manliness."[18] He did not just have "virility," he had "uncommon virility."[19]

As Mary Louise Adams notes, twentieth-century dance writers often "borrowed heavily from discourses of sport and male athleticism" in advocating for the art form because "the similarity between the sporting body and the dancing body has been offered by dancer writers as evidence of the manliness of male dancers. Male athletes are considered manly; dancers look like athletes; therefore, dancers must be manly too."[20] Although Adams does not mention the National Ballet in her article, David Adams's athleticism and physical strength were frequently stressed by the press in the 1950s. A few years prior to the creation of the National Ballet, for instance, Don West, a young University of British Columbia Thunderbird football player interviewed Adams and Smith for the *Vancouver Daily Province Magazine*. In the resulting article, West chummily called Adams "Dave" as if to intimate the two were buddies and Adams reciprocated by confiding, "I've played some football back East when I was at school." In his own estimation, West felt he did not have the same level of strength as Adams. He claimed that he had almost dropped Smith "trying to lift her to arm's length the way Dave does so easily," and when jumping beside Adams, the dancer's elevation was "a good three inches higher" than that of the Thunderbird guard.[21]

Perhaps it was not a leap – balletic or otherwise – from "athlete" to "ideal heterosexual man." In his ongoing embodiment of 1950s heterosexual masculinity, Adams was frequently depicted as an ordinary fellow who, as one Vancouver writer stated, "dresses and acts more like the guy next door than a man who is the idol of thousands of ballet lovers."[22] The focus on Adams's offstage activities redirected attention away from the more difficult task of convincing readers and potential audience members that not all male dancers were homosexual and instead offered male-identified physical activities as an embodied shorthand for acceptable masculinity. For instance, much was made of Adams's hobbies, including creating movies of the company on tour, amateur photography, and the most manly of all hobbies: woodworking.[23] According to a 1957 article about the couple that appeared in *Maclean's* magazine, Adams and Smith had decided to use money given to them as a wedding present to buy a circular saw so Adams could make furniture for their apartment (although one wonders about Smith's vote).[24] The message was clear: through his physical labour Adams could provide for his marriage just like any other husband with access to power tools.

Arguably the most convincing assertion of male heterosexuality at the disposal of the National Ballet in the 1950s were the marriages of Adams and Smith as well as that of two other principal dancers – Jury Gotshalks and Irene Apiné. The couples, particularly Adams and Smith, were often the topic of human-interest stories about the Company. Moreover, the dancers' comments and the way the stories were written, stressed the "normalcy" of dancers' lives, as if to quell any suspicions about the moral rectitude of ballet artists that readers and/or audience members might harbour (see Figure 8.1).[25]

A frequent refrain in the press was that both married couples were the kind of people readers would like to have as neighbours. They were "bright intelligent young people and wouldn't be a bit above lending that cup of sugar or giving that mud-logged car an extra push."[26] As if to confirm the conventionality of ballet dancers in terms related to domesticity, the same writer even noted that meat loaf was the specialty dish in the Gotshalks-Apiné household. The Adams-Smith marriage was especially depicted as stable and harmonious: "Although David Adams and Lois Smith have been dancing together for nine years, and have been married for eight years of that time, they have less [sic] fights than the average couple … And the way they looked fondly at each other, the evidence seemed all on their side."[27] In short, the marriages of the leading National Ballet dancers conveyed the message that ballet dancers

Figure 8.1 Lois Smith and David Adams in *Giselle*, ca. 1953. Photo by Ken Bell; courtesy of the National Ballet of Canada Archives. GISE 300 SMI ADA 6.

were average Canadians. Or, as Adams commented in 1959, "We are ordinary people off stage."[28] In other words, the normalcy of the dancers'
domestic lives was often subtly couched in corporeal terms, specifically
equating the marriages as satisfying the bodily need for nourishment,
neighbourly goodwill manifest through physical action, and martial
affection conveyed through physical cues such as gazing at each other
lovingly.

If marriage signalled male heterosexuality as well as the "normalized"
state of ballet dancers' private lives, children complicated the image.
The creation of a baby served as the perfect corporeal symbol of heterosexual virility and fertility, but the reality of the ballet family usually did
not adhere to traditional expectations of the nuclear family, rendering
the children living, breathing liabilities for their parents' careers. A few
of the dancers in the National Ballet during its first decade had children,
but their familial arrangements often did not conform to 1950s ideals of
"normal" family life. Company member Angela Leigh, for instance, was
a single parent.[29] When Gotshalks and Apiné joined the National Ballet
in 1951, their son Gunnar was only five years old, and during their tenure at the Company, the couple lamented that they did not have much
time to spend with their child.[30] Smith and Adams also had a young
child – a daughter, Janine – born in April 1951, barely half a year before
the National Ballet's first performance. She did not live with her parents
most of the year, but instead resided in Vancouver with Adams's parents.
Although the concept of the nuclear family was central to the stereotypical 1950s narrative of domesticity, the hectic rehearsal and performance schedules of the dancers, compounded by touring engagements,
prevented ballet families in the Company from functioning according
to social expectations. Nevertheless, these parents were sympathetically
depicted in the press. According to publicity stories, Smith and Adams
were good parents because they wanted to protect their child from the
spotlight.[31] The physical absence of their daughter was a hardship, particularly for Smith, who was portrayed as the devoted mother who had
a "heart-breaking emptiness" because their daughter did not live with
them.[32] These stories re-enforced the "naturalness" of close physical
proximity between parents and their offspring. Rarely did other narratives escape the apologist script of the regretful dancing parent, but in
1959, when asked if she missed "normal life" as a "homemaker," Smith
confessed, "Only when I'm home."[33]

Smith's admission that she did not often miss playing the role of a
homemaker (and therefore did not conform to social expectations for

mothers) serves as a reminder that female dancers could not escape gender stereotypes. Beyond the difficulty of applying traditional narratives of motherhood to female dancers, one of the most persistent negative gendered stereotypes about professional dance has involved the connotations inherent in the image of women being paid to perform in public. During the nineteenth century, young male season subscribers were allowed to mingle in the Foyer de la danse at the Paris Opera with female dancers – dancers who, for a variety of economic reasons, often allowed themselves to become the subscribers' mistresses.[34] Moreover, the flowing tunics and the barefooted modern dances of Isadora Duncan, and the salacious Salomé-mania, inspired, in part, by the Canadian-born dancer, Maud Allan, were both representative of the kinds of theatrical performances in the early years of the twentieth century that physicalized the questionable morals of dancers who willingly transgressed the social proprieties of the time. The relentless global touring of Anna Pavlova arguably did much to reposition classical ballet as spiritually transcendent, but a paradox remained: while it was acceptable and even desirable for young girls to take dance lessons in the hopes they would achieve grace, the stage was arguably viewed more critically.

In the 1950s, the National Ballet and the news media both slyly capitalized on the traditional theatrical commodification of female sexuality by emphasizing the physical attractiveness of the Company's ballerinas while carefully remaining within the bounds of respectability; the dancers were simultaneously physically desirable and morally decent. One male interviewer told his readers that Smith was "constructed along lines which would have turned the head of the late Flo Ziegfield [sic], she's the kind of girl who could make a wolf forget to howl. It came as a bit of a shock to discover that she is the mother of a two-year-old daughter."[35] Similarly, in 1959, the National Ballet performed at Pensacola for Dominion Day, and some of the dancers visited the Naval Air Station. A resulting publicity shot featured three female dancers wearing Navy anti-gravity suits and helmets along with pumps (see Figure 8.2). Two midshipmen posed with their arms around the women. One newspaper ran the photograph with the caption, "The girls like the airplanes. The cadets like the girls."[36] In this way, the National Ballet used female bodies to attract and cultivate audiences by carefully and quietly orchestrating public images of its female dancers' sexuality.[37]

The sexual allure of the National Ballet dancers' bodies, however, was always carefully contained within respectable limits of decorum, even though other dancers in Canada during the 1950s were depicted in

Figure 8.2 Sally Brayley, Jacqueline Ivings, and Cecily Paige with Canadian Naval Cadets, 1959. Photo by Norm La Coe, courtesy of the *Pensacola News Journal* and the National Ballet of Canada Archives, 1959-1.

more lascivious ways. In a story about Theatre Under the Stars (TUTS), the summer musical theatre company in Vancouver, an accompanying photo showed a female dancer wearing a bikini that "weighs only a few ounces even when wet."[38] Although backstage photographs of National Ballet dancers meeting dignitaries were standard, photographs of young female TUTS dancers doing the cancan with middle-aged Kiwanis members provided an arguably more lecherous version of the trope.[39] Moreover, if the photograph of the National Ballet dancers and midshipmen was framed by a flirtatious caption and appeared in a paper to announce (and sell tickets) for an upcoming performance by the Company, a more sexualized photograph of TUTS female dancers pretending to hitch-hike that was used to promote the TUTS production *Blossom Time* included a man leaning out of his car to gawk eagerly at them. The caption accompanying the TUTS photograph left no question that the dancers' bodies were being used to entice audience members to attend the production: "The lithesome three, Anita Barnett, Gene Lussin and Diane Bourne, feel assured one interested gentleman is going to buy his tickets early."[40]

The beauty of the female dancers employed by the National Ballet was often conflated with their capabilities. In other words, technical excellence was often couched in terms of physical attractiveness: "Long of leg and line, lofty and strong in extensions, fluent and straight in pirouettes, Miss Smith danced with the superlative command and beauty of movement, her musical awareness producing some ever-so-delicate and subtle phrasing."[41] Another reviewer similarly praised dancer Lilian Jarvis in 1959: "Miss Jarvis, a winning blonde, almost stole the show with her beauty in this and the succeeding number. The prettiest of many pretty girls in the company, she also danced appealingly and brought an appealing quality of acting to her work."[42] The effect was to diminish the female dancers' dedication and self-discipline to hone their craft as working artists and, instead, to emphasize innate ability and beauty, always couched in stereotypical feminine terms.

Even Franca, arguably the most powerful woman in dance in Canada during the 1950s, did not escape the metonymic implication that her body represented who she was. The toughness required of Franca in her position as the artistic director or by the unglamorous daily lives of the female dancers were aspects of the ballet world rarely broached. Instead, female agency was recast as idealized, trivialized, and stereotypical femininity. For instance, there were several newspaper stories about Franca's hair. One newspaper story featured photographs of Franca modelling theatrical hairdos, intimating to readers that "Miss Franca reserves this flirtatious hairdo to portray the Operetta Star in *Offenbach in the Underworld*. Crown of curls, some of which are false, gives it its nickname – the 'cigar box.'"[43] Another story about Franca similarly focused on the various styles she could create quickly between performances, including the "classical ballerina style" for *Giselle*, the "cigar box" (again) for *Offenbach in the Underworld*, the "medieval" look for *Swan Lake*, and the off-centred bun that Franca called the "Hindu style" that she liked to wear for rehearsals and receptions. Readers learned that Franca did not have a hairdresser, but instead preferred to do her own hair because, as she mused, "One always knows one's own head best, don't you think?"[44] Franca was also portrayed as an expert on proper hair care: "Miss Franca, whose waist-length hair has escaped the scissors since she began dancing, pampers her hair with a weekly liquid shampoo and perpetual combing, brushing and scalp massage."[45] Neatly groomed hair, as the story implied, equalled professionalism for female dancers. "Come to think of it," the writer continued, "we can't imagine a Sugar Plum Fairy with untidy locks."

On the rare occasions that the toughness Franca required for her job as the artistic director was discussed, her administrative authority and responsibilities were moderated by her unthreatening physicality. She was described by one reporter in competing terms that simultaneously reinscribed and highlighted her gendered and embodied frailty while expressing awe at the fact she had leadership skills and stamina: "[The] driving force behind the undertaking is the 110-pound daughter of an English tailor who looks as if a strong breeze would blow her away but who puts in a day – and every day – that would stagger a stevedore. Celia Franca dancing behind the footlights is a breath-takingly ethereal. Celia Franca, the choreographer, producer, director, teacher and general factotum, reveals so much executive ability and drive that she leaves strong men panting from exhaustion in her wake. Only those equally dedicated can keep up with her."[46]

Thus, while her strength was acknowledged, it was done so in terms that conveyed incredulousness and was contained within the context of stereotypical femininity. Franca was a force of nature, but still a wisp of a woman. This emphasis on female dancers' etherealness as expressed through the public disclosure of Franca's body weight is perhaps one aspect of the art form that has not changed significantly since the 1950s. Interviewers were interested in what female dancers ate to keep themselves slim.[47] Statistical information regarding female dancers' bodies was published in newspapers perhaps as a benchmark for readers' own diets and weight aspirations. In 1959, for instance, the *Toronto Daily Star* informed its readers that Smith was 5'4" and weighed a trim 110 pounds.[48]

Publicizing Corporeal Patriotism

Publicizing highly personal information about dancers' bodies and private lives constructed a false intimacy between prospective supporters and the Company's performers – an intimacy that implicitly invited audiences and readers to see themselves and dominant social values reflected in the personas offered for public consumption. The campaign to legitimize and popularize ballet, however, also was conducted in broader, nationalist terms as the National Ballet employed a variety of strategies to assert itself as a Canadian entity and ballet as a Canadian art form by using the bodies of the dancers to equate ballet with established Canadian symbols, including hockey. Moreover, the Company stressed its patriotic allegiance to the country by acting as cultural ambassadors when touring internationally. Photographs of the dancers chatting with dignitaries and attending diplomatic functions, often while wearing theatrical costumes, were published in the National Ballet's souvenir programs and underscored how the dancers' corporeal presence could be used as nationalistic propaganda.

The National Ballet specifically used clothing and the association with physical activities synonymous with "Canada" to demystify and naturalize ballet as a national pastime. In 1957, for instance, National Ballet dancers participated in a demonstration of ballet syllabi at the Canadian National Sportsmen's Show at the Coliseum. Among the booths for fishing, trapping, boat motors, and wildlife exhibits, young female dancers in ballet costumes performed exercises from their daily classes.[49]

In her study of the construction of dominant culture and ideologies in Canada, Eva Mackey notes that symbols are "important strategic tools in the pan-Canadian nationalist cause."[50] In this light, it is possible to see that the National Ballet capitalized on the power of national symbols, joining the patriotic campaign to promote a sense of national pride while simultaneously using dancers' bodies to equate ballet with more recognizably Canadian symbols. Photographs printed in the Company's 1957–1958 souvenir program, for instance, showed Franca dropping the puck in a face-off between George Armstrong, the captain of the Toronto Maple Leafs, and Maurice ("The Rocket") Richard, the captain of the Montreal Canadiens. The photograph caption informed patrons that Franca had been in attendance at the Montreal Forum for the opening game of the season between the two teams and had seen The Rocket score his 499th career goal. Two other hockey-themed photographs appeared on the same page of the souvenir program. In one, Franca, wearing a classical ballet costume with a long, layered tutu and pointe shoes holds a hockey stick like she is about to take a slap shot. In the other, female members of the National Ballet, all in costumes with tiny flower garland headbands crowd around Nick Tomiuk, the captain and "most popular player" of the Sudbury Wolves as he autographs a pointe shoe.

Figure 8.3 Betty Pope, Lilian Jarvis, Angela Leigh, and Lois Smith wearing hockey sweaters, ca. 1957. Photographer unknown; courtesy of the National Ballet of Canada Archives, 1957-4.

The photo caption states that the "delighted" National Ballet ballerinas "collected enough sticks and sweaters to play floor-hockey in their rehearsal hall. Fortunately the windows are high enough to be out of puck-range"[51] (see Figure 8.3). Similarly, another photograph distributed to the media showed female dancers – Betty Pope, Lilian Jarvis, Angela Leigh, and Lois Smith – sporting the sweaters with the emblems and leg warmers in the colours of their supposedly favourite National Hockey League teams: Chicago Black Hawks, New York Rangers, Detroit Red Wings, and Boston Bruins.[52] (It is curious that the Canadian teams were not represented, but perhaps the Company did not want to alienate any Canadian hockey fans by appearing to favour certain Canadian teams over others.)

These two contexts – sportsmen's shows and hockey games – were stereotypically male-oriented; publicity strategies incorporated a stereotypical understanding of masculinity into the typical ballet-attending audience by using the female dancers' bodies to convey an image of the National Ballet as friendly to husbands who might rather go hunting or watch a hockey game than attend a ballet performance.[53] Thus, the publicity surrounding the Company placed the dancers in environments and dressed their bodies in costumes with sports logos that invited viewers who might feel the art form was elitist to associate ballet with the quintessential and arguably more accessible images of Canadian athleticism provided by outdoor sports and hockey.

If promoting ballet as compatible with sporting goods, and hockey was the populist approach to "Canadianizing" the art form, another strategic tactic involved demonstrating that the National Ballet could function as a propaganda agenda for the government. By touring internationally to places like the United States, the National Ballet reminded foreign neighbours of Canada's friendship and common interests through the "soft diplomacy" of non-political engagement.[54] In this way, the corporeality of the dancers physicalized the message that ballet had an important cultural contribution to make by projecting Canada's image internationally as a genial and artistically advanced nation. Moreover, ballet performances and receptions gave diplomats and other Canadian citizens abroad an opportunity to establish and renew relationships on a social level away from more formal and overtly political settings.

The National Ballet capitalized on its representation of Canada internationally, and the dancers' bodies were the conduit for publicity that carried the ideological message that the Company was in the service of the nation. The Company's 1956–1957 souvenir program, for instance, contains several photographs from a tour to Washington, DC.[55] Among the photographs, Arnold Heeney, Canada's ambassador to the United States chats with Smith and Adams after a performance of *Swan Lake*. Lilian Jarvis, dressed in a tutu poses with two Mounties outside of the

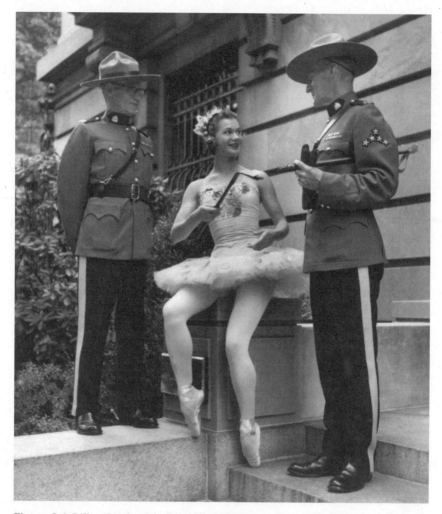

Figure 8.4 Lilian Jarvis with Canadian Mounties on tour in Washington, 1956. Photo by Ken Bell; courtesy of the National Ballet of Canada Archives. JARL 100 1956 4.

Canadian Embassy (see Figure 8.4). Franca, in a light-coloured dress resembling a Romantic tutu, plants a maple tree to commemorate a visit to Alexandria, Virginia, as tutu-wearing dancers and male dignitaries stand behind her. In yet another photograph, three National Ballet dancers pose with the Lincoln Memorial in the background. Perhaps most interesting in the context of Cold War politics, one photograph is a backstage shot of dancers Beverly Banfield and Catherine Carr laughing with Soviet Ambassador to the United States Georgi Zarubin, previously the Soviet ambassador to Canada, from 1944 to 1946. The dancers were wearing their costumes so there could be no mistaking who they were as they participated in ambassadorial functions or conversed with dignitaries and government officials. The photographs were part of a publicity strategy to impress patrons who purchased the souvenir program, but the dancers' smiles for the camera also signalled that, as unofficial agents of the country, they were engaging in the project of solidifying Canada's relationship with its foreign friends and Cold War foes.

Conclusion

In the 1950s, the newly formed National Ballet had to convince potential audience members and government officials that ballet was not socially deviant, morally threatening, elitist, or frivolous. To do so, the National Ballet's publicity materials (echoed and augmented by the press) used information and images related to the corporeality of the Company's dancers to suggest that ballet was compatible with dominant definitions of gender norms as well as popular national symbols and propagandist agendas. As a result, documentary evidence from the Company's first decade provides historians with an opportunity to consider how artists' bodies were malleable tools of persuasion not only onstage, but beyond the footlights as well.

The various ways that the bodies of the National Ballet's dancers were used to legitimize and popularize ballet as examined in this chapter are not intended to imply that oppositional views about gender roles and national identities were absent in Canada during the 1950s. Instead, by reinscribing established social norms and by implicitly asserting that dance was benignly at the service of mainstream culture, the National Ballet demonstrated how strategies of conformity were embodied, and how contested values were quietly concealed.

Notes

I would like to thank the staff at Dance Collection Danse (DCD), especially Carolyne Clare, as well as Marian McGraw at the University of Victoria for their research assistance during the preparation of this essay.

1 There are numerous scholarly studies addressing embodied values, including the following anthologies and introductory texts: Alexandra Carter and Janet O'Shea, eds., *The Routledge Dance Studies Reader*, 2nd ed. (New York: Routledge, 2010); Jane C. Desmond, ed., *Meaning in Motion: New Cultural Studies of Dance* (Durham, NC: Duke University Press, 1997); Ann Dils and Ann Cooper Albright, eds., *Moving History/Dancing Cultures: A Dance History Reader* (Middletown, CT: Wesleyan University Press, 2001); and Susan Leigh Foster, ed., *Choreographing History* (Bloomington, IN: Indiana University Press, 1995). Among the relatively few studies that consider dance in Canada, see Ann Cooper Albright, "Techno Bodies or, Muscling with Gender in Contemporary Dance," *Choreography and Dance* 5, no. 1 (1998), 39–51; Lisa Doolittle, "The Trianon and On: Reading Mass Social Dancing in the 1930s and 1940s in Alberta, Canada," in *Ballroom, Boogie, Shimmy Sham, Shake: A Social and Popular Dance Reader*, ed. Julie Malnig (Urbana, IL: University of Illinois Press, 2009), 109–25; and Barbara La Blanc, "Changing Places: Dance, Society, and Gender in Cheticamp," in *Undisciplined Women: Tradition and Culture in Canada*, ed. Pauline Green Hill and Diane Tye (Montreal and Kingston: McGill-Queen's University Press, 1997), 101–12.

2 The issue of bodies and advertising is also explored in this anthology by Cheryl Krasnick Warsh and Greg Marquis.

3 Alexandra Howson, *The Body in Society: An Introduction* (Cambridge: Polity, 2004), 95.

4 Herbert Whittaker, "Show Business," *Globe and Mail*, 5 Sept. 1951, 10.

5 Iro Valaskakis Tembeck, "Dance, the Church, and Repressive Morals in Catholic Quebec," in *Right to Dance: Dancing for Rights*, ed. Naomi M. Jackson (Banff: Banff Centre Press, 2004), 34. For a more detailed discussion of the Ballets de Paris incident, see Tembeck, "Dance, the Church, and Repressive Morals in Catholic Quebec," in ibid., 42–3.

6 J.W. Pickersgill, *My Years with Louis St Laurent: A Political Memoir* (Toronto: University of Toronto Press, 1975), 139.

7 Vincent Massey et al., *Report of the Royal Commission on National Development in the Arts, Letters and Sciences, 1949–1951* (Ottawa: King's Printer, 1951), 201.

8 Richard Dyer, *White* (London: Routledge, 1997), 1.

9 "Canada's Famed Ballet Group Here," *Vancouver Province*, 8 March 1954, 25.

10 For example, see M.E.K., "Small but Receptive Audience at Ballet," Newspaper Clipping (1952), Lois Smith Portfolio (Smith Portfolio), Dance Collection Danse Archives (DCD), Toronto; Beatrice Taylor, "National Ballet Improved by Experience of Year," Newspaper Clipping (1953), Smith Portfolio, DCD; Anson B. Cutts, "National Ballet of Canada Impressive in Two Shows Here," Newspaper Clipping (1958), Smith Portfolio, DCD.

11 For more detailed examinations of the history of responses to men in dance, see Ramsay Burt, *The Male Dancer*, 2nd ed. (London: Routledge, 2007); Jane Desmond, ed., *Dancing Desires: Choreographing Sexualities on and off the Stage* (Madison, WI: University of Wisconsin Press, 2001); Jennifer Fisher and Anthony Shay, eds., *When Men Dance: Choreographing Masculinities across Borders* (Oxford: Oxford University Press, 2009); Julia L. Foulkes, *Modern Bodies: Dance and American Modernism from Martha Graham to Alvin Ailey* (Chapel Hill, NC: University of North Carolina Press, 2002); Lynn Garafola, "Reconfiguring the Sexes," in *The Ballets Russes and Its World*, ed. Lynn Garafola and Nancy Van Norman Baer (New Haven, CT: Yale University Press, 1999), 245–68; Lynn Garafola, "The Sexual Iconography of the Ballets Russes," *Ballet Review* 28, no. 3 (2000), 70–7; David Gere, *How to Make Dances in an Epidemic: Tracking Choreography in the Age of AIDS* (Madison, WI: University of Wisconsin Press, 2004); Stavros Stavrou Karayanni, *Dancing Fear and Desire: Race, Sexuality and Imperial Politics in Middle Eastern Dance* (Waterloo: Wilfrid Laurier University Press, 2004); Kevin Kopelson, *The Queer Afterlife of Vaslav Nijinsky* (Stanford, CA: Stanford University Press, 1997); Peter Stoneley, *A Queer History of the Ballet* (London: Routledge, 2007).

12 Richard O'Hagen, "Lois Smith and David Adams and Their ... Life Sentence with the Ballet," *Maclean's*, 7 Dec. 1957, 68.

13 Frank Tumpane, "Take a Look, Men!" *Globe and Mail*, 17 April 1954, 3.

14 Grant Strate, *Grant Strate: A Memoir* (Toronto: Dance Collection Danse Press/es, 2002), 62.

15 Although, as Mary Louise Adams notes, there is a history of dance writers lamenting the effeminacy of male ballet dancers on stage throughout the twentieth century. See Mary Louise Adams, "'Death to the Prancing Prince': Effeminacy, Sport Discourses and the Salvation of Men's Dancing," *Body and Society* 11, no. 4 (2005), 63–86. I would like to thank Jane Nicholas for bringing this article to my attention.

16 "Ballet Isn't for 'Sissies,' Top Dancer Tells Students," Newspaper Clipping (1959), Smith Portfolio, DCD. For a similar story, see Herbert Whittaker, "The Rise of David Adams: Spindly Boy to Star Dancer," *Globe and Mail*, 17 April 1954, 10.

17 "Children Make Receptive Viewers, Says Danseur," *St. Thomas Times-Journal*, 7 Dec. 1959.

18 Larry Henderson to Lois Smith, letter, 27 Feb. 1959, Smith Portfolio, DCD; Thomas Archer, "Sight and Sound," Montreal *Gazette*, 1 March 1955.

19 "Canadian Ballet in Los Angeles Draws Crowd, Praise for Ballerina," Newspaper Clipping (1958), Smith Portfolio, DCD.

20 Adams, "'Death to the Prancing Prince,'" 64.

21 Don West, "Buckin' the Ballet Line," *Vancouver Daily Province*, 22 Oct. 1949, 3.
22 Ted Greenslade, "Ballet Beauties Dazzle Reporter," *Vancouver News-Herald*, 8 March 1954.
23 "Canadian Ballet to Be Given Thurs. by Artist Series," Newspaper Clipping (1957), Smith Portfolio, DCD; Helen Parmelee, "The Many Faces of Talent," Newspaper Clipping (1959), Smith Portfolio, DCD; "Lots of Work as well as Play for Toronto's Favorite Ballet Stars," Newspaper Clipping (1955), Smith Portfolio, DCD; Jean Whitehead, "Camera Big Hobby for Ballet Troupe," Newspaper Clipping (1955), Smith Portfolio, DCD.
24 O'Hagen, "Lois Smith and David Adams," 68.
25 "Plot Loves Real for Ballet Stars," *Kitchener-Waterloo Record*, 11 Jan. 1955, 7. Also see "Dancers Mix Marriage, Careers," Newspaper Clipping (1954), Smith Portfolio, DCD.
26 "Lots of Work as well as Play," Newspaper Clipping (1955).
27 Frank Morriss, "Fights? Very Few Says this Dancing Couple," *Winnipeg Free Press*, 14 May 1958, 3. For similar comments, see Blaik Kirby, "National Ballet's Lois Smith: A Star of Our Own," *Toronto Daily Star*, 7 Feb. 1959, 21.
28 "Ballet Isn't for 'Sissies,'" Newspaper Clipping (1959).
29 Zoe Bieler, "A Little Opposition Aids Dancers' Careers," *Montreal Star*, 22 Nov. 1955, 30.
30 "Lots of Work," Newspaper Clipping (1955).
31 Kirby, "National Ballet's Lois Smith," 21.
32 Parmelee, "Many Faces of Talent."
33 Kirby, "National Ballet's Lois Smith," 21.
34 Victoria Huckenpahler, "Confessions of an Opera Director: Chapters from the *Mémoires* of Dr. Louis Véron," Pt. 1, *Dance Chronicle* 7, no. 1 (1983), 54. For more detailed critical discussions about moral anxiety, sexuality, and female dancing bodies, see Anne Middleboe Christensen, "Deadly Sylphs and Decent Mermaids," in *The Cambridge Companion to Ballet*, ed. Marion Kant (Cambridge: Cambridge University Press, 2007), 126–37; Sarah Davies Cordova, "Romantic Ballet in France, 1830–1850," in *The Cambridge Companion to Ballet*, ed. Marion Kant (Cambridge: Cambridge University Press, 2007), 113–25; Karen Eliot, *Dancing Lives: Five Female Dancers from the Ballet d'Action to Merce Cunningham* (Urbana, IL: University of Illinois Press, 2007), 49; Joellen A. Meglin, "Feminism or Fetishism? *La Révolte des femmes* and Women's Liberation in France in the 1830s," in *Rethinking the Sylph: New Perspectives on the Romantic Ballet*, ed. Lynn Garafola (Hanover, NH: Wesleyan University Press, 1997), 69–90.
35 Greenslade, "Ballet Beauties Dazzle Reporter."

36 Norm La Coe, "'Dance, Ballerina, Dance,'" Newspaper Clipping (1959), Smith Portfolio, DCD.

37 The National Ballet experience anticipated and resonated with the issue of using the bodies of women to promote organizations that is raised in the chapters in this volume by Tarah Brookfield, who examines of how femininity was performed on stage in the Edmonton-based Miss United Nations pageants of the 1960s, and Mary-Ann Shantz, who analyses the 1970s Miss Nude World pageants held in southwestern Ontario.

38 "Clothes Are a Burden these Days," Newspaper Clipping (1952), Gordon Wales Portfolio, DCD.

39 "'Kick a Little Bit Higher, George,'" Newspaper Clipping (1950), Gordon Wales Portfolio, DCD.

40 "Look Out Mister, You'll Twist Your Neck," Newspaper Clipping (c. 1949), Gordon Wales Portfolio, DCD.

41 Merita Mills, "Artistry of Top Rank Is Shown in City Auditorium Performance by National Ballet of Canada," Newspaper Clipping (1959), Smith Portfolio, DCD.

42 Warner Twyford, "Canadian Ballet Gives Enjoyable Performance," Newspaper Clipping (1959), Smith Portfolio, DCD.

43 Glenna Syse, "How Ballet Star Keeps Hair Tidy," Newspaper Clipping (1955), Smith Portfolio, DCD.

44 Ruth Carlton, "Ballerina's Shining Glory Sports Short-Order Styles," Newspaper Clipping (1955), Smith Portfolio, DCD.

45 Syse, "How Ballet Star Keeps Hair Tidy."

46 Helen Beattie, "National Ballet: Has It a Future?" *Canadian Home Journal* (Jan. 1953), 14–15.

47 Linda Curtis, "Ballet Dancers May Float but Cannot Live on Air," Newspaper Clipping (1954), Smith Portfolio, DCD.

48 Kirby, "National Ballet's Lois Smith," 21.

49 Lotta Dempsey, "Learn to Chat in French at the Salon Français," Newspaper Clipping (1957), Smith Portfolio, DCD.

50 Eva Mackey, *The House of Difference: Cultural Politics and National Identity in Canada* (Toronto: University of Toronto Press, 2002), 56.

51 *National Ballet of Canada Souvenir Program, 1957–1958*, Smith Portfolio, DCD.

52 For example, "Ballet Troupe Here," *San Francisco Chronicle*, 9 April 1958, 32.

53 Tellingly, these publicity photographs and events featured female dancers, not their male counterparts. The absence of the male dancers was probably strategic. It offered the men who traditionally attended sportsmen's shows

and hockey games the opportunity to view pretty female dancers as interested in and supportive of stereotypically male pursuits without the hurdle of addressing "men in tights."

54 For more about the role of arts in cultural diplomacy, see Evan Potter, *Branding Canada: Projecting Canada's Soft Power through Public Diplomacy* (Montreal and Kingston: McGill-Queen's University Press, 2009). For an international example, see Naima Prevots, *Dance for Export: Cultural Diplomacy and the Cold War* (Hanover, NH: Wesleyan University Press, 1998).

55 *National Ballet of Canada Souvenir Program, 1956–1957*, Smith Portfolio, DCD.

9 Gender, Spirits, and Beer: Representing Female and Male Bodies in Canadian Alcohol Ads, 1930s–1970s

CHERYL KRASNICK WARSH AND GREG MARQUIS

Alcoholic beverage advertisers used the female and male forms in various ways in Canadian print media from the 1930s to the 1970s. Alcohol ads, and how bodies were used in them, were representative of Canada's ambivalent response to alcohol. Producers associated their beverages with pleasure, while regulators reflected society's continued anxieties about products and practices associated with immorality, danger, and health risks. These anxieties paralleled the findings of Smith and Wakewich on the female "citizen body" during the Second World War, and Syperek's discussion of the female nude in Canadian art and the concept of "gendered codes." The gendered marketing of products and lifestyle is also explored in Colpitts's chapter on Canada's interwar fur coat industry.[1] To examine alcohol and the depiction of gender, we analyse the urban, middle-class–oriented magazines *Saturday Night* and *Maclean's*, newspapers such as the Montreal *Gazette* and the Toronto *Globe and Mail*, and two American publications with high numbers of Canadian readers, *Time* and *Life*.[2]

In Canadian-produced alcohol ads, depictions of male and female bodies were governed not by the market, public taste, or industry self-regulation, but state bureaucracies committed to discouraging consumption. Following the end of prohibition in the 1920s, print advertising was regulated at the provincial level, with considerable variation among the provinces. "Commercial speech" was controlled to protect society in general rather than individual consumers. Radio and television alcohol commercials were regulated by the federal government. In most provinces, the regulation of liquor ads was fairly strict until the early 1970s, when more liberal attitudes gave rise to controversial "lifestyle" ads that eventually drew the attention of experts and governments.

The primary tactic of alcohol advertising is to associate products with a "desirable lifestyle."[3] Such image advertising, mastered by tobacco companies in the early twentieth century, stressed not simply the product but how it supposedly enhanced the lifestyle of the consumer.[4] Canadian attitudes towards alcohol, gender roles, and what constituted a desirable lifestyle, changed over the period under review. At various times, advertisers emphasized masculinity (men in work and leisure situations), mixed-gender socializing (married couples in domestic, suburban settings), and the female form (exploited most notoriously in beer ads).[5] Advertisers also appealed to the female consumer, both before and after the start of second-wave feminism and the entry of more women into the workforce. From the 1970s, alcohol producers marketed new products aimed at female consumers, such as coolers, as well as targeting this demographic with advertisements associating drinking with "independence, good health, and professional accomplishment."[6] Yet, this was not a simple evolution.

Media Regulations and Alcohol Advertising

Control of alcohol advertising was a form of state regulation with roots in the pre-prohibition temperance era. Following the gradual dismantling of provincial prohibition, beginning with British Columbia and Quebec in the early 1920s and ending with Prince Edward Island in 1948, alcohol policy pursued contradictory objectives. The state sought to curb consumption while at the same time collect "sin tax" revenues through excise taxation and retail profits.[7] In the transition from prohibition to "government control," provincial legislators placed strict controls on the advertising of alcoholic beverages, largely as a political compromise to placate the prohibitionist minority.[8]

Prior to the age of prohibition, alcohol ads in Canadian newspapers and magazines usually promoted the product itself, with minimal imagery, although by the early 1900s, some advertisements included images related to production and consumption. Well into the twentieth century, some manufacturers publicized the alleged health and nutritional benefits of their products, as well as their safety and "purity." Gender-specific marketing pitched female "health tonics" such as Vin Mariani (containing alcohol and cocaine).[9] On the eve of prohibition, Budweiser and other major American brewers placed in Canadian newspapers expensive ads portraying middle-class and elite men, and couples, enjoying beer in restaurants, at home, and at social functions, sometimes served by African-American waiters (more reflective of the ads' U.S. origins rather than Canadian society). Major advertising agencies like New York's J. Walter Thompson used findings from John B. Watson and other modern psychologists to determine that beer was a "middle-class drink meant for unpretentious sociability."[10] After repeal, the alcohol industry and its advertisers developed a voluntary code, albeit unenforced, banning the depiction of women and children in ads, to avoid future temperance backlash.[11]

Beer and spirits ads, already reflecting "market segmentation," depicted elderly drinkers, as well as male, blue-collar workers, or men engaged in masculine pursuits, such as fishing or relaxing with a cigar and a newspaper (see Figure 9.1). Alcohol ads were also placed on newspaper sports pages.[12] Pre-prohibition newspapers and magazines featured pictorial institutional or public service ads, such as a series by Molson Breweries dedicated to Quebec history.[13]

Temperance opinion, strong in many Protestant churches, had long warned that the "liquor traffic" would employ advertising to further insinuate alcohol into Canadian life. The "traffic" would supposedly carry out its anti-social mission by portraying beverage alcohol as a harmless consumer product, akin to radios, soap, iceboxes, or automobiles.[14] For the architects of government control, the main manifestation of which was the heavily regulated liquor store, alcohol was a politically sensitive and socially hazardous commodity whose distribution required considerable state oversight. Yet, voices of modernity, such as *Saturday Night*, distanced themselves from the "antiquated" attitudes reflected in Canada's temperance-influenced liquor control regimes. In 1934, the journal contrasted strict Canadian consumption laws, particularly in "blue-nosed" Ontario, with the more liberal laws of post-prohibition America.[15]

The underlying philosophy of provincial liquor control into the 1960s, in most jurisdictions, was that alcohol was a privilege, not a citizenship right. Post-prohibition provincial governments tread carefully as did alcohol producers, who until the 1940s, feared the possible return of prohibition. Despite lobbying to the contrary, Ontario's liquor legislation in the 1920s and 1930s outlawed magazine, newspaper, and billboard alcohol advertisements.[16] By contrast, according to an English temperance speaker, beer was advertised in Great Britain as "a training diet for athletes, an aid to rheumatism, a cure for indigestion – in fact ... a remedy for every conceivable human ailment."[17] Producers also engaged in self regulation. The distillery industry was most cautious about market-

Figure 9.1 The Industrial Worker. Institutional beer ad with masculine, working-class collective focus. *Maclean's* 15 November 1947.

ing, largely because spirits had been associated with the excesses of the pre–First World War saloon. Following the repeal of prohibition in the United States, in 1933, Seagram's, owned by Canada's Bronfman family, began a "drink moderately" campaign that attempted to associate drinking whisky with social responsibility, not human misery. The campaign was a subtle yet effective form of indirect advertising that reinforced the social status of consumers of whisky over that of beer drinkers.[18]

Print media regulations varied by province, and no province was able to ban U.S. magazines and newspapers, or those published in more liberal jurisdictions. Publishers avoided restrictive regulations in their home provinces by producing "split editions," so that magazines such as *Atlantic Advocate*, with "wet" ads, could be shipped to neighbouring provinces.[19] *New Liberty*, published in Quebec, was a favourite target of temperance critics as it was owned by E.P. Taylor, head of Canadian Breweries Limited, as was *Canadian Homes and Gardens*. Unionized printers, and newspaper and magazine publishers, protested that the publishing sector in "no ad" provinces faced unfair competition from Quebec and American publishers.[20]

Prior to the Second World War, Quebec's print media were unique in Canada in that they depicted men, women, couples, and mixed-gender groups in beer ads. In the 1930s, the Montreal *Gazette* featured not only a photograph and a personal endorsement for Labatt's beer from a Montreal sports writer, but also a photograph of a group of men in suits drinking beer in a tavern.[21] Most common were cartoon or comic strip–style features for the Dow and Dawes breweries, such as Dow's "Where's Joe?" (1939) and "Gone for a Dow," featuring middle-aged men enjoying a quiet glass of ale. The message was that for men, drinking a beer was a relaxing interlude in modern urban society. It was a masculine, but not necessarily a blue-collar, activity. Dawes ads depicted a respectable, middle-aged cartoon figure enjoying a Black Horse Ale in a social setting. "Now for Dow" (1936) was a rarity in the masculine world of beer ads in that it featured a drawing of a young couple in bathing suits returning from a swim. Combining sex appeal with sports was the Dow Girl campaign (1933), which featured a photo of a young woman who answered sports trivia in the newspaper's pages and who was on Montreal radio station CKAC.[22]

At the beginning of the Second World War, prohibitionists pressured the federal and provincial governments to restrict the production and sale of alcohol in the name of the war effort.[23] In 1943, the Mackenzie King government prohibited alcohol product advertising under the Wartime Alcoholic Beverages Control Order (WABCO). Despite the lack of product advertising, and the imposition of rationing at the provincial level, the number of drinkers increased with wartime prosperity and the constant mobilizing of tens of thousands of young Canadians for military duty and work in war-related industries.[24] Manufacturers of beverage liquor, under the WABCO, were allowed "institutional, educational" advertising, most of which supported the war effort or praised Canada's history, political culture, social institutions, workforce, and natural resources. Institutional ads depicted men and women not as consumers, but as citizens contributing to the national challenge. Yet, brewers were aware of the sensitive nature of promoting consumption during wartime, and ran moderation and "V for Victory" spots in newspapers from 1940.[25] The happy consequence of institutional advertising for the brewers and distillers was their alignment with producers of tobacco, soft drinks, and candy, among other consumer goods, as patriotic Canadian corporate citizens doing their part for the war effort.

Gendered Bodies in Postwar Advertisements

The fluidity of gender roles during wartime (for more on this issue, see Smith and Wakewich in this volume) was apparent in institutional ads. Dow's Joe character disappeared from having lunch beside a female worker in the munitions factory, and left a game of checkers to lecture women at the bridge club to volunteer for war work, while Dawes Brewery and Bright's Wines encouraged both women and men to consider farm work.[26] Institutional ads, promoting Victory Bonds and the challenges of demobilization of the Canadian forces, were acceptable advertising in *Saturday Night* and *Maclean's* for O'Keefe's Brewing and other companies. Yet, the pictures of handsome soldiers in battle fatigues, denoting courage, resolve, and strength, were attractive role models of heroic drinkers for both men and women,[27] and even for children. Another O'Keefe institutional ad showed a resolute young boy (or pre-drinker) with his train set, with the caption, "Me? I'm gonna be an Engineer!" In 1949, Gooderham and Worts Distillers placed an institutional ad for Remembrance Day that pictured a young boy and girl. Similarly, a grandmother and granddaughter in rocking chairs, knitting warm socks for the troops, was another opportunity for Dawes to sanitize its image with its appeal to timeless homeliness and good service, by invoking two figures more commonly found in earlier Woman's Christian Temperance Union campaigns.[28]

Following the expiration of federal orders-in-council, in 1947, control of print and other non-electronic advertising reverted back to the provincial level. At first, the Ontario government honoured its 1946 pledge to block all forms of liquor advertising, although indirect ads continued. By the mid-1950s, its rules had been considerably loosened, and existing regulations were often interpreted quite generously.[29] Toronto-based *Saturday Night*, an influential but limited-circulation periodical, was awash with liquor advertising in the 1950s, and there were striking differences apparent in the thematic campaigns relative to earlier years. The portrayal of women as equal contributors to the war effort never was at the cost of strong masculinity, since, of course, masculinity equalled combat. By the 1950s, however, despite the "redomestication" of women as homemakers, there were hints of gender insecurity, if not confusion. A couple of Labatt's ale ads, depicting narrow-chested, underweight male figures, urged "de-masculinized" Canadians to recapture their gender identity with "the hearty kind of ale our fathers enjoyed. But why dream? Labatt's India Pale Ale [IPA] is yours for the asking … the answer to a MAN'S dreams."[30] Another series for IPA shifted the manly focus to space; cartoon figures displayed the beer label on chairs and walls "to show that it's a *man's* room." And this display of masculinity was even approved by women, one of whom put a beer label flag outside her house as a "way of saying she's got herself a *man*."[31]

Due to continued public ambivalence towards their public drinking, women were relatively scarce in 1950s liquor advertising, and they were usually limited to spots for table and fortified wines. In one two-page spread for Canadian wines, a "sought-after fashion model" was pictured beside the Eiffel Tower, touting the virtues of Canadian wine.[32] In two Bright's Wines ads (one portrayed a Punch and Judy puppet couple, another two gloved female hands), sherry was promoted as an accompaniment for a dinner party at home. It was rare to depict a woman actually serving wine in the 1950s.[33] Provincial regulations usually excluded women from ads for spirits in this decade, and brewery marketing tactics minimized their use in beer ads. One popular exception was Carling's Black Label beer, with its slogan "Hey Mabel, Black Label."[34]

Unlike later ads, where drinkers would be young and fit, some 1950s liquor advertisements did nod, perhaps unintentionally, to the realities of alcohol consumption and the average consumer. In a Calvert House whisky ad, two men in suits were depicted as sitting down to watch television.[35] One Canadian campaign in 1947 highlighted not "bodies" but places that sheltered them – Blue Top beer ran a series of print ads that featured drawings and floor plans of affordable houses, suitable for war veterans and their young families. In an age when breweries owned professional sports franchises, the established link among men, beer, and sports continued to be a standby in advertising. Beer, like spirits, was often framed within a homosocial context. Johnnie Walker whisky presented sporting ads in the 1950s, with both participants (hockey players, jockeys) and observers (coaches, bettors), so that those of varying athletic ability could identify with the product.[36] As in other forms of advertising, at this time, there were few allusions to non-White cultures. One exception was a Jameson whisky ad with Black longshoremen carrying crates, combining traditional tropes of race, class, and colonialism.[37]

Postwar anxieties about alcohol were fuelled by wartime excess (with rising arrest rates for public drunkenness), the new discourse on alcoholism, and debates about the morality of cocktail bars and other sites of public drinking. As of 1948, only Quebec and British Columbia permitted product advertisements produced within the province, and Manitoba, Alberta, Ontario, and New Brunswick allowed institutional ads. In 1959, Alberta actually tightened its rules by banning all advertisements produced within the province.[38] By the mid-1960s, provincial alcohol regulations across Canada were a patchwork. In 1966, Newfoundland, which had joined the Dominion in 1949, was described as an "ad man's paradise" because of its liberal alcohol promotion regime. Quebec prohibited testimonials, medicinal claims, and scenes that depicted imbibing. Ads produced in Manitoba could not show bottles, labels, or prices. The Liquor Control Board of Ontario permitted the portrayal of bottles in print advertisements only in 1968. British Columbia and Alberta prohibited colour spots in magazines. Alberta's Social Credit government, citing the influx of advertisements from outside the province, charted a more liberal course for print media in 1965 by permitting images of labels and brand names as well as slogans and recipes, but no bottles, glasses, or "family scenes."[39] Quebec was another example of how postwar alcohol consumption patterns and advertising controls could take divergent paths. In 1964, the province instituted gender-specific regulations that owed more to puritanical Catholicism than concerns about what later would be deemed "sexism." Under the new code, young, attractive female models were to be replaced by "persons of maturity, dignity and moderation," and females were not to be portrayed in "immodest or provocative dress or situations." Male models were permitted to hold a glass or bottle, yet they were forbidden from sipping, while female models could not hold bottles or glasses.[40]

"Spill Over" and the Bodies of Female Consumers

By the early 1950s, as more Canadian families living close to the border purchased television sets, American TV shows sponsored by alcohol companies became the newest threat to provincial liquor control.[41] Although imported American beer did not sell well, and Canadian breweries did not begin to bottle or distribute it until the 1970s and 1980s, critics warned that "spill over" advertising of U.S. brands such as Miller and Budweiser, encouraged consumption. American beer commercials, much like the ads in the American mass-circulation magazines flooding into Canada, were more liberal in their depiction of situations involving men and women than their Canadian-produced counterparts.[42] During the 1960s and early 1970s, alcohol continued to gain widespread acceptance in Canadian society, where a majority of adults were drinkers. In addition to more liberal attitudes, consumption levels were augmented by the falling real cost of alcohol; the proliferation of liquor stores, licensed premises, and occasions for social drinking; rising affluence; and a greater presence of young adults in the population as a result of the Baby Boom. In the words of the British Columbia Liquor Inquiry Commission, by 1970, alcohol control was perceived by many to be based on "outdated theories, opinions and tenets."[43]

Throughout the era of liberalization, drinking at home and in public was becoming more popular among women.[44] As consumers as well as drinkers, women were usually portrayed as controlling not only household budgets but also family purchasing habits. Earlier generations had sought to limit women's access to alcohol, based in part on cultural biases that drinking was a male activity, or that beer parlours and taverns would attract "bad" women who would prey on male customers, engage in prostitution, and spread venereal diseases. The compromise solution, where permitted, had been separate sections in taverns (called "ladies beverage rooms" in Ontario), exclusively for women and their male escorts.[45] One argument in favour of cocktail lounges in the 1940s and 1950s was that they would normalize public drinking by women and mixed-gender drinking.[46] Although, by the 1950s, most Canadian women were drinkers, they consumed smaller amounts of alcohol than men. Nonetheless, the growing women's market was pursued by winemakers and distillers. By the early 1960s, advertisers clearly respected the purchasing power of women and made a "pitch" for that demographic by picturing young, attractive couples in magazine ads. Brewers, despite some attention to women as consumers in past magazine ads, usually did not run marketing campaigns geared specifically towards women.[47] One exception was Schlitz's 1965 Malt Liquor campaign. Although the product was probably not available in Canada, Canadian readers of *Life* magazine were treated to an ad with an inquisitive young female model closely examining a glass of malt liquor and exclaiming, "I like it. What is it?" The visual message here was that although beer knowledge was "men's knowledge," it could be imparted to female consumers.[48]

Although women began popping up with more frequency in 1960s liquor ads, the demarcation of masculinity was still evident.[49] In a 1964 series in *Time*, couples drank a variety of liquor products together in social situations such as after dinner, after work in bars, or at glamorous cocktail parties.[50] *Maclean's*, although operating under stricter regulations, still managed to connect premium products such as V & O or Calvert House whisky with sophisticated, mixed-gender social occasions. A number of beer and spirits ad campaigns in the 1950s and 1960s used images of mixed-gender relaxation and socializing, often with suburban overtones. A Dow ad depicted a case of beer with a husband and wife in the kitchen as they unpacked groceries. A Carling Cinci Lager ad depicted no bottles or glasses, but two couples playing bridge.[51] Products not traditionally considered women's drinks, such as beer and whisky, were marketed for their "lightness" or "sparkling" qualities, again with images of couples dating or hosting family barbeques.[52] A series of Labatt's ads for its India Pale Ale was one of the brewery's more "manly" campaigns: a 1960 spot in *Maclean's* portrayed a middle-aged man studying a glass of IPA, "a Real Man's Ale ... with an honest, masculine directness ... full strength, full bodied." Labatt's had run a similar campaign in the mid-1950s, with a series of photo-based ads featuring real Canadian men in a variety of occupations. The message was that beer both reinforced and restored masculinity.[53]

In these ads, women generally were not portrayed as drinking alone or with other women, and the implication was that they are usually married or in a relationship. In Figure 9.2, a young suburban Grace Kelly–type of woman who has brought her husband a beer is content to watch him enjoy it. Reflecting market research by beverage alcohol and advertising companies, a number of campaigns played on women's roles as consumer, hostess, and homemaker. Bright's Wines appealed to middle-class women to purchase sherry and other products for entertaining, ministering to "tired husbands" arriving home from work, and for cooking. In one 1950s magazine ad, a woman recalls how her first drink of sherry was given to her by her husband. Bright's provided consumers with recipes

Figure 9.2 Domestic bliss in the suburbs: Beer as a non-threatening consumer good, courtesy of Molson's Brewery: *Saturday Night*, 29 March 1958. Note that the woman is not drinking.

and meal planning information, much like Seagram's did, with the booklet *The Spirit of Hospitality*, which provided women with ideas for theme
parties, meals, and hors d'oeuvres, with the proper accompanying mixed
drinks.[54]

Lifestyle, Liberalization, and Sexing the Drinking Body

In contrast with the controversial beer lifestyle commercials of the 1970s,
many of the models in the print ads from the 1960s were middle-aged
or older. Yet, there were suggestions, often subtle, that middle-class Canadians were interested in marketing that reflected the more liberal
sexual attitudes of the decade. Regulations kept the scenes being depicted more in the traditions of heterosexual romance and glamour,
but there were hints of the "permissive society." The American men's
magazine *Playboy*, readily available in Canada, carried ads for alcohol
and other consumer products.[55] So did *Cosmopolitan*, the "single girl's"
magazine, which was read mainly by married women. By the mid-1960s,
the automobile, tobacco, alcohol, and home electronics industries were
consciously marketing to the so-called Mustang generation, young, educated single men and women who supposedly lived in "pads" (apart-
ments) and spent much of their income on socializing and consumer
goods. Alcohol ads developed for this market emphasized not only the
carefree single lifestyle, but also a less "uptight sexuality.[56] A 1965 ad for
Dubonnet Blonde, an imported wine-based apéritif, depicted a bottle
and two models as "Three Blondes from Paris."[57] Smirnoff vodka ran a
series in *Maclean's* and in U.S. magazines that displayed how "Smirnoff
people" enjoyed themselves at brunches, fondues, cafes, cocktail parties,
and other sophisticated gatherings.[58]

Lifestyle marketing, which was both a cause and an effect of liberalization, was not a new concept by the late 1960s. Since the 1920s, the mul-
tinational Coca-Cola Company had been depicting "active, contented,
good-looking, successful young men and women" enjoying its beverage,
despite its controversial origins and caffeinated contents.[59] By the 1970s,
the issue of lifestyle ads had set off a spirited alcohol policy debate. The
key public health concern was their impact on youthful Canadians, including those below the drinking age. This was related to not only the
maturation of the Baby Boom generation but also the lowering of the
minimum legal drinking age (MLDA) between 1970 and 1974. Provincial medical societies began to speak out against commercials that appeared to encourage youthful consumption. Another emerging issue

was public safety – the enactment of the impaired driving sections of the *Criminal Code* of Canada in 1969 had made a link with alcohol-involved traffic accidents and teenage drinking. With the appearance of a victims' rights movement in the 1970s that eventually sparked the establishment in Canada of organizations such as Please Reduce Impaired Driving Everywhere (PRIDE) and Mothers Against Drunk Driving (MADD), controversial alcohol commercials gained another group of critics. A third body of opinion arose out of the consumer rights movement, which was critical of products perceived to be socially, physically, or medically harmful, and of advertising that was dishonest.[60]

One important exception to liberalization was the continuing ban on spirits commercials in electronic media. Federal broadcasting regulations in the period under review prohibited commercials for spirits, reflecting the North American belief that distilled beverages were a greater potential problem than beer or wine.[61] Canadian distillers, as in the United States, were bound by a voluntary industry code that banned product advertising on the airwaves. The Association of Canadian Distillers (ACD) explained, in 1977, that members voluntarily avoided "outdoor" advertisements (billboard signs). Yet, members of the ACD kept the magazine industry afloat, judging by the number of ads for whisky, vodka, gin, rum, and other premium spirits in publications such as *Saturday Night* and *Maclean's* by the 1970s. For the most part, these were classic product shot ads, although sometimes they depicted people socializing or suggested "sophisticated" leisure activities such as tennis, golf, or yachting.[62] On occasion, they hinted at a link between the product and a successful love life. A 1970 Normandie wine spot in *Maclean's*, for example, depicted a man and a woman in close proximity, as if about to embrace, with the slogan, "All Normandie can promise is that she'll adore the wine. The rest is up to you."[63]

In the 1960s, private broadcasters lobbied to gain equality with magazines and newspapers with respect to alcohol advertising revenues. In 1964, the Board of Broadcast Governors (BBG), the federal regulator, permitted minute-long wine and beer commercials on radio and television. At that time, electronic liquor ads were permitted only in Ontario, Quebec, Nova Scotia, and Newfoundland. Beer or wine could not be depicted being poured from bottles or being "lifted to the mouth."[64] In 1968, the BBG was replaced with the Canadian Radio Television Commission (CRTC), which permitted the promotion of beer, wine, and cider on radio and television on the understanding that it did not promote the "general use" of alcohol, only "brand preference."[65] The CRTC permitted alcohol commissions to dictate the specifics of beer and wine radio and TV commercials in each province, with considerable regional variation. The provincial authorities had no control, however, over wine and beer commercials on American cable television, which was becoming more popular in the 1970s.[66] The revised Nova Scotia Liquor Control Act permitted alcoholic beverage advertisements, under certain restrictions. Neither print nor electronic ads were authorized in Saskatchewan.[67]

Lifestyle ads were against regulations in a number of provinces by the 1970s, and even where they were not, they provoked a backlash from experts and governments throughout the decade. The biggest challenge was in how provincial regulations were interpreted. In 1971, British Columbia introduced a short-lived total ban on alcohol advertisements produced within the province. In 1974, Federal Health Minister Marc Lalonde reportedly "blindsided" Canada's brewers for "pandering to the fantasies of a population that has already been conditioned to glamour and sophistication."[68] By the mid-1970s, advertisers in general were spending more money on television commercials than on magazine and newspaper campaigns, and Canadians, increasingly, were forming impressions about beer in particular from TV. The backlash against the promotion of alcohol, apparent on the federal and provincial levels by 1974, prompted one advertising executive to write a polemical piece in the trade publication *Marketing* that predicted a future fascist society, devoid of consumer choice.[69]

Ontario, home of the Addiction Research Foundation, reflected ambivalent attitudes towards liberalization throughout the 1970s. Policy decisions in this province were important because of the size of its population and alcohol market, as well as the influence of its media. A poll in 1977 suggested that 38.1 per cent of Canadians favoured banning lifestyle commercials and 35.4 per cent supported restricting them.[70] Ontario's minister of consumer affairs, in 1974, joined the chorus of addictions experts, public officials, and newspaper editors criticizing breweries for their offensive television marketing. Four years later, the Ministry of Consumer and Corporate Relations announced updated regulations governing lifestyle ads, which removed them from publications directed primarily at audiences below the MLDA.[71] In Quebec, regulations announced in 1975 prohibited advertisements that portrayed alcoholic beverages as a "factor of importance" for consumers, or suggested that they could somehow solve personal problems.[72]

Media, interest group, and government concerns about excessive alcohol consumption in Manitoba led to a counterattack on lifestyle marketing in 1974. According to the Manitoba Liquor Control Commission, print ads by distillers and radio and television commercials for wine producers were within the bounds of good taste. But television beer commercials had been equating personal happiness with drinking, and they appeared to be aimed at a young audience.[73] Revised content regulations limited alcohol promotions to "brand advertising only." Ads were to avoid associating consumption with "personal or collective merit," or creating an impression that the product "enhances social prestige, success in business, relationships with the opposite sex," or improves "performance in sports or helps solve personal problems." No group scenes, social functions, or "lifestyle" activities were to be depicted in published advertisements.[74] The industry adjusted to Manitoba's rules against the depiction of the "party environment" or implying sexual activity, and most advertisements submitted to provincial officials for review were accepted, sometimes with minor adjustments.[75]

Most of the attention in the debate on alcohol advertising was directed at TV beer commercials, but the entire policy environment was affected by the battle between brewers and regulators. As late as 1981, Ontario prohibited alcohol commercials that suggested sports prowess, and British Columbia refused to clear an ad featuring men drinking beer at a campsite. Provincial liquor commissions continued to impose content guidelines and, for electronic commercials, place weekly limits on airtime. Alberta's regulations prohibited depictions of groups of more than five persons, and the Nova Scotia Liquor Commission retained its traditional proscription against the "female form or face" in ads produced for consumption within the province.[76]

The industry response, represented by organizations such as the Brewers Association of Ontario, was that lifestyle advertisements did not affect overall consumption, only brand choice. This assertion was repeated by the ACD.[77] The Brewers Association of Canada usually stressed that beer was a beverage of moderation and on this basis should be under less regulation than spirits or wine.[78] Distillers, who had long engaged in self-regulation, were aware of the dangers of public reactions to promotion campaigns deemed excessive, such as the heavy use of magazine spots near Christmas. Regulators were not always unsympathetic; in 1980, the Manitoba Liquor Control Commission recommended that the province's ad regime be loosened. Specifically, it suggested allowing breweries and other advertisers to depict larger groups of people in their commercials.[79]

Expert studies on the actual effects of alcohol promotion in the 1970s showed mixed results, with most suggesting that overall consumption was not affected.[80] The most famous Canadian examples by the late 1970s were British Columbia and Saskatchewan, where alcohol ads were banned but consumption levels were no different from those in provinces that permitted beer and wine ads. British Columbia's initial 1971–1972 electronic commercial ban, according to a study by Smart and Cutler, was ineffective. The alcohol industry was quick to seize on the equivocal results of this research in order to ward off threats to marketing and advance arguments for further liberalization.[81]

One of the social movements of the "permissive society," feminism, became another factor influencing definitions of public acceptability in alcohol advertising. The issue of sexism and gender stereotyping in print and electronic ads, although evident in the public realm in Canada in the 1970s, would become more prominent in the 1980s and early 1990s.[82] Yet, given the increased media attention to gender stereotypes and inequality during the 1970s, and rising education, incomes, and workforce participation rates for women, the links between gender and advertising in general did surface occasionally. Feminism's reactions to the issue of alcohol advertising revealed the movement's internal tensions. On the one hand, there was anxiety and outright hostility towards ads that depicted women in traditional situations or exploited them sexually; on the other, the women's movement demanded that women be treated as citizen consumers. *Ms.*, a feminist magazine published in the United States, did convince a number of wine and spirits advertisers that women were a worthwhile advertising audience, but as Gloria Steinem notes, brewers avoided the publication in its first eight years.[83]

Academic research was examining the degree to which mainstream advertising played on, and reinforced, gender stereotypes. Two American academics, Hawkins and Pinegree, engaged in pioneering research on the issue in the mid-1970s, based on television and prominent magazines such as *Time* and *Newsweek*, which had a large readership in Canada. They developed a typology of gender imagery in advertising; level one depicted women as "sex objects"; level five, as "individuals." They found that most mainstream U.S. magazines portrayed women at level one or level two, traditional stereotypical roles. One example would be a 1970 *Newsweek* ad that depicted a man and woman on a snowmobile, with the man driving. The slogan, for Canadian Club whisky, urged the man to make the woman "earn" her CC by enduring this rugged sporting experience. Dewar's, a spirits manufacturer, was an exception in that it portrayed men and women as equals (level four). The general message of mainstream advertising in mid-decade America, especially on television where most ads were level two, was that women's place in society was limited. Beer commercials, for example, featured "strong, robust men."[84]

Stereotypical male gender roles, a traditional tool for marketing beer, were recognized by addictions experts as a social norm legitimating harmful levels of consumption. In the mid-1970s, Canada's Department of Health and Welfare and Ontario's Addiction Research Foundation cooperated on the Dialogue on Drinking project, an attempt to raise awareness at the individual and community levels about alcohol abuse. In an age supposedly more concerned about definitions of femininity, Dialogue on Drinking questioned the contributions of masculinity to alcohol problems. A 1977 commentary explained that television, magazine advertisements, and society in general expected men to drink: "the macho image" represented a "real 'he man'" as a "hard drinking hero."[85] Although understated, spirits ads in *Maclean's* had continued to associate drinking rum, vodka, gin, and whisky with healthy, outdoor activities and romantic success. One sign of the concerns of the next decade came in 1979, when the federal government appointed a committee to monitor sexism in radio and television commercials in general.[86]

Conclusion

What Mariana Valverde calls "enlightened hedonism," moderate social drinking in the post-1945 period, took place primarily not in beer parlours, cocktail lounges, or Legion halls, but in the home, and the idealized home was in the suburbs.[87] Advertisers, constrained by state regulation, associated a controversial product with non-threatening situations and non-threatening bodies, at the same time attempting to cater largely to middle-class desires. The depiction of the body, therefore, indicated the tension between social ideals and social anxieties. These anxieties, articulated via the media and experts, could counter the general trend towards liberalization, as evident in the early 1970s.[88] Most print alcohol ads produced in Canada prior to the 1970s focused on the male drinker – usually by depicting drawings or photos of men in situations associating drinking with camaraderie, masculinity, relaxation, escape, and enjoyment.[89] On occasion, female figures, as with automobile ads, were employed to attract the attention of male consumers, but usually not in an overtly sexual way. This began to change in late 1960s, as evident in influential U.S. publications such as *Life*, as advertisers consciously appealed to young and/or unmarried consumers, or to older consumers who aspired to be part of the "Mustang generation."[90] Ads for spirits and wine commonly displayed sophisticated, relaxed, mixed-gender socializing, with hints, by the late 1960s, of the "swinging" singles lifestyle. Beer, although more a drink of the masses, was also marketed to middle-class, suburban couples. These domesticated bodies, also portrayed enjoying products in catalogues and newspaper advertisements for national retail chains such as Eaton's and Canadian Tire, epitomized consumer society. Yet, in most beer ads, the man was the one suggesting, offering, or holding the glass or bottle; advertisers were, and remain, concerned not to depict beer as a "woman's" product.[91] The bodies depicted were not only respectable, but also mature. Men in their thirties and forties wearing ties, dress shirts, and sports jackets seem a far cry from the casually dressed young males depicted in the frivolous beer commercials of the 1980s and 1990s. Certain brewers also consciously appealed to working-class male drinkers by depicting blue-collar bodies. The general assumption, however, was that drinkers were moderate, knew how to enjoy themselves and entertain, and belonged to the middle class. As consumer organizations and regulators complained in the 1970s, the bodies depicted in alcohol ads invariably were not only class specific, but also White. This was part of a larger problem of exclusion in Canadian advertising. In spirits advertising, the world consisted of men and couples, with the occasional female model thrown in for "sex appeal." When women were depicted alone or in pairs or small same-sex groups in wine ads in the 1950s, invariably, it was in the context of being homemakers or hostesses. As more women entered the workforce in the 1960s, and their public drinking became more socially acceptable, they began to be given equal billing in wine ads.

Advertisers were not setting out to "create culture," but to sell their products in a manner that did not offend the general public nor run afoul of regulators. The images and messages described above were all examples of what advertisers call market segmentation. Many of them were based on gender stereotypes and anxieties, but they also announced impending social change. The backlash against lifestyle beer commercials in the electronic media in the 1970s affected the print media, which were declining in importance. The relative absence in the 1970s of female –and male – bodies from English Canada's premiere middle-class magazine, *Maclean's*, indicates continuing anxieties associated with linking alcohol to the human form.

Notes

The authors wish to recognize the assistance of research assistants Jordan Stanley and Nicole Wilson.

1 All in this volume.

2 The popular Canadian version of *Readers' Digest*, published in Quebec, carried alcohol ads, unlike its influential American counterpart. See *Wall Street Journal*, 15 Mar. 1956, 1.

3 Michael Messner, *Out of Play: Critical Essays on Gender and Sport* (Albany, SUNY Press, 2007).

4 Penny Tinkler and Cheryl Krasnick Warsh, "Feminine Modernity in Interwar Britain and North America: Corsets, Cars, and Cigarettes," *Journal of Women's History* 20, no. 3 (2008), 113–43.

5 For appeals to masculine values in other marketing campaigns, see Michael E. Starr, "The Marlboro Man: Cigarette Smoking and Masculinity in America," *Journal of Popular Culture* 17, no. 4 (1984), 45–57.

6 Christine Lubinski, "Are We Addicted to Alcohol Advertising?" *Health* 20, no. 20 (2000), http://www.health20-20.org/article/23/for-your-information/alcohol-drug-abuse/are-we-addicted-to-alcohol-advertising

7 George MacAdam, "Quebec's Temperate Law Solving the Liquor Question," *New York Times*, 30 Apr. 1922. Overviews of Canada's experience with alcohol include Reginald G. Smart and Alan C. Ogborne, *Northern Spirits: A Social History of Alcohol in Canada* (Toronto: Addiction Research Foundation, 1996), and Craig Heron, *Booze, A Distilled History* (Toronto: Between the Lines, 2003).

8 Cheryl Krasnick Warsh, "Advertising Regulations (Canada)," in *Alcohol and Temperance in Modern History: An International Encyclopedia*, vol. 1, ed. Jack S. Blocker, Jr., David M. Fahey, and Ian Tyrell (Santa Barbara: CA, ABC-CLIO, 2003), 6–7.

9 Toronto *Globe*, 2 Sept. 1907. Saint John *Daily Telegraph* 1914: 4 May, 7; 6 May, 3; 27 May, 7.

10 James Playsted Wood, *The Story of Advertising* (New York, Ronald, 1958), 488–9. See Cheryl Krasnick Warsh, "Smoke and Mirrors, Gender Representation in North American Tobacco and Alcohol Advertisements before 1950," *Histoire Sociale/Social History* 31, no. 62 (1998), 187.

11 Otis Pease, *The Responsibilities of American Advertising: Private Control and Public Influence, 1920–1940* (New Haven, CT: Yale University Press, 1958), 183.

12 Saint John *Daily Sun*, 11 Sept. 1909, 3. Saint John *Telegraph*, 15 Sept. 1911, 7; 14 June 1912, 5; 9 Sept. 1913, 2; 18 May 1914, 3.

13 Montreal *Gazette*, 1 July 1929; 2 July 1931, 16. See also Craig Heron, "The Boys and Their Booze: Masculinities and Public Drinking in Working-Class Hamilton, 1890–1946," *Canadian Historical Review* 86, no. 3 (2005), 411–52.

14 *Globe and Mail*, 20 May 1937, 12; 26 Sept. 1956, 8.

15 *Saturday Night* [*SN*], 9 June 1934, 5.

16 Toronto *Globe,* 9 Feb. 1935, 4; 24 Oct. 1935, 11.

17 Toronto *Globe,* 12 Aug. 1935, 1.

18 Saint John *Evening Times Globe,* 17 June 1975, 30. Michael R, Marrus, *Samuel Bronfman: The Life and Times of Seagram's Mr. Sam* (London: Brandeis University Press, 1991), 195, 231.

19 *Globe and Mail,* 10 May 1952, 11. Of course, American state governments, as alcohol producers and the advertising industry repeatedly complained, also maintained a patchwork of advertising controls. *Washington Post,* 29 Sept. 1963, E9.

20 *Globe and Mail,* 27 Aug. 1953, 10.

21 Montreal *Gazette,* 3 Dec. 1931, 13; 6 May 1932, 4; 2 Feb. 1938, 3.

22 Montreal *Gazette,* 1 May 1933, 15; 3 Aug. 1936; 2 Jan. 1939, 12.

23 *New York Times,* 17 Dec. 1942, 31. Saint John *Evening Times Globe,* 1 Apr. 1944, 2.

24 Montreal *Gazette,* 10 Feb. 1944, 6; 5 May 1945, 3. *Globe and Mail,* 15 Feb. 1945, 3.

25 Montreal *Gazette,* 1 Apr. 1940, 5; 2 May 1940, 2; 4 Aug. 1941, 16; 5 Jan. 1943, 7. *SN,* 1944: 22 Apr., 24; *SN,* 3 June, 19; 6 May, 27; 17 June, 27; 29 July, 31.

26 *SN,* 1944: 22 Apr., 24; 23 Dec., 22; 9 Sept., 17; 24 June, 40.

27 *SN,* 15 Jan. 1944, 13.

28 *SN,* 15 Apr. 1944, 16; 12 Aug. 1944, 36; 2 Sept. 1944, 31; 8 Nov. 1949, 1.

29 *Globe and Mail,* 2 Apr. 1947, 8; 8 July 1949, 4; 3 Mar. 1961, 4.

30 *SN,* 1954: 2 Jan., 20; 9 Jan., 26; 23 Jan., 9; 30 Jan., 26; 6 Feb., 9; 20 Feb., 10–11.

31 *SN,* 1954: 30 Oct., 15; 16 Oct., 17; 11 Dec., 25.

32 *SN,* 20 Feb. 1954, 20.

33 *SN,* 1954: 23 Oct. 23; 10 July, 14; 11 Dec. 28.

34 *SN,* 1954: 15 May, 27; 2 Oct., 16. *Globe and Mail,* 1 June 1962, 3.

35 *SN,* 1954: 23 Jan., 16; 24 Apr., 12.

36 *SN,* 15 Oct. 1947, 28; 30 Jan. 1954, 27; 10 Apr. 1954, 20.

37 *SN,* 13 Feb. 1954, 28.

38 *Globe and Mail,* 31 Mar. 1965, B01.

39 Ibid. Montreal *Gazette,* 13 Aug. 1966, 3. *Globe and Mail,* 27 Jan. 1968, 11.

40 Victoria *Advocate,* 18 May 1964, 5. *Globe and Mail,* 5 May 1964, B02.

41 *Globe and Mail,* 3 Oct. 1950, 5; 21 Sept. 1955, 5. Ottawa *Citizen,* 7 June 1963, 8.

42 Montreal *Gazette,* 16 June 1984, 61.

43 British Columbia, *Report of the British Columbia Liquor Inquiry Commission* (Victoria, B.C.: Queen's Printer, 1970), 10. See also, Archives of Ontario (AO), RG 31-1, Box 29, George Kitchin to John C. Clement, 24 Nov. 1972.

44 *New York Times*, 11 Feb. 1954, 1.

45 *Globe and Mail*, 21 July 1945, 4.

46 *Globe and Mail*, 2 Apr. 1947, 15.

47 *New York Times*, 18 Oct. 1963, 63. Addiction Research Foundation, *Task Force Report: The Treatment of Alcoholics, An Ontario Perspective* (Toronto: ARF, 1978), 131–2.

48 *Life*, 59, no. 1(2) (1965), R8.

49 *Time*, 24 Jan. 1964, 73.

50 *Time*, 1964: 7 Feb., 96; 14 Feb., 101; 21 Feb., 6.

51 *Maclean's*, 18 Jan. 1958, 4; 2 Jan. 1960, 49; 9 Apr. 1960, 71.

52 *Time*, 1964: 13 Apr., 113; 13 Mar., 68; 7 Aug., 38.

53 *SN*, 28 May 1955, 64; *Maclean's*, 23 Apr. 1960, 1.

54 *SN*, 29 Mar. 1958, 38. *Maclean's*, 15 Mar. 1958, 48; 23 Apr. 1960, 62. Seagram's, *The Spirit of Hospitality: A Guide to Successful Entertaining* (Montreal: Joseph E. Seagram's and Sons, 1973).

55 *Time*, 1964: 21 Feb., 97; 11 Sept., 114; 18 Dec., B7; 28 Aug., 45. Paul Rutherford, *A World Made Sexy: From Freud to Madonna* (Toronto: University of Toronto Press, 2007), chapter 3.

56 *Wall Street Journal*, 23 Feb.1967, 1, 11.

57 *Maclean's*, 16 Oct 1965, 34.

58 *Maclean's*, Sept. 1970, 7.

59 Mark Pendergast, *For God, Country and Coca-Cola: The Unauthorized History of the Great American Soft Drink and the Company That Makes It* (Toronto: Collier, 1994), 164.

60 Montreal *Gazette*, 28 July 1983, 40. Toronto *Star*, 24 Dec. 1985, A1. *Globe and Mail*, 11 Nov. 1977, 4. *Report of the Ministerial Committee on Liquor Control* (Winnipeg: Government of Manitoba, 1981), 2.

61 Thomas Babor et al., *Alcohol: No Ordinary Commodity* (Toronto: Oxford Medical Publications, 2003), 42–3.

62 *New York Times*, 3 Feb. 1971. *Globe and Mail*, 27 Sept. 1977, B05. *SN*, 92 (1977). *Maclean's*, 92 (1979). *New York Times*, 21 Mar. 1982. Ontario, Advisory Committee on Liquor Regulation, *Report of the Advisory Committee on Liquor Regulation* (Toronto, ON: Queen's Printer, 1987), 69.

63 *Maclean's*, Sept. 1970, 51. See also *Maclean's*, Jan. 1975, 47, 51; and July 1975, 9.

64 Ottawa *Citizen*, 11 Sept. 1963, 1.

65 Debra Scoffield, *Public Policy and Alcohol Consumption in the Maritime Provinces* (Halifax: Atlantic Provinces Economic Council, 1976), 35.

66 *Report of the Ministerial Committee on Liquor Control*, 14. *Globe and Mail*, 13 Sept. 1975, 8.

67 Scoffield, *Public Policy*, 35–6. For self-regulation see, AO, RG 31-1, Box 39, File 39, Ontario Brewers' Code of Ethics, 1973.

68 *Globe and Mail*, 3 Apr. 1971, 10. Montreal *Gazette*, 27 Sept. 1974, 20.

69 Rob Gerssbeck, "Near Death Experience," *Marketing*, 11 Aug. 2008. *New York Times*, 26 May 1985, E16.

70 Montreal *Gazette*, 9 Dec. 1977, 10.

71 Ottawa *Citizen*, 5 Oct. 1974, 30; 31 May 1978, 1.

72 *Globe and Mail*, 18 Jan. 1975, B01.

73 MACLC, MLCC, Exhibit D, 1980.

74 *Report of the Ministerial Committee on Liquor Control*, 143–4. *Globe and Mail*, 13 July 1977, 9.

75 Montreal *Gazette*, 28 July 1983, 40.

76 Fredericton *Gleaner*, 23 July 1981, 2.

77 Toronto *Star*, 15 Sept. 1985, B2. Ontario, Advisory Committee on Liquor Regulation, *Report of the Advisory Committee*, 8–9, 14.

78 Brewers Association of Canada, *Perspectives on Beer in Canada* (Ottawa: BAC, 1979).

79 *Globe and Mail*, 27 Sept. 1977. Observations of the Manitoba Liquor Control Commission, submitted to the Ministerial Advisory Committee on Liquor Control, 14 May 1980.

80 Babor et al., *Alcohol: No Ordinary Commodity*, 173–4, 182–3. A.C. Ogborne and R.G. Smart, "Will Restrictions on Advertising Reduce Alcohol Consumption?" *British Journal of Addictions*, 75, no. 3 (1980), 293–6. AO, RG 31-01, Ministry of Consumer and Corporate Affairs, Box, 29/2 memo, 5 June 1972.

81 *Report of the Ministerial Committee on Liquor Control*, 15, 150–1. See also Reginald G. Smart, "The New Drinkers – Teenage Use and Abuse of Alcohol," *Addictions* 23 (Spring 1971), 21; *Globe and Mail, Report on Business*, 23 Nov. 1985, B2; Smart and Ogborne, *Northern Spirits*, 163–7.

82 Montreal *Gazette*, 16 June 1984, 61. Schenectady *Daily Gazette*, 15 Apr. 1991, 1. *Toronto Star*, 27 June 1990, A2.

83 Gloria Steinem, "Sex, Lies and Advertising," *Ms. Magazine*, July/August, 1990, 18–28.

84 *Milwaukee Journal*, 13 Apr. 1976, 16. *Newsweek*, 5 Jan.1970, 85. For "avoiding the feminine" in marketing, see Diane Barthel, *Putting on Appearances, Gender and Advertising* (Philadelphia, PA: Temple University Press, 1988), 175.

85 *Globe and Mail*, 29 Oct. 1977.

86 Gerssbeck, "Near Death Experience." *Globe and Mail*, 7 May 1990, B04. For example, see *Maclean's*, Jan.–Dec. 1975.

87 Mariana Valverde, *Diseases of the Will: Alcohol and the Dilemmas of Freedom* (Cambridge: Cambridge University Press, 1998).

88 This theme is prominent in the chapter by Smith and Wakewich, this volume.

89 *New York Times*, 26 May 1985, E16.

90 *Wall Street Journal*, 23 Feb. 1967, 1.

91 Barthel, *Putting on Appearances*, 8–9.

10 Nudity as Embodied Citizenship and Spectacle: Pageants at Canada's Nudist Clubs, 1949–1975

MARY-ANN SHANTZ

Over the past fifteen years, the seemingly trivial beauty contest has become the subject of academic study. Scholars have highlighted how the beauty pageant has served as a platform for the staging of dominant cultural ideals and norms of femininity, race, and sexuality. But they have also demonstrated how beauty contests, "by choosing an individual whose deportment, appearance, and style embodies the values and goals of a nation, locality, or group, expose these same values and goals to interpretation and challenge."[1] Building on both of these currents of analysis, I explore how, after the Second World War, nudist clubs and organizations embraced the medium of the pageant to embody the nudist philosophy and represent it to the Canadian public. In staging their own versions of the beauty contest, an institution that reached its height of popularity during this period, nudists proclaimed both their distinctiveness from, and their likeness to, mainstream Canadian culture.[2] Nudist pageants contested conventional attitudes towards nudity by promoting the practice of nudism and, more critically, by inviting audience members to gaze upon nude bodies and by imbuing the act with positive potential. At the same time, the staging of a pageant enabled nudists to highlight what they shared in common with their fellow Canadians, notably their acceptance of mainstream gender and sexual norms and their embrace of pleasurable leisure pursuits.

Organized nudism has its roots in industrializing Germany at the turn of the twentieth century, when nudism developed as one strand of a broad "life reform" movement aimed at moderating the impact of polluted cities, poor working conditions, and overcrowded housing on the health of the German people. German nudism was ideologically diverse, with middle- and working-class currents, and included gymnastics programs, youth hiking groups, and nudist recreational parks. The core message of nudism was that nudity was a natural state of being, that all parts of the body were pure and wholesome, and that social nudity offered a means to achieve physical, mental, and moral health and fitness. Through the renewal of the individual citizen, nudism promised to form the basis of a healthier, stronger nation.[3]

During the interwar period, nudism spread to France, England, and the United States. Canada's oldest nudist club, the Van Tan Club, was formed in Vancouver in 1939. Nudism established a firm foothold in Canada only after the Second World War as European immigrants with nudist experience and Canadian war veterans, who had encountered nudist magazines and clubs while serving overseas, provided an influx of leaders and members to the fledgling Canadian movement.[4] By 1960, there were about twenty nudist clubs operating in Canada, with memberships ranging from ten at the smallest to well over a hundred at the largest.[5] Canadian nudism was concentrated in southwestern Ontario and the greater Vancouver area, but clubs were active in cities across the country. Nudist camps were not utopian places of residence or "colonies" – a common misnomer – but places for weekend and summer retreat, functioning as nudist alternatives to modern public beaches and campgrounds.

A central aim of the international nudist movement was to achieve "a healthy mind in a healthy body." As Ruth Barcan explains, "In its medical underpinnings, nudism overlapped with heliotherapy, or suncure, which enjoyed some popularity in Europe at the beginning of the twentieth century ... Heliotherapists were concerned about modern city-dwellers' lack of access to sunlight and fresh air – caused by the wearing of clothing and the soot-choked skies of industrial cities." Notable advocates of heliotherapy included Dr. Auguste Rollier and British physician Caleb Saleeby. Rollier established a world-renowned heliotherapy centre in Leysin, Switzerland, in 1903, where he used nude sunbathing to treat diseases such as tuberculosis and rickets. Saleeby founded the English Sunlight League, in the 1920s, to agitate for the reduction of coal pollution and champion urban planning that would maximize the presence of sunlight. Early nudist writers similarly extolled the health-giving effects of the sun and fresh air and endorsed nude sunbathing as the way to obtain optimum benefit.[6]

Nudism and Postwar Canada

Postwar Canadian nudists emphasized their movement's benefits to mental, more than physical, health. In the first half of the twentieth century,

Western society experienced a sharp decline in mortality rates through measures such as improved sanitation and the development and availability of antibiotics and vaccines to treat and prevent infectious disease. At the same time, the new field of psychology carried increasing social authority. In this context, nudism was cast as the solution to social problems such as juvenile delinquency and mental illness, social problems nudists believed to be rooted in repressive cultural attitudes towards nudity.[7] They argued that clothing should not be worn out of a sense of bodily shame based on "outdated" social taboos, and they offered nudism as the antidote to the shame and inhibitions engrained by society. Canadian nudists viewed their movement as a means, however unconventional, of realizing the widely shared objective of creating healthy, well-adjusted citizens. In contrast to the early German movement, Canadian nudists placed far less emphasis on the movement's ability to reform the physical body and instead understood nudism as an embodied practice with the power to reform self-identity and social relationships.

A pageant to select a nudist king, queen, and often, prince and princess, was a highlight of the summer season at Canadian nudist clubs. Canadians followed the lead of English and American nudists in incorporating pageants into their local and national gatherings, and the election of a "royal family" became a staple of the Canadian movement early in its history.[8] A national nudist body, the Canadian Sunbathing Association (CSA), was founded in 1947, drawing together recently formed clubs and independent nudists from across the country, and the first CSA king and queen were selected at the organization's third annual convention held in British Columbia, in 1949.[9] The pageant, along with business meetings and a volleyball tournament, became a regular feature at Canadian nudist conventions each summer. The Eastern and Western Canadian regional conferences often selected royal families of their own, and Canadians in attendance at the conventions of the American Sunbathing Association also routinely participated as pageant contestants. In addition, individual clubs from British Columbia to Quebec ran contests to bestow an array of titles on club members including May Queen, Nudist Mother of the Year, and Miss/Mrs. and Mr. honorary club name-bearers.[10] While generally not taken overly seriously by the nudists themselves, nudist pageants were, nevertheless, promoted as a visual representation of the nudist philosophy that provided positive publicity for the movement and encouraged Canadians to see the body in a new light. These events took place on nudist club property and were not open to the public; however, members of the press were invited to cover the pageants and frequently did. As a result, the pageants became a means of introducing the wider public to the nudist movement within Canada.

I approach nudist pageants as bodily performances. My analysis follows Belgian historian Evert Peeters in positing that the "perception of the body and sexuality within nudist writing did not simply reflect a discursive message; rather, the physical techniques of nudism became a means of cultural criticism."[11] Like Peeters, I am influenced by Judith Butler's concept of performativity, defined as the construction of an identity through the very acts that affirm it as natural. For Butler, performativity carries both a regulatory effect and transgressive potential. Despite the apparently all-encompassing nature of hegemonic identities, Butler locates weakness in the necessity of repetition to their maintenance. She observes, "That this reiteration is necessary is a sign that materialization is never quite complete, that bodies never quite comply with the norms by which their materialization is impelled. Indeed, it is the instabilities, the possibilities for rematerialization, opened up by this process that mark one domain in which the force of the regulatory law can be turned against itself to spawn rearticulations that call into question the hegemonic force of that very regulatory law."[12] Butler's ideas illuminate the operation of cultural norms and taboos surrounding nudity within postwar Canadian society as well as nudist resistance to them by highlighting the possibility for disruption or resignification. This is in the same vein as what Michel de Certeau called "the practice of everyday life" by which social groups or individuals "make innumerable and infinitesimal transformations of and within the dominant cultural economy in order to adapt it to their own interests and their own rules."[13] Viewed through this lens, pageants offered a stage on which contestants both constructed and embodied nudist identities and represented these identities to the broader Canadian public.

Nudist Pageants, Spectacle, and Criteria

Nudist pageants were hypothetically based on a similar set of criteria, which included "all-over tan," "general good health" or attractiveness, and personality and "contribution to nudism."[14] Since winners were generally determined by audience applause, judging standards were admittedly flexible and relaxed. Rather than acting as objective measures by which the field of participants was judged, the pageant criteria served to underscore central tenets of the nudist philosophy. An "all-over tan" served as a badge of nudist membership, in contrast to the tan lines that marked non-nudists and new club members. More importantly, it represented physical evidence of contestants' commitment to nudism through exposure of their entire bodies to the sun and air. It was, in the words of one Canadian nudist, "nature's mark of goodness and health" – physical *and* mental health, since the act of social nudity signalled a wholesome attitude towards one's own body and those of other members.[15] For these reasons, nudists saw themselves as embodying citizenship, and believed it was individuals such as the pageant contestants who would be "the pioneers of a happier, healthier and cleaner generation."[16]

In addition to its philosophical import, nudists viewed a full-body tan as aesthetically pleasing, and overall physical appearance was also a criterion in the judging of nudist pageant contestants. This factor was alternately described as "general good health," physical fitness, or attractiveness. Sander Gilman convincingly argued "the equation of beauty with health and ugliness with illness is fundamental in the Western understanding of the body."[17] Nudists were, therefore, in no way exceptional in correlating beauty with physical health. But beyond valuing physical attractiveness as material evidence of the beneficial impact of nudism on bodily well-being, the nudist philosophy affirmed aesthetic appreciation of the body in its own right. Nudist writer and club leader Ray Connett reflected, "We all enjoy a pretty face, a lovely tan, and a handsome figure, be it male or female."[18] Nina Morris suggests that sensory perception held a prominent place within nudist thought and practice.[19] The pageant criterion of physical appearance embraced the visual pleasure to be derived from looking at the body, a pleasure that nudists defined as "natural" rather than sexual in character. This constituted the nudist gaze, a way of viewing the body that affirmed embodiment as an important and positive aspect of being human but that displaced sexuality from the centre to the periphery of this experience. Scholars of visuality have identified a nineteenth-century reconceptualization of sight from something mechanical and objective to something corporeal and unstable. Nudist pageants emerged from the latter understanding, and provide a fitting case study of what Lianne McTavish has called "localized visual practices and forms of resistance to dominant modes of looking." Like the members of the New Brunswick Natural History Society studied by McTavish, nudists believed that "learning to see properly could have a positive moral effect on society."[20] Nudists rejected cultural concerns about the corrupting potential of looking at nude bodies, countering that it was beneficial to do so as a means of loosening the hold of social taboos that cast nudity as shameful, exhibitionist, or sinful.[21] When approached in the proper way, they believed, gazing upon nude bodies promoted a healthy body image and a well-adjusted (meaning hetero-) sexual identity.

Personality or personal contribution to nudism through service to the club or organization constituted the third area on which nudist pageant participants were evaluated. This criterion worked to democratize the pageant to a certain extent and, particularly in the local club contests, encouraged participation by members representing a range of ages, shapes, and sizes. In the 1957 competition for title of Miss/Mrs. Sun Valley Gardens, a young woman and her mother both received thirty-six votes from club members. The club newsletter reported that the title was awarded after the mother declined it in favour of her daughter.[22] Rose, a Calgary Sunny Chinooks Club member who was a pageant participant in the 1970s, recalled, "The King and Queen had to be over eighteen, and often the queen had pretty saggy boobs and a flabby tummy. All contestants had to answer questions. I don't remember what the questions were, but often they had to do with the role that nudism played in their life."[23] Rose insisted that "the pageants were not beauty contests," echoing a sentiment expressed by officials of a wide range of pageants including the Miss Canada and Miss America Pageants. As Patrizia Gentile explains, "This oft-repeated phrase sought to recast beauty contests as respectable and viable enterprises for women. Insisting that beauty contests were not really *beauty* contests became a crucial strategy in maintaining a hold on the values of chastity and virtue even as the last vestiges of the Victorian era disappeared."[24] Rose inferred that the questioning of contestants about the role of nudism in their lives, their contributions to their club or the nudist cause, distinguished nudist pageants from conventional beauty contests by conveying the sense that the contest was about more than appearance. It also functioned to distinguish those participants who would be the best ambassadors for nudism, as pageant winners often became the focus of press coverage, especially in the case of the woman chosen as queen.

Nudist Pageants: Celebrations of the Nude Body or Profit Makers?

Not everyone was as convinced as Rose that the pageants were anything more than superficial beauty contests, and they were not without controversy in Canadian nudist circles. In 1956, the Eastern Division of the Canadian Sunbathing Association declared that it was not in favour of the election of a royal family and returned the Bowman Trophy for

CSA Queen to the Western Canadian Division. In spite of their apparent opposition, the Eastern Division did not avoid contests altogether, and replaced the royal pageant with the election of a Mr. and Miss/Mrs. Suntan.[25] The change was presumably intended to minimize a focus on physical attractiveness in favour of the more principled "all-over tan" criterion. But, in spite of the semantic distinction, appearance was quite evidently still a factor. And the change appears to have been short-lived. By 1966, nudist royalty pageants were again noted as a main feature of the Eastern Division of the Canadian Sunbathing Association (ECSA) Convention.[26] Marcus Meed, one of the first presidents of the CSA and the leader of the New Brunswick club, the Maritans, expressed his philosophical opposition to nudist pageants in his club newsletter. Meed reported favourably that New Zealand nudists did not hold pageants, referencing the editor of the *New Zealand Naturist* magazine, who reportedly stated that such contests "were inconsistent with New Zealand naturism's acceptance of all, irrespective of looks." To which Meed responded, "Well friends, some of us in Canada feel much the same way."[27]

While some viewed the pageants held at Canada's nudist clubs as superficial, organizers of the Miss Nude World Contest made innovations to the beauty pageant format in order to place greater emphasis on physical appearance. Founded in 1970, at the Four Seasons Nature Park, a nudist club located between Guelph and Hamilton, Ontario, the Miss Nude World Pageant became a popular event that the club hosted each summer for the next six years. As the name suggests, it featured only female contestants, and tickets to the two-day event were sold to the public.[28] According to Four Seasons owner and Miss Nude World Contest producer Lisa Stein, "This is the most honest beauty contest there is. If you are beautiful in the nude then you are beautiful."[29] Her reasoning was consistent with the attitude expressed by California nudist club owner Mel Hocker, in a published rant against conventional pageants:

> In my opinion there is only one way to hold a beauty contest. Require the contestants to appear in the nude, where they can naturally and normally display themselves with no girdle bathing suits, nor built-in foam rubber creations to deceive the onlookers. Many a doll would fall flat on her face without the archaic bathing suit to build her up ... an event which began with the selection of the gal with the most gorgeous figure, the Atlantic City Miss America Pageant, has deteriorated into a "talent" contest. Today's winners must be so diversified as to be able to make music on a tissue paper comb, play pattie-cake, operate a yo-yo, or compete in such mundane

events as wearing formal gowns correctly. All this down-grades the contest into one which qualifies any mis-shapen miss who happens to have a good publicity agent.[30]

Not mincing any words, Hocker suggested that only a beauty contest conducted in the nude, without a talent portion to the competition, would offer a "true" assessment of beauty. And this is what the Miss Nude World Contest set out to provide.

In a departure from the nudist royalty pageants in which men, women, and children competed, the Miss Nude World Contest was open only to female contestants, single or married, between the ages of eighteen and thirty. Tickets were sold to the public, but contest rules required that pageant participants be members of a nudist club. This requirement was easily fulfilled: the winner of the 1974 Miss Nude World Contest revealed to a CBC radio interviewer that she had joined a nudist club for the first time the day before the pageant began.[31] The Miss Nude World Contest was not the first of its kind – between 1965 and 1969 clubs in California, Indiana, and Florida had hosted similar events – but it was a first for Canada, and it quickly became the pre-eminent "Miss Nude" event, to which winners of Miss Nude contests hosted by several clubs in Canada and the United States advanced.[32]

In contrast to the informal manner in which the nudist royalty pageants were judged based on the applause of their fellow nudists, Miss Nude World contestants were judged by a panel comprised of local community members and minor celebrities, including business owners and members of the media. The women were interviewed in private by the judges, and then competed on stage in three events, progressively revealing more skin as they transitioned from evening gown, to bathing suit, to the nude portion of the contest. There was no talent portion to the competition. Pageant director Carl Alkerton explained, "Even the simplest gesture in the nude could be misconstrued by the vice squad as … of a suggestive or obscene nature."[33] But a talent portion would also have gone against the grain of a contest intended to offer "the ultimate in beauty contests."[34] The three criteria on which Miss Nude World participants were evaluated were personality, poise, and appearance. Judges were supplied with a points system for scoring. Personality, which could be awarded a possible total of fifteen points, was subdivided into categories consisting of character, conversation, and manner. This was primarily assessed in the contestant's private interview with the judges, and was intended to ensure that the winner would be a suitable representative for the pageant. Poise, also worth a total of fifteen points, was based on walk, posture, and composure. Appearance, worth twenty-five points, was broken down into the following five subdivisions: bathing suit, face and hair, hips and legs, bust, and coloration or tan. Each subdivision was judged on a scale from one to five, in which three was considered "average," while five was "superior," and one was "poor." The 1976 Contest Rules informed contestants that they would "be judged on natural beauty. Natural make-up will be accepted. No breast surgery. No wigs. No shaved pubic area. No artificial means can be used to simulate a tan … White high heel pumps or sandals are preferred."[35] Jewellery was worn at the participants' discretion.

Both the Miss Nude World Contest and the nudist royalty pageants were intended to provide publicity to the nudist movement. In the early 1950s, it became CSA policy that all pageant contestants permit their pictures and their names to be printed in nudist and mainstream publications. The royalty pageants generally took place during a club's Open House weekend or at a convention, events that were regularly covered by the press. The nudist pageant was a favourite subject for journalists. One reporter dubbed it "a beauty contest to end all beauty contests," and declared, "If there's a reporter … who wouldn't like to watch a beauty contest at a nudist camp there's something the matter with that reporter."[36] Nudist pageants became a gateway for media coverage of Canadian nudism more broadly, raising public awareness of the movement.

Lisa Stein conceived the Miss Nude World Contest as a source of publicity for her club. In a 1974 radio interview, she offered the following explanation of the contest's origins: "to get a new idea across you have to try and sell it. But how do you sell it? You sell any new product only with a gimmick! So we were thinking, what would the media pick up? What is a good gimmick for, for us to use? We had a new club, we had an indoor pool, we had certain facilities, and uh, we had no people. And we didn't want people from the other clubs, we wanted new people to become interested. So here it comes, the Miss Nude World Contest."[37]

The event provided publicity both through the spectators it drew and the media coverage it attracted. The contest was open to the public, and attendance figures suggest that the event succeeded in drawing a crowd. The 1971 Miss Nude World Contest drew approximately three thousand spectators. Reportedly, over five thousand people were turned away from the 1972 event after the venue reached capacity: "According to a police spokesman, the highway leading past the Four Seasons was backed up some four to six miles with traffic waiting to gain admission to the Four

Seasons."[38] In the days leading up to the contest, organizers took local contestants on a promotional circuit around southern Ontario that included press conferences and radio and television interviews.[39] In addition, reporters annually descended on the Four Seasons on the July weekend when the contest took place. Pageant director Carl Alkerton estimated that in its first three years the Miss Nude World Contest had resulted in $500,000 worth of free publicity for the club and for nudism, although this claim cannot be verified.[40] Regardless of the monetary value of the publicity, the Steins considered the Miss Nude World Contest a public relations triumph, surpassing their expectations. They maintained that the Miss Nude World Contest "promoted more interest in the nudist movement in Canada and the United States than any other event."[41]

While both the nudist royalty pageants and the Miss Nude World Contest were devised as promotional measures, the Miss Nude World Contest was also a commercial enterprise. This was despite Lisa Stein's declaration that hers was "a contest run in good taste ... with no exploitation of the girls, except to promote nudism."[42] The Four Seasons sold admission tickets to the public as well as advertising space in the pageant program. Volunteer labour and solicited prizes from sponsors kept costs at a minimum.[43] The event also claimed new members, and more membership dues, for the Four Seasons. Stein gauged the success of the pageant in financial terms: "Our Miss Nude World Contest the first year was a big success, financially as well as member-wise, which is financially again. We were nine months in operation and we could afford to build an outdoor pool, we could afford to extend our facilities, our shower and toilet facilities." She believed that as a result of the pageant, "we could afford to put here country club facilities, and compete with every country club in the southern Ontario area."[44]

The commercial use of nudity by the Miss Nude World Contest was distasteful to some other nudist club leaders. Contest director Carl Alkerton himself acknowledged that from the outset many nudist club owners regarded the Miss Nude World Contest "with a lot of suspicion as it was felt that a promotion of this nature would have harmful repercussions on the Nudist Recreation Movement."[45] It was clear that nearby Sun Valley Gardens club owner Karl Ruehle had the Four Seasons in mind when he complained that "there are some camps which compete with the others for the most facilities, and have a really country club atmosphere of commercialism, even to the point of exploitation, in some instances."[46] Even Summerset Nature Park owner Ted Lisiecki, in announcing that his club would play host to the first Miss Nude Ontario Contest in 1973, expressed mixed feelings about the idea. In his club newsletter he reflected:

> I know that the biggest percentage of the attending public will be coming to the contest with the idea of looking over the pretty girls on the stage. From my point, I can visualize that some of these visitors will form a different outlook on social nudism, and won't form the idea in their minds that we are exploiting the nude body at all times. One may think that the financial aspect plays the main part to influence us in staging this contest. It is practically true, because like everyone else we need cash to operate the park. This seems to be the only way we can offer the serenity at other times.[47]

Lisiecki seemed barely convinced of his own rationalization for hosting the contest and uncertain that the contest would do more good than harm.

As desired, the nudist royalty pageants and the Miss Nude World Contest generated publicity for the nudist movement, and the latter was also a financially profitable venture for the Four Seasons. But what were the messages these contests conveyed about nudist views of the body? The most obvious feature of these contests, and the reason they captured the attention that they did, was that they put nude bodies on display and encouraged viewers to look. In doing so, nudists underscored their departure from the mainstream by challenging the conventional notion that nudity was inherently obscene.[48] According to Ontario club leader Karl Ruehle:

> The human body is just a body, and whether it is nude or clothed has no influence upon its moral standard ... Most people have no idea what a wonderful work God did. Generally they do not think about it at all unless they are sick and pain forces it to their attention. Did you ever look in the mirror of your bathroom to see your whole body? Did you ever notice those wonderful lines of your limbs and your chest? All the muscles are in the proper place to fulfil their important functions which keep you moving. There is nothing ugly or superfluous. Even your sexual parts have their functions in relation to your entire life and your body ... Their functions are as decent as those of your heart, stomach, or any other organ of your body ... There is nothing evil or disgusting about the sexual organs except in an evil mind.[49]

Nudists frequently contrasted the "wholesomeness" of nudist attitudes to the body with the sexually suggestive display of the body, particularly the female body, in popular culture. Trying to walk a line between being typecast as "prudes" or as "perverts," nudists argued that it was clothing, not nudity, that heightened sexual tension. Reflecting on this point with reference to nudist pageants, one American nudist writer speculated, "To the many witnessing for the first time a contest unhampered with bathing attire, will come the revelation that here, indeed, is a presentation having none of the erotic implications so evident where a portion of the body remains concealed. And to them, future contests, considered 'acceptable by society,' will be viewed with considerable cynicism."[50] German historian George Mosse argues that nationalism and respectability became integrally linked in modern European society, and that control over sexuality was a critical element of this alliance. In particular, modern manliness demanded "freedom from sexual passion, the sublimation of sensuality into leadership of society and the nation."[51] This is precisely what nudists invoked when they extolled the practice of "body freedom," not sexual licence but "freedom from sexual passion" and "perversions." As Ruehle, leader of a large Niagara area nudist club, explained, "We are working for the day when nudity will not be an invitation for sexual exploitation but a challenge for self-control which is the root of all good beginnings."[52]

The philosophy that nudity was natural and not erotic informed both the nudist royalty pageants and the Miss Nude World Contest. However, these contests exploited the social taboo against nudity of which the nudist movement was so critical by making a display of nude bodies for the sake of publicity. In the case of the Miss Nude World Contest, the public ticket sales, the non-nudist judging panel, and the staging of nudity as the culmination of the pageant turned nudity into a spectacle. The judging of various parts of a contestant's physique seemed at odds with nudism's philosophical emphasis on bodily integrity. While contest organizers protested that what they offered was "clean" and "in good taste," and "that the burlesque and erotic have no part in nudism," the message that nudity was "natural" was easily lost in the mix.[53] In a moment of frankness, Lisa Stein admitted that the Miss Nude World Contest "goes against the whole philosophy of nudism, we agree to that. But it has done a job, it has shown people who know nothing about nudism a nudist club, and what kind of people go to a nudist club, and that was the whole idea behind it."[54] The hope was that as they gazed at the Miss Nude World contestants' bodies, audience members would take note of the club setting and all that it had to offer, rather than that they would find their gaze redirected towards their own views and assumptions about nudity.

Like the Miss Nude World Contest, the nudist royalty pageants made a display of nude bodies to arouse public interest in the movement. But the latter provided a different context for the nudity on display, which enabled them to embody the nudist message more successfully. Significantly, the bodies of the contestants and the audience members worked together to perform this task. Contestants' tanned and attractive physiques symbolized physical health, while their uninhibited attitude towards nudity and lack of shame stood as evidence of a healthy mental outlook. Audience members at these pageants were integral to the consistency and effectiveness of this message, in particular, as it was transmitted to visiting journalists. As fellow nudists, many of whom were also nude during the pageant, audience members provided a context in which the contestants' nudity was naturalized, mitigating the potential for it to be interpreted as exhibitionist in nature. Nudist audience members also embodied the nudist philosophy by displaying an appreciation for the contestants' bodies, on the one hand, and no signs of sexual arousal, on the other. In doing so, audience members signalled their conversion to the nudist gaze, providing evidence that nudism could disrupt socialized ways of looking and re-educate people to see the body in a new light.

While both types of nudist contests pushed the bounds of social tolerance for nudity, in other respects, the events worked to affirm nudists' normalcy, in particular, by underscoring their adherence to sexual and gender norms. At a fundamental level, the royalty pageants were about gender, selecting a male as "king" and a woman as "queen." Gender difference and complementarity were an integral aspect of the nudist philosophy. A newsletter for the B.C. Meadowbrook Club declared, "We, more than any other group of people, realize that humans ... come in two varieties, male and female."[55] Nudist promoter and club owner Ray Connett reasoned, "A basic fact of human nature ... is the desire of both men and women to talk to, to see and to engage in various social activities with members of the opposite sex. This does not mean that sex activities have any part or place in a nudist club, but the fact remains that in any activity, nudist or others, man seeks the company of woman, and vice versa. This is ... even more true in a nudist club."[56] Nudists feared being perceived as sexually deviant, and the mixed-sex composition of nudist clubs and the selection of a male king and a female queen at nudist pageants underscored their embrace of normative heterosexuality. It was a strictly regulated heterosexuality, however, lest the public equate nudity in a mixed-sex setting with sexual permissiveness. The first rule of many North American nudist clubs was to "conduct yourself like a gentleman or a lady." There were to be no displays of physical contact between members, including married couples. Men were advised that erections were not acceptable in the club setting and could be avoided through activity and mental discipline. Connett described nudist clubs as having a "Sunday school picnic ... morality," and clubs demanded that people regulate themselves even more carefully than they would in most clothed public contexts.[57] Nudism shared postwar society's veneration of heterosexual marriage, and Canadian nudists hoped to convey that their practice strengthened rather than undermined the institution of marriage.[58]

In different ways, the royalty pageants and the Miss Nude World Contest accepted the culturally dominant treatment of women as objects of gaze, or what Laura Mulvey has termed women's "to-be-looked-at-ness."[59] The Miss Nude World Contest made an overt spectacle of women's bodies. Even though nudist royalty pageants elected both a king and queen, it was the queen who garnered the most attention from nudists and nonnudists alike. The CSA queen was the only pageant winner to receive a trophy, and she was subject to the greatest media scrutiny, something that nudists anticipated and encouraged. Canadian nudist magazine *Sunbathing for Health* columnist Mildred Harris described the reaction of the media covering the 1954 CSA Convention at the Sunny Trails Club in Surrey, B.C., upon their introduction to the past CSA queen: "Our Queen of last year, Arleigh, had an amusing experience on Sunday when reporters and photographers were present from almost every paper, including the press services such as Canadian Press and British United Press. When they found she was last year's Queen they pestered her for some good pictures, in the nude of course. And one particularly aggressive photographer was kidding her about being backward so she said, 'O.K., if you'll join me you can have my picture.' And he did!"[60]

As hoped, this female pageant winner became the attractive face of nudism in the campaign to promote the movement to the public. Gentile has argued that workplace beauty contests worked to mitigate social fears about a loss of femininity that attended women's increased workforce presence in the mid-twentieth century.[61] Her observation translates well into the context of nudist pageants. Given the strong cultural associations between femininity and modesty, nudists were at pains to demonstrate that the practice of nudism did not entail women's rejection of gender norms. Female pageant participants demonstrated that despite exchanging their clothes for the "natural state," nudist women continued to embrace standards of female beauty and a feminine identity. The desire for an attractive physical appearance was constructed as something innate to women, thus rendering the ways women disciplined their bodies to conform to gender norms compatible with nudism. Female nudist pageant contestants played an important role by underscoring the femininity of nudist women.

In addition to affirming sexual and gender norms, nudists hoped that the contests they put on would communicate that the movement was not a fanatical cult but a pleasurable leisure activity pursued by regular Canadians. As Alkerton explained it, Miss Nude World Contest organizers hoped to demonstrate "that people who belong are just like their next-door neighbours."[62] While the royalty pageants stressed the family-friendly respectability of nudism, the Miss Nude World Contest offered a modern take on the movement as being "not a health thing anymore … just another form of recreation."[63] Pageants demonstrated that nudism was "good fun" and that nudists did not take themselves too seriously, that like their fellow Canadians nudists sought pleasure and relaxation in their free time. One Canadian nudist explained:

> a nudist club does not consist solely of deadly serious people, their minds directed exclusively to the job of improving their health, figures and skin pigmentation. They have fun too, and it is this enjoyment, reflected in their faces, freed from obsessions and confusion, which provide them with an outlook on life which many envy. Because they are content and healthy, they are better citizens and their contribution to their country's progress is far greater and more creative in the respective sphere in which they direct their efforts. Being a nudist helps a man to do his job better, and therefore his country is the gainer … Our mission is the improvement of mankind and nations, and we are already well on the road towards our target.[64]

Shirley Tillotson argues that the postwar public recreation movement in Canada was premised on a belief that "democracy was a matter of everyday culture, and that only in leisure were people truly at liberty to practice living as citizens of a free society."[65] From this perspective, nudists embodied citizenship not only through improvements to their physical and mental health, but also by engaging in pleasurable recreation.

Conclusion

A close reading of Canadian nudist pageants reveals that these contests were sites of both social contestation and conformity. They sought to upset mainstream definitions of nudity as inherently obscene or immoral and affirm the body as being more than a sexual object. Nudists cast their lifestyle as a form of embodied citizenship; the practice of nudism offered a path to physical and mental health that would enable individuals to achieve their fullest potential as functioning members of society. They rejected cultural concerns about the corrupting potential of looking at nude bodies, countering that it was beneficial to do so as a means of loosening the hold of social taboos. However, while nudist pageants were purportedly intended to encourage the public to see the body in a new light, the public appeal of these events depended on an exploitation of the taboo nature of nudity and made a spectacle of nude bodies. In doing so, these pageants were as revealing of the tensions within nudism as they were of the contestants on stage.

In other respects, nudist pageants worked to affirm nudists' normalcy. The election of a king and queen in a nudist pageant underscored their commitment to sexual and gender norms and visibly demonstrated that while nudists shed their clothes they did not shed their femininity or masculinity. In addition, the contests were intended to signal that nudists were not fanatics or crusaders, but ordinary people who enjoyed a beauty contest as much as their neighbours. Postwar Canadian nudists employed pageants to differentiate their philosophical approach to nudity from the mainstream public and to assert their position as "ordinary" Canadians.

This essay exposes the cultural negotiations of a group of people who moved back and forth across the bounds of normative categories, pushing the limits of social tolerance for nudity while aspiring to "normalcy" and respectability. As a result, I believe it has implications for the ways the body operated as a site of inclusion *and* exclusion, situating embodiment as an experience of both social regulation and cultural resistance. It is this tension that characterizes nudism's relationship to postwar Canadian society and makes it such a rich area of study. As anthropologist Adeline Masquelier observes, "The body surface ... can simultaneously mediate the 'self' and the 'social' and exclude one from the other. It is precisely this paradoxical potential of the bodily surface to signify inclusion in the community as well as separation or deviation from it that makes it such a powerful vehicle of moral contestation."[66]

Notes

I am grateful to the Federation of Canadian Naturists for providing me access to their archive of records. I also thank the American Nudist Research Library in Kissimmee, Florida, and the volunteers that run it. Permission to quote from the CBC radio program "Identities" was granted by the CBC. This research was funded by a SSHRC Canada Graduate Scholarship.

1 Cohen, Colleen Ballerino, Richard Wilk, and Beverly Stoeltje, eds., *Beauty Queens on the Global Stage: Gender, Contests, and Power* (New York: Routledge, 1996), 2. Also see Sarah Banet-Weiser, *The Most Beautiful Girl in the World: Beauty Pageants and National Identity* (Berkeley, CA: University of California Press, 1999); Elwood Watson and Darcy Martin, eds., *"There She Is, Miss America": The Politics of Sex, Beauty, and Race in America's Most Famous Pageant* (New York: Palgrave Macmillan, 2004); Patrizia Gentile, "Queen of the Maple Leaf: A History of Beauty Contests in Twentieth-Century Canada," doctoral dissertation, Queen's University, 2006. Also see Tarah Brookfield, this volume. Pageants were not unique in using bodies to convey a message. As Valerie Minnett points out, this volume, "the female body," in particular, "has been used historically to personify abstract qualities."

2 Watson and Martin, *"There She Is, Miss America,"* 8; Gentile, "Queen of the Maple Leaf," 3.

3 German nudism is discussed at length in several recent studies. See Michael Hau, *The Cult of Health and Beauty in Germany: A Social History, 1890–1930* (Chicago, IL: University of Chicago Press, 2003); Chad Ross, *Naked Germany: Health, Race and the Nation* (Oxford: Berg, 2005); John Williams, *Turning to Nature in Germany: Hiking, Nudism, and Nature Conservation, 1900–1940* (Stanford, CA: Stanford University Press, 2007).

4 James Woycke, *Au Naturel: The History of Nudism in Canada* (Etobicoke, ON: Federation of Canadian Naturists, 2003), 7–11.

5 Due to spotty record keeping and concern over members' privacy, it is difficult to arrive at more precise figures. According to the secretary of the American Sunbathing Association (ASA), the umbrella organization with which the majority of Canadian clubs were affiliated, in 1963 there were 557 Canadian members of the ASA belonging to 13 affiliated clubs. However, this number excludes two of the largest Canadian clubs that were no longer affiliated: Sunny Trails in Surrey, B.C., and Sun Valley Gardens in Fonthill, Ontario. Federation of Canadian Naturists, Toronto, Ontario (FCN), Secretary's Report, ASA Annual Report, 1963.

6 Ruth Barcan, "'Regaining What Mankind Has Lost through Civilization': Early Nudism and Ambivalent Moderns," *Fashion Theory* 8, no.1 (2004), 71.

7 For more on the influence of psychology and the preoccupation with juvenile delinquency in postwar Canada, see Mary Louise Adams, *The Trouble with Normal: Postwar Youth and the Making of Heterosexuality* (Toronto: University of Toronto Press, 1997); and Mona Gleason, *Normalizing the Ideal: Psychology,*

Schooling, and the Family in Postwar Canada (Toronto: University of Toronto Press, 1999).

8 The Canadian nudist magazine, *Sunbathing for Health,* frequently noted the occurrence of English and American nudist pageants or contained photos of pageant winners. References include *Sunbathing for Health* 7, no. 10 (1954), 31; Ray Connett, "Sunny Trails: A Nudist Call to Canada," *Sunbathing for Health* 8, no. 6 (1954), 11; 8, no. 12 (1955), 18–19; 9, no. 5 (1955), 28; 9, no. 10 (1956), 2–3, 31.

9 Ray Connett, "Sunny Trails: A Nudist Call to Canada," *Sunbathing for Health* 3, no. 10 (1950), 10.

10 Clubs that ran their own local pageants included Sunny Trails (Surrey, B.C.), Sun Valley Gardens (Fonthill, Ont.), the Four Seasons Nature Park (Freelton, Ont.), and Paradise Terrestre (Quebec).

11 Evert Peeters, "Authenticity and Ascetism: Discourse and Performance in Nude Culture and Health Reform in Belgium, 1920–1940," *Journal of the History of Sexuality* 15, no. 3 (2006), 432–61.

12 Judith Butler, *Bodies That Matter: On The Discursive Limits of "Sex"* (New York: Routledge, 1993), 2.

13 Michel de Certeau, *The Practice of Everyday Life,* trans. Steven Rendall (Berkeley, CA: University of California Press, 1984), xiv.

14 See, e.g., Perc W. Cousins, "New Zealand's First Naturist Rally," *Sunbathing for Health* 7, no. 6 (1953), 13; Ray Connett, "Sunny Trails: A Nudist Call to Canada," *Sunbathing for Health* 7, no. 8 (1954), 10.

15 Mildred Harris, "The Woman's Page," *Sunbathing for Health* 5, no. 4 (1951), 17.

16 FCN, "East Haven Sun-Club du soleil levant," *Newsletter* (Jan. 1959), n.p.

17 Sander Gilman, *Picturing Health and Illness: Images of Identity and Difference* (Baltimore, MD: Johns Hopkins University Press, 1995), 93.

18 Ray Connett, "Sunny Trails: A Nudist Call to Canada," *Sunbathing for Health* 8, no. 6 (1954), 11.

19 Nina J. Morris, "Naked in Nature: Naturism, Nature and the Senses in Early 20th Century Britain," *Cultural Geographies* 16 (2009), 283–308.

20 Lianne McTavish, "Learning to See in New Brunswick, 1867–1929," *Canadian Historical Review* 87, 4 (2006), 553.

21 For more on cultural concerns about the effect on the viewer of gazing upon the body, see Lindgren, Minnett and Syperek, this volume.

22 FCN, *Sun Valley News* 3, no. 9 (Sept. 1957), n.p.

23 *Warm Winds on Bare Bodies: A Collection of Stories Chronicling the First Fifty Years of the Sunny Chinooks Association,* 2nd ed. (Calgary: Sunny Chinooks Association, 2003), 26.

24 Gentile, "Queen of the Maple Leaf," 51.

25 Ray Connett, "Sunny Trails: A Nudist Call to Canada," *Sunbathing for Health* 10, no. 7 (1956), 8.

26 FCN, *Silva Sun Bulletin* (Spring/Summer 1966).

27 FCN, *Maritan News* (March 1963). New Zealand nudists had not always been so dismissive of pageants. A 1953 report on the first nudist convention in that country by prominent New Zealand naturist, Perc Cousins, noted the election of a royal family. Perc Cousins, "New Zealand's First Naturist Rally," *Sunbathing for Health* 7, no. 6 (1953), 13. On the subject of nudism's inclusiveness, the Canadian and American Sunbathing Associations stipulated that clubs not discriminate on the basis of "race, colour, or creed," and nudists also bragged that the shedding of clothes eliminated class distinctions. In reality, however, very few racial minorities were members of Canadian nudist clubs, and while they did have many working-class members, club fees and the near necessity of car ownership to travel to the clubs were real financial barriers to nudist club membership.

28 Much to the organizers' dismay, on at least one occasion, a male entered the Miss Nude World Contest and successfully "passed" through the first rounds of the contest. The Four Seasons Nature Park also played host to a Mr. Nude World Contest, but it took place on a different weekend and did not receive the publicity that the women's contest did. As a result, sources on the Mr. Nude Contest were scarce and I have confined my discussion here to the Miss Nude pageant.

29 Lisa Stein, "Everything Is Beautiful," *Bare in Mind* (Aug.–Sept. 1972), 2.

30 American Nudist Research Library, Kissimmee, Florida (ANRL), clipping, Mel Hocker, "Leave the Beauty Contests to the Nudists," *Sundial* 1, no.1 (1961).

31 ANRL, Pageants file, "A Contest Run in Good Taste," 1972 Miss Nude World booklet; CBC Broadcasting Centre, Radio Archives, Toronto, Ontario (CBC RA), "Identities" program, 11 Nov. 1974.

32 Winners of these pageants generally had their way paid to the Miss Nude World Contest as part of their prize package, but it was not necessary to have won a qualifying event in order to enter. Despite its name, the vast majority of contest participants were Canadian or American.

33 CBC RA, "Variety Tonight" program, 9 June 1980.

34 ANRL, clipping, Charles Remsberg and Bonnie Remsberg, "Here She Comes, Miss Nude America," *Esquire* (May 1970).

35 ANRL, Pageants file, 1976 Miss Nude Florida Souvenir Program. As a pageant affiliated with the Miss Nude World Contest, the Miss Nude Florida Contest used the same system of scoring.

36 BC Archives, Sunny Trails Nudist Club file, T4201:0005 (CBC radio clip, Reporter Bill Good, 1957).

37 CBC RA, "Identities."

38 FCN, clippings, "Miss Nude World 1971 Swiss-Born Montrealer," *Victoria Daily Times*, 26 July 1971; "Miss Nude World Pageant," *Bare in Mind* (Aug.–Sept. 1972), n.p.

39 Stein, "Everything Is Beautiful," 2.

40 Carl Alkerton, "Promotion and Nudism," *Bare in Mind* (Aug.–Sept. 1972), 1.

41 ANRL, Club files, Four Seasons Nature Park, 1971 Miss Nude World Pageant Program.

42 ANRL, "A Contest Run in Good Taste."

43 The grand prize was typically a trip to Florida or the Caribbean, courtesy of a Toronto travel agency, but an assortment of other prizes were also donated by local businesses. The 1972 prize list included a fur coat, a diamond and emerald ring, a bikini, a bicycle, a portable TV, and a radio – "A Sincere Thanks," *Bare in Mind* (Aug.–Sept. 1972), 4.

44 CBC RA, "Identities."

45 Alkerton, "Promotion and Nudism."

46 CBC RA, "Identities."

47 FCN, "Miss Nude Ontario Special Edition," *Summerset Strip* 9, no. 6 (1973).

48 For examples of cultural tensions concerning bodily displays, especially those of women's bodies, see Syperek and Minnett, this volume.

49 Karl Ruehle, "Promoting Nudism," *Sunbathing for Health* 9, no.11 (1956), 26–7.

50 ANRL, clipping, Ramon Williams, "Realism in Pageantry," *American Nudist* (Winter 1965).

51 George Mosse, *Nationalism and Sexuality: Respectability and Abnormal Sexuality in Modern Europe* (New York: Howard Furtig, 1985), 13.

52 Karl Ruehle, "Juvenile Delinquency," *Sunbathing for Health* 12, no. 4 (1958), 25.

53 "A Contest Run in Good Taste"; FCN, Press file, "A Revealing Site at Britannia Hotel," *Barrie Examiner*, undated [1976].

54 CBC RA, "Identities."

55 ANRL, *The Meadowlark*, 14 Feb. 1977, n.p.

56 Ray Connett, "Sunny Trails: A Nudist Call to Canada," *Sunbathing for Health* 9, no. 1 (1955), 8, 10.

57 FCN, clipping, "A Positive Attitude to Nudism Given," *Saskatoon Star-Phoenix*, 22 July 1972.

58 For more on the creation and function of heterosexual norms in postwar Canada, see Adams, *The Trouble with Normal.*

59 Laura Mulvey, *Visual and Other Pleasures*, 2nd ed. (New York: Palgrave Macmillan, 2009), 19.

60 Mildred Harris, "The Woman's Page," *Sunbathing for Health* 8, no. 6 (1954), 17.

61 Gentile, "Queen of the Maple Leaf," 28, 115–61.

62 ANRL, Pageants file, "The Producer," 1972 Miss Nude World booklet.

63 CBC RA, "Identities."

64 Peter Jackson, "The International Scene," *Sunbathing for Health* 10, no. 2 (1956), 20.

65 Shirley Tillotson, *The Public at Play: Gender and the Politics of Recreation in Post-War Ontario* (Toronto: University of Toronto Press, 2000), 11. Also see Caroline Daley, *Leisure and Pleasure: Reshaping and Revealing the New Zealand Body, 1900–1960* (Auckland: Auckland University Press, 2003), 162, 255. On the concept of citizenship in postwar Canada more generally, see Magda Fahrni, *Household Politics: Montreal Families and Postwar Reconstruction* (Toronto: University of Toronto Press, 2005); and Nancy Christie and Michael Gauvreau, eds., *Cultures of Citizenship in Postwar Canada* (Montreal and Kingston: McGill-Queen's Press, 2003).

66 Adeline Masquelier, ed., *Dirt, Undress, and Difference: Critical Perspectives on the Body's Surface* (Bloomington, IN: Indiana University Press, 2005), 5.

11 Modelling the U.N.'s Mission in Semi-Formal Wear: Edmonton's Miss United Nations Pageants of the 1960s

TARAH BROOKFIELD

The crowning of Miss United Nations 1963, Anita Pearl, a high school student and contestant representing the Scandinavian benefit society Sons of Norway was supposed to symbolize Canada's commitment to internationalism, Edmonton's embrace of multiculturalism, and the inclusivity of women within the United Nations. Edmonton's United Nations Association created the pageant to increase the participation of young women in their association and to generate public awareness and support for the United Nations. Women between the ages of sixteen and twenty-five living in Edmonton and its environs competed based on their beauty, personality, poise, and most importantly, their knowledge of the U.N.'s mission. The overall theme of the pageant was internationalism, the ideology that encouraged political and economic cooperation among nations. Certainly, the pageant captured this spirit by promoting Canadian support of the United Nations, but it also answered the call to internationalism by recruiting contestants from a variety of ethnic backgrounds, including those from Edmonton's visible minority communities. Having the pageant stage duplicate the diversity found within the U.N. General Assembly was supposed to demonstrate that both Edmonton and Canada were living examples of the U.N. values necessary for building peace. This short-lived spectacle, that was neither a traditional beauty pageant, nor a truly egalitarian model, was an opportunity for young women that both reinforced and subverted traditional understandings of feminine beauty, achievement, and agency. Likewise, the contest represented 1960s Canada's newfound enthusiasm for celebrating multiculturalism, if only with gestures of tokenism. Furthermore, the pageant's existence, evolution, and eventual cancellation can be used as a way to measure the Canadian public's waning enthrallment with the United Nations in the 1960s.

The UNA: Bringing the World to Edmonton and Edmonton to the World

In the aftermath of the Second World War, Canada's Department of External Affairs supported internationalism via the newly created U.N. as a means to help rebuild war-torn Europe and establish security, stability, and allies in an increasingly fragmented Cold War world.[1] The Canadian government supported the U.N.'s dual mission, on the one side, promising to intervene and avert war, and on the other, spreading peace through economic development, social justice, and human rights. A $10,000 annual grant from External Affairs made it possible for U.N. supporters to organize a national office and local branches of the United Nations Association, an international organization dedicated to educating the public about the United Nations and encouraging civic participation in the U.N. mission. Founded in 1946, the UNA was seen as a way for ordinary citizens to assist their nations and the world in achieving the U.N.'s goals. Edmonton was just one of dozens of Canadian cities and international locales that hosted a branch of the UNA in the 1960s. Overall, UNA members hoped Canadians would see themselves not only as citizens of their nation, but of the world, taking interest, responsibility, and leadership in global affairs. Given the tense Cold War geopolitics and arms race, James S. Thompson, Canada's first national UNA president, believed international engagement was critical to Canada's postwar national identity and survival, saying, "This is surely the time for all who believe in international co-operation to speak out, insisting that a new world-conflict is madness that need not happen."[2]

Like Thompson, who was the moderator of the United Church of Canada, the UNA's first executive members were deemed to be "opinion leaders," described as professors, teachers, clergy, Members of Parliament, former Canadian Armed Forces officers, and journalists, who could "have direct influence on many other people."[3] Membership was drawn more broadly from the civic-minded middle class, and in the 1960s, the majority of members in Edmonton were women. Together, the executive and members organized branch activities devoted to introducing the new international organization to the public by hosting mass meetings with renowned speakers such as Lester B. Pearson explaining Canada's position in the Korean War, and Eleanor Roosevelt promoting the U.N.'s Educational, Scientific, and Cultural Organization.[4] The UNA also produced radio broadcasts on U.N. achievements, distributed free U.N. posters and literature, screened U.N. films, and raised money for U.N. agencies. As the Cold War progressed, the UNA supplemented

their boosterism with constructive criticism, lobbying the Canadian government to propose structural and policy reforms that would make the
United Nations more effective as a global leader.

The UNA's most industrious time was each October, when it honoured the U.N.'s anniversary. In 1960s Edmonton, this translated into a
week-long celebration that typically began with a flag-raising ceremony
and included parades, lecture series, teas and lunches, cultural exhibits and festivities, and the Miss United Nations pageant. The Edmonton
UNA claimed it held the biggest anniversary celebration for the United
Nations in Canada, if not the world. Although Edmonton's UNA membership was approximately half that of Canada's largest branches in
Montreal, Toronto, Vancouver, and Winnipeg, it was consistently praised
in the UNA's National annual reports for its number of events and high
per capita fundraising.[5] The enthusiasm could be attributed to Edmonton's postwar boom in population, infrastructure, and economy. In the
1960s, Edmonton was Canada's seventh largest metropolitan area. Due
to the expansion in oil and gas pipelines, the city was experiencing relative prosperity, increased immigration, and was known as the "core of
Canada's Energy Empire."[6] Undoubtedly, Edmonton's UNA hoped the
city could also be the heart of Canada's internationalism which is why
it did not hesitate to issue an invitation to U.N. Secretary General U
Thant to lead the parade that kicked off its 1964 U.N. anniversary celebrations because "it is the only city celebrating the United Nations so
extensively."[7]

U Thant's attendance would have proved to the Edmonton UNA that
its work was significant. At both the local and national levels, Canadian
branches of the UNA consistently fretted about the impact of their work.
They argued that their efforts fostered "mutual understanding, goodwill and cooperation between the people of Canada and those of other
countries, with the object of promoting international peace."[8] They
also recognized how lofty their aims were and how difficult they were
to achieve, let alone measure. Furthermore, Canadians' support for the
United Nations in the postwar years could be characterized as erratic.
Initially, there was great enthusiasm and optimism for the organization's
founding, but in 1950, *Maclean's* rated the U.N.'s first five years by stating, "It has been fashionable, in public, to take for granted that the U.N.
is worthwhile. It is even more fashionable, in private, to sneer at the U.N.
as an empty futile debating society."[9] Canadian opinion of the United
Nations wavered during and after the Korean War, especially in regards
to the wisdom in sending and sacrificing Canadian troops. The U.N.'s

popularity steadily rose in 1956 when Pearson's peacekeeping mission in the Suez brought Canada worldwide recognition; however, the fiscal crisis caused by subsequent peacekeeping missions brought uncertainty about the U.N.'s ability to survive in the early to mid-1960s.[10] Despite an ambiguous faith in the U.N.'s security plans, Canadians continued to give generously to the U.N.'s relief and development programs, most notably the United Nations Children Fund (UNICEF).

The UNA could quantify some of its own success in reaching hundreds of thousands of youth. Seen as the leaders of tomorrow, children and adolescents were deemed critical players in achieving the U.N. dream. Working with school boards, home and school associations, and groups like the Girl Guides and Boy Scouts, the UNA organized guest speakers for school assemblies, recruited for UNICEF's Halloween "Trick or Treat" campaign, and made U.N. clubs, model U.N. forums, and pen pal programs a staple of afterschool activities in the 1960s. Lorraine Oak, Miss United Nations 1967, who was a youth volunteer for UNICEF, recalls: "I was acutely aware at a young age of the Bay of Pigs and world peace or we blow up, and of course we had the air raid practices and the sirens went off and we all went home, presumably to be annihilated. It was a time where serious kids were very aware about the dangers of the Cold War ... I had absolute faith. I truly believed in the United Nations and that would be our salvation."[11]

The UNA contextualized its educational and service work with youth as a character-building exercise for Canadian children. Building future leaders keen to support the United Nations was viewed as a way to foster peace and preserve democracy.[12]

Creating a youth event specifically for young women, such as the Miss United Nations pageant, coincided with the U.N.'s interest in gender equality and an understanding that women were interested in world affairs. As a result, while women were often underrepresented within the actual United Nations and on UNA executives, they dominated in terms of individual and group membership. In 1962, the national branch of the UNA listed 301 secular and 178 faith-based women's groups in their ranks, compared with participation from only 49 men's groups and 44 mixed-gender groups.[13] Within the same year, women represented 57 per cent of individual memberships in the Edmonton UNA, compared with 26 per cent of male members, 12 per cent of members who joined as a couple, and 5 per cent whose sex was undetermined.[14] Women's high participation in the UNA could be linked to the specific focus on youth, as well as expanded opportunities in the postwar period for Canadian women to participate in public life, including politics and paid work outside the home. One of the Edmonton UNA's most prominent members was Cora Taylor Watt Casselman, a former teacher from Ontario who had been active all her life in women's organizations and had previously been a member of the League of Nations Society. When her politician husband died, she ran and won his seat in Edmonton West and served in Parliament between 1941 and 1945, becoming the first female Speaker of the House of Commons and the only female in Canada's first delegation to the United Nations.[15] Women's high participation in the UNA suggests they found the U.N. mission appealing and relevant. Just as women organized around issues of security and peace during the First and Second World wars, women continued to be engaged in these pressing matters during the Cold War. Using explicit maternalistic language that claimed the U.N.'s work was a woman's issue, Toronto UNA member Kay Livingstone, a radio personality and founder of the Congress of Black Women stated, "No longer can women afford to let someone else look after the world while they look after their homes. To protect our homes we must look after the world."[16] As Miss United Nations contestants, the young women assumed the role of ambassadors for internationalism.

Although a beauty pageant might seem like a contradictory initiative to promote young women's role within the U.N. mission, pageants were and still are a setting for the performance of a specific image of womanhood and fostering of a group identity. The context and setting for Miss United Nations differed from other contemporary beauty pageant contests such as Miss Canada or the Nudist Queen and King pageants analysed by Mary-Ann Shantz in the previous chapter, but in all cases, these events produced a winner who would best represent an image and vision determined by the pageant sponsors. Colleen Ballerino Cohen, Richard Wilk, and Beverly Stoeltje argue in *Beauty Queens and the Global Stage: Gender, Contests, and Power* that "as universal and diverse as beauty contests are, what they do is remarkably similar ... They showcase values, concepts, and behavior that exist at the centre of a group's sense of itself and exhibit values of morality, gender, and place ... The beauty contest stage is where identities (local, ethnic, regional, national, international) ... [are] made public and visual."[17]

Within this context, a pageant stage is a familiar and appropriate setting for the construction of a specific identity; in this case, one Canadian city's endorsement of internationalism. Singling out young women as the specifically gendered and racialized representation of internationalism gave the impression that girls could be informed citizens, capable leaders, and role models in international relations, an area usually considered to be a male domain. At the same time, restricting this message to a competition that included traditional pageant elements, which focused on the contestant's bodies, implied that the young women might be mere ornaments for internationalism.

"Pert" and "Pretty" Girls: Crowning Inner and Outer Beauty

For young women in 1960s Edmonton, there was no shortage of beauty contests.[18] The two biggest pageants were Miss Edmonton, whose winner would go on to compete in Miss Canada, and Miss Edmonton Eskimo, who would go on to represent Edmonton at the Canadian Football League's Miss Grey Cup. During the selection process for these two popular queen contests, the *Edmonton Journal* included large photos and lengthy profiles of the finalists and winners, and lists of the contests' prizes, most often printed in the "Women's Journal" section of the newspaper. These features, which almost always included the contestants' measurements and hair colour, as well as their interests and talents, generally acted as a "how to" guide that demystified what made a beauty queen. The quantitative and qualitative description of one Miss Edmonton Eskimo winner was typical: "A very knowledgeable girl, Jacqueline is 19 years of age, stands five feet five, weighs 123 pounds. Her measurements are 36, 24, 35."[19] The article then went on to list Jacqueline's interests in cooking, travel, sports, music, and French. In order to represent Edmonton, queens needed to be well rounded, not only with appropriately dimensioned figures, but in attitude and motivation, too.

Starting in 1963, Miss United Nations offered a new type of pageantry for Edmonton's young women, one that placed more attention on a contestant's intellectual abilities. The UNA explained that their "Queen would be chosen on account of both her talent and beauty," with talent being a contestant's knowledge about the United Nations and her ability to communicate this awareness.[20] It was determined that three male and three female judges would be selected from within and outside the UNA on the basis of their expertise in different pageant elements, including fashion, grooming, and international relations.[21] Contestants would be judged in three separate portions, each worth one-third of the final score. The first part consisted of an essay about the United Nations, approximately three hundred words long, which was to be judged on content rather than grammar or structure. A private interview would occur after the essay was written to help the judges to further gauge the contestants' understanding of the United Nations. Finally, beauty, posture, and poise were to be judged when the contestants attended the UNA's International Ball during U.N. Week, where they would be interviewed for a second time by the judges. To keep with the serious mission of the United Nations, there was no bathing suit component; rather, the young women were presented to the public in semi-formal clothing.[22] Devoting two-thirds of the final score to U.N.-related elements meant that an ideological commitment to internationalism and awareness of the United Nations were the most highly sought queenly qualities. Still, by including a section devoted to beauty, it was clear that one needed a certain degree of attractiveness and style to represent the United Nations.

Despite the pageant's emphasis on substance over style, the media's coverage of Miss United Nations made it sound and look more like a typical pageant. As it did with other pageants, the *Edmonton Journal* included photos of smiling Miss United Nations contestants and crowned queens accompanied with brief biographies. Although the press did not go so far as to ever list the Miss United Nations contestants' measurements, the newspaper often framed the contest as being for "pretty girls" and ignored the intellectual and ideological components. This can be seen in a write-up of the contest's second year, which stated, "No celebration is complete without a pretty girl to reign as queen. When United Nations Week officially gets underway in Edmonton Saturday an attractive Miss United Nations will reign over activities."[23] The photo accompanying this article does suggest a more sedate contest than Miss Edmonton or Miss Edmonton Eskimo. While those contestants were often pictured in exotic and erotic fashions – bathing suits, fur coats, dance costumes, and evening gowns – the 1964 Miss United Nations contestants posed in modest dresses and skirts appropriate for the school day, seated much like in a class photo (see Figure 11.1).[24] The contestants could be described as pleasant looking, but few would stand out as being particularly glamorous, and two wore eyeglasses.[25] The prizes were also humble in scope. The anointed queen won a crown, a Miss United Nations sash, a gift certificate for a local restaurant, and a bouquet of roses. All contestants received a book about the United Nations.[26]

The structure and publicity for Miss United Nations did not call attention to the young women's bodies in an overly dramatic manner, at least not in comparison to other pageants. Yet, the choice to promote young women's involvement in the United Nations in the form of a pageant that invited the scrutiny and ranking of women's attractiveness, suggests

Figure 11.1 Miss United Nations contestants pose with costumed child, 1964. Courtesy of the *Edmonton Journal.*

a limited vision of women's uses and image. Lorraine Oak, Miss United Nations 1967, recalls that she found the competition to be "a genuine attempt to include women in the United Nations" and a desire to involve women in international relations. Yet, Oak remembers finding it "so bizarre to couch it in almost all the trappings of a beauty contest."[27] Interestingly, the 1963 meeting minutes that discussed the creation of a Miss United Nations noted, "Disadvantage to this type of contest were [sic] expressed."[28] It is unknown which aspects of the pageant were considered to be problematic, nor was it recorded who brought this point up. This comment may have referred to the organizational headaches of mounting a large event or perhaps someone questioned if a queen contest would be the best forum to showcase U.N. values. Despite the scholarly sections of the contest being worth more points, the essay writing and interviews happened behind closed doors.[29] Meanwhile, the one event open to the public's gaze focused on the fashionable presentation of candidates in their semi-formal wear, suggesting the winner was merely a pin-up girl for the United Nations, rather than an active participant in internationalism. If the UNA was concerned about the contradictory message, it was not recorded in the organization's records or media accounts. Perhaps the UNA hoped that crowning a woman on the basis of her knowledge of the United Nations would itself be an example of women's equality and, therefore, negate any other potentially exploitative elements. At the same time, it was perfectly clear that for financial reasons the UNA was consciously relying on the excitement that came from displaying women's bodies and inviting an audience to scrutinize and judge them.

Seeing the pageant as having an economic value made sense given the Edmonton UNA's financial difficulties in the 1960s. There was pressure to increase the anniversary week ticket sales. Membership fees comprised the UNA's main source of revenue. Across the country, UNA branches were failing to grow or even maintain their membership, and in the case of Edmonton's UNA, membership numbers were dropping. Speculation surrounding the lack of interest in the UNA included the U.N.'s inability after three decades to build real peace and consistent security or, alternatively, that the current period of Cold War detente made them appear less necessary. As original UNA members died and retired, Wilson Woodside, the UNA national president in 1963 noted that younger Canadians were joining like-minded but more radical organizations such as the Voice of Women, the Campaign for Nuclear Disarmament, or the World Federalists.[30] Therefore, choosing to promote the U.N. mission in the form of a pageant went beyond the event being a traditional space to champion a specific identity. It was an occasion known to draw attention, financial sponsorship, and a large audience, something the UNA struggled to achieve through its traditional programming. In the early 1960s, beauty pageants were considered a big deal and big business. This went alongside what Joan Sangster argues was "the increased presence of alluring female bodies" in postwar popular culture, be it in movies, fashion magazines, advertising or beauty pageants.[31] In fact, the meeting minutes discussing the creation of a Miss United Nations pageant show that increasing revenue was the only reason for implementing it: "Mr. Willford explained a suggested queen contest to help with the sale of tickets."[32] Selling the United Nations through the image of "pert" and "pretty" girls was one way to spice up the dull and oft-heard message on the importance of internationalism.[33] In this way, Edmonton's Miss United Nations contest was akin to a typical beauty pageant where young women's bodies were put on display not only for the promotion of an ideal, but for the purposes of spectacle and commodification.

The latter was confirmed when changes made to the contest placed the contestants' bodies under more scrutiny. As a means to gain publicity and improve ticket sales, the pageant quickly abandoned some of its unique academic features. In 1966, the essay of three hundred words was replaced by a poster contest to be displayed alongside its creator in a public venue. The year before, a popularity ballot had been added so that family, friends, and the general public could participate by casting votes for their favourite contestant.[34] Each returned ballot was considered to be the equivalent of one point towards the contestants' final marks, a move that had nothing to do with rewarding knowledge of internationalism, and all to do with the further ranking of the contestants based on criteria unrelated to the U.N. mission. Meanwhile, the 1967 contestants sought more glamour and asked to wear a formal, rather than semi-formal, dress for the ball.[35] Given these changes, it is most likely that the pageant was viewed by the UNA as an annual spectacle aimed to increase interest rather than a serious attempt to build a strong relationship with young women. The lack of post-pageant follow-up with the contestants or winners seems to confirm this. Lorraine Oak remembers that in her year of the competition she was never called upon again to attend any UNA events, such as presenting a youth perspective at a meeting or being used to recruit other youth.[36] It appears that the Edmonton UNA's main objective was for the anniversary celebrations (and by proxy the U.N. mission) to benefit from the spotlight and financial reward typically associated with beauty pageants.

Adding a "Dash of Colour": Racialized Bodies on the Pageant Stage

If the financial incentives and superficiality of the pageant stage meant that Miss United Nation's feminist goals met with mixed success, so did the contest's multicultural aspirations. When soliciting contestants, the Edmonton UNA invited local ethnic associations, women's clubs, and other civic organizations to nominate exceptional young woman to compete for the title of Miss United Nations. In the first year of the contest, eight associations came forward with nominees: the Canadian Ukrainian Society, the Dante Alighieri Society, the Canadian Polish Congress, Sons of Norway, the Icelandic Society, the Edmonton Student UNA, the Canadian Native Friendship Association, the Imperial Order Daughters of the Empire, and Job's Daughters.[37] The inclusion of ethnic associations in the nomination process ensured the contestants were drawn from all corners of Edmonton's population. In 1963, the city's population was estimated to be just over 303,000, which was predominantly made up of the descendants of the region's first Anglo-Saxon settlers (70%) as well as later immigrants from Ukraine and Poland (15%) and Germany and Scandinavia (8%). The remaining population came from a more recent wave of postwar immigration from Europe, including Belgium, Holland, Hungary, Greece, and Italy. There was a small community of Chinese residents who had settled in Edmonton after the Western Canadian railways were built in the late nineteenth century, along with an equally small number of African Canadians, many of whose ancestors had emigrated from the United States at the turn of the century. Living in the city or on nearby reserves were the region's first inhabitants, the Blackfoot, the Cree, and the Metis.[38] The election of William Hawrelak, the son of Ukrainian immigrants, as mayor of Edmonton in 1951 (a position he held until 1959, and was re-elected to again between 1963 and 1965 and again in 1974 and 1975) has been cited as evidence of the city's smooth ethnic integration, at least among its European population.[39] The Edmonton UNA felt its city's friendly diversity made it an ideal symbol of the U.N.'s internationalism, representing not only a microcosm of Canada, but the world. The association believed that holding a multi-ethnic and interracial contest would demonstrate the importance of inclusivity and harmony championed by the United Nations. This meant that in addition to the contestants presenting an image of modern womanhood, their bodies were deliberately racialized to fit both as individuals and as a collective portrait of diversity. The multicultural recruitment of the contestants embodied the following message: we are from multiple nations and races, but as a whole, we are Edmonton, we are Canada, we are the world. This fit with Canada's nation-building goals in the 1960s, which for the first time were beginning to openly embrace the idea of multiculturalism.

Official recognition and celebration of Canada's plurality was mediated through the nation's postwar identity crisis. Diminishing economic and cultural ties to Great Britain, an uncertain and unequal relationship with the United States, heightened nationalism issues in French Canada, and the growing pool of immigrants coming from non-traditional sending nations led to a fear of an increasingly fragmented country. Rebranding Canada as pluralistic was seen as one solution. This process often occurred in the form of public festivals and cultural events. Since the early 1960s, the federal government's Canada Day festivities made it a point to recognize the nation's Aboriginal, French, and British heritage on the anniversary of Confederation and later would include newer immigrant groups. Matthew Hayday argues that 1 July celebrations presented an opportune moment to respond to changing demographics by constructing a unified Canadian identity. By acknowledging rather than ignoring diversity and making it a symbol of Canada, the government hoped multiculturalism would create a new and unifying national identity.[40] Along these lines, Canada's centennial project Expo 67 also used multiculturalism as a form of nation building. The summer-long exhibition was divided into pavilions devoted to specific cultural groups and nations, but taken together, it was supposed to represent the compilation of peoples and traditions that made up Canada as a national entity and a global citizen.[41] The Miss United Nations contest practised these ideals on a much smaller scale, placing the responsibility to model national and international visions on a handful of young women.

Women of all ethnic and racial backgrounds were invited to compete in the Miss United Nations contest. This differed greatly from the majority of queen pageants active in the 1960s, which practised official or unofficial segregation. Contests such as Vancouver's Miss Chinatown or the nationwide Miss Indian Princess were organized for specific ethnic communities, and reinforced an outsider or "other" identity. Meanwhile, Miss Canada only featured White, Anglo-Saxon women as contestants.[42] Most of the Miss United Nations contestants appeared to have British or European backgrounds, but it is significant that in the first three years of the contest, contestants included women from visible minority communities. In the 1964 contest, Rosalind Ardell Harper, a seventeen-year-old African Canadian, nominated by Edmonton's Co-operative Association, and Fae Seto, an eighteen-year-old Asian Canadian, nominated by the Citizenship Council, joined ten other contestants from European backgrounds.[43] These women shared the pageant stage together, presenting a multicultural and interracial vision that suggested inclusivity in terms of citizenship and representations of beauty. Supposedly, to be Miss United Nations, the colour of your skin, eyes, and hair was irrelevant, and you could be a newcomer to Canada or from one of the founding nations.

Although there does not appear to be an Aboriginal candidate in 1964, both the 1963 and 1965 contests featured a First Nations contestant. In 1965, the Canadian Native Society nominated Sharon LaRoque as their candidate for Miss United Nations. During the contest, she was

Figure 11.2 Sharon LaRoque, Miss United Nations contestant, at Native Music Festival, 1965. Courtesy of the *Edmonton Journal.*

photographed attending the Alberta Native Festival of Music, where she demonstrated a traditional dance. The photo shows her in mid-dance wearing a ceremonial dress, her Miss United Nations contestant sash, and a spectacular beehive – a hybrid of symbols worn on her body that represented her Aboriginal heritage, her global citizenship, and her status as a fashionable modern women (see Figure 11.2).[44] Although La-Roque would not be named queen, her image captured everything the UNA hoped Canadians would achieve: the successful balance of individual, national, and global citizenships and identities.

Even though the pageant's structure emphasized a particular vision of multiculturalism, it was important for the UNA that the ultimate image be internationalism. Therefore, beginning in 1965, contestants were assigned a pageant identity associated not with the organization nominating them, but with a U.N. agency. This meant that Corrine Arnfinson, nominated by the Icelandic Society, became known as Miss UNESCO, while LaRoque was identified as Miss Commission on Human Rights. Bestowing humanitarian agencies as official sponsors for each contestant, similar to traditional markers such as the names of hometowns or provinces, suggests the erasure of borders and local identities, and implies a global family working together in cooperation. In addition, contestants simply wore sashes, which stated "Miss United Nations Contestant," which labelled everyone as being part of the world organization, without mentioning their individual roots, their residence in Edmonton, or their Canadian nationality.

To cement the pageant's vision of internationalism, Miss United Nations contestants were initially crowned during the UNA's Festival of Song and Dance, a theatrical event that acted as the anniversary week's closing ceremonies. The performers were Edmonton residents and visitors performing songs and dances from their homelands, which in the 1960s included nations whose cultures had long been in Alberta, since the nineteenth century: England, Ireland, Wales, Scotland, Germany, Poland, Ukraine, Norway, and Iceland. The festival also included dancers and singers representing nations that were becoming more prominent due to postwar immigration: Italy, Greece, Spain, India, Lebanon, Burma, and Israel.[45] In particular, the U.N.'s festival took on a folksy feel-good atmosphere that emphasized the smallness of the world, cultural pluralism, and tolerance. One account of the 1964 festival described it as "a colourful pot-pourri of international song and dance, well received by 1200 spectators" and noted that the audience was "as colourful and cosmopolitan as the 16 different sketches … Turbans, Tyrolean hats and quilts attested to the true United Nations spirit."[46] It appears that the visual identification of diversity through the presence of multiple types of fashions and cultural performances were the main means of ascribing something as bearing "the true United Nations spirit."

Despite the noble intentions, it is unclear if Edmonton's Festival of Song and Dance or Miss United Nations were anything more than cross-cultural window dressing. As one UNA member explained, the festival was a "tangible way to recognize the various groups [in Edmonton] and identify them," and it "would add colour to the festival."[47] "Adding colour" in no way called attention to the discrimination and economic inequality frequently experienced by minority groups or new immigrants, one element preventing a culture of peace being built in Canada. Festivities representing what Franca Iacovetta calls "unity in diversity" were a popular means of giving an "appreciated nod to newcomers" in the 1950s and 1960s, yet it was a form where "these cultures were valued mainly for their capacity to enrich Canadian society, and not to change it in any way."[48] In other ways, the festival and Miss United Nations contest may have reinforced the power dynamics of Edmonton's Anglo-Saxon elites by creating a temporary space that contained and domesticated difference. As anthropologist Liisa Malkki argues, "The projection of internationalist logic onto domestic cultural difference, provid[es] a conceptual frame for ordering and domesticating the dangerous difference with what otherwise threatens the whole logic of 'nation-state.'"[49] As a result, this makes multicultural spectacles, be they festivals or beauty pageants, "an appealing but flimsy ritual shield against – narrow nationalisms, jingoisms, chauvinisms, racisms, and xenophobia."[50] It was not until the 1970s that the Edmonton UNA moved beyond the token celebration of ethnicity and included anti-racism training as part of its human rights programming.[51]

Making Miss United Nations a multi-ethnic, interracial pageant allowed for the presentation and celebration of a non-hegemonic vision of beauty and femininity. Despite these inclusions, it is important to note that none of the winners appear to have come from a visible minority community, and after 1965, neither did any of the contestants.[52] Was this a coincidence or did this pageant mimic the hierarchy of internationalism seen within the United Nations itself? Although any nation could join the United Nations, and democratic principles informed the General Assembly, real power was held by the permanent members of the U.N. Security Council, each of which had the power to veto any U.N. resolution. Did Miss United Nations play upon the same principles that invited anyone to the table, but privileged those whose ethnicity and race were associated with a certain power? Although a pageant with only fifty contestants over six years is not a huge sample from which to draw conclusions, one could speculate that the multicultural aspect of the Miss United Nations contest was an example of temporarily "adding colour," rather than creating a space for meaningful inclusion for ethnic and racial groups at the margins of Canada's population in the 1960s.

Conclusion

The number of Miss United Nations contestants declined from twelve in 1964 to seven in 1967 and three in 1968, the last year of the pageant. The pageant's cancellation can be linked to three reasons associated with changing times. Throughout the 1960s, the UNA was forced to scale down its annual anniversary celebrations due to budget woes and falling membership.[53] Edmonton's UNA continued to exist, but with the exception of programs like UNICEF's Trick or Treat for Halloween, the association's public presence never regained the popularity it had in the 1940s and 1950s. Second, women's consciousness rising across North America positioned beauty pageants under a critical light. In 1968, women held a protest in Atlantic City at the site of that year's Miss America contest where bras and other feminized "instruments of torture" were thrown in a trash can, rumoured to have been burned later, an event that one protester referred to as the "first major action of the current wave of feminism in the United States."[54] Even before the Atlantic City protest, the plans for Canada to host a Miss Centennial Pageant at Expo 67 were cancelled for fear of negative connotations.[55] This critique made it to the pages of the pageant-loving *Edmonton Journal*, when columnist June Sheppard applauded the efforts of university student Liz Law for asking the University of Alberta student council to stop funding campus beauty contests.[56] Finally, the shifting requirements and events associated with Miss United Nations must have been confusing for any young woman with an interest in the United Nations, but who would not have been attracted to the traditional elements of a beauty pageant. Nor would the scholarly elements necessarily appeal to the women typically drawn to beauty pageants.

The short-lived Miss United Nations pageant in Edmonton interrogates several social and political tensions brewing within Canada in the 1960s. Here, both the pageant stage and the United Nations represent powerful spaces created to imbue values and identity. Merged together for the Miss United Nations contest, they represent a moment in time that identified young women as valid participants and leaders in internationalism. This could be viewed as the prelude to the demands by Canadian women and their allies for more citizenship and economic rights during the feminist movements of 1970s. At the same time, Miss United Nations subverted its goals by creating a system that ranked participants and placed value on attractiveness and fashion. Miss United Nations also used the young women's mixed ethnicity and racialized bodies to paint a picture of peaceful coexistence and community in multicultural Edmonton. This had a double purpose; it could be a visual checkmark for Canada's newfound expressions of nation building that needed to accept diversity to avoid fragmentation and could act as proof of Canada's internationalist credibility. Yet, the sense of tokenism that pervaded the pageant and other UNA events and the disappearance of minority contestants suggests only a provisional commitment to or understanding of multiculturalism. The superficiality in how Miss United Nations performed feminism and framed multiculturalism demonstrates the problems of employing a queen contest to promote agency, acceptance, and equality. The inclusive dimensions were further complicated by financial incentive being the pageant's primary goal, turning the contestants' bodies into a valuable fundraising domain. Ultimately, for the young women who competed to be Miss United Nations, they were used by the UNA to fulfil the association's ideological and financial mandate. At the same time, the contestants' attempts to change the contest or simply stop participating suggests they were not willing to endlessly perform for something that did not satisfy their own wants and needs.

Notes

1 Adam Chapnick, *The Middle Power Project: Canada and the Founding of the United Nations* (Vancouver: UBC Press, 2005).
2 Library and Archives Canada (LAC), United Nations Association (UNA) Fonds, MG 28, I202, UNA in Canada, box 54, file 8, Branch Officers – Correspondence 1946, Memo to Branch Secretaries from National President James S. Thompson, 23 Sept. 1946.
3 LAC, UNA Fonds, MG 28, I202, UNA in Canada, box 45, file 5, Annual Meetings 1962, Public Relations Study, Toronto UNA, July 1962, 1.
4 These are a sample of talks hosted by the UNA in Toronto, advertised in the *Globe and Mail*, 1950, on 19 Jan., 17 March, and 15 Nov., and 17 May 1955. Smaller branches had a more difficult time attracting such well-known speakers.
5 City of Edmonton Archives (CEA), Bertha Lawrence (BL) Fonds, MSS 688, box 3, UNA in Canada, "National Directors Report" by Willson Woodside, 26 May 1963.
6 James G. MacGregor, *Edmonton: A History*, 2nd ed. (Edmonton: Hurtig, 1975), 14.
7 "Society Asks U Thant to Come to Edmonton," *Edmonton Journal*, 2 Oct. 1964, 26.

8 LAC, UNA Fonds, MG 28, I202, UNA in Canada, box 60, file 9, General corr. 1949, Memo to members of executive committee from Sidney Smith, National Secretary, 15 July 1949.

9 "The U.N. Proves Its Worth with the Blue Chips Down," *Maclean's,* 1 Aug. 1950, 2.

10 Michael K. Carroll, *Pearson's Peacekeepers: Canada and the United Nations Emergency Force, 1956–67* (Vancouver: UBC Press, 2009), 71.

11 Interview, Lorraine Oak, 8 Feb. 2010.

12 CEA, BL Fonds, MSS 688, box 3, UNA in Canada, Hallowe'en for UNICEF for children everywhere – Planning Manual Produced by the National UNICEF Committee, Toronto, 1960.

13 LAC, UNA Fonds, MG 28, I202, UNA in Canada, box 1, file 1 Affiliated Community Organization – correspondence, 1965.

14 An estimation of membership by gender was taken from various documents in the CEA, BL Fonds, MSS 688, boxes 1–4.

15 CEA, MSS 688, BL Fonds, Box 4, UNA in Canada, UNA in Canada Edmonton Branch, 1956.

16 Archives of Ontario (AO), Toronto Local Council of Women Fonds, F805-2-0-5 "Report from U.N. Association in Canada – Women's Section," *The Councillor: Official Bulletin of the Local Council of Women of Toronto,* March 1963.

17 Colleen Ballerino Cohen, Richard Wilk, and Beverly Stoeltje, eds., *Beauty Queens and the Global Stage: Gender, Contests, and Power* (London: Routledge, 1996), 2.

18 Other contests advertised in the *Edmonton Journal* included Miss Federal Civil Service, Miss Stampeder, Miss Stylemakers, Miss University of Alberta (for students in the Department of Education), Miss University of Alberta Frosh Queen, Teen Queen of the Montgomery Branch Legion, and Miss Northern Alberta. The results of American contests like Mrs. America, Miss Railway, and Miss Teen-ager were also announced.

19 "University Student Wins Miss Eskimo Title," *Edmonton Journal,* 22 Oct. 1962, 13.

20 CEA, MSS 688, BL Fonds, Box 3, UNA in Canada, Minutes of the Citizen's Committee for Celebration of U.N. Week, 7 May 1963.

21 CEA, MSS 688, BL Fonds, Box 3, UNA in Canada, Minutes of the Citizen's Committee for Celebration of U.N. Week, 14 Sept. 1963.

22 "Sons of Norway U.N. Contestant Wins Folk Dance Festival Title" and "Miss United Nations," *Edmonton Journal,* 28 Oct. 1963, 18, 29.

23 "Miss United Nations Contestants," *Edmonton Journal,* 13 Oct. 1964, 17.

24 "Miss Edmonton Princess Finalists," *Edmonton Journal,* 5 Oct. 1965, 20.

25 "Miss United Nations Contestants," *Edmonton Journal,* 13 Oct. 1964, 13.

26 "Sons of Norway U.N. Contestant Wins Folk Dance Festival Title" and "Miss United Nations," *Edmonton Journal*, 28 Oct. 1963, 18, 29.

27 Interview, Lorraine Oak, 8 Feb. 2010.

28 CEA, MSS 688, BL Fonds, Box 3, UNA in Canada, Minutes of the Citizens' Committee for Celebration of U.N. Week, 7 May 1963.

29 Patrizia Gentile, "Queen of the Maple Leaf: A History of Beauty Contests in Twentieth-Century Canada," doctoral dissertation, Queen's University, 2006, 231.

30 CEA, MSS 688, BL Fonds, Box 3, UNA in Canada, "National Directors Report" by Willson Woodside, 26 May 1963.

31 Joan Sangster, "'Queen of the Picket Line": Beauty Contests in the Post–World War II Canadian Labor Movement, 1945–1970," *Labor: Studies in Working-Class History of the Americas* 5, no. 4 (2008), 85.

32 CEA, MSS 688, BL Fonds, Box 3, UNA in Canada, Minutes of the Citizens' Committee for Celebration of U.N. Week, 7 May 1963.

33 "College Teenager Crowned Miss U.N.," *Edmonton Journal*, 23 Oct. 1964, 3.

34 CEA, MSS 688, BL Fonds, Box 1, UNA in Canada, New rules, 1965.

35 CEA, MSS 688, BL Fonds, Box 1, UNA in Canada, Remarks Miss U.N. Contestants 5th annual, 1967.

36 Interview, Lorraine Oak, 8 Feb. 2010.

37 "Festivities for U.N. Week," *Edmonton Journal*, 18 Oct. 1963, 17.

38 MacGregor, *Edmonton*, 184; *City of Edmonton Municipal Census*, 1963.

39 Edmonton Public Library, *Edmonton: A City Called Home*, 2004, http://www.edmontonhistory.ca, accessed 17 Feb. 2010.

40 Matthew Hayday, "Fireworks, Folk-Dancing, and Fostering a National Identity: The Politics of Canada Day," *Canadian Historical Review* 91, no. 2 (2010), 287–314.

41 For an interesting discussion on how Expo 67 exhumed Canada's legacy of colonialism, see Myra Rutherdale and Jim Miller, "'It's Our Country': First Nations' Participation in the Indian Pavilion at Expo 67," *Journal of the Canadian Historical Association* 17, no. 2 (2006), 148–73.

42 For a discussion on the presentation of ethnicity in Canada's pageant history, see Gentile, "Queen of the Maple Leaf," chapter 3.

43 "Miss United Nations Contestants," *Edmonton Journal*, 13 Oct. 1964, 13.

44 "High-Stepping at Native Music Fest," *Edmonton Journal*, 18 Oct. 1965, 7.

45 CEA, BL Fonds, MSS 688, box 1, UNA in Canada, "1961 UN Week Program" and "1965 UN Week Festival Program."

46 "College Teen-Ager Crowned Miss U.N.," *Edmonton Journal*, 24 Oct. 1964, 3.

47 CEA, BL Fonds, MSS 688, box 3, UNA in Canada, Minutes of the Citizens' Committee for Celebration of U.N. Week, 7 May 1963.

48 Franca Iacovetta, *Gatekeepers: Reshaping Immigrant Lives in Cold War Canada* (Toronto: Between the Lines, 2006), 76.

49 Liisa Malkki, "Citizens of Humanity: Internationalism and Imagined Community of Nations," *Diaspora* 3, no. 1 (1994): 60.

50 Mallkki, "Citizens of Humanity," 56.

51 CEA, BL Fonds, MSS 688, box 2, UNA in Canada, Minutes of the UNA, 1 Dec. 1971.

52 The winning queens were Miss Anita Pearl, Sons of Norway, 1963; Paula Gaudette, unknown affiliation, 1964; Janet Eggelton, Queen Elizabeth High School U.N. Club, 1965; Lorraine Oak, UNICEF, 1967, and Beth Kuhnke, unknown affiliation, 1968. It is unknown who the 1966 queen was as the UNA records made no mention of it, and the *Edmonton Journal* only mentioned the contest and that it had 10 contestants, but did not mention their names or include a photo.

53 CEA, BL Fonds, MSS 688, box 3, UNA in Canada, "National Directors Report," by Willson Woodside, 26 May 1963.

54 Bonnie J. Dow, Feminism, "Miss America and Media Mythology," *Rhetoric and Public Affairs* 6, no.1 (2003), 130.

55 Gentile, "Queen of the Maple Leaf," 84.

56 June Sheppard, "Beauty Contests a Bore," *Edmonton Journal*, 22 Oct. 1969, 22.

PART THREE

Regulating Bodies

12 Obesity in Children: A Medical Perception, 1920–1980

WENDY MITCHINSON

Healthy children represent a strong future for a nation; unhealthy children threaten it. The failure of many young men to pass a medical test in order to fight for their country during the First World War raised fears in Canada that the bodies of young people were less than robust. Today, the focus is on overweight and obese children and the cost to society of responding to the perceived physical and social problems obesity causes and will cause when those children reach adulthood and demand help in fighting their lower life expectancy.[1] In 2004, approximately a quarter of all Canadian children aged two to seventeen were overweight and 8 per cent were obese.[2]

Historical studies of children and adolescent bodies have been increasing in recent decades and have joined the plethora of literature in the field of body history.[3] Little work, however, exists on obesity in children. The few studies that mention it tend to focus more on adult than on child obesity and more on the United States than elsewhere. Nevertheless, these studies offer the beginnings of a historiography. In looking for the causes of child obesity blamed are parenting patterns, the culture of consumerism, and the changing culture of youth. Dating public awareness of it varies from the early years of the last century, to mid-century, to the present century.[4]

This essay is a first attempt to study the medical history of obesity in Canadian children between 1920 and 1980. The main primary sources are three medical journals – the *Canadian Medical Association Journal* (*CMAJ*), the leading medical publication in the country; *Canadian Doctor* (*CD*), designated as a business journal for the profession; and the *Public Health Journal* (*PHJ*), later called the *Canadian Public Health Journal* (*CPHJ*) and the *Canadian Journal of Public Health* (*CJPH*), the periodical of the Canadian Public Health Association. From the 1920s to the 1950s, most health commentators worried about malnutrition in children, using weight as a measurement of nutritional health – malnourished children were underweight. Eventually, emphasis on weight led to an understanding that being overweight was another form of malnourishment, so that by 1980 child obesity had become part of the wider medical discourse about obesity in Canada. It did not reach panic proportions, however, but remained part of the world of nutritional concerns and a fear that the sedentary and intense consumer society that followed the Second World War was undermining the health of the most vulnerable in Canada and their ability to become fully contributing citizens.

While scholars today are sensitive to divisions among Canadians based on gender, ethnicity, and class, physicians and nutritionists in the past were less so. Often they referred to children in a generic way when they really were referring to White, middle-class children from urban centres. That being said, children (from pre-school to the end of adolescence) were grouped by age, a reflection of much of the data on weight being generated by nutritional studies in the schools. There was some sensitivity to social class because of concerns that the Depression would constrain the ability of poorer Canadians to eat well and that the Second World War, in taking away too many family breadwinners, would do the same. After the war, immigrants coming to Canada with different foodways caught the eye of nutritionists as did a decline in the health of Native children in the far north, a result of the shift to a normative southern diet, one high in carbohydrates and sugar. Throughout the years, worry about teen-aged girls and their poor eating habits persisted.

What and how Canadians ate are reflective of wider changes in society, including Canadians leaving the farm and relying on others to raise the food they ate, new ways of processing food that led to the rise of canned products by the 1920s, and increasingly afterwards, the emergence of food studies with often conflicting advice on how to eat better being offered to Canadians, women carving out careers for themselves as dietitians and nutritionists, and mothers being increasingly bombarded by advertisements and advice by experts on how to feed their children. While such experts were few and far between, their messages were easily accessible through their writings in popular magazines.[5] Studying children's nutritional health was ongoing through school surveys, often not overseen by practising physicians but by individuals in the employ of local health units, the provincial or federal departments of Health, or university academics. In part, all of the above coalesced in the post–Second World War world that seemed foreign to an older generation – a world in which children ate TV dinners, consumed fast food, and seemed to be more sedentary than previous generations.

Awareness of obesity in children stimulated a medical discussion of its causation and treatment. Perceived causes included physiological problems, learned habits, and/or psychological anxiety. Mothers were the major caregivers of children, and not surprisingly, physicians blamed them for improperly feeding their children. While practitioners repeated the trope of mother blaming throughout the decades, some also acknowledged children's agency in refusing to eat the food given to them or not being willing to engage in physical activities to offset the extra weight caused by the food they ate. As for treatment efforts, physicians had many ideas on how to effect weight loss, varying from better eating habits to pharmacological control of children's metabolic rate, appetite, and energy level. None of them were particularly successful. The medical perceptions of child obesity, its causes, and treatment are fascinating, particularly as they reflect wider cultural and social themes in the history of medicine and childhood: the rise of pharmaceutical use in medicine, the increasing role of psychology in understanding children, concern about the development of a sedentary society and the consequent lack of fitness among Canadians, and the centrality of children's health as a bellwether for adult health and the health of the nation.[6]

Children's Health and Recognition of Obesity

Awareness of childhood obesity came early in the century because of concern about malnutrition in children. The poor health of many potential recruits in the First World War brought to the fore the health problems (many of them nutritional) of Canada's youngest citizens since the assumption was that much of the poor health in recruits began in childhood. Children represented the future, and for a country that had lost too many young adults to war, the health of children who would replace them was paramount.[7] Thus, soldiers' bodies were connected to children's bodies and their future physical development and how that would effect what they would be able to offer their country.

By the 1920s, a better understanding of nutrition had emerged, promoted by the discoveries of various food nutrients.[8] Such knowledge, however, was of little use unless health experts could assess the nutritional intake of Canadian children. Schoolchildren were a captive audience and, consequently, studies throughout the decades to determine their nutritional health took place, sometimes comparing them with children in the past or with their contemporaries in their own schools or elsewhere. Based on a nutritional survey of five Toronto schools chosen to represent different socioeconomic groups, estimates in 1921 were that just over 25 per cent of schoolchildren were underweight, that is, malnourished. The potential consequences were significant: for the child – poor health, bad behaviour, and lack of focus on school; for the nation – "stunting of the race," a phrase that reflected a eugenic fear for a nation that had lost too many young men considered the cream of Canadian manhood.[9]

Studies of children based on height and weight charts continued as well as studies of food consumed. In 1934, the results of a survey of 2,050 children, aged eight to sixteen in Ontario schools were reported. Almost one-third of the participants did not have a cereal component for breakfast, girls skipped breakfast too often, and older children in general tended to eat "undesirable" food. This study, and subsequent ones, provided practitioners with a sense of what children were eating, what the nutritional deficiencies of their diet were, and how both related to their health.[10] The studies were all predictable in their negative findings. Indeed, determining a nutritional problem seemed to justify the study and became the raison d'être for the next one. In the early 1970s, the Nutrition Canada Survey, the most significant undertaken in the country until that time, emphasized what most in the field already knew, children were below standard in intake of iron and vitamin C and teenagers were deficient in calcium intake.[11] Despite generations of nutritional advice, Canadian children were not optimally healthy.

The concern about child obesity emerged out of the awareness of malnourishment, although mention of it was sporadic in the early decades. Equating health with a certain weight not only revealed those who were underweight and presumed undernourished but also some who were overweight and equally malnourished. In 1941, Dr. Lionel M. Lindsay of Montreal published one of the first overviews of obese children in Canada, using what had become the normative adult measurement of obesity: 20 per cent above the norm for age, height, and sex. He noted that while some fat children experienced health problems, most fat children were physically healthy. Psychologically they were less so, prone to the "taunts" of other children, their own sensitivity to their appearance (a particular issue for girls), and at risk of "personality changes or behavior problems ... detrimental to the whole future of the individual." Obese children, then, didn't "fit" into their society.[12] Despite his concern for what he saw as the psychological and limited physical problems of obesity in children, Lindsay found "stout" children attractive and believed that their parents were similarly positive, seeing in their child's weight a sign of health. Such a perception was shared more broadly in society, with advertisers using the chubby young child as the epitome of health, in part, because the high infant and child mortality rates of earlier years were well imprinted on the memories of adults.[13] In 1953, G.T. Haig, author of "Suppose Tommy Won't Eat," described one mother who was worried that her two-year-old daughter was not eating enough. The child looked healthy, had lots of energy, and seemed to be of normal weight and height, so Haig asked the mother what the child ate. The breakfast was "substantial" consisting of "4 oz. of orange juice, ½ cup oatmeal, an egg, a piece of whole wheat toast and 6–8 oz. milk. Lunch and dinner were comparable in quality and size." As Haig told his readers, here was a healthy child and an overly worried mother, the latter because she simply did not know the food needs of her child.[14] She also had a specific image of what a healthy two-year-old should be. Eventually, that image would come back to haunt mothers who would bear the brunt of blame for their children's obesity.

By the 1970s, obesity in the young was no longer seen as an individual problem. Experts considered it a consequence of living in a modern, developed nation in which "overnutrition, underactivity, and poor level of fitness" were becoming the hallmarks of the teenage years. Unlike in young children, being overweight was not a sign of health in a teenager. Teenaged bodies were judged by a different criterion, a more adult one. Clearly, commentators feared that society had changed in ways to undermine youth – they no longer entered the workforce at a young age or engaged in significant physical activity. Such concerns reflected the perceived disconnect of teenagers from the generation of their parents. For some, the rejection of society and its values by "hippies" epitomized the disconnect. For the teenagers referred to in the above quote, it was by a generation that too often revelled in the fast food and sedentary recreation available to them.[15] Estimates were that child obesity rates were close to those of the United States, somewhere between 2 and 15 per cent. And Canadians and Americans were not alone. French physicians, too, worried about the obese child.[16] While child obesity was not at an "epidemic" stage, it had become a more global problem.

Causes of Obesity

Once physicians accepted obesity as a problem in some children, they needed to find its cause. Because the concern about adult obesity dominated discussions of obesity, not surprisingly, the causes of obesity in adults were applied to obesity in children, even while acknowledging differences due to age and the fact that children and youth were still growing. Physicians' first step in determining causation was to seek a physiological factor. They had long looked to an endocrine disturbance (more often than not focused on the thyroid) as a cause of obesity in adults, and Lindsay in his 1941 article specifically discussed it in children, seeing child obesity as a "result of a peculiar metabolism, which in the last analysis is probably governed by glandular action."[17] The focus on "glandular action" was significant; it suggested that the fat child was not at fault, and it presented physicians with a physical cause that either the child would outgrow or that medical science could manage. While mention of metabolic and/or endocrine obesity continued, its supporters had one difficulty. Most individuals who were obese did not have a glandular disorder.[18]

A more compelling cause was what and how much children ate. As early as the 1920s, F.W. Tidmarsh complained that too often parents allowed their children to "rule" the household, drinking tea or coffee instead of milk and eating candy "at all hours," consequently, ruining their appetite for good and nourishing food.[19] Underlying the complaint was a sense of children running amok. Yearning for a time believed to have existed when children knew their place, commentators concluded modern children did not. No wonder nutritional experts were determined to educate Canadians about proper nutrition, but even the Canadian Nutrition Program, introduced during the Second World War, couldn't offset the perils of family dynamics that often worked against it. Lindsay, in his seminal article, certainly had no doubt about the cause of child obesity – obese children ate too much. Little changed in the ensuing decades.[20] But the relationship between food and obesity was not as clear as researchers thought. In the 1960s, studies reported that while obese children ate more than their non-obese counterparts, obese girls of high-school age did not.[21] Studies also revealed that Inuit children were heavier not because they were eating more and better, but because they had adopted a southern diet that included a fourfold increase in sugar.[22] Their weight gain was not a healthy one. More disturbing about the relationship between weight gain and food consumption were findings of its impact on the cellular level of the body, that is, overeating in infancy and childhood could lead to the development of additional fat cells that once created did not disappear but could only change in size.[23] Such cells explained much of the intractability of obesity.

While the fat cell number and size provided a physiological explanation for what happened when children overate, physicians linked the reason for them doing so to other factors such as heredity. Like physiological causation, it made the obese child "blameless." Although studies suggested a positive relationship between the obesity in children and obesity in their parents, the environmental aspects so integral to family such as eating habits made separating heredity from them "nearly impossible."[24] Nevertheless, part of the physiology of the child was what she or he had inherited. The genetic factor allowed both doctor and parents to understand why the obesity occurred in the child and why treatment seldom worked. Like the endocrine theory, what it didn't explain was the growing rate of obesity among children.

Because physicians were dealing with children and youth, the family situation had to be of interest – eating habits in children and youth were a result of learned behaviour. Tidmarsh's comment on children ruling the household comes to mind. Obesity researchers in the post–Second World War years suggested that "overzealous or misguided" mothers were the problem.[25] Yet, given the concern about malnutrition that had existed in the past and still existed at mid-century, that mothers wanted to encourage their children to eat was not surprising. Linked to family as well were its cultural norms, which with increased immigration after the Second World War were recognized as playing a part in eating habits.[26] But whether the fault was the mother's or cultural practice, the conclusion for A.M. Bryans, head of the Department of Pediatrics at Queen's University, was clear: "in our efforts to ensure an adequate diet for everyone we are feeding some children too much."[27]

The family dynamics of eating touched on the role psychology played. By mid-century, Canadians had become familiar with hearing about psychological theories and explanations of their own and others' behaviour, and for those in child and nutrition studies, it seemed logical to ask why some children ate too much.[28] The biggest name in the field of child obesity from a psychological perspective was Hilde Bruch, a German-born American psychoanalyst. Of particular interest to Bruch was the child-mother relationship. She found that mothers of obese children were often overprotective of their children and that their children tended to be immature for their age and often the youngest or the only child in a family.[29] Daniel Cappon, an associate professor in the Department of Psychiatry at the University of Toronto, considered Bruch's work "brilliant," although he questioned her research methodology. Where were the controls in her study? Where was the "proof that any one family constellation of interpersonal dynamics and values will result in obesity"? Cappon was a Freudian analyst and, not surprisingly, took Freud's rather gendered theories as "proof" of what was more or less standard across families. With respect to girls he accepted that "a girl's overeating may result from penis envy expressed also with the phantasy of incorporating the male phallus. In childhood the sex theory of oral impregnation is prevalent. To the child's mind, rather logically if the baby is in the tummy, it gets there through the mother's eating too much."[30]

Although an intriguing theory, very little of what Cappon described as causation could be changed or verified. No wonder most practitioners focused on overeating and left it at that. Theories were not useful unless they led to treatment modalities. The psychological was certainly something that the medical and health literature continued to recognize, but more often than not, in passing. Indeed, for some physicians, psychological problems were a consequence of obesity not the cause.[31]

The equation that dominated obesity studies was energy intake balanced by energy expenditure. That being the case, practitioners did mention the need for children (and adults) to be active. By the 1950s, commentators warned that, instead of walking, youth "jumped" into cars to go a block. In the 1960s, a study of Toronto schoolchildren confirmed significant problems, especially in girls who had "poor strength and aerobic power."[32] The medical focus on exercise and fitness, however, was never significant but, like the psychological, was listed among a myriad of causes. Physicians had little experience or knowledge of the new science of kinesiology, and they never really saw lack of exercise as a primary cause of obesity, only a secondary one.

The perceived causes of obesity in the young were clearly multidimensional. As A.M. Bryans concluded in 1967, "Juvenile obesity is probably a reflection of undefined, complex, and inherited and metabolic factors, aggravated by diet, lack of exercise and other environmental influences. There seem to be both psychological and physiological reasons which make obesity, once established, a self-perpetuating entity."[33] Where that left the obese child, his or her parents, nutritionists, and physicians is unclear. But every possibility seemed covered and, taken together, led to many treatment possibilities.

Treatment of Obesity

Although some children might be overweight or even obese, practitioners did not always approve of treating them. Lindsay believed that if the child seemed healthy and strong and not worried about how she or he looked, then keeping her or him under observation might be enough. After all, children's growth patterns were individual and with growth the problem could disappear. If the child did complain, either about physical or psychological problems, however, treatment should ensue.[34]

Although dieting was the main treatment for adults, practitioners did not advise it for children because they were still growing. In the 1930s, only if they were "grossly obese" did Toronto's Walter R. Campbell think that the young should diet. This advice was followed throughout the decades. But if children were not to be placed on a diet, that is, reduced calories, the nature of their food intake could be altered. In 1941, Lindsay was giving the accepted dieting advice – cut back on fats and carbohydrates and consume protein and green vegetables. Marketing of food products supported such a strategy for everyone. In its advertisements, the Canadian Banana Company Ltd. reminded physicians that "bananas satisfy without fattening, for a medium banana contains only 88 calories." And bananas had nutrients, which is more than could be said for "the soft-drink-cake diet" favoured by teenagers.[35]

Exercising became the partner to dieting, not specifically for weight loss but as a preventative for weight gain. Yet, getting obese children to be more active was not going to be easy. As Lindsay admitted, their weight made some "indolent and lazy."[36] More problematic was that by the 1970s some argued that physical activity heightened appetite. That being the case, the balance between weight gain and weight loss in children was delicate and challenging.[37] What exercise did offer was fitness and better health, both of which it was hoped might improve an obese child's self-image and result in a change in his or her eating habits.[38] Fitness was a goal for Canadians in general, and concern about fitness had led to the government supporting sports and exercise initiatives such as ParticipACTION. Even before that, however, Canadians had become aware of the need to exercise – the mention by Prince Philip of Canadians' lack of fitness in 1958 and the popularity of the RCAF's 5BX and 10BX exercises.[39]

If dieting and exercise were not central in treatment, what was? Although the belief in the metabolic cause of obesity in some children was a debatable issue, the influence of the thyroid over the metabolic rate suggested to some that thyroid extract might be helpful in weight loss even in obesity that wasn't endocrine in origin. By speeding up the metabolic rate, the body would process food (fat) faster. Other drugs for those without an endocrine problem were also put forward by the

1940s. Lindsay, for example, suggested to his colleagues that benzedrine sulphate in small doses was helpful. It stimulated physical activity and Lindsay had heard that it also depressed the appetite.[40] But not all were happy with the use of benzedrine. Edmonton doctors, Leonore Hawirko and P.H. Sprague, in 1946 reported that physicians elsewhere did not believe young people tolerated it well. What they recommended was dextro-amphetamine. In their estimation, it worked like benzedrine without its potential side effects: "insomnia, irritability, edginess and tenseness."[41]

Physicians continued to prescribe amphetamines. In the late 1950s, the makers of Dexedrine (dextro-amphetamine) came out with a low-dose version useful for treating children and geriatric patients. Advertised also were Probese TD & VM (phenmetrazine) in a newer and milder form "for the pediatric case."[42] But some practitioners were questioning the use of amphetamines. In 1957, Dr. Antonio Martel wrote an article on Preludin (phenmetrazine) in which he criticized many of the amphetamine-based drugs used as appetite suppressants. According to Martel, Preludin appeared to be longer lasting than amphetamines and safe, even for the treatment of children. The latter phrase was how many studies were presented in advertisements. The real tests were done on adults; the mention of its safety for children a throwaway line.[43]

Drug advertisements in the 1960s appealed to the anxiety adolescent girls often had about their body image. One advertisement for Ambar #2 Extentabs (methamphetamine hydrochloride and phenobarbital) depicted an adolescent girl at a dance sitting on the sidelines. The text read, "She tries to lose weight – but her emotions won't let her."[44] The answer for her physician was to prescribe Ambar #2 Extentabs. They would stabilize her emotions so that she could stay on a diet and also would suppress her appetite. Such products were to make losing weight less stressful and the physician's task easier and ultimately successful, a powerful promise on both counts. Even problematic drugs appealed to the need to fight child obesity. Advertisements for Durabolan warned that its composition (nandrolone phenpropionate) meant taking care when giving it to women and children since they "are more sensitive to any degree of androgenic stimulation and should be watched for signs of virilization." Indeed, too large a dose could "inhibit" menstruation.[45] The use of drugs in obesity treatment for both children and adults was part of a broader adoption by practitioners and Canadians of pharmacological solutions for both physical and psychological conditions.

Drugs were to work to make dieting less stressful and in doing so control the psychological component of the urge to overeat. Doctors offered more traditional psychological treatment, as well, especially in the 1970s. As practised, it tended to be based on common sense. Physicians counselled their child patients, trying to find from them and their parents (mostly mothers) what their home life was like and what factors might be at work to make the child overeat. The goal was behaviour modification, altering the established patterns of eating.[46] "Self-acceptance" among the young was especially important, and practitioners considered psychological support, whether through sympathetic counselling or other means, vital.[47] After all, the postwar years were highly focused on "feeling good" about yourself, something that had not been particularly strong in pre–Second World War society. At the very least, visits to the doctor to "talk" would make the child feel that she or he was not alone. Psychotherapy, however, as treatment was rare. The medical profession was not particularly supportive of it, and there were few psychoanalysts in Canada.[48]

Despite the variety of treatment modalities tried, one commonality among them was their lack of success. In 1975, estimates were that any "long-term" success in treating obesity in children was under 20 per cent.[49] The problem with treatment was twofold – the patients were children and their bodies were still growing and because they were children, physicians had to deal with other family members, in particular the mothers who, as we have seen, physicians often blamed for their child's obesity. Much of the treatment offered by physicians was not particularly therapeutic – advice on what to eat and encouragement to exercise could come from health experts other than general practitioners. Drug treatment, however, could not, and it loomed large as an adjunct to dieting, exercising, and improving how the children or adolescents felt about themselves. In looking at treatment, none of the efforts could promise a cure. Remission could occur, that is, the loss of weight was possible, but whether that weight could stay off could only be judged over time. If the increased obesity rates of both children and adults in recent years are accurate, time has given a negative answer.

Conclusion

Compared with the medical concern about adult obesity, worry about children was limited in the period 1920–1980. Until mid-century, the emphasis on the younger members of Canadian society was on nutrition. That continued to be the case, but by mid-century, obesity in children had become a variant of this anxiety. For physicians, the questions to answer were what caused obesity and what were the best ways to treat it. Once they had eliminated physiological and genetic reasons, neither of which could account for any increase in obesity rates, Canadian practitioners were left with poor eating habits and psychological factors. The former could only be blamed on the parents and family situation and the parent who controlled that aspect of family life was the mother. The psychological focus was quite prominent in the literature on children from the 1950s onward; however, it didn't seem to result in any sustained treatment. What did were efforts to teach children what to eat, and if they proved incapable of keeping to a new way of eating, to assist them with drug aids.

Obesity (and malnutrition for that matter) in children focused attention on bodies largely ignored in the historical literature. Obesity raised the issue of what a normal weight was and what it should be. Seldom asked was whether the norm was a healthy weight; it was simply assumed to be, based on what was known about the nutritional needs of the body. Child obesity called attention to the needs of those who were the future of the nation. Gender, ethnicity, and class were aspects that entered various discussions of who was malnourished, who was obese, and why and how to overcome the problem. Bodies varied, and children's bodies especially so, as they followed the trajectory of growing from childhood to adulthood. What the literature on child obesity reveals, however, is the belief in an idealized body and the fear that another, less attractive, and more "weighty" body had taken its place.

Notes

Funding support for this essay came from Associated Medical Services in partnership with the Canadian Institutes of Health Research and from the Canada Research Chair Programme. Work on an earlier version began at the Liguria Study Center, Bogliasco, Italy, in 2007. Thanks to my research assistants, Carol Cooper, Cheryl Hulme, Nicole Fera, and Sarah Morse.

1 See Greg Critser, *Fat Land: How Americans Became the Fattest People in the World* (Boston, MA: Mariner Books, 2004), 133–40; Timothy Lobstein, "What Are the Factors Contributing to the Obesity Epidemic among Children and Youth?" Presentation Abstracts, International Conference on Physical Activity and Obesity in Children, Toronto, 24–7 June 2007; Roger Kersh and James A. Morone, "Obesity, Courts and the New Politics of Public Health," *Journal of Health Politics, Policy and Law* 30, no. 5 (2005), 843. Note that

much of the concern about obesity today is reminiscent of a moral panic. See Heather Orpana et al., "BMI and Mortality: Results from a National Longitudinal Study of Canadian Adults," *Obesity* 18, no. 1 (2009), 214–18. http://www.nature.com/oby/journal/v18/n1/full/oby2009191a.html, accessed 8 July 2011. Orpana's study suggests being overweight is a protective factor and class I obesity is not linked to increased mortality.

2 Maya Villeneuve (Nutrition Survey Section, Nutrition Research Division, Health Canada), "What Are Canadians Eating?" Report from The Sixth Annual Health and Nutritional Symposium, Toronto, 26 Nov. 2007, 1–2. Statistics on obesity are based on figures that have reflected contingency over time.

3 For literature on the health and bodies of children and youth, see Terry Copp, *The Anatomy of Poverty: The Condition of the Working Class in Montreal, 1897–1929* (Toronto: McClelland and Stewart, 1974); Jocelyn Motyer Raymond, *The Nursery World of Dr. Blatz* (Toronto: University of Toronto Press, 1991); Cynthia Comacchio, *"Nations Are Built of Babies": Saving Ontario Mothers and Children, 1900–1940* (Montreal and Kingston: McGill-Queen's University Press, 1993); Katharine Arnup, *Education for Motherhood: Advice for Mothers in Twentieth-Century Canada* (Toronto: University of Toronto Press, 1994); Gaston Desjardins, *L'amour en patience: La sexualité adolescente au Québec, 1940–1960* (Sainte-Foy: Presses de l'Université du Québec 1995); Steven Maynard, "'Horrible Temptations': Sex, Men, and Working-Class Male Youth in Urban Ontario, 1890–1935," *Canadian Historical Review* 78, no. 2 (1997): 197–235; Mona Gleason, "Embodied Negotiations: Children's Bodies and Historical Change in Canada, 1930–1960," *Journal of Canadian Studies* 32, no. 1 (1999), 112–38; Mona Gleason, "Disciplining the Student Body: Schooling and the Construction of Canadian Children's Bodies, 1930–1960," *History of Education Quarterly* 41, no. 2 (2001), 189–215; Cynthia Comacchio, "'The Rising Generation': Laying Claim to the Health of Adolescents in English Canada, 1920–1970," *Canadian Bulletin of Medical History* 19, no. 1 (2002), 139–78; Mona Gleason, "Race, Class, and Health: School Medical Inspection and 'Healthy' Children in British Columbia, 1890–1930," *Canadian Bulletin of Medical History* 19 (2002), 95–112; Mona Gleason, "From 'Disgraceful Carelessness' to 'Intelligent Precaution': Accidents and the Public Child in English Canada, 1900–1950," *Journal of Family History* 30, no. 2 (2005), 230–41; Robert M. Stamp, "Teaching the 'Children of Silence': Samuel Greene and the Hearing-Impaired," *Historical Studies in Education/Revue d'histoire de l'éducation,"* 17, no. 1 (2005), 165–8; Cheryl Krasnick Warsh and Veronica Strong-Boag, eds., *Children's Health Issues in Historical Perspective* (Waterloo: Wilfrid Laurier University Press, 2005); Mona Gleason, "Be-

tween Education and Memory: Health and Childhood in English Canada, 1900–1950," *Scientia Canadensis* 29, no. 1 (2006), 49–72; Aleck Samuel Ostry, *Nutrition Policy in Canada, 1870–1939* (Vancouver: UBC Press, 2006); Mona Gleason, "Size Matters: Medical Experts, Educators, and the Provision of Health Services to Children in Early to Mid-Twentieth English Canada," in *Healing the World's Children: Interdisciplinary Perspectives on Child Health in the Twentieth Century*, ed. Cynthia Comacchio, Janet Golden, and George Weisz (Montreal and Kingston: McGill-Queen's University Press, 2008), 176–202; Mona Gleason, "Lost Voices, Lost Bodies? Doctors and the Embodiment of Children and Youth in English Canada from 1900 to 1940," in *Lost Kids: Vulnerable Children and Youth in Twentieth-Century Canada and the United States*, ed. Mona Gleason, Tamara Myers, Leslie Paris, and Veronica Strong-Boag (Vancouver: UBC Press, 2009), 136–53; Denyse Baillargeon, *Babies for the Nation: The Medicalization of Motherhood in Quebec, 1910–1970* (Waterloo: Wilfrid Laurier University Press, 2009); Tasnim Nathoo and Aleck Ostry, *The One Best Way? Breastfeeding History, Politics, and Policy in Canada* (Waterloo: Wilfrid Laurier University Press, 2009). An important American study is Joan Jacobs Brumberg, *The Body Project: An Intimate History of American Girls* (New York: Vintage, 1998).

4 Peter Stearns, *Fat History: Bodies and Beauty in the Modern West* (New York: New York University Press, 2002), 162, 195–201; Harvey A. Levenstein, *Revolution at the Table: The Transformation of the American Diet* (Berkeley, CA: University of California Press, 2003), 8; Hillel Schwartz, *Never Satisfied: A Cultural History of Diets, Fantasies and Fat* (London: Collier Macmillan, 1986), 269; Laura Lovett, "The Popeye Principle: Selling Child Health in the First Nutrition Crisis," *Journal of Health Politics, Policy and Law* 30, no. 5 (2005), 803–38.

5 In 1922, the Canadian Society for the Study of the Diseases of Children had 13 members and in 1951, 216. Nathoo and Ostry, *The One Best Way?* 100. Even in 2010 there are only 2,300 practising paediatricians in the country, http://www.cma.ca/index.php/ci_id/16959/la_id/1.htm#1, accessed 2 Sept. 2010.

6 While Smith and Wakewich, this volume, mention the gaze directed at women and their work clothing during the Second World War, and Minnett, this volume, refers to the gaze directed at Lady X, a transparent plastic, larger than life representative "woman," the gaze directed at obese or overweight children, both boys and girls, focused on their bodies.

7 For the impact of the First World War and concern about children's health, see A.B. Dawson, "Recreation as a Public Health Measure," *PHJ* 11, no. 3 (1920), 120; n.a., "Standards of Nutrition," *CMAJ* 14, no. 6 (1924), 531; R.G. Sinclair, "The Nutritional Significance of Fat," *CMAJ* 38, no. 5 (1938), 492.

8 Aleck Ostry, "The Early Development of Nutrition Policy in Canada," in *Children's Health Issues in Historical Perspective*, ed. Krasnick Warsh and Strong-Boag, 191–206. See also Ostry's *Nutrition Policy in Canada*.

9 Alan Brown and G. Albert Davis, "The Prevalence of Malnutrition in the Public School Children of Toronto," *CMAJ* 11, no. 2 (1921), 124–6. On the nation, see Claire Campeau, "Nature of Milk as a Food," *Canadian Nurse* 18, no. 4 (1922), 223.

10 J.T.H. Phair, "Survey of Health Habits among School Age Children," *CPHJ* 25, no. 8 (1934), 382. For examples of other studies, see Gordon E. Swallow, "Anorexia," *CMAJ* 49, no. 1 (1943), 43; M.T. Doyle, M.C. Cahoon, and E.W. McHenry, "The Consumption of Recommended Foods by Children in Relation to Sex, the Use of Sweet Foods, and Employment of Mothers," *CJPH* 44, no. 7 (1953), 259–62; M.W. Partington and Norma Roberts, "The Heights and Weights of Indian and Eskimo School Children on James Bay and Hudson Bay," *CMAJ* 100, no. 11 (1969), 506; J. Ellestad-Sayed, J.C. Haworth, and H. Medovy, "Nutrition Survey of School Children in Greater Winnipeg," *CMAJ* 116, no. 5 (1977), 490.

11 Z.I. Sabry, "The Cost of Malnutrition in Canada," *CJPH* 66, no. 4 (1975), 291.

12 Lionel M. Lindsay, "The Overweight Child," *CMAJ* 44, no. 4 (1941), 504–6.

13 Alphamette Liquid ad, *CMAJ* 51, no. 5 (1944), 489.

14 G.T. Haig, "Suppose Tommy Won't Eat," *CJPH* 44, no. 1 (1953), 18.

15 R.J. Shepard et al., "The Working Capacity of Toronto Schoolchildren," *CMAJ* 100, no. 15 (1969), 710.

16 A. Angel, "Pathophysiology of Obesity," *CMAJ* 110, no. 5 (1974), 540. For concern in France, see S.S. Gilder, "The Fat Child," *CMAJ* 107, no. 11 (1972), 1068.

17 Lindsay, "The Overweight Child," 504.

18 For continuing discussion of endocrine/metabolic causation, see D.E. Rodger, J. Grant McFetridge, and Eileen Price, "The Management of Obesity," *CMAJ* 63, no. 3 (1950), 265; Probese ad, *CMAJ* 78, no. 6 (1958), 70; book review of *Adolescent Nutrition and Growth*, ed. Felix P. Heald (New York: Appleton-Century-Crofts, 1969), *CMAJ* 102, no. 3 (1970), 433; Richard Goldbloom, "Obesity in Childhood," *CMAJ* 113, no. 2 (1975), 139.

19 F.W. Tidmarsh, "Malnutrition," *CMAJ* 13, no. 6 (1923), 426.

20 Lindsay, "The Overweight Child," 504, 506; see also Rodger, McFetridge, and Price, "The Management of Obesity," 265–6. For reference to the Canadian Nutrition Program, see Smith and Wakewich, this volume.

21 John R. Beaton, "Energy Balance and Obesity," *CJPH* 58, no. 11 (1967), 481–2.

22 O. Schaefer, "Pre- and Post-natal Growth Acceleration and Increased Sugar

Consumptions in Canadian Eskimos," *CMAJ* 103, no. 10 (1970), 1059. For concern about Inuit, see also M.K. Rajic et al., "Height-Weight Comparison of Canadian Schoolchildren," in *Physical Fitness Assessment: Principles, Practice and Application*, ed. Roy J. Shephard et al. (Springfield, IL: Charles C. Thomas, 1978), 73.

23 N.a., "Obesity in Children Equally Intractable," *CMAJ* 112, no. 3 (1975), 350; Angel, "Pathophysiology Changes in Obesity," 1402.

24 W.W. Hawkins, "Some Medical and Biological Aspects of Obesity," *CJPH* 54, no. 10 (1963), 479.

25 Rodger, McFetridge, and Price, "The Management of Obesity," 266.

26 D.A. Hill, "A Wetzel Grid Survey in Toronto," *CJPH* 44, no. 8 (1953), 286. For concern about how immigrants ate, see Franca Iacovetta and Valerie J. Korinek, "Jell-O Salads, One Stop Shopping, and Maria the Homemaker: The Gender Politics of Food," in *Sisters or Strangers? Immigrant, Ethnic and Racialized Women in Canadian History*, ed. Marlene Epp, Franca Iacovetta, and Frances Swyripa (Toronto: University of Toronto Press, 2004), 190–230.

27 A.M. Bryans, "Childhood Obesity – Prelude to Adult Obesity," *CJPH* 58, no. 11 (1967), 488.

28 On psychology and children, see Mona Gleason, *Normalizing the Ideal: Psychology, Schooling, and the Family in Postwar Canada* (Toronto: University of Toronto Press, 1999).

29 On Bruch, see n.a, "The Emotional Obese," *CD* 14, 3 (1948), 92; Rodger, McFetridge, and Price, "The Management of Obesity," 265; Antonio Martel, "Preludine (Phenmetrazine) in the Treatment of Obesity," *CMAJ* 76, no. 2 (1957), 119.

30 Daniel Cappon, "Review Article, Obesity," *CMAJ* 79, no. 7 (1958), 571–2.

31 Maurice Jetté, William Barry, Lyon Pearlman, "The Effects of an Extra-curricular Physical Activity on Obese Adolescents," *CJPH* 68, no. 1 (1977), 39. See Christopher J. Greig, "The Idea of Boyhood in Postwar Ontario, 1945–1960," doctoral dissertation, University of Western Ontario, 2008, 119, for link between overweight boys and being effeminate.

32 News Brief, "Decline of Walking," *CD* 21, no. 6 (1955), 55; R.J. Shepard et al., "The Working Capacity of Toronto Schoolchildren," *CMAJ* 100, no. 15 (1969), 710. On the lack of exercise, see D.M. Sinclair, "Obesity as a Public Health Problem," *CJPH* 58, no. 11 (1967), 520; Richard Goldbloom, "Obesity in Childhood," *CMAJ* 113, no. 2 (1975), 139.

33 Bryans, "Childhood Obesity – Prelude to Adult Obesity," 488.

34 Lindsay, "The Overweight Child," 505.

35 Walter R. Campbell, "Obesity and Its Treatment," *CMAJ* 34, no. 1 (1936), 42; Lindsay, "The Overweight Child," 505. For bananas, see Canadian Banana

Co. ad, *CMAJ* 79, no. 6 (1958), 51. For the poor diet of teenagers, see Doris
L. Noble, "Eating," *CJPH* 43, 10 (1952), 432; Preludin ad, *CMAJ* 93, no. 16
(1965), 45.

36 Lindsay, "The Overweight Child," 506.
37 Gilder, "The Fat Child," 1068.
38 Barbara A. Davis and Daniel A.K. Roncari, "Behavioural Treatment of Obes-
    ity," *CMAJ* 119, no. 12 (1978), 1423, and Jetté, Barry, and Pearlman, "The
    Effects of an Extracurricular Physical Activity on Obese Adolescents," 39.
39 For lack of fitness in Canadians, see Minnett, this volume.
40 Lindsay, "The Overweight Child," 506.
41 Leonora Hawirko and P.H. Sprague, "Treatment of Obesity by Appetite-
    Depressing Drugs," *CMAJ* 54, no. 1 (1946), 29.
42 For Dexedrine ad, see *CD* 24, no. 5 (1958), 18. For Probese ad see *CMAJ* 78,
    no. 6 (1958), 70.
43 Martel, "Preludin (Phenmetrazine)," 117–20. For Preludin for children, see
    Preludin ad, *CMAJ* 78, no. 2 (1958), 59. Preludin turned out to be addictive
    if taken incorrectly, and reports of some cases of psychosis were reported in
    subsequent years. http://en.wikipedia.org/wiki/Preludin, accessed 9 Feb.
    2009.
44 Ambar Extentabs ad, *CD* 32, no. 11 (1966), 6.
45 Durabolin ad, *CMAJ* 91, no. 21 (1964), 46.
46 N.a., "Obesity in Children Equally Intractable," *CMAJ* 112, no. 3 (1975),
    350; Davis and Roncari, "Behavioural Treatment of Obesity," 1423; Anthony
    W. Myers and David L. Yeung, "Obesity in Infants: Significance, Aetiology,
    and Prevention," *CJPH* 70, no. 2 (1979), 117.
47 N.a., "Obesity in Children Equally Intractable," 350; n.a., "Controversies in
    Medicine Fanned during Association Scientific Meeting," *CMAJ* 113, no. 1
    (1975), 64.
48 See Alan Parkin, *A History of Psychoanalysis in Canada* (Toronto: Toronto
    Psychoanalytic Society, 1987).
49 N.a., "Obesity in Children Equally Intractable," 350.

13 Public Body, Private Health: *Mediscope*, the Transparent Woman, and Medical Authority, 1959

VALERIE MINNETT

In 1959, the physicians of the Ontario Medical Association (OMA) staged *Mediscope*, an exhibition designed to instil public confidence in scientific medicine by demystifying the professional care of the body. Billed as the first exhibition of its kind in Canada, *Mediscope* featured "graphic demonstrations of the workings of the human body, from the development of a baby to the illnesses of old age."[1] Physicians from across the province of Ontario planned and orchestrated the entire event from designing the large-scale exhibits, fundraising, and advertising to manning the displays over the course of the exhibition. The Woman's Auxiliary of the OMA also contributed; 750 physicians' wives and student nurses gave guided tours and hosted visiting school groups. *Mediscope* opened on Thanksgiving weekend, running from 12 to 17 October, and conservative estimates placed attendance at between 125,000 and 150,000 visitors over that duration. The exhibition was held in the Queen Elizabeth Building on the Canadian National Exhibition grounds.[2]

The *Globe and Mail* reported that *Mediscope* was "designed to increase understanding between the medical profession and the public ... [It] will provide an opportunity for the public to see, in exhibit form, aspects of the history, present status and future of medicine." Doctors and medical technicians were stationed at each exhibit, and "they will constitute the largest force of medical men ever assembled in Canada to demonstrate medical techniques and answer questions from the public."[3] Exhibits featured doctors in action performing major surgery, highlighted their technical skills such as reading X-rays and using laboratory equipment, and sharing specialized knowledge with the public, for example, following the development of a baby from conception to birth or diagnosing disease or illness (see Figure 13.1).

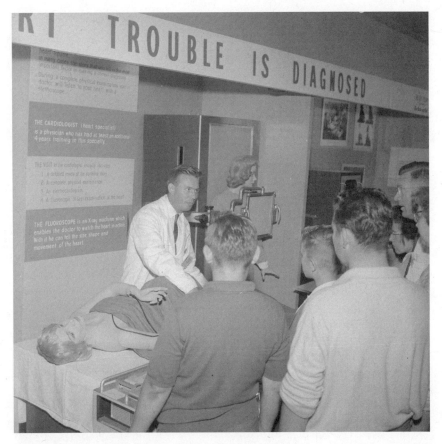

Figure 13.1 A physician demonstrates the diagnosis of a heart condition to *Mediscope* '59 visitors. CNE Archives MG5–0–0–0–435–10.

Mediscope evolved partially in response to remarks made by Prince Philip, Duke of Edinburgh, and president of the Canadian Medical Association (CMA), in July 1958. Philip noted the "sub-health" of Canadian citizens and challenged doctors to pledge their wholehearted support to reverse worrisome health trends.[4] This was a major concern for Ontario's physicians, who offered up numerous insights into their work and world in exchange for increased confidence from patients. Visitors to the exhibition were presumably invited to share what Michel Foucault has termed the "medical gaze," signifying the way modern physicians

are trained "to see" and "to know," and the OMA was loudly congratulated for taking the public "into their confidence."[5] By extending this
trust, the OMA believed that the general public would assume greater
responsibility for their own health, visiting the doctor's office more readily if they could identify perceptible signs of illness. Ontario's education
minister also praised the OMA for giving laypeople a small glimpse of
how certain medical procedures worked, demonstrating what and how a
physician was scientifically trained to see.[6]

   Mediscope featured fifty large-scale exhibits, each staffed by a corps of
volunteer physicians who gave instructive talks and answered the public's
questions. Although the huge range of displays impressed visitors and
media, the most popular and well-attended exhibit came at the end of
the show: a transparent, life-sized anatomy model of a woman that narrated a 17-minute tour of the body – focusing on major organs, arteries,
and veins – which lit up as she pivoted on stage (see Figure 13.2). OMA
committee members approached Toronto businesses to help underwrite
the cost of exhibits, and the *Toronto Daily Star* purchased the transparent
woman, or "Lady X," as she was referred to in the media, for *Mediscope*.
Built in Cologne, Germany, Lady X was modelled after a twenty-eight-
year-old German woman whose body was cast to make a mould. Her
bones were made of metal, veins and arteries were represented by wire,
and major organs were rendered in plastic, all encased in Lucite – a
hard, transparent thermoplastic popular in the 1940s and 1950s. Experts
in the United States implanted an electronic voice system in Lady X before she was shipped to Toronto. The model also arrived with a hefty
price tag; the *Star* shelled out $20,000 for her purchase.[7]

   Historicizing *Mediscope* and the exhibition of the transparent woman
is an opportunity to interrogate the complex responses to the public display of medical knowledge, especially as it pertained to women's bodies.
Although the model was see-through, Lady X was anything but transparent. The transparent body, José van Dijck argues, is a "complex product
of our culture – a culture that capitalizes on perfectibility and malle-
ability."[8] The ideal of transparency governed the possibilities and limits
of putting medical knowledge on display. Lady X reinforced the idea
that to see is to know, and promulgated the notion that gazing into the
body produced easy solutions to complex medical mysteries. The media
compounded the idea that seeing is knowing by devoting large portions
of text and images to *Mediscope*, consistently noting the enlightenment of
the lay public who visited the exhibits. The very nature of the exhibition,
however, contradicted true clinical observation as defined by Foucault:

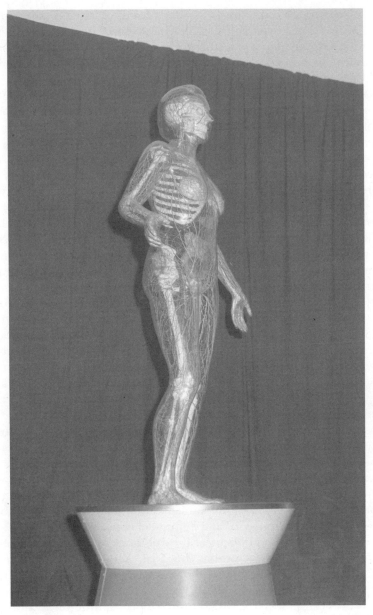

Figure 13.2 The Transparent Woman on display at *Mediscope* '59. CNE Archives
MG5–0-0–0-435–33.

"The observing gaze refrains from intervening: it is silent and gesture-less. Observation leaves things as they are; there is nothing hidden to it in what is given. The correlative of observation is never the invisible, but always the immediately visible, once one has removed the obstacles erected to reason by theories and to the senses by the imagination."[9]

Mediscope fulfilled familiar categories of spectacle rather than offering an opportunity for unmediated clinical observation. The exhibition of Lady X represents, in particular, a carefully orchestrated juncture be-tween medical knowledge and popular entertainment. The model was presented as an object of medical knowledge that invited curious spec-tators to gaze upon and into the body without fear of social censure; it offered a privileged viewing usually reserved for high art or (less respect-able) sideshow exhibitions.[10] I argue that Lady X is an example of the transparent body as a cultural artefact, an idealized feminine form whose display sought to elicit specific responses and actions from spectators. In this regard, the exhibit followed long-standing traditions in the medi-cal or scientific display of women's bodies. The transparent woman pre-sented viewers with two narratives, one dealing with the performance of gendered citizenship and the other reinforcing the power of the medical gaze. Medical knowledge and media technologies worked together to in-form these narratives, fuelling public perceptions about the importance of maintaining the social and physical health of the body, and promising increased access to and understanding of medical knowledge about the body through *guided* observation. In the broader context of *Mediscope*, Lady X was invested with traditional gendered assumptions but simul-taneously challenged the dominant discourses that defined the body as private. Throughout the exhibition, women's bodies were strongly as-sociated with motherhood, the home, and their importance in main-taining a healthy citizenry through reliance on clinical medicine. By becoming a public body through exhibitionary display, Lady X imbued private, household issues with an impetus to focus on citizenship. In the broader context of *Mediscope*, the transparent woman identified the body as an important site for social and cultural change.

Despite the fact that public health exhibitions such as *Mediscope* have received little scholarly attention, they were key components in popu-larizing and normalizing medical discourses. In this case, medicine's gendered assumptions were highlighted, the body was identified as an important site for social and cultural change, and the distinctions be-tween public and private were blurred as physicians sought to increase their standing as experts. Lady X's display facilitated this endeavour –

her sex communicated ideas about gender, her transparency displayed medical confidence in the public, and her mechanics suggested how the body was central to appropriate citizenship. As an object of medical knowledge, the transparent woman presented the body as technology – the body as machine – in a visually graphic way. Her lucidity signified the willingness of physicians to initiate the lay public into their way of seeing by educators and government officials. Alternatively, the transparent woman gave legitimacy to these physicians, who used her display to showcase their specialized and exclusive knowledge of the body. *Mediscope* reinforced a discourse that gendered medicine masculine by virtue of its definition as scientific and rational, justified in assuming a penetrating gaze. Patients, meanwhile, were feminized, expected to comply with expert knowledge, and dependent on physicians for the maintenance of healthy bodies.

The Transparent Woman

The decision to purchase and display a transparent anatomy model was enthusiastically promoted by members of the OMA. A committee of Ontario physicians dedicated to the idea of staging an exhibition convened in 1957, buoyed by the recent visit of several members to a similar event hosted by doctors in Cincinnati. There, they noticed that exhibits were "calculated to bring to the public, something of the progress made by medicine and the services being rendered by the medical profession." More importantly, doctors in Cincinnati felt that the exhibition had "enhanced their status ... it proved to be an excellent public relations project."[11] The OMA's exhibition committee travelled to other venues as well: American Medical Association Headquarters, the Museum of Industry and Science, and the Hindsdale Health Museum (a privately endowed institution) in Chicago, and museums that featured health-related exhibits in Buffalo and Cleveland. The committee returned with this proclamation:

> two exhibits stood out above all others and must be in our exposition if it is to be a first class show. These exhibits are:
>   (i) the plastic figure commonly referred to as JUNO
>   (ii) the Birth of a Baby – which is also called Life Before Birth.[12]

"Juno" was the first known transparent woman to be displayed in North America, making her debut at Manhattan's Museum of Science and Industry in August 1936. Advertised as "the woman without mystery,"[13] this model was built at the Hygiene Museum in Dresden, Germany, for a private philanthropist in Michigan, who took it on the road across the United States. The two-year, hundred-city tour was promoted mostly to scientists, public health officers, and the medical profession, but the transparent woman was wildly popular with lay audiences as well.[14] Four transparent men had been constructed prior to this, all originating in Dresden, and were displayed across Europe and the United States.[15] Despite the earlier success of these exhibits, Lady X was the first transparent model to be displayed publicly in Canada.

Notwithstanding the spectacular appeal of such an exhibit, advertisements for *Mediscope* and the general discourse among OMA members appealed to the public by imbuing the transparent woman with a gendered, and highly charged sexual identity. Dr. S.F. Robertson, chairman of the OMA's Exposition Committee, set the tone for the event, stating, "As is the case in every day life, WOMAN has captured the spotlight in MEDISCOPE '59."[16] Robertson's comments reflected the mood of OMA physicians, who were eager to win public favour by promoting and hosting a successful show. The transparent woman was ensured sustained media attention since the *Toronto Daily Star* underwrote the cost of purchasing the model. The pages of the OMA's journal, *Ontario Medical Review*, also emphasized the transparent woman's feminine charms in updates to their readership:

> Our fragile young lady, as yet unnamed, is receiving her final curves and appropriate dimensions before taking an airplane trip across the Atlantic where she will learn to speak with the assistance of American electronic experts. Like all of her sex, she will be a show stopper … [her] audible utterances will be confined to educating viewers with the workings of the human body. To her creators in Cologne, Germany, she is JUNO, the namesake of the goddess Juno, mythologically recognized as … *the sublime embodiment of virtue and the protectress of women everywhere.* (original emphasis)[17]

Although her plastic construction facilitated the medical display of the body's interior, Lady X was constructed to idealized female bodily proportions. She was touted in the media as having an "average figure," but newspapers also ran details of her bust, waist, and hip measurements, making comparisons between Lady X and the Venus de Milo. Rather than emphasize Lady X's medico-educational value, the OMA and the media situated the anatomy model as an object of visual pleasure and titillating sexuality.[18] This strategy places the display of Lady X historically alongside other "scientific" exhibitions of women's bodies, perhaps most famously Saartjie Baartman, the "Hottentot Venus," and among centuries of anatomy illustration.[19]

The *Toronto Daily Star* sponsored a contest to name the transparent woman in the months leading up to *Mediscope*. This was an important step in promoting the show and endearing Lady X to the public. First prize in the naming competition was a $1,000 scholarship in health education. Setting aside any pretext of medical or scientific objectivity, the ads for this naming contest and the newspaper's promotional features for *Mediscope* endowed Lady X with a sexualized identity and advertised her idealized feminine form. The week before *Mediscope* officially opened, the *Star* ran this description of the transparent woman: "She stands 67 ½ inches tall. Her bust is 37 ¾, waist 31 ½, and hips 38 ½. She is three and one-half inches taller than Venus, almost the same in bust and waist as Venus, and not nearly as hippy as the Greek Goddess of Love."[20]

An advertisement for the contest to name Lady X appeared in the paper that same day and every subsequent day for the next two weeks. Urging readers to "Stop Whistling! Give her a name," the *Star*'s contest made obvious reference to the sexual identity attributed to the transparent woman.[21]

Lady X was touted as having an "average" figure, but her comparison to the Venus de Milo and the overt sexual message of the ads for the naming contest in the *Star* made her into an object of desire. Lady X's plastic construction allowed her to exhibit ideal proportions that were anything but representative of real women. Consider this comparison of Lady X to the average American woman from a *Star* reporter: "A few years ago American women received a rude awakening when, from the measurements of 15,000 women, the late Dr. Robert L. Dickenson found the average American woman tends to be rather short, plump, big-busted and broad-hipped. A model, named 'Norma,' was made from these measurements. Lady X is four inches taller than Norma, more than two inches bigger in the bust, two inches smaller in the waist, and just a half inch bigger in the hips."[22]

Despite this revelation, Lady X was advertised as "a physical counterpart of all women," which not only enhanced her mystique, but set a physical standard for health and, by extension, beauty. The contest to name Lady X reveals that the model was perceived to be a doll of sorts rather than an object of medical knowledge; among the colourful entries were "Cassie, the Lassie with the Glassy Chassis"; "Cutie, the beauty on medical duty"; "Fetchin' Gretchen"; "Plastic Pat"; "Suzie Sawbones"; and "Transparent Tilly." The doctors who judged the competition opted for a more serious name in the end, and Lady X was dubbed "Lehra" from the German verb "to teach." Miss Jean McCrimmon submitted the winning name, and the *Star* coyly reported, "When Lehra and Miss McCrimmon met ... for the first time, both were speechless."[23]

The contest to name Lehra united the two narratives that she embodied through her public display: gendered performance and the primacy of the medical gaze. Naming "Lady X" bridged the gap between clinicians and laypeople by providing an opportunity for the public to participate in one small, but widely publicized, part of the exhibition. It established a relationship between Lehra and her public, proving both the metaphorical, as well as physical, aspects of her transparency.

Historian Ludmilla Jordanova argues that medicine, traditionally, is not primarily part of the public domain. It is generally understood in terms of privacy and is defined by words like "confidentiality" and "secrecy."[24] Displaying Lehra was an important part in the exchange of information from clinician to layperson and legitimated the degree of "confidence" imparted on the public. Media images catered to this physician-driven mandate, in one case using a photograph featuring Lehra's transparency to denote the sharing of a secret, woman to woman (see Figure 13.3). The photo's caption reads, "'Lehra' bares inner self to confidants." Divulging medical secrets entailed the public display of knowledge, and Lehra's lucidity reinforced the notion that physicians had nothing to hide. Despite this show of good faith, newspaper evidence suggests that some members of the public were uneasy with this transfer of information. Alongside photographs and advertisements that overtly sexualized the model, some reporters questioned the suitability of the transparent woman's exhibition by drawing attention to the perceived immodesty of displaying "private" parts to a public audience. This was not only an issue of displaying "appropriate" nudity, but also a much deeper and possibly perverse, to some, look into the body's interior.[25] Science reporter Leonard Bertin, for example, left his children, aged eleven and nine and a half, at home until he had satisfied himself that the exhibits were wholesome enough for children to view.[26] More explicitly, *Star* columnist Lotta Dempsey voiced concern about the appropriateness of both the public display of a woman's body and the public accumulation of medical knowledge. In an edition of her column "Private Line," Dempsey recounts a conversation with a physician friend in the weeks leading up to *Mediscope*:

I've always thought of your Hypocrates zone as the original no-layman's land. No trespassing ... Now don't imagine I'm not in favor of enlightenment, doc. But don't you think there's a little danger in giving too much book, chapter and verse in this big Inside You expose? ... First thing you know, every woman will be constructing her own, transparent talking woman, like she does a papier-machier dressmaker dummy for sewing. Even maybe putting pins in where it hurts ... And take husbands. You know how they like to tinker. There could be an epidemic of do-it-yourself operating rooms off suburban garages; home body repair shops ... togetherness periods in pathology and anatomy with the children Sunday afternoons.

Dempsey's editorialized observations speak to the concern physicians' voiced – the public was uninformed in basic matters of anatomy and personal health. Dempsey's column expresses doubt about the public's ability to receive and digest medical knowledge and articulates a palpable concern about the public display of a woman's body. Reading from a press release, Dempsey continues: "'As the theatre lights dim, the audience will only be conscious of the human figure before them. Her brain will light up first, and she will explain it ... She will then take you on a tour of the human anatomy, stopping ... at her larynx, thyroid gland, lungs, heart, liver, gall bladder, spleen, pancreas gland, stomach, etc. etc. etc.' (I found myself unaccountably pulling my coat modestly around me and buttoning it up)."[27]

In both Dempsey's description and transcripts of Lehra's narration, the "tour of the human anatomy" is strictly gender neutral, featuring internal body parts and organs that both males and females possess. There is no mention of breasts, the uterus, or womb. Why then, is Dempsey so concerned about modesty, only articulating concern when she reads how Lehra will publicly describe her body despite the exclusion of so-called private parts? Medical historian Ludmilla Jordanova posits that the distinctions between male and female, public and private, are central to conventions that regulate the human body.[28] Dempsey's dramatic reaction to reading about Lehra's performance – pulling her own coat closer around her, as if to elude the probing gaze of an imagined audience – spoke to the long-standing, and tenuous, boundary between public and private. This duality worked on the premise that women understood their bodies to be exclusively private in nature and that their public lives were contingent on modesty. When Lehra went on display, privacy became public. Dempsey could not reconcile the public display of a body with her understanding of what it meant to be a woman.

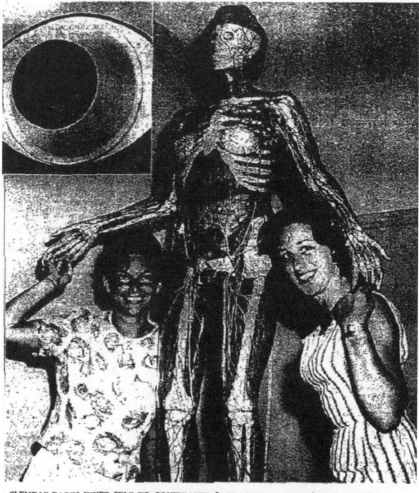

"LEHRA" BARES INNER SELF TO CONFIDANTS SANDI EKSTEIN AND DVORA BLITSTEIN
The Star donated $20,000 to bring transparent woman to CNE from Cologne, Germany

Figure 13.3 *Mediscope* and Lehra were put on display as part of the CNE two years following the initial 1959 show. *Toronto Daily Star*, 10 August 1961.

The allure of Lehra's outer beauty – her form, and the display of her inner mechanics – her function, exemplifies what women's bodies as artefacts can represent culturally. I argue that in becoming a public body, Lehra imbued private household issues with an impetus to focus on citizenship. In spite of her imagined sexual persona, potential to instil public confidence in the medical profession, and the question of her affect on audiences, Lehra's narrative sends a message quite apart from, yet inextricably linked to, these gendered qualities. An excerpt from her recorded narrative states: "I have made the unseen visible to you. You have seen the intricate parts which function harmoniously together to keep us in good health of mind and body. Please guard them· in your daily living by using good sense in the care of the house in which you live but once."[29]

Lehra's gender provided viewers with a familiar point of reference for imagining the metaphorical connections between body and house. The relationship between body and house has long been recognized as a vital component in the construction of fit citizens. Speaking about mid-Victorian England, literary theorist Pamela Gilbert says, "Preparation for citizenship came to be seen less as a matter of acquiring a public and political identity than of shaping the familial, moral and physical environment required to foster a natural and healthy body and mind ... fitness for citizenship ceased to be simply a political issue and became instead explicitly a social matter rooted in the private and domestic spheres."[30]

Citizens were not only the moral products of education, but also they became physical products of good domestic hygiene and health. Links between poor housing and poor health were a well-established part of the Sanitarian movement in mid-nineteenth century England, where it was not uncommon for the house to be regarded as an extension of the body.[31] Couple this tradition with early twentieth-century concerns that chronically unhealthy bodies would not result in fit citizens, and the relationship becomes clearer. The female body has been used historically to personify abstract qualities as a "ready substratum onto which shared values and collective commitments can be projected, even if these have not been consciously articulated."[32] Visually and verbally, Lehra communicated the importance of maintaining the body as a good "house," a private domain for healthy, fit citizenship. Housing and respectable domesticity are recognized as vital in demonstrating appropriate social standing and announcing prosperity and well-being. Elsewhere in this collection, Smith and Wakewich argue for the primacy of the home in understanding the connections between women's bodies and appropriate citizenship. They describe the home as "the arena for negotiating the boundaries of the social skin and the place in which the female ... body was to be restored to the conventional ideal."[33] The display of Lehra took this a step further by presenting her as an embodied expression of home. Lehra's transparency made her body into an open-house that demonstrated how private matters had implications for civic and social health, and entrenched the connection between ideal femininity and home.

Gendering citizenship was an important part of this discourse, and *Mediscope* expressed the integral role of the doctor in shaping healthy citizens. The overall narrative of *Mediscope* confirmed that women were defined medically by childbirth and motherhood through its layout. Physicians crafted the exhibition around the life story of a girl, beginning with her conception, and ending when she gives birth herself under the watchful care of the medical practitioner who was present for every step of her journey. The catalogue description reads: "The doctor delivers a baby girl and cares for her through infancy, childhood and adulthood. She receives treatment for tonsil and appendix conditions and a skin rash; her grandfather is treated for a heart ailment, and grandmother for a broken wrist. This demonstration of the versatility of the General Practitioner concludes as the girl, now grown to adulthood, looks forward to the care of the same family doctor during her pregnancy."

Lehra was displayed at the conclusion of this story as an embodied ideal that balanced private action and public responsibility. The OMA crafted this exhibitionary narrative to "improve the health standards of the people of Ontario" by suggesting a specific vision of citizenship, one that imagined women as mothers and featured a healthy, professionally cared-for, body at its core.[34]

Media reports, however, were careful to promote the focus of *Mediscope* on women's health in a measured tone. Eliciting a feminist response in one breath, and quelling fears about the pervasiveness of women's issues in the next, one reporter wrote:

> Contrary to popular belief, women are stronger than men. They are stronger biologically and psychologically, though not physically. But Lady X, the talking transparent woman, does not boast about this in her talk about anatomy that thousands of people will hear next week … Scientists are learning that women are biologically quite different from men in more pervasive ways than the obvious physical differences. Femaleness has an elusive quality. It shows in the way a ball is thrown, a needle is threaded. It shows in the approach to a problem, in the reaction to a crisis.[35]

The narrative of *Mediscope* seemingly privileged the health-story of women to attract the attention of audiences by revealing those "elusive" qualities that governed the female body. This was one more part of the secret, or specialized, knowledge physicians could offer up in hopes of attracting the public's attention.

Medical Authority

Plans for *Mediscope* were prompted by the belief on the part of many physicians that people were reluctant to seek a doctor's care because they lacked confidence in professional medicine. Inviting the public to watch doctors in action and to see the intricate workings of the body was a calculated move to dispel anti-professional attitudes that physicians interpreted as fear or misunderstanding. Doctors sought to control, from the very beginning, the way their profession was represented to the public. Some balked at the idea of attempting to educate the layperson, claiming the undertaking "wasn't the professional thing to do" or that "the people wouldn't come."[36] Concerns about drawing the attention and attendance of the public were unfounded, but physicians maintained strict control over the way exhibits were experienced and viewed. Each display was manned by at least one doctor, who answered viewers' inquiries and, in some cases, provided demonstrations (see Figure 13.1). The OMA was conscious to exert this control from the time planning *Mediscope* began, stating, "Conducting this Exposition will be the passing of a milestone in improving doctor-patient relations. The [medical] profession has the responsibility of making sure the public gets its medical information from the most authoritative source ... the doctors."[37]

Most exhibits were designed specifically to feature physicians' knowledge. Medical technologies were demonstrated, diseases were diagnosed, and complex medical procedures were explained and illustrated with the aid of an initiated interpreter. Lehra's display was slightly different. Yet, in spite of her autonomous speech, audience members could only expect to walk away from Lehra's performance with a rudimentary understanding of the placement and function of a few major organs. Answers to specific questions about the material reality of the body's interior relied on the cooperation and expertise of trained medical practitioners.

Conclusion

Historians agree that medical distance from the public is a crucial element in the maintenance of professional status, especially separating medical display from popular entertainment.[38] The knowledge and training required to read medical displays and images ultimately reflects a level of professional authority. It is crucial to understand how these performances of professional power inform issues of control and agency in mitigating access to medical knowledge. Foucault suggests that clinical knowledge is jealously guarded and does not lend itself easily to simple explanation: "Description, in clinical medicine, does not mean placing the hidden or the invisible in reach of those who have no direct access to them; what it means to give speech to that which everyone sees without seeing – a speech that can only be understood by those initiated into true speech."[39]

Exhibiting the transparent woman expressed physicians' confidence in the public to understand the relationship between seeing and knowing. This confidence, however, was tempered by the lay public's limited medical knowledge. Exhibition-goers were confronted with a diluted version of the specialized information that practitioners in the modern medical profession demanded, and potential for Foucault's observing gaze was eliminated by exhibits designed and mediated by physicians. The transparent woman was intended strictly for lay education, which differentiates her from other forms of medical imaging. The model was not a diagnostic aide for physicians, nor a teaching tool for clinicians-in-training, but merely a spectacle for public consumption. In some respects, Lehra's narrative was a ruse that diverted attention away from medical or true corporeal knowledge and focused instead on the performance of gendered citizenship.

Lehra's triumph as a scientific artefact negated the desire for a more comprehensive look into the body. The progress of medical science, van Dijck argues, relies in part on confidence in the medical gaze, and partly on the exaltation of technology; imaging tools that penetrate the body and help see inside lead to more knowledge, and more knowledge to better cures. Overall, the transparent woman helped to entrench the primacy of the medical practitioner in matters of health by embodying both. Her transparency complicated the visuality of the body with its tangle of wires and plastic parts, rather than making it clearer. Lehra's sex influenced this way of seeing, and she suggested particular ways of thinking about the body not only medically, but also socially and culturally.

Lehra remains on display today, the flagship exhibit in the Ontario Science Centre's "Human Body" hall, although she has lost her voice box and Lucite shell.[40] Her longevity can perhaps be attributed to the constancy of the ideal of transparency. The public still seeks intimate knowledge of the body's interior: to see what cannot be seen. Notwithstanding the proliferation of medical imaging currently available to the lay public, the interior of the body still retains a certain mystique (to which the success of Gunther von Hagens's *Body Worlds*[41] and like exhibitions attests). Lehra remains a three-dimensional reminder of the mediated body as artefact, an object of medical technology that has persisted in the wake of sophisticated digital, magnetic, and ultrasound imaging. At *Mediscope*, the visuality of the transparent body was complicated by the public's inability to see and to know. Although laypeople were given a glimpse into the body, their untrained eyes could not translate vision into medical knowledge. Instead, medical practitioners were upheld as vanguards of health and as unquestionable authorities.

Notes

Many thanks to Linda Cobon at the CNE Archives for bringing *Mediscope* to my attention, and Gus Dassios at the Ontario Science Centre for introducing me to Lehra.

1 *Globe and Mail*, 26 Feb 1959.
2 "A Permanent Mediscope?" *Globe and Mail*, 19 Oct. 1959.
3 *Globe and Mail*, 26 Feb. 1959.
4 J. Clarence Boyle, "Mediscope and Sub-Health," *Globe and Mail*, 22 Oct. 1959.
5 "All Major Exhibits Attract Long Queues," *Globe and Mail*, 13 Oct. 1959.
6 "30,000 at Mediscope Opening," *Globe and Mail*, 13 Oct. 1959.
7 The *Star's* purchase of the model seems to be purely for the purposes of publicity. Underwriting the cost of Lady X provided ample opportunity for promoting the newspaper and its role in bringing an unprecedented and technologically sophisticated medical display to the citizens of Ontario.
8 José van Dijck, *The Transparent Body: A Cultural Analysis of Medical Imaging* (Seattle, WA: University of Washington Press, 2005), 5.
9 Michel Foucault, *The Birth of the Clinic: An Archaeology of Medical Perception*, trans. A.M. Sheridan (London: Routledge, 2003), 131.
10 Jane Nicholas is especially helpful in contextualizing the public display of women and outlining culturally acceptable or understood categories of gazing at bodies in early twentieth-century Canada. See Nicholas, "'A Figure of a Nude Woman': Art, Popular Culture, and Modernity at the Canadian National Exhibition, 1927," *Histoire sociale/Social History* 41, no. 82 (2008), 313–44.

11 "Reports to Council and Transactions of Council: Committee on Medical Exposition," *Ontario Medical Review* 26, no.11 (1959), 114.

12 "Reports to Council and Transactions of Council: Committee on Medical Exposition," *Ontario Medical Review* 26, no.11 (1959), 116.

13 "Woman without Mystery on Display in New York," *Science News Letter*, 29 Aug. 1936.

14 Juno is still on display at HealthSpace, Cleveland, Ohio, part of the Cleveland Museum of Natural History.

15 "Medicine: Museum Piece," *Time*, 31 Aug 1936, http://www.time.com/time/magazine/article/0,9171,756568,00.html.

16 Dr. S.F. Robertson "Woman Steals Spotlight as Mediscope '59 Imports Mythical Goddess from Germany," *Ontario Medical Review* 26, no.4 (1958), 396.

17 Ibid.

18 Lisa Cartwright argues that medical anatomy has traditionally regarded with "contempt and dismissal" parts of the female body because they bear sexual meanings. See "A Cultural Anatomy of the Visible Human Project," *The Visible Woman: Imaging Technologies, Gender and Science*, ed. Paula A. Treichler, Lisa Cartwright, and Constance Penley (New York: New York University Press, 1998), 23.

19 Although the exhibition and legacy of these two women's bodies differs significantly, Baartman and Lady X share the distinction of becoming sexualized, public bodies appropriated for the dissemination of scientific knowledge. For further reading about the display and afterlife of Saartjie Baartman's body, see Rachel Holmes, *The Hottentot Venus: The Life and Death of Saartjie Baartman* (London: Bloomsbury, 2007), and Clifton Crais and Pamela Scully, *Sara Baartman and the Hottentot Venus: A Ghost Story and a Biography* (Princeton, NJ: Princeton University Press, 2009). For a discussion of emerging illustrations of sex and sex difference in anatomy during the eighteenth and nineteenth centuries, see Londa Schiebinger, "Skeletons in the Closet: The First Illustrations of the Female Skeleton in Eigtheenth-Century Anatomy," in *The Making of the Modern Body: Sexuality and Society in the Nineteenth Century*, ed. Catherine Gallagher and Thomas Laqueur (Berkeley, CA: University of California Press, 1987), 36–82, and Ludmilla Jordanova chapter 3, "Body Image and Sex Roles," in *Sexual Visions: Images of Gender in Science and Medicine between the Eighteenth and Twentieth Centuries* (Madison, WI: University of Wisconsin Press, 1989), 43–62.

20 "Name Transparent Lady Get $1,000 Star Bursary," *Toronto Daily Star*, 6 Oct. 1959.

21 The sexual appropriation of medical objects and images has a long-standing history, perhaps most popularly in the twentieth century through the trope

of "X-ray vision." X-rays' visual penetration of clothing and skin exposed bodies, and especially women's bodies, to a "lustful" gaze, giving rise to new forms of cultural consumption for medical imaging. See Bettyann Holtz-mann-Kevels, *Naked to the Bone: Medical Imaging in the Twentieth Century* (New Brunswick, NJ: Rutgers University Press, 1997), 27–30.

22 "Name Transparent Lady Get $1,000 Star Bursary."
23 "Woman Names Mediscope Model," *Toronto Daily Star*, 31 Dec. 1959.
24 Jordanova, "Body Image and Sex Roles," 136.
25 Pandora Syperek shows that Canadians found artistic value in the "right type" of nude figure in art during the interwar years, while other nude figures invoked cultural disquietude in their public display. See Syperek, this volume.
26 Leonard Bertin, "Something for Everyone at 'Mediscope' Show," *Toronto Daily Star*, 15 Oct. 1959.
27 Lotta Dempsey, "Doctors Now Let Us Peek Inside Us," *Toronto Daily Star*, 3 Oct. 1959.
28 Jordanova, *Sexual Visions*, 138.
29 *Mediscope* catalogue, 21.
30 Pamela Gilbert, *The Citizen's Body: Desire, Health, and the Social in Victorian England* (Columbus: Ohio State University Press, 2007), 3.
31 See Annmarie Adams, *Architecture in the Family Way: Doctors, Houses and Women, 1870–1900* (Montreal: McGill-Queen's University Press, 1996).
32 Jordanova, "Body Image and Sex Roles," 135.
33 Smith and Wakewich usefully employ Terence Turner's concept of the "social skin" to describe the surface of the body as a significant cultural medium for communicating ideas about social identity. See Smith and Wakewich, this volume.
34 *Mediscope* catalogue, 3.
35 Ben Rose, "Star Offers $1,000 Health Scholarship for Naming Proud 'Lady X,'" *Toronto Daily Star*, 8 Oct. 1959.
36 "Doctors' Show a Hit It Will Go on the Road," *Toronto Daily Star*, 14 Oct. 1959.
37 B.T. McLaughlin, "Medicine Opens the Door to the Public Next October with Medical Exposition," *Ontario Medical Review* 26, no. 2 (1958), 137.
38 See Jordanova, "Body Image and Sex Roles," 137, and *The Visible Woman: Imaging Technologies, Gender and Science*, ed. Paula A. Treichler, Lisa Cartwright, and Constance Penley (New York: New York University Press, 1998), 5.
39 Foucault, *Birth of the Clinic*, 141.
40 Lehra was donated to the Ontario Science Centre prior to its opening in 1969 and has been on display ever since.

41 Anatomist von Hagens invented a technique called Plastination in 1977 as a way of preserving human tissue with plastics. Originally limited to preserving small samples, von Hagens is now able to preserve entire human corpses that are displayed in the spectacular, if controversial, *Body Worlds* exhibition. Human bodies are posed in lifelike scenarios and dissected to reveal different aspects of human anatomy. Von Hagens has staged *Body Worlds* globally since 1995.

14 Trans/Forming the Citizen Body in Wartime: National and Local Public Discourse on Women's Bodies and "Body Work" for Women during the Second World War

HELEN SMITH AND PAMELA WAKEWICH

During the Second World War, the Canadian national ideal of gendered citizenship and its accompanying anxieties were inscribed in distinctive ways on, and through, the female body. Consequently, representations of the female body and women's "body work" for the national war effort function as a historical record of those ideals and anxieties. For this essay, we emphasize the function of the home as the site for protecting and restoring the body's integrity during the war, when there was the need for a more flexible gender order. We draw on the materials featured in a national health periodical, the *Canadian Public Health Journal* (renamed the *Canadian Journal of Public Health* in 1943 and henceforth *CPHJ/ CJPH*),[1] and a regional newspaper, the *Fort William Daily Times Journal* (*FWDTJ*), as two examples of the many sites of public discourse in which women's participation in the war effort was discussed. We demonstrate how tensions about women's war work and "stability in the gender order" were reflected in contested representations of the in/flexible and im/ permeable female body, as well as in public health messages calling for the production of a less vulnerable and more fit citizen body for the war effort.[2] We demonstrate how navigating the boundaries of "the social skin" in relation to wartime demands for productivity was presented as a dilemma for female war workers.[3] Finally, using an example from our oral history collection of women aircraft workers at the Canadian Car and Foundry war plant in Fort William, Ontario, we also explore "bodies as [marked] sites of experience" in which subjectivities are negotiated and renegotiated over time in relation to both representations and embodied experience.[4]

Situating the Wartime Body/Work Nexus[5]

The work of making the body social is common to all societies. However, whose bodies require work, the type and extent of work to be done, and who is expected to carry out the labour of body work varies over time and place.[6] Taking a historical perspective enables us to explore the changing social relations of embodiment and body work and how they are constituted in relation to gender, class, and racialization at particular moments in time.[7]

In his discussion of the historical construction of American worker bodies, Slavishak argues that in a capitalist system, a labouring body not only produces, but "also consumes."[8] As the twentieth century progressed, increasingly "industries approached working bodies as fragile but malleable resources that could be augmented and adjusted with the assistance of consumer goods."[9] Workers became responsible for using their "leisure time" outside of work to keep their bodies fitted to the optimal production needs of their workplace. As anthropologist Jason Pine further notes, "body modification" becomes a major component of "embodied capitalism."[10] Consequently, both "real" and imagined bodies could be used "as short-hand to celebrate national pride and prosperity" in times of peace and war.[11]

Peniston-Bird's research has demonstrated that both "public and private attention to the body" and "sensory experience" are heightened during wartime.[12] This was certainly true in the Canadian context where, as we will argue, messages about women's body work were carefully prescribed through public health rhetoric about the necessity of enhancing the physical and emotional well-being of individuals, families, and communities for the success of the war effort and the good of the postwar nation.

To ensure that women's wartime employment in traditionally masculine jobs was truly temporary, clear boundary limitations had to be set in terms of when and which female bodies were allowed to work, the space allotted to working bodies, and the depth and extent to which the work could be embodied.[13] Home became the arena for negotiating the boundaries of the social skin and the place in which the female worker body was to be restored to the conventional ideal. As Minnett has noted, maintenance of the private female body as a "good house" was viewed as a marker of healthy citizenship and a significant contributor to the health of the larger social body.[14]

While workers and their families were left largely responsible for monitoring the limits of embodied flexibility outside of the workplace, numerous sources of information were available to guide their understandings of the parameters of social acceptability. Articles and advertising in the *CPHJ/CJPH* set the tone for experts' advice to women concerning the ways in which they should monitor and manage the integrity and permeability of individual bodies, to ensure the stability of the larger social and political body in the postwar era. The message to Canadian women during wartime was that the body/work nexus, both in the home and at the war plant, required careful and ongoing monitoring and negotiation.[15]

Public Health Messaging and Women's Body Work in the Home

As the official journal of the Canadian Public Health Association, the *CPHJ/CJPH* served as a forum for debate and discussion among health professionals and public health advocates during the war. Articles addressed the state of the nation's health, advances in public health research, and directions for health policy and advice.[16] Two key messages about the healthy citizen body were emphasized in the journal throughout the war: (1) the need to increase the physical capacity of individual bodies in order to meet the productivity demands of wartime and set the nation up for a prosperous postwar experience, and (2) the need to monitor the flexibility and permeability of the body to safeguard both individual and collective bodies from war-related external threats. In both instances, women were defined as having a distinctive role to play in this body work, but only under the careful tutelage of experts whose advice would ensure the development of a healthy national body in wartime and beyond. As Mitchinson argues, women's responsibility for the proper feeding of children, the future recruits of the nation, was central to medical discussions of childhood obesity and nationhood through the early and mid-twentieth century.[17]

The *CPHJ* prominently advertised the Canadian Medical Association's 1940 publication, *Food for Health in Peace and War: What Canadian Doctors Suggest for Wholesome Meals at Low Cost*, as a valuable resource for doctors to display in their offices.[18] With the exhortation on its front cover "Keep This Book in Your Kitchen," the pamphlet set the tone and context for housewives' contribution to body work/labour (caring and support for other people's bodies) and body-making work (labour done to produce particular body effects) on the home front.[19] Under the careful guidance of medical, scientific, and home economics experts who "have learned about food through years of study and research," Canadian wives and mothers were tasked with the production and protection of a healthy citizen body against the perceived vulnerabilities of war.[20] They were also asked to foster the growth of a strong and fit citizen body to lead the nation into the postwar era. As the pamphlet counselled, "We have a war to win. We must be fit for whatever task is required of us. Every housewife can do her bit – and help others do theirs – by keeping her family's health at a high level."[21]

The links between science, nutrition, national defence, and the necessity of building a better physical citizen body were perhaps best expressed in a 1942 address to the Health League of Canada by Thomas Parran, surgeon general of the United States Public Health Service. Reflecting on cross-national meetings of health officials concerned to improve health defence policy, Dr. Parran states: "We know that if ... we *can* put science to work to solve the two problems of undernourishment and malnourishment, we shall have the power to build a nation of people more fit, more vigorous, more competent; a nation with better morale, a more united purpose, more toughness of body and greater strength of mind. We know we shall need all those qualities for the grim days that lie ahead."[22]

As his statement clearly suggests, the building of a strong physical body was viewed by health policy advocates as central to cultivating the "united purpose" or the collective national will and morale needed to support the war effort, as well as the resilience to meet its ongoing demands. Echoing other policymakers, Parran argued that not only soldiers, but "every citizen is on the front lines" and that medical science had a distinctive role to play in the war effort by "promoting national efficiency" through health policy development and dissemination.[23]

The importance of a Canadian nutrition program, founded on scientific principles and widely disseminated to Canadian housewives who would do the work of producing fit bodies, was reinforced in the *CPHJ/CJPH* throughout the war years.[24] Women's work in body making through nutrition was also extended to the war plant cafeteria, where women laboured as food producers for war workers, and female plant workers were encouraged to bolster their own bodies as food consumers. In a 1942 article on "Nutrition in War Industry," cafeteria manager Florence Ignatieff argued that economically produced, "attractive meals," following the "principles of nutrition," should be available to war industry workers throughout the country.[25] She emphasized the importance of plant experts using the training period to encourage workers to "discourage consumption of poor lunches," and help them "develop good eating habits," with the goal of increasing the efficiency and health of those whose diet "is not up to standard at home"[26]

The message to health professionals and public health workers about housewives' body-making labour to produce the fit bodies required for war work under the guidance of knowing professionals was also reinforced in advertising published in the *CPHJ/CJPH* during the war years. Ads sponsored by the American Can Company of Hamilton and Vancouver modelled professional counselling and education about "diet planning for good nutrition" through a series of gendered, racialized, and classed vignettes.[27] In the images, an older male physician or dietary expert is typically pictured at his desk, his expertise affirmed by the diploma and scientific nutritional charts prominently displayed on the wall behind him (see Figure 14.1). The accompanying text presents him as offering reassuring "expert" counsel to concerned middle-class homemakers and female health care workers. The women are described as asking "intelligent questions" about wise and protective food choices for those under their "care" in the home, or the hospital setting, and seeking advice on how to meet demands for good dietary and nutritional planning while living on the "moderate food budget" of wartime.[28]

Bently has argued that in the "politics of domesticity during wartime" the expanded need for female bodies in the paid labour force and accompanying anxieties about the long-term transitions this might generate in the larger social and political body were expressed through contradictory images of women, food, and family.[29] On the one hand, presenting the "kitchen as battlefront" elevated the wartime status of homemakers by emphasizing women's expanded role as consumers and food managers – a role of particular importance given the economic exigencies of life on the home front.[30] On the other hand, wartime rhetoric "accentuated gendered messages of a woman's love and nurturance for her family implicit in the act of cooking and serving meals."[31] Such representations functioned to naturalize and diminish the body-producing work done by women. While the emphasis on improving the nutritional status of the population reflected real public health concerns about the vulnerability of the individual physical body to disease and loss of productivity for the war effort, "the iconography of the family meal – ordered, gendered, [and] racialized" was also intended to quell anxieties about disruptions to the social body in wartime.[32] With many women having left pre-war employment in low-paid and unrewarding domestic service to seek the

QUESTION: *In these patterns of diet planning for good nutrition, at least 21 servings of fruits and vegetables, in addition to 11 servings of potatoes or sweet potatoes, per week are recommended (1). How can I manage this on only a moderate food budget?*

ANSWER: You will note that these methods of diet planning have provisions which assist in modifying your food purchases according to fluctuations in individual food costs with season and location. Also, the fresh or canned varieties of the fruits and vegetables have similarly nutritive values and may be used interchangeably. In diet planning, full consideration should be given to the many canned fruits and vegetables which are readily available at reasonable cost during all seasons in all sections of the country.

American Can Company, Hamilton, Ontario;

American Can Company Ltd., Vancouver, B.C.

(1) 1939, Food and Life: Yearbook of Agriculture
U. S. Dept. Agriculture, U. S. Gov't
Printing Office, Washington, D. C.

Figure 14.1 American Can Company of Hamilton: Diet and nutrition ad. *Canadian Public Health Journal* 33, no. 12 (December 1942).

higher wages and more highly valorized work of the war industry, reassuring messages about order and social stability grounded in the daily routine of women's body work in the home were deemed important to maintaining morale and a smooth return to the status quo in the postwar era.[33] As noted above, such themes and tensions were evident in the *CPHJ/CJPH* articles and advertisements concerning Canadian women's body-producing work for the war effort.

Home and the Body/Work Nexus for Female War Plant Workers

With "expert" advice from sources such as the *CPHJ/CJPH* arguing that the welfare of the citizen body depended on women's body work in the home, the government's wartime departure from this gender system in order to recruit women into the traditionally male workspace had to be carefully monitored to ensure only a temporary body displacement. As Peniston-Bird has argued within the British context, while the wartime military transformation of the male body was officially valorized, any transformation of the female body that challenged hegemonic gender roles was represented as "on the surface only: a question of clothing – a uniform – which changed neither her physicality nor her role."[34] In the case of female war-plant workers, official propaganda promised that women's masculine work required for wartime productivity altered her body only as far as her overalls which would easily come off at war's end – her productive body was a temporary necessity. However, there existed alternative wartime discourses that were less assured of this smooth postwar return to the hegemonic gender order of carefully marked-out masculine and feminine spheres of influence, with equally rigid demarcations of the masculine and feminine bodies both representing and performing within these spheres. These variant messages of anxiety over the possible permanency of the flexible wartime gender order were found within the media forms traditionally associated with highlighting social anxieties – advertising and cartoons

A local newspaper like the *Fort William Daily Times Journal* demonstrates a regional "flexibility" when adapting these national discourses to local issues. Advertising and cartoons found in the Fort William paper shared the national concerns about whether wartime flexibility would allow too great a disruption to the gendered spheres of home and workplace, with masculinized female bodies contaminating both spheres. However, ads differed from cartoons by not only depicting the anxiety but also providing product solutions. As Toews designates, this was a capitalist consumer discourse constructing a capitalist consumer body of workers.[35] A running narrative theme within advertising offered the home as the site in which the masculinized female worker body could be restored to its proper femininity through various consumer items, carrying her safely into the postwar world.

In the shadow of the Depression, postwar employment for returning soldiers was a concern across Canada. This was particularly true for the twin cities of Port Arthur and Fort William, where unemployment hit particularly hard given the region's fragile dependency on the economic patronage of southern Ontario and Montreal. Establishing and keeping up the Canadian Car and Foundry war plant in Fort William depended on persuading British and American governments that the "isolated" region could find the bodies to build the war planes. Consequently, the Can Car recruitment of women locally and from across Canada transformed the plant and the twin cities, filling the region with employed consumer bodies whose pay cheques, it was hoped, would boost Depression-starved local businesses.[36] However, throughout the war years, the Fort William newspaper interspersed its announcement of local success stories with concerns about continuity of employment from one contract to another and fears of returning to the earlier bad days of the Depression.

During the war, advertising campaigns were designed specifically to target the female war plant worker with a storyline depicting her masculine work as damaging to her feminine body and, therefore, requiring restorative products and the leisured home time in which to apply them. These campaigns played on the broader cultural discourses tagging women who performed masculine work as "mannish, failed heterosexuals" who "destabilized marital and family relations."[37] Feminine restoration of the social skin involved soap to wash away the masculine workspace from the surface of the skin, creams to restore the skin's surface delicacy, dresses as costumes in place of masculine pants, and hairstyles that easily transferred from the masculine to the feminine worlds. In their wartime advertising campaign, Palmolive soap included the image of a smiling industrial female war plant worker in kerchief and overalls. Oversized letters positioned in the middle of the ad shouted, "I'M A WOMAN IN A MAN'S WORLD – BUT I'M STILL A WOMAN!" (see Figure 14.2).[38] The advertisement constructs the dilemma of preserving the feminine body and its heterosexual attractiveness put at risk by having to don masculine clothes and perform masculine work. To underline further the wartime attack on femininity, the Palmolive company line warns, "Now more than ever you need Palmolive to keep that schoolgirl complexion."[39] The ad's

Figure 14.2 "I'M A WOMAN IN A MAN'S WORLD – BUT I'M STILL A WOMAN!" *Fort William Daily Times Journal,* 8 October 1942.

focus isn't really about war work, but rather the fear that such work will result in a permanent loss of femininity with the resulting loss of dates and future marriage prospects. Hindes hand cream continues this narrative by promising to restore the delicacy of hands damaged by war work, as well as racializing the beauty norm with promises of "whiter" skin.[40]

In July 1943, a special edition of the *FWDTJ* was published as a patriotic salute to the Can Car workers in which local businesses were given the opportunity to say "thank you" to the "Can Car family." This also allowed companies to advertise their products specifically to attract the plant pay cheque. In recognition of the increasing numbers of female Can Car workers, local businesses designed their own advertisements to promote the products required to assist women with their daily transformations between work and leisure time – the home providing the

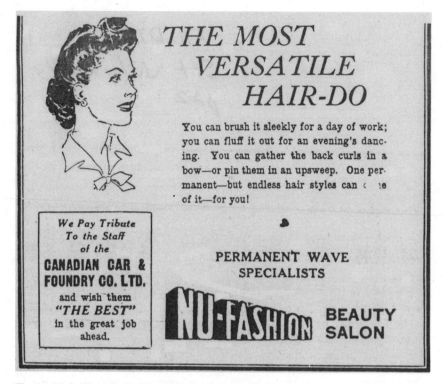

Figure 14.3 The Nu Fashion Beauty Salon ad offered "The Most Versatile Hair-Do." *Fort William Daily Times Journal,* 10 July 1943.

space in which this costume change would take place. The ads used images of White-skinned fashion models, usually blonde and willowy with delicate features. The Nu Fashion Beauty Salon ad offered "THE MOST VERSATILE HAIR-DO" (see Figure 14.3).[41] The Fashion Shoppe advised women workers that while "it is a great thing you do when you don your uniform to keep our freedom," it is equally important to keep up appearances – "It's Smart to be Feminine! After a day in the plant it's refreshing to don a smart frock."[42] The iconic young blonde is dressed in opposition to what would be acceptable on the plant floor – dress, wide hat, high heels, and delicately gloved hands holding a clutch bag. The Nu-Mode Dress Shoppe ad hoped to attract women by including an air force officer gazing in admiration, suggesting the promise of a future heterosexual romance through the restoration of less flexible gender distinctions (see Figure 14.4).[43]

While wartime advertising campaigns helped to perpetuate a climate of anxiety over the possibility that the bodies of women war workers might become too flexible, they also provided the antidote to this potential threat to the nation. Like advertising, cartoons also participated in supporting the hegemonic gendered body and added to the climate of fear concerning the evil necessity of wartime flexibility. However, unlike the advertising campaigns, cartoons played with the frightening possibilities of such flexibility creating an increasingly deviant body that would not return to the norm at war's end. Belonging to the "eminently transgressive" genre of the satirical text, cartoons could draw on the literary tradition of equating "out-of-place" women with the "monstrous."[44] According to Holman and Kelly, wartime cartoons had the flexibility to reinforce and undermine the official propaganda, simultaneously.[45] The body becomes the central signifier through which to humorously "articulate the unsayable" – the fear that wartime patriotic gender disruptions will remain permanent.[46] Consequently, women's wartime flexibility at home and at work is presented as absurdly incongruous with the norm. In the case of certain cartoons found in the Fort William newspaper, the humour lies in the disjuncture between "natural" female bodies and their position within the masculine workplace and jobs, and the ways masculinized female bodies disrupt the feminine space of home. The "unspeakable" anxiety here is that the necessary wartime flexibility required for the productive female citizen body might extend into the postwar period. What if women were unwilling to give up their embodiment of male power and rejected the home's function of restoring their femininity?

The Fort William newspaper included a selection of cartoons from the well-known American cartoonists E. Simms Campbell and J.N. "Ding" Darling, possibly reflecting stronger ties between Canadians and Americans after 1942, when the local plant won the American contract for building Curtiss Helldivers to fight the Japanese in the Pacific. While these cartoons were created within an American context, they were dropped as isolated texts within the local paper to be read and interpreted in the regional context of the Can Car war plant. Campbell had a running theme in his cartoons of women being more disruptive than helpful to the American war effort. He used a stereotypical White, usually blonde, pin-up body as the generic feminine form in all situations. However, rather than being simply the inept "dumb blonde," this pin-up

Figure 14.4 Nu-Mode Dress Shoppe Ad. *Fort William Daily Times Journal,* 10 July 1943.

is portrayed as having the potential, with her masculine work and pay cheque, to emasculate men through gender role reversal, a common theme in wartime cartoons.[47] For example, in a July 1943 cartoon, a man sits up in bed angrily yelling at his wife, who is in the process of putting on her industrial uniform for work at a war plant (see Figure 14.5). The caption reads, "You've got my trousers on again!"[48] The cartoon draws on a very old metaphor of the wife wearing the "man's pants" to represent undermining the paterfamilias by depicting her as the pin-up dressed in man's clothing to perform as the "breadwinner," while the husband is "trapped" within the domestic sphere of the bed. Drawing on the carnivalesque tradition of the hen-pecked husband, here the working wife "embodies the most despised aspects of 'strong' femininity, and her subordinate position in society is in part underlined in this enactment of power reversal."[49] In October 1944, with the end of the war in sight, Campbell goes a step further by having his pin-up not only performing in men's clothing but also developing a more masculine body which further undermines patriarchal authority in the home. In the cartoon, one uniformed female riveter shows off her exaggeratedly muscular arm to another with the caption reading, "'War work is wonderful! I won every fight I had with my husband last week!'"[50] Portrayed here is the deviant incongruity not only of having her performing masculine work dressed in masculine clothes, but also having a pin-up body with a muscular arm. Although the scene takes place in a war plant, they are discussing her home life in which her masculinized body now has the physical strength to subdue her husband – she has gone beyond merely wearing his clothes to now visibly wearing his body.

Darling's 1943 cartoon dispensed with any ties to the pin-up stereotype, and instead depicted women's performance of men's industrial jobs as creating a monster in the form of a giant "mannish" female worker towering over her small, "everyman" husband. Darling draws on a popular film image of the time with a caption reading, "A Genie Out of a Bottle" (see Figure 14.6).[51] The cartoonist positions the female war worker in the public space between home and factory as she leaves for work at the industrial plant in the distance. Her tiny husband is left standing at the front door in an apron and carrying a frying pan and broom, calling after her, "But remember you gotta come right back as soon as the war is over!"[52] With home as the bottle from which she has been released, she rises up above him through the black cloud of smoke emanating from the dinner burning in the kitchen. Her overalls pocket contains an envelope labelled, "Her own man's size pay envelope."[53]

"You've got my trousers on again!"

Figure 14.5 July 1943 cartoon: "You've got my trousers on again!" *Fort William Daily Times Journal,* 7 July 1943.

Figure 14.6 Darling cartoon (1943), "A Genie out of a Bottle." Courtesy of the Jay N. 'Ding' Darling Wildlife Society. The University of Iowa Libraries.

Her huge boots look like they might trample him and her enormous muscular arms carry, like weapons, her giant lunchbox and machine tool. The image may be a play on Rockwell's muscular "girl-next-door," Rosie the Riveter. However, here she is a wickedly smiling, fearful monster who cannot be controlled. Her body has been so transformed by the masculine work that she no longer fits into the feminine sphere of home. This menacing genie obviously has no intention of granting her husband's wishes as her cheeky response, "Oh yeah?" suggests. Read in relation to his later cartoon depicting Japan as an even more dehumanized trampling genie with fangs, hands, and sword dripping with blood, Darling's female genie takes on a racialized "domestic foreignness" that defines the "real enemy [as] within."[54] By rejecting the home, the female worker body has transgressed not only the gender limits of the social skin, but human norms as well.[55]

Embodying the Wartime Home/Work Nexus

In the final section of this essay, we attempt to "anchor [the experience of embodiment] in the particularity of places and bodies, and to flesh out one of the ways [embodiment] feels," as illustrated through one woman's memories of her wartime experiences while working at Can Car. We try to avoid situating our analysis "too simply in terms of resistance/subjection."[56] Rather than suggesting that experiences can easily be polarized as belonging to one category or the other, we suggest a more "flexible" framework that allows shifting forms of engagement between representation and experience throughout an individual's embodied life story.[57] In this particular case, we look at "how 'the record of war survives in the bodies'" through the intertwining processes of memory and embodiment, discursive coercion, and agency.[58] Here we profile Angie's story because of her use of "sensory experience" in memory formation, her identification of a specific wartime embodiment, and the ways in which her story demonstrates layered meanings of flexibility. As with many of the women we interviewed, her wartime experience of embodiment was much more complicated than the patriotic expectation of protecting her femininity from the wartime flexibility required by masculine work. Although she understood and accepted that her war work belonged to men and would be returned to them at war's end, the physical experience of such work and the resulting pay cheque allowed for an embodied flexibility both inside and outside of work that remained with her long after.

Angie was born in 1925 in Fort William. Her parents were born in Italy, where they lived in what Angie described as "extreme poverty."[59] Before the war, her father worked as a labourer at various jobs, her older sisters as domestics, and her brother as a bush worker, while she briefly worked as a sales clerk in the Eaton's department store – "if you got to grade nine, boy you were lucky."[60] Angie described her mother more as the domestic producer for her family, rather than consumer, by keeping a garden and "Noah's ark" in the backyard.

When the Can Car plant began its recruitment campaign, eighteen-year-old Angie, her father, and her older sister found jobs, while her brother enlisted. Angie connected with the patriotic wartime body by accepting the gendered nature of the work that allowed continuing post-war employment for her father and only temporary positions for herself and her sister. She identified her sister's riveting job and her own job in the stores department as being "men's work" that would be returned to them at war's end – they would both require more flexible worker bodies than their father's, to be able to patriotically shift from the war-time to postwar job market. However, she was very aware of the physical competence of the female workers in fulfilling this masculine work, and her own body in particular. Angie remembered with great pride and nos-talgic laughter how she and her female co-worker performed their jobs, climbing up and down the mountain of bins in the stores department to fetch supplies for the other plant workers:

We used to holler and go up there like monkeys. We were just climbing. I never took a ladder once! Whoa, physical! ... We were in good shape.[61]

She recognized that part of her physical ability to do the work stemmed from her home life where, as the youngest in the family, she fulfilled the role of "go-for" as she fetched and carried for the rest of the family, as she now fetched for her co-workers. In contrast to the advertisements, rather than identifying the masculine workplace as unfamiliar terrain that threatened her established sense of femininity, Angie identified the interconnectedness between home and work skills that eased and inten-sified her embodiment of the new job.

Angie provided a number of examples of slippages between work and home that allowed for an easier transfer between masculine and femi-nine performances, as suggested by the local business advertising cam-paigns but on a more playful, and less anxious, level. While Angie did embody some aspects of the feminine ideal, she was also able to make light of certain expectations, suggesting that certain elements of femininity remained lightly inscribed. Although her eldest sister regularly wore pants at home and at work, Angie was not comfortable in her pants outside of her own work department and identified the issue as being primarily about what the pants signified. She disliked having to report to an upstairs office where

> the men were in suits and ties and that, and the girls were dressed and nicely, and I come in like this farmer from outside ... I was very comfortable in my place, but not in the office [where she felt like] the labourer entering into the upper crust.[62]

She'd wear her slacks at work, but change back into dresses as soon as she got home. While this suggests that her sense of feminine embodiment was deeply affected by the classed and gendered elements of clothing regulations, there were also occasions in which she enjoyed the opportunity of subverting the masculine workspace by wearing her dresses to work. She emphasized throughout her interview the constant pressure from management to keep up production, which frequently required double shifts and sudden calls for overtime. She and her co-workers would find ways to make the regulations and schedules more flexible to their social needs:

> There were intervals when we would go to a party, and then we had to go in at midnight. Well, of course, we had to dress to go to a party, and we'd come in, dressed. Oh it wasn't really appropriate. They'd frown upon it because we had to climb bins ... You couldn't climb bins unless you wanted to make a spectacle of yourself.[63]

She said the problem did not involve the physical ability to work productively in a dress, which she could do. This was a proscriptive issue concerning the unruly female as "public spectacle" with her "loss of boundaries" in a masculinized space requiring a masculine costume.[64] In Angie's comic retelling, the dress becomes the means by which she embraces the gendered "spectacle" for its "liberatory and transgressive effects."[65]

Conclusion

When we asked Angie whether she ever talked to her son about her wartime work, she related the following conversation with him:

"You see me limping around here," and I says "if you'd only seen me when I was twenty, climbing those bins like an ape." I says, "You wouldn't believe I was the same girl. Not only that, let me tell you something, the summer of 1944, I climbed [Mt. McKay] three times" ... It's been a good life in a lot of ways.[66]

Angie's sense of her own aging body formed her memories of her wartime work as an experience that extended beyond the workplace. As she looked back on her life, the war stood out as a chance to expand the social skin and be physically fit not only on the national government's terms, but on her own terms as well, allowing for greater flexibility between home and work and of bodily performance. Ironically, postwar national reconstruction reduced the gender flexibility between the spheres of domesticity and the workplace just as Angie needed it most. As both Llewellyn and Schmidt discuss, in this volume, postwar Canadian national discourses continued to monitor women's employment in relation to safeguarding the "marriageable body" within the home.[67] Rather than transforming into middle-class housewives, many of the women Angie knew returned to the reduced pay of domestic and retail service jobs, as she returned to her poorly paid employment at Eaton's department store. As Angie described it, "I was the working poor."[68] The proper female citizen body was supposed to return to the home and her dependency on the husband's pay cheque. Angie did have a brief postwar experience of marriage, which she described as "a disaster." She did stop working for as long as the marriage lasted, "so it was a very short-lived interruption."[69] She remained the breadwinner for her son until her retirement. To some degree, her postwar body was the "genie" refusing to go back in the bottle in that she transgressed the ideal gender order by working as a lone-parent mother. However, she was certainly not a monstrous genie as she no longer had the option to carry a "man's size pay cheque" in the pocket of the dress she wore to work at Eaton's. Yet, she carried with her the embodied memory of climbing bins and mountains, with enough gender flexibility to reject the idealized goal of married domesticity. She chuckled,

I went out on my own. And there were times I could have got married but it just didn't seem right.[70]

Notes

Our sincere thanks to Tory Tronrud from the Thunder Bay Historical Society for assistance with cartoon images from the FWDTJ and his ongoing support of our project.

1 The *Canadian Journal of Public Health* (CJPH) remains the official journal of the Canadian Public Health Association.
2 Deborah Montgomery, *The Women's War: New Zealand Women, 1939–1945* (Auckland: Auckland University Press, 2001), 4.
3 Anthropologist Terence C. Turner uses the concept of "the social skin" to describe the ways in which the surface of body functions as both a biological and psychological boundary between individuals and the cultural medium "through which we communicate our social status, attitudes, desires, beliefs and social identity." Terence C. Turner, "The Social Skin," in *Not Work Alone*, ed. J. Cherfas and R. Lewyn (Beverly Hills, CA: Temple Smith, 1980), 114.
4 Kathleen Canning, *Gender History in Practice: Historical Perspectives on Bodies, Class and Citizenship* (Ithaca, NY: Cornell University Press, 2006), 169. See P. Wakewich, H. Smith, and J. Lynes, "Women's Wartime Work and Identities: Women Workers at Canadian Car and Foundry Co. Limited, Fort William, Ontario, 1938–1945," in *Framing Our Past: Canadian Women's History in the Twentieth Century*, ed. S. Cook, L. McLean, and K. O'Rourke (Montreal and Kingston: McGill-Queen's University Press, 2001), 409–17, and P. Wakewich and H. Smith "The Politics of 'Selective' Memory: Revisioning Women's Wartime Work in the Canadian Public Record," *Oral History* 34, no. 2 (2006), 56–68, for a description of the larger project.
5 Carol Wolkowitz, "The Social Relations of Body Work," *Work, Employment and Society* 16, no. 3 (2002), 498. In her sociological analysis of labour and embodiment, Wolkowitz argues that the "body/work nexus is crucial to the organization and experience of work relations" and people's embodiment is deeply influenced by work. Carol Wolkowitz, *Bodies at Work* (London: Sage, 2006), 1.
6 Wolkowitz, 'Social Relations,' 501.
7 Ibid., 503, and P. Wakewich, "Contours of Everyday Life: Women's Reflections on Embodiment and Health Over Time," in *The Gendered Society Reader: Canadian Edition*, ed. Michael S. Kimmel, Amy Aronson, and Amy Kaler (Don Mills, ON: Oxford University Press, 2008), 22, 327–8.
8 Ed Slavishak, "'Made by the Work': A Century of Labouring Bodies in the United States," in *The Body Reader: Essential Social and Cultural Readings*, ed. Lisa Jean Moore and Mary Kosut (New York: New York University Press, 2010), 148.
9 Ibid., 162.
10 Jason Pine, "Embodied Capitalism and the Meth Economy," in Moore and Kosut, *Body Reader*, 165.

11 Slavishak, "'Made by Work,'"148.
12 Corinna Peniston-Bird, "Classifying the Body in the Second World War: British Men In and Out of Uniform," *Body and Society* 9, no. 4 (2003), 31–48.
13 H. Smith and P. Wakewich. "'I Was Not Afraid of Work': Female War Plant Employees and Their Work Environment," in *Canadian Environments: Essays in Culture, Politics and History*, ed. Robert C. Thomsen and Nanette L. Hale (Brussels: P.I.E. Peter Lang, 2005), 229–47.
14 Valerie Minnett, this volume.
15 The regulation of the socially prescribed "healthy" female body in the wartime workplace is discussed in Smith and Wakewich, "Regulating Body Boundaries and Health during Wartime: Nationalist Discourses, Media Representations and the Experiences of Canadian Women War Workers," *Gender and History* 24, no. 1 (2012), 56–73.
16 See, e.g., Enid Charles, "Canadian Vital Statistics during the War Years," *CJPH* 35, no. 11 (1944), 439–51, and Grant Fleming, "Public Health in Wartime," *CPHJ* 33, no. 4 (1942), 145–7.
17 Wendy Mitchinson, this volume.
18 Canadian Medical Association (hereafter CMA), *Food for Health in Peace and War: What Canadian Doctors Suggest for Wholesome Meals at Low Cost* (Toronto: Canadian Medical Association, 1940).
19 Sociologist Debra Gimlin has developed a useful typology describing four kinds of body work typically ascribed to women, in "What Is Body Work?" *Sociology Compass* 1, no. 1 (2007), 353–70. Two of these – body-labour work and body-making work – were emphasized in *CPHJ* discussions of the health of the citizen body during wartime.
20 CMA, *Food for Health*, 2.
21 Ibid.
22 Thomas Parran, "Health, Nutrition and National Defence," *CPHJ* 33, no. 3 (1942), 101.
23 Ibid., 99.
24 See Mitchinson, this volume, for a discussion of nutritional messaging to Canadian mothers promoting development of the "healthy child body."
25 Florence Ignatieff, "Nutrition in War Industry," *CPHJ* 33, no. 12 (1942), 572.
26 Ibid.
27 *CPHJ* 33, no. 1 (1941): 1.
28 American Can Company, "When Your Patients Ask about Vitamins," *CJPH* 34, no. 7 (1943), 1, and American Can Company, *CPHJ* 33, no. 12 (1942), 1.
29 Amy Bently, *Eating for Victory: Food Rationing and the Politics of Domesticity* (Urbana, IL: University of Chicago Press, 1998).
30 Ibid., 5–6.
31 Ibid., 70.

32 Ibid., 6–7.
33 See Smith and Wakewich, "Regulating Bodies," for a more in-depth discussion of this issue.
34 Peniston-Bird, "Classifying the Body," 44. While her article discusses the British military, her argument holds for wartime gendering of industrial workers in Canada.
35 Anne Frances Toews, this volume.
36 Smith and Wakewich, "I Was Not Afraid of Work," 2005.
37 Susan K. Cahn, "From the 'Muscle Moll' to the 'Butch' Ballplayer: Mannishness, Lesbianism and Homophobia in U.S. Women's Sports," in *The Politics of Women's Bodies: Sexuality, Appearance, and Behavior*, ed. Rose Weitz (New York: Oxford University Press, 1998), 67, 73. For a recent discussion of shifting gender prescriptions in Canadian advertising from before the Second World War through to the postwar period, see Emily Spencer, *Lipstick and High Heels: War, Gender and Popular Culture* (Kingston, ON: Canadian Defence Academic Press, 2007).
38 *Fort William Daily Times Journal* (hereafter *FWDTJ*), 8 Oct, 1942, 2.
39 Ibid.
40 *FWDTJ*, 3 April 1944, 9.
41 *FWDTJ*, 10 July 1943, 22.
42 Ibid.
43 Ibid, 25.
44 Rosi Braidotti, "Mothers, Monsters, and Machines," in *Writing on the Body: Female Embodiment and Feminist Theory*, ed. Katie Conboy, Nadia Medina, and Sarah Stanbury (New York: Columbia University Press, 1997), 64. Within this Western cultural tradition, Braidotti defines "monster" as "the bodily incarnation of difference from the basic human norm" (62) and, consequently, "woman" as "a sign of difference is monstrous" (65).
45 Valerie Holman and Debra Kelly, "War in the Twentieth Century: The Functioning of Humour in Cultural Representation," *Journal of European Studies* 31 (2001), 256.
46 Ibid., 251.
47 Montgomerie, *The Women's War*, 10.
48 *FWDTJ*, 7 July 1943, 15.
49 Mary Russo, "Female Grotesques: Carnival and Theory," in Conboy et al., *Writing on the Body*, 322.
50 *FWDTJ*, 12 Oct. 1944, 10.
51 *FWDTJ*, 18 Feb. 1943, 2. As the microfiche newspaper cartoon is of poor quality, we have substituted a digital copy of the original, courtesy of the Jay N. "Ding" Darling Wildlife Society. Darling's genie coincides with the popu-

lar 1940 British film *Thief of Bagdad*, which familiarized the American public with the ambivalent nature of a genie – djinn – as appropriated for Western audiences.

52 Mark Bryant, *World War II in Cartoons* (London: Grub Street, 1989), 8. After the First World War, depictions of larger-than-life male heroes were replaced with "smaller character types" representing "the common man" (ibid.).

53 *FWDTJ*, 18 Feb. 1943, 2.

54 Rosi Braidotti, "Signs of Wonder and Traces of Doubt: On Teratology and Embodied Differences," in *Feminist Theory and the Body: A Reader*, ed. Janet Price and Margrit Shildrick (New York: Oxford University Press, 1999), 293.

55 In Darling's 11 Aug. 1945 cartoon, captioned "The evil genie goes back in the jar," the evil genie Japan is being shoved into a jar labelled "crime does not pay."

56 Canning, *Gender History*, 173.

57 For a discussion of women's reflections on changing embodiment over time, see Wakewich, "Contours of Everyday Life," 2008.

58 Ibid, 174. Canning quotes from Elaine Scarry, *The Body in Pain: The Making and Unmaking of the World* (Oxford: Oxford University Press, 1985).

59 Canadian Car Interview, #38. A pseudonym is used to protect confidentiality.

60 Ibid.

61 Ibid.

62 Ibid.

63 Ibid.

64 Russo, "Female Grotesques," 318. Spectacle is understood as "a specifically feminine danger."

65 Ibid., 322.

66 Interview, #38.

67 Kristina Llewellyn, this volume, and Bonnie Reilly Schmidt, this volume.

68 Interview, #38.

69 Ibid.

70 Ibid.

15 "Flesh, Bone, and Blood": Working-Class Bodies and the Canadian Communist Press, 1922–1956

ANNE FRANCES TOEWS

Canadian workers shivering through the winter of 1924 may have experienced an additional shudder not entirely attributable to the January temperatures when they opened their weekly *Worker* newspaper to the terrifying headline, "Glands Stolen by Highwaymen."[1] Reading on, they discovered that a "robust" twenty-six-year-old Chicago taxi driver on his way home from work had been kidnapped at gunpoint, then chloroformed, by "medically trained students working in the pay of some surgeon and some decrepit millionaire." The victim, Charles Reims, emerged from the effects of anaesthesia and made his way to a hospital where doctors determined that certain unnamed glands were missing. Luckily for Reims, it seemed that the organ theft was performed by a skilled surgeon, who took some pains to stitch him up neatly and prevent infection, thus ensuring the patient's survival.

This tale lent itself well to the goals of the *Worker*'s publisher, the Communist Party of Canada (CPC).[2] Folklorist Véronique Campion-Vincent positions narratives of organ theft in contemporary society as "commentary on the issues of difference and justice;"[3] class differences and the injustice inherent in capitalism were exactly what the CPC wanted emphasized in the early 1920s, as it sought "to enthuse [sic] revolutionary life into the inert masses of the workers."[4] Readers were likely to believe rumours of organ theft: Campion-Vincent argues that these kinds of tales are credible because they are "perfect parable[s] about the evils to be denounced in the materialistic modern world."[5] Capitalism was (and is) the greatest of these evils, according to Canada's communists, one that placed working-class bodies in mortal danger.

Bodies, more usually with all organs still intact, were ubiquitous in the *Worker* and other Canadian Communist papers from 1922 through

1956.[6] Dead and alive, young and old, male and female, worker and capitalist, strong and weak, healthy and diseased, starving and well-nourished, in whole and in part, they peppered the pages of the Party press. By juxtaposing representations of bodies as threatened and weak or as "the picture of health," the CPC was able to illustrate the benefits of socialism over capitalism in a manner that did not rely on any prior theoretical knowledge. The flexibility and efficacy of the body as a tactical didactic tool is evident in its deployment as such in the service of the CPC's changing strategies during these years. Invoking the body to call on Canadian workers to identify their interests as coinciding first with others of their class, no matter their gender, ethnicity, or nationality, communists promoted a transnational solidarity that disrupted the concept of a Canadian nation.[7]

The Communist Press

Founded in 1921, the Communist Party of Canada brought together a group of Canadian socialists eager to follow the model of the apparently successful Russian Bolsheviks and their leader, V.I. Lenin. Lenin conceptualized communist parties as a vanguard tasked with educating the working class in socialist ideology and leading it in the coming overthrow of capitalism. He argued that a communist party should be built around its newspapers because although workers were eager for knowledge, if the party did not "imbue the proletariat with the *consciousness* of its position and the consciousness of its task," it would be susceptible to the false doctrines fed to it in bourgeois propaganda.[8] Party workers ran labour colleges and organized an endless round of lectures, meetings, and rallies, but these means of delivering its message were to some extent preaching to the converted – union members and others who were already willing to invest time and money in hearing what the CPC had to say. Purchasing a copy of the *Worker* required less of an investment and commitment, and the Party anticipated from the beginning that its press would provide an effective means of fulfilling its mission.

Along with coverage of current events, the *Worker* delivered a version of Marxist-Leninist theory adjusted to fit the changing Party line: instructive editorials, reviews of Marxist literature, articles about the history of socialism, and essays by prominent Canadian or European communists. In 1926, for example, a weekly feature drawn from the works of the recently deceased Lenin was introduced as part of "a systematic theoretical education" for *Worker* readers.[9] Articles with titles such as "Three Ele-

ments of Marxism: Historical Materialism, Surplus Value and Class Struggle" credited the reader with both the intelligence and the will to "make
good any gaps in his understanding of the fundamental principles involved in the struggle between Capital and Labour."[10]

This cerebral approach to educating the worker complemented what
one might call a visceral approach, exemplified by the story of Charles
Reims and his stolen glands. Did shocking stories of violence done to
human bodies, often described in gruesome detail, produce a physical
effect on readers? It would not be surprising if they were to shudder, gag,
clench their fists, feel their skin crawl, or perhaps in this case, tense their
muscles in subconscious protection of their own organs. Readers' involuntary reactions may well have contributed to an embodied awareness
of the CPC's message; Joy Parr reminds us that, "humans 'make sense'
of the world ... directly through their sensing bodies."[11] However, even
if such articles elicited no physical response whatsoever, they could pro-
voke an emotional response and thus reach those who might otherwise
miss the Party's message. Speaking to and through the body by inscrib-
ing lessons in history, political science, and economics on human bodies
could therefore be seen as a useful pedagogical approach for the CPC.

The immediate purpose of these lessons changed in accordance with
national and international political and economic conditions: readying
the working class for world-wide socialist revolution in the early 1920s,
supporting whatever foreign policy might be most beneficial to the Soviet Union during the Second World War, or promoting trade with the
Soviet Union rather than closer relations with the United States at the
onset of the Cold War. The underlying message of CPC publications continued to echo Karl Marx's position that capitalism itself, not the "will,
either good or bad of the individual capitalist," caused the destruction,
degeneration, and consumption of working-class bodies.[12] Literal and
metaphorical accounts of assaults on working-class bodies were certainly
not limited to the Communist press, but for a party with limited financial
and human resources, the use of corporeal language gains significance
because the word was the CPC's main weapon.[13] Following Marx, then,
the *Worker* and its successors set themselves apart by making it clear that
the amelioration of working-class living conditions by means of better labour standards, higher wages, or more widely available health care could
only be an interim solution: socialism provided the only physically safe
and healthy alternative to capitalism.[14] Ridiculing the labour and mainstream papers for their failure to recognize this, the CPC's point was
not simply to offer an alternative discourse but, as Marx had advised, to
change the world.[15]

The Body as Metaphor

References to human bodies in the Party press took both metaphorical and literal forms. Reflecting common practice in the Soviet Union, the state, the Party, and various social groups were described as living organisms. Tricia Starks notes, "Corporeal metaphors, used since ancient times to describe the health of a society, became a mainstay of the social sciences in the nineteenth century, with the organic nature of the state the dominant metaphor."[16] Starks explains that in the 1920s this metaphor, combined with "faith in the beneficial and transformative power of science," became the basis for government policy; nations thus acquired bodily qualities of hygiene, health, order, and purity.[17] Increasingly, Pavlovian theory influenced organic models of the state by the late 1940s in the Soviet Union.[18] Ivan Pavlov criticized Western medicine's over-attention to "the microscopic study of diseases," and he emphasized that the body's social and physical environment affect "all pathological upsets, [and] all disturbances of bodily function."[19] Relying on these theoretical underpinnings, the CPC linked the health of workers to the health of the economic system in which they toiled: both the Soviet Union and the Soviet worker were healthier under socialism, and the same was possible in Canada.

Anthropologist Mary Douglas has noted that social groups under threat also commonly express the threat through corporeal metaphors.[20] Political enemies might thus be demonized by describing them as "infection spots." Leon Trotsky's fall from grace, for example, occasioned articles accusing him of trying to "behead the Soviet Union," and likening him to "a cancer."[21] The CPC had justification for describing Canada's working class as a threatened group in the 1920s and beyond. Workers and their families struggled to balance periods of unemployment with dangerous working conditions and wages that were often insufficient to meet basic needs, all the while monitored, rebuked, regulated, and disciplined by educators, employers, publishers, clerics, doctors, legislators, police officers, and judges.[22] The Party press repeatedly emphasized the connections between all these groups. As Marx had explained, "The executive of the modern State is but a committee for managing the common affairs of the whole bourgeoisie."[23] To communists, then, the working class was a threatened and inert body and the CPC was its head, becoming, in fact, "the incarnated will of the working class."[24] The *Worker* was itself wrapped in corporeal metaphor that lent it life and substance, introducing itself as "a paper that will be flesh, bone and blood of the living every-day experiences of the working class."[25] However, despite the Party's declaration that the paper would provide workers with "their ... own means to express their needs, their demands, their hopes," the voice of the paper was the Party's voice.[26]

Certain body parts carry with them obvious symbolism that was put to use in the Party press. Hands, for example, could represent oppression, as in "the bare fist of Tsarism," or class solidarity, as in headlines such as "British Miners Grasp Hand of Russian Labour."[27] A highly unpopular appendage oft mentioned in the pages of all left-wing papers was the "Iron Heel of Ruthlessness" belonging to Depression-era Prime Minister R.B. Bennett; Bennett rarely made an appearance without it.[28] The worker's back was sometimes strong and straight, signifying competence and power, and at other times, bent under the burdens placed on it by capitalism. The backs of the "boss class" served very little purpose other than to transport unnecessarily extravagant clothing to social engagements and the bank.[29]

Splashed across page after page, blood was usually the most common body part in a Communist newspaper. A versatile metaphor, blood has a long history as the ultimate symbol of life and of death.[30] Blood connected the worker with the martyrs of socialist history, most notably the Paris Communards, "pioneers" in proletarian revolutionary action and remembered each year on the anniversary of their 1871 uprising. The blood of thousands of Communards could carry a powerful didactic message, as it did in a 1926 *Worker* editorial explaining that capitalists were able to crush the Commune because it "lacked the direction of a strong, single-willed Communist Party through which the workers could exercise rule."[31] Moreover, blood had a symbolic significance that Communists held dear, like the red flag and the song that bore its name. While the flag was the international emblem of revolution, the Party also pressed it into service to mark less dramatic steps towards its own goals. In 1924, for example, the *Worker* heralded the first issue of the CPC's Yiddish newspaper, *Der Kampf*, with the headline, "Red Flag Flies in Montreal."[32] The melancholy anthem, *Red Flag*, was so well-loved in the 1920s that South African rebels defiantly sang it on their way to the gallows.[33] As the song's lyrics indicate, the red-dyed flag signifies the blood of working-class martyrs.

The Party was well aware of the potential persuasiveness of language. The power of blood as metaphor was certainly understood by *Worker* writer Trevor Maguire, who referred to the British Empire as the "British Vampire" – and by the Canadian state, which tried him for sedition for doing so.[34] In response to a woman whose son had been injured in a shooting, a *Worker* writer declared that her letter to the paper surely "pierces through the body of a class conscious worker just as the policeman's bullet pierced the body [of her son]."[35] Bodies and parts thereof appeared in the Party press not only as metaphor but as topic; the blood that was splashed through the pages of the *Worker* often took the form of literal accounts of the spilled blood of workers.

Capitalism's Assault on Working-Class Bodies

Whether blood was spilled at the barricades or in the factory, the Party press was careful to link it with capitalism. As Marx had shown in his study of nineteenth-century England, capitalism consumed the bodies of workers through work-related disease, industrial "accidents" that tore workers' bodies apart, or the stunted growth and degeneration that resulted from poor nutrition, lack of rest, or unhealthy living conditions.[36] The lives of individual workers were of little importance as long as the labour force continued to reproduce itself, and the *Worker* related the many ways in which workplaces could chew up bodies.[37] Construction projects, logging operations, battlefields (understood as workplaces), railways, hotels, and even the bourgeois homes where workers toiled – all provided stories of fingers severed, limbs ripped off, and bodies burned, crushed, drowned, buried, or otherwise destroyed.[38] Factories were seen as inherently dangerous places – even something as seemingly innocuous as the underwear produced in the factories of Paris, Ontario, was described as "stained with the blood and suffering" of the women who made it.[39] Instead of taking measures to improve safety, owners introduced often-fatal "speed-ups." This allowed the CPC to claim that workers were not just consumed, they were deliberately "sacrificed on the altar ... of capitalist industry ... [T]heir flesh, bone and blood are ground into dust by the industrial machine."[40]

Workers in some industries, such as mining, were at high risk of workplace injury or death; extracting profit from the earth simultaneously extracted the life from working-class bodies.[41] The British Empire Steel Company (BESCO) was singled out for the especially "appalling conditions under which workers [ground] out profits." After four fatal "accidents" over a five-day period, the *Worker* described its Cape Breton coal mines as a "slaughterhouse."[42] Occupational illness was another hazard that the Party press brought to the worker's attention: garage workers driven "stark mad" by "loony gas" (ethyl gasoline), for example, or watch factory workers poisoned by radium in the paint used for luminous dials.[43] Silicosis, endemic among gold miners, was known to result from improper ventilation, but it was capitalism's drive for ever-greater profit that led mine owners to resist slowing down production by introducing safer operating procedures.[44]

It was not just in workplaces that the physical dangers of capitalism were present; workers' dwellings could also be a "menace to health."[45] Several *Worker* articles described how the "drama of capitalism" played out in Glace Bay, essentially a BESCO company town: families living in chicken coops, with sanitary conditions "almost unknown," open sewers, an inadequate water supply, and wages too low to provide anything but a starvation diet.[46] The Great Depression made things worse for many Canadian working-class families. A 1932 headline informed readers that in Montreal, jobless workers were "forced to burrow in holes" and "live as the cliff-dwellers of old on top of Mount Royal."[47] In Vancouver, a "beloved comrade [died] of capitalist greed," suffering from "lack of proper medical attention and nourishment."[48] As the Christmas of 1935 approached, jobless workers suffering the physical pain of hunger could be expected to quickly grasp the message of a satirical item about a sojourner in the USSR entitled, "No Freedom in Soviet Russia: Vancouver Woman Forced to Eat Several Times a Day."[49]

Drawing on improved knowledge of nutrition (see Wendy Mitchinson in this volume), a series entitled "The Worker's Health under Capitalism" appeared in the *Worker* in 1929.[50] The author ("a medical doctor") explained that capitalists could afford the best of food, while workers and their families were sold "louse-lizard sugar" and the like, food that was "debauched, adulterated and rendered foodless." This was one means by which "the ruthless capitalist machine grinds the life out of [the worker] in about 48 years." A 1940 review of a book entitled *Picture of Health* ridiculed its author's prescription for "sensible living," noting that it "lacks a sense of reality" because "the food, exercise and rest recommended are beyond [the] reach" of working-class families.[51] The problem was systemic; the system had to change.

However, any attempt to bring about change exposed all working-class bodies – those of men, women, children, and even the unborn – to the prospect of targeted violence. CPC newspapers carried numerous articles about violent labour conflict around the world, but they also made it clear that Canada was not immune to this aspect of capitalism. Reporting on a Canada-wide wave of massive protests in March 1930, the *Worker* noted that in Montreal, police used "horses, clubs, whips, and every form of brutality" to prevent workers from "protesting against starvation and the capitalist system that produces it among the working class."[52] After leading Party member Tom Ewen was "almost killed ... at [a Toronto] police station," in 1929, the *Worker* asked, "Is murder the next step? Will workers be beaten to death or shot down in cold blood by the police thugs of Toronto?"[53] The Party press reported instances when striking workers *were* killed. In 1925, for example, private BESCO "Cossacks" fired on Cape Breton strikers, killing miner William Davis, and in 1931, three Saskatchewan coal miners participating in a street march were "murdered" by RCMP fire in what the CPC would call "The Estevan Massacre."[54] Many working-class bodies bore the physical scars of "police terrorism."[55]

The CPC's exposition of the negative effects of capitalism depended in part on the assumption that the categorization and re-categorization of bodies corresponded to an unspecified and shifting hierarchy of vulnerability. The bodies of infants, children, youth, the aged, women of any age, and the disabled were especially vulnerable; so too were the unemployed, recent immigrants, French Canadians, Canada's Indigenous peoples, returning war veterans – in short, anyone other than a fit Anglo-Canadian male worker in the prime of his life. Age and gender were particularly salient but not fixed categories: a fourteen-year-old could be classified as a "small boy."[56] A woman's body might be presented simply as a working body, but female bodies acquired higher levels of vulnerability if they were pregnant or marked by age. A story about the brutality of company thugs was that much more effective when the thuggery was visited upon a "working class babe." The "black crime of capitalism" that caused a train derailment was that much blacker when the severed arm of an infant was found in the wreckage.[57]

The particular problems faced by the aged were encapsulated in the story of an Ontario woman, "ill for years with asthma, heart trouble and a work-worn ill-nourished body," who had been unable to receive permission for her son to draw relief on her behalf. After having dragged herself from her sick bed to the welfare office, she "died ... while standing in line awaiting her grocery order."[58] The *Worker* also reprinted a bizarre reversal of the organ theft narrative, an American account of medical rejuvenation experiments perpetrated on residents of a San Francisco home for the aged. The story forecast "poorhouses depopulated by the dumping of gland-renewed old people on the labor market to fight and scrabble for jobs," thus reinforcing the point that, under capitalism, working-class bodies were useful only for as long as they could be compelled to productivity.[59] A full discussion of the differential levels of vulnerability applied to bodies in the Communist press is well beyond the scope of this essay, the point of which is to demonstrate that the CPC used *all* bodies as slates on which it could write lessons about capitalism and socialism.

The CPC's ability to present various kinds of damaged bodies as evidence of capitalism's harmful effects was premised on the existence of an assumed ideal, a naturally healthy pre-capitalist body sustaining itself through work, "life producing life."[60] Dan Irving argues that in the capitalist regime of the late twentieth century, this has come to mean that an important condition on access to the benefits of citizenship and the ability to fully participate in society is the capacity of individual bodies to demonstrate their economic productivity.[61] Although this capacity to be productive is now, in a post-industrial society, less likely to involve heavy physical labour or overt violence to the body, Carol Wolkowitz suggests that "the human body continues to be deeply involved in every aspect of paid work" while "our bodies are built out of and through our roles as paid workers."[62] As Helen Smith and Pamela Wakewich's interview with Angie demonstrates (this volume), even under capitalist relations of production this shaping of the body through work can be and has been seen as constructive rather than destructive. The Communist press argued that this was more likely to be the case in a socialist state, where work was valued as a constructive process, produced by and producing healthy bodies and, through those bodies, a healthy society. Whether its effects on the body were constructive or destructive, the understanding of work as an embodied experience underlay CPC discourse.

Against this ideal of healthy bodies at work, the Communist press presented capitalist bodies as parasitic and unnatural by emphasizing their most salient physical characteristic: obesity.[63] Abhorrent examples of overconsumption, they embodied capitalism and violated the underlying principle of socialism. Communists were unequivocal about the cause and the reciprocal nature of the worrisome problems of obesity and malnutrition. By describing capitalists as "gorged plunderers" interested only in the "distending of their own bellies while tightening the belts on the already lean and hungry slaves," the *Worker* made it clear that the extra girth displayed by capitalist bodies was gained at the expense of working-class bodies.[64]

Union leaders who were more absorbed with preserving their own comfortable posts than with engaging in class struggle acquired some of the physical characteristics of capitalists in the pages of the Party press, often referred to as "fat boys." The bodies of capitalists' allies, such as "stool pigeons," labour spies, and police officers, were often represented as malformed and either brutish or puny; they might display visible signs of disease, especially sexually transmitted disease.[65] The bodies of "class traitors" who took work that required them to cross picket lines were utterly repugnant; the *Worker* predicted that the drowned body of one such traitor would eventually be found "intact, as even the scavenger fish will pass up scab meat."[66]

The CPC's ultimate goal of replacing capitalism with socialism was always seen as a threat by Canada's political and business elite and the agencies that they controlled or influenced, although the perceived and actual magnitude of the threat varied considerably, as did the Party line. While by 1922 the Soviet Union was much less vocal about advocating armed uprisings in support of a world proletarian revolution than it had been two years earlier, after Lenin's death, in 1924, this goal was abandoned altogether in favour of Stalin's doctrine of ensuring the survival of "socialism in one country" (that country being the Soviet Union). Still, even without the expectation of world revolution, the CPC considered itself to be part of an international communist movement. By the late 1920s, Communists had identified signs of an imminent and cataclysmic "crisis of capitalism"; the system was about to fail spectacularly, and the CPC sought to make the Canadian working class fully aware that its interests did not lie with prolonging the death throes of capitalism. In the 1920s and through the Great Depression, the CPC's negatively framed articles about the effects of capitalism on working-class bodies emphasized that point.

Eliciting Transnational Solidarity in the Cold War Era

The CPC's immediate goals shifted during and after the Second World War, but bodies continued to feature prominently in the Party press. The war ended both the crisis of capitalism and, temporarily, the Party's estrangement from the rest of the Left. After July 1941, when the Soviet Union entered the war on the side of the Allies, the CPC emphasized an often-capitalized UNITY at home and in Europe in an all-out effort to end the war that was exhausting the Soviets. International worker solidarity was once again vociferously encouraged in the final months of the war and afterwards when the Western nations, having overcome the fascist menace, turned a suspicious gaze on their former ally, the Soviet Union. During this period, the CPC once again argued for class loyalty over national loyalty. Articles encouraged Canadian workers to interpret violent conflict around the world in terms of class struggle and to identify themselves with others of their class, even if those others lived in, say, Indonesia, a country that "most Canadians [had] never heard of."[67] On 28 April 1945, the *Pacific Advocate* featured a front-page drawing of an embodied transnational "World Labor" dwarfing the North American continent and looking down watchfully on the San Francisco Conference on World Security from somewhere in the vicinity of Russia.

With the deepening chill of the Cold War, pressure to protect the Soviet Union intensified; for Communists, class continued to trump nation. A key move in mobilizing Canada's workers to protest against any aggression towards the Soviet Union was to portray the latter as the ideal workers' state, inhabited by people like themselves. While the CPC press had, since 1921, diligently and delightedly reported on the good life in Russia, in the postwar years it published a flood of these positively framed articles. At a very uncomplicated level, Canadian workers could be expected to think well of a place where workers were valued, work was part of a healthy life rather than a source of danger, food was abundant, and the benefits of an obviously superior health care system were available to all. The 1952 *Canadian Tribune* series, "World of Socialism, People's Democracy," gave details of Soviet housing projects, cultural events, health care, and scientific advances. Party leaders such as National Education Director Beckie Buhay travelled to the Soviet Union and attributed declines in the incidence of heart disease and tuberculosis in the USSR to "the complete absence of tensions, pressure and hysteria" there.[68] Buhay reported enthusiastically on the excellent treatment she herself received in a Georgian sanatorium. Underscoring the link between good health and socialism, she informed readers that her Soviet physicians advised her against returning home before she was fully recovered because, "While we're changing the environment for the better here every day, we cannot export it to Canada."[69]

Articles about the healthier bodies of Soviet citizens served a dual purpose, helping to instil and sustain positive feelings about the Soviet Union and suggesting that closer economic ties could provide immediate benefits, in Canada, for Canadian workers. Buhay made this point explicit by asking readers to "think how application of the advanced Soviet knowledge of the treatment of arthritis, for example, could benefit thousands of Canadian sufferers."[70] Dyson Carter, president of the Canadian-Soviet Friendship Society, argued that cooperation with Moscow could mean a share in the promise of "limitless development" offered by the peaceful application of nuclear power, as well as "an end to wars and economic crisis, unemployment and premature death."[71]

But the *Canadian Tribune* made it clear that even if the Soviets were willing to share their advanced medical knowledge, Canada would be unable to provide workers with the level of care available in the Soviet Union unless it scaled back defence spending. In 1954, a front-page article documented Prime Minister Louis St. Laurent's refusal to institute a national health insurance plan because, as he stated, "Canada is spending so much on armaments."[72] The article linked St. Laurent's decision with that year's "polio scourge," and it was illustrated by two photos of children, neatly labelled with directional arrows pointing to "health insurance or crippled children." Party intellectual Stanley B. Ryerson criticized "Yankee warlords," who advocated "arming to defend democracy" in Europe rather than spending on social programs: "It is up to us to … extricate our country from the machinations of Wall St.'s 'Murder Incorporated.'"[73]

During the 1950s, the most reprehensible work of Murder Incorporated, and the subject of numerous alarming articles in the Communist press, was the development of "ABC" (atomic, biological, and chemical) weapons. The *Canadian Tribune* reprinted the Soviet demand that "the whole mass of atomic material be directed completely to peaceful aims."[74] Because the Americans had already demonstrated their willingness to use atomic bombs, workers could be expected to believe them equally capable of using biological weapons against Communist Korea and China. Indeed, an enlarged photograph of "an insect dropped in Korea," offered to readers as evidence, demonstrated that the Americans had already done so.[75] Many column inches were devoted to this topic, including homegrown rumours of "top secret … work in germ war weapons" in Quebec.[76]

Chemical weapons were not new. In the early 1920s, the *Worker* had described the effects of poison gas on soldiers' bodies during the First World War. In 1929, the paper had warned of major "improvements" that would allow more potent poisons to "fall like rain" from specially built aircraft and cause victims to "tear their windpipe[s] right out in order to get air."[77] A 1952 description of the effects of napalm on the bodies of Korean women and children was no less graphic. A witness to this "flaming horror" reported that as napalm burns heal, "the hands become drawn backward like the claws of birds, the eyelids are pulled up and down, leaving bulbous eyeballs [staring] … from wide red frames of the out-turned [eye socket] itself."[78] Perhaps, today, these descriptions still elicit an involuntary physical reaction in the reader.

Conclusion

The Communist press painted a vivid picture of the physical harm that capitalism could inflict on working-class bodies, eliciting, it hoped, the reader response that it intended. The specifics of the message changed in much more nuanced ways than this short essay can explore, but the themes of the vulnerability of the body, countered by the strength of solidarity and the leadership of the CPC, were constants. Party newspapers framed these articles to support Communist claims of knowing the best way of ordering the world. But beyond political purpose and any attempt to manipulate the reader's reaction, the palpable sense of outrage that colours these accounts of bodily harm is also indicative of the deep level of commitment shared by the men and women who printed them in the expectation of changing the world for the better.[79]

On 5 March 1953, Communists the world over mourned the death of the man that Party leader Tim Buck eulogized as "the greatest of all champions of peace and friendship between peoples," Josef Stalin.[80] In 1956, Stalin's successor, Nikita Khrushchev, revealed something of the extent of his predecessor's abuses of power, forcing Canada's Communists to reassess the meaning of Soviet-style communism, and making it difficult for them to continue to argue for the Soviet Union as a workers' paradise. However, from 1921 through 1956, the CPC could plausibly recruit support by casting the difference between capitalism and socialism very literally as a matter of life and death. A continuing but changing discourse centred on the health and physical integrity of the body was clearly one of the Party's most important proselytizing tools. It was through and to working-class bodies that the CPC delivered both its negative critique of capitalism and the positive promise of socialism, demonstrating its recognition that the impulse to action – be it revolutionary or reactionary – is inseparable from the living flesh in which it is contained.

Notes

This essay is derived, in part, from research conducted for my M.A. thesis, "For Liberty, Bread, and Love: Annie Buller, Beckie Buhay, and the Forging of Communist Militant Femininity in Canada, 1918–1939," Simon Fraser University, 2009, for which I gratefully acknowledge the support of the Social Sciences and Humanities Research Council of Canada.

1 "Glands Stolen by Highwaymen," *Worker*, 5 Jan. 1924.

2 The Communist Party of Canada also operated briefly in the 1920s as the Workers' Party of Canada, and in the 1940s as the Labor Progressive Party.

3 Véronique Campion-Vincent, "Organ Theft Narratives as Medical and Social Critique," *Journal of Folklore Research* 39, no. 1 (2002), 35.

4 V.I. Lenin, *What Is to Be Done? Burning Questions of Our Movement*, trans. Joe Fineberg and George Hanna (Marxists Internet Archive, http://www.marxists.org/archive/lenin/works/1901/witbd/index.htm). Quotation is from a letter from A. Kent to Presidium of the Comintern, 16 Aug. 1922. Library and Archives Canada (LAC), Communist International Fonds, MG 10 K-271, file 3.

5 Campion-Vincent, "Organ Theft Narratives," 33, 45. David McNally explicates how "persistent body-panics" derive from "threats posed to bodily integrity" by the generally invisible workings of capitalism in *Monsters of the Market: Zombies, Vampires and Global Capitalism* (Boston: Brill, 2010), 2, 9. This is not to deny the present-day commodification of bodies and their parts; on this, see Nancy Scheper-Hughes and Loïc Wacquant, eds., *Commodifying Bodies* (London: Sage, 2002).

6 This essay draws primarily on material from the *Worker*, the Party's official newspaper from 1922, published in Toronto. Renamed the *Clarion* in 1936, it appeared for a time as the *Daily Clarion*, and was succeeded in 1940 by the *Canadian Tribune* (hereafter *CT*). Published in Vancouver, the *Pacific Tribune* (*PT*) was also a Communist newspaper, although not an official party organ; it was known at various times as *B.C. Workers' News* (*BCWN*), *People's Advocate*, *Advocate*, *People*, and *Pacific Advocate* (*PA*). *National Affairs Monthly* (*NAM*), the "theoretical organ" of the CPC, began publication in 1944.

7 On a theoretical level, the CPC explicitly included women in the category of "worker," and on an organizational level it strove to recruit women, with varying levels of commitment and success. But in representations, and especially in imagery, the ostensibly "universal" worker (and the *Worker* itself) was in reality generally gendered male. Elizabeth Faue has argued, in the American context, that this was a widespread and long-standing tactical error of the labour movement as a whole. See Elizabeth Faue, "Gender, Language, and the Meaning of Class Struggle, 1929–1949," in *Community of Suffering and Struggle: Women, Men, and the Labor Movement in Minneapolis, 1915–1945* (Chapel Hill, NC: University of North Carolina Press, 1991), 69–99. On women, feminism, and the CPC, see Joan Sangster, *Dreams of Equality: Women on the Canadian Left, 1920–1950* (Toronto: McClelland and Stewart, 1989). For an examination of a Ukrainian-Canadian Communist newspaper that illustrates how gender and ethnicity "might reinforce class consciousness but also contradict it," see Sangster, "'*Robitnytsia*, Ukrainian

Communists, and the 'Porcupinism' Debate: Reassessing Ethnicity, Gender, and Class in Early Canadian Communism, 1922–1930," *Labour/Le Travail* 56 (Fall 2005), 51–89.

8 Lenin, *What Is to Be Done?* Original emphasis.

9 "Marxist Education," *Worker*, 13 Feb. 1926.

10 Ibid.

11 Joy Parr, *Sensing Changes: Technologies, Environments, and the Everyday* (Vancouver: UBC Press, 2010), 12. Parr draws on an extensive body of scholarship to assert that we are, in Francisco Varela's words, "embodied minds." Francisco Varela, Evan Thompson, and Eleanor Rosch, *The Embodied Mind: Cognitive Science and Human Experience* (Cambridge, MA: MIT Press, 1991). Parr borrows the phrase "make sense" from Laura Gowing, *Women, Touch and Power in Seventeenth-Century England* (New Haven, CT: Yale University Press, 2003).

12 Karl Marx, *Capital: A Critique of Political Economy*, vol. 1, trans. Ben Fowkes (New York: Vintage, 1977), 381. Erin O'Connor notes that accounts of bodies malformed by work abound in Victorian critiques of industrialism, revealing prevailing anxieties as well as more hopeful imaginings about the seemingly permeable border between "selves" and "stuff." Erin O'Connor, *Raw Material: Producing Pathology in Victorian Culture* (Durham, NC: Duke University Press, 2000), 6–10, 16.

13 Van Gosse, drawing on the work of Gareth Stedman Jones, has noted, "'Language' *is* the everyday material reality of practical organizing under any conditions short of guerrilla war and clandestinity." Van Gosse, "'To Organize in Every Neighborhood, in Every Home': The Gender Politics of American Communists between the Wars," *Radical History Review* 50 (1991), 135. However, the focus on material bodies in the Communist press reflected Marx's disdain for idealist philosophers who dwell solely in the abstract realm of language, as well as the Party's efforts to focus attention on the material conditions of life faced by those compelled, under capitalism, to sell their labour power in order to survive. David McNally explains that "bodiliness" is in itself a trait that male bourgeois philosophers ascribed not to themselves but to non-elite social groups (marked by differences of gender, race, ethnicity, and sexuality, as well as by class). David McNally, *Bodies of Meaning: Studies on Language, Labor, and Liberation* (Albany, NY: SUNY Press, 2001), 4–5.

14 Scott Vokey provides an example of how this also set the *Worker* apart from liberal and conservative papers. Scott Vokey, "Inspiration for Insurrection or Harmless Humour? Class and Politics in the Editorial Cartoons of Three Toronto Newspapers During the Early 1930s," *Labour/Le Travail* 45 (Spring 2000), 141–70.

15 "Theses on Feuerbach," in *Karl Marx: Selected Writings*, 2nd ed., ed. David McLellan (Oxford: Oxford University Press, 2000), 173.

16 Tricia Starks, *The Body Soviet: Propaganda, Hygiene, and the Revolutionary State* (Madison, WI: University of Wisconsin Press, 2008), 24.

17 Ibid., 20–4.

18 Ruscoe Clarke, "The Theoretical Base of Soviet Medicine," *NAM* (Nov. 1951), 18. In contrast, Cynthia Comacchio describes how organic metaphors were replaced by mechanistic models of both society and the body in industrializing Canada during the first half of the twentieth century. Cynthia Comacchio, "Mechanomorphosis: Science, Management, and 'Human Machinery' in Industrial Canada, 1900–45," *Labour/Le Travail* 41 (Spring 1998), 35–67; see esp. 38–41, 55, 57, 65–6. She concludes that an extended campaign "to transform humans into machinery" for increased industrial efficiency was "disappointing" despite the best efforts of various "experts" in science, health, and the management of labour (65).

19 Clarke, "Theoretical Base of Soviet Medicine," 15, 21.

20 Mary Douglas, *Purity and Danger: An Analysis of Concepts of Pollution and Taboo* (London: Routledge, 1966); as cited in Campion-Vincent, "Organ Theft Narratives," 41.

21 Starks, *The Body Soviet*, 24; "Trotsky Plotted with Nazis to Behead the Soviet Union," *Clarion*, 27 Jan. 1937.

22 Elsewhere in this volume, Wendy Mitchinson explains that concerns about the future of the nation in the years following the First World War fuelled scientific research into the causes of obesity and malnutrition; we might therefore add nutritionists, public health workers, and psychologists to this list. As workers responsible for shaping the nation, "monitors" were also regulated themselves, often in gendered ways, as Kristina Llewellyn and Bonnie Reilly Schmidt remind us in their discussions of, respectively, teaching bodies and policing bodies, in this volume.

23 Marx, "The Communist Manifesto," in McLellan, Karl Marx: *Selected Writings*, 247.

24 Jack Macdonald, "Lenin and the Communist Party," *Worker*, 23 Jan. 1926.

25 "'The Worker' – Our Paper – Your Paper – The Workers' Paper," *Worker*, 15 March 1922.

26 Ibid.

27 Leon Trotzky, "How Capitalists Mould Mentality of Workers," *Worker*, 15 Jan. 1923; *Worker*, 29 May 1926.

28 Beckie Buhay, "The Hungry Thirties," *NAM* (Jan.–Feb. 1949), 29.

29 "The 'Globe' Makes a Slimy Attack," *Worker*, 24 Nov. 1923.

30 Piero Camporesi, *Juice of Life: The Symbolic and Magic Significance of Blood*, trans. Robert R. Barr (New York: Continuum, 1995).

31 "The Paris Commune," *Worker*, 20 March 1926.
32 *Worker*, 22 Nov. 1924.
33 "Capitalist Democracy," *Worker*, 15 Jan. 1923.
34 "The Trial of Clever Satire," *Worker*, 1 Dec. 1922.
35 "Who Is It Likes Blood?" *Worker*, 1 Jan. 1925.
36 Marx, *Capital*, 355–6, 364–7.
37 Ibid., 381. Unlike most of his contemporaries, Marx attributed these out-comes not to industrialization itself but to the profit motive inherent in the capitalist relations of production. The Communist press repeatedly stressed that, under socialism, miners, factory workers, and other toilers could expect safer and healthier working conditions. See, e.g., "Miner Compares Conditions Here and in USSR," *Worker*, 16 Nov. 1929.
38 See, e.g., "Blood Stains on Bosses' Profits," *Worker*, 1 Feb. 1930; Untitled [p. 2], *Worker*, 2 June 1926; "Sacrificed to Profit," *Worker*, 8 Dec. 1923.
39 Leslie Morris, "Concerning Underwear," *Worker*, 8 Dec. 1923.
40 "Three More Miners Sacrificed," *Worker*, 28 Nov. 1925. Some of the material for this paragraph and the next are drawn from my MA thesis. See Toews, "For Liberty, Bread, and Love," 57-58.
41 See, e.g., "Coal and Blood in the Crow's Nest Pass," *Worker*, 17 Sept. 1927; Charles Crozier, "Blood Stained Gold in Alaska," *PT*, 30 Aug. 1935.
42 "Slavery in Besco Slaughterhouse," *Worker*, 22 Aug. 1923; "Five Days in a Besco Slaughter House," *Worker*, 20 Nov. 1926.
43 "Provincial Health Department Warns against 'Loony Gas,'" *Worker*, 26 March 1927; "Workers Dying a Painful Death from Radium Poison," *Worker*, 26 May 1928.
44 "Gold Miners Prepare to Fight Conditions that Breed Silicosis," *PT*, 1 Nov. 1935.
45 "Workers' Shacks Menace to Health," *Worker*, 1 Dec. 1923.
46 Beckie Buhay, "In the Grip of Steel and Coal," *Worker*, 9 April 1927; Beckie Buhay, "Besco Gets The Wheat – The Miners Get the Chaff," *Worker*, 16 Jan. 1926.
47 "Workers Forced to Burrow in Holes," *Worker*, 30 July 1932.
48 "Death after Long Illness," *BCWN*, 12 April 1935.
49 *BCWN*, 13 Dec. 1935.
50 The three articles were signed with what was presumably a pseudonym, N. Lectarius; they appeared 2, 9, and 21 Nov. 1929.
51 J.C.B., "Your Body," *CT*, 14 April 1940.
52 "20,000 in Demonstration at Montreal," *Worker*, 15 May 1930.
53 Oscar Ryan, "Workers Savagely Beaten by Toronto Police Thugs," *Worker*, 3 Jan. 1931.

54 "Mine Picket Killed by Besco Thugs," *Worker*, 20 June 1925; "The Estevan Massacre," *Worker*, 3 Oct, 1931. See also "Awful Brutality of Besco Cossacks," *Worker*, 18 July 1923.

55 "Young Working Class Fighter to Tour Ontario for C.L.D.L." *Worker*, 8 Feb. 1930.

56 "Master Class Justice and a Small Boy," *Worker*, 29 Nov. 1924.

57 "In Memoriam," *Worker*, 18 July 1923; "C.P.R. Train Wreck Is Black Crime of Capitalism," *Worker*, 24 Dec. 1927.

58 F.B. Rose, "Old Woman Drops Dead at Welfare," *Daily Clarion*, 31 Nov. 1936.

59 "Glands for Open Shoppers," *Worker*, 15 Dec. 1923. It was the potential for capitalist exploitation of workers' bodies that prompted communist outrage in this instance, not the prospect of "rejuvenation" itself. For Soviet attitudes towards sex gland transplantation experiments in the 1920s, see Stephen Lovell, "Soviet Socialism and the Construction of Old Age," *Jahrbücher fur Geschichte Osteuropas, Neue Folge* 51, no. 4 (2003): 568–9.

60 Karl Marx, "Economic and Philosophic Manuscripts," in McLellan, *Karl Marx: Selected Writings*, 90.

61 Dan Irving, "Normalized Transgressions: Legitimizing the Transsexual Body as Productive," *Radical History Review* 100 (Winter 2008), 38–59.

62 Carol Wolkowitz, *Bodies at Work* (London: Sage, 2006), 54–5.

63 This was especially evident in cartoons, which often portrayed wealthy men and women as almost spherical in shape. On the effectiveness of editorial cartoons as "a conclusion without an argument," see Vokey, "Inspiration for Insurrection or Harmless Humour?" 143–4.

64 "Shrinking Stomachs vs. Bulging Bellies," *Worker*, 15 Feb. 1923. Here Canadian communists were elaborating on a well-established early socialist discourse. See Ian McKay, *Reasoning Otherwise: Leftists and the People's Enlightenment in Canada, 1890–1920* (Toronto: Between the Lines, 2008), 20, 73.

65 "Degenerate Tools of the Capitalist Courts," *Worker*, 15 Feb. 1923.

66 "Davy Jones Receives Scab," *Worker*, 5 Jan. 1924.

67 "Indonesian People Victims of Brutal Imperialist Suppression," *PA*, 1 Oct. 1945.

68 Beckie Buhay, quoted in John Stewart, "Complete Health Care Services Available to Everyone," *PT*, 17 July 1953. See also Toews, "For Liberty, Bread, and Love," 58–9.

69 Ibid.

70 Beckie Buhay, "Canadian-Soviet Friendship Month," *NAM* (Jan. 1952), 22.

71 Dyson Carter, "There Are Jobs in Friendship," *CT*, 25 Jan. 1954; Stewart, "Complete Health Care Services Available to Everyone."

72 "Kill Health Plan: 'More Guns' – Gov't," *CT*, 14 Dec. 1953.

73 Stanley B. Ryerson, "Timetable of Life or Timetable of Death," *CT*, 12 May 1952.

74 "Put *All* Atomic Power to Use for Peace – USSR," *CT*, 28 Dec 1953.

75 "Science, Law, Religion on Impartial Body to Probe Germ War," *CT*, 14 April 1952. On the possibility of germ warfare in Korea, see Reg Whitaker and Gary Marcuse, *Cold War Canada: The Making of a National Insecurity State, 1945–1957* (Toronto: University of Toronto Press, 1994), 368-369, along with sources cited in their footnotes 12 and 13, pp. 478–9, and footnote 15, p. 442.

76 "Sinister Experiments in Quebec," *CT*, 14 April 1952.

77 "Disclosures by a Worker in the British Navy," *Worker*, 17 July 1929.

78 Allan Winnington, "Eyewitness Describes Flaming Horror," *CT*, 11 Aug. 1952.

79 Memoirs and biographies of CPC members illustrate the level of commitment and sacrifice demanded of CPC workers; see, e.g., Andrée Lévesque, *Red Travellers: Jeanne Corbin and Her Comrades*, trans. Yvonne M. Klein (Montreal and Kingston: McGill-Queen's University Press, 2006).

80 Tim Buck, "His Name Will Endure through the Ages," *CT*, 16 March 1953.

16 "Better Teachers, Biologically Speaking": The Authority of the "Marrying-Kind" of Teacher in Schools, 1945–1960

KRISTINA R. LLEWELLYN

In the early twentieth century, the ideal woman teacher was married to her school and community. This changed following the Second World War. School boards lifted bans on married women's employment and campaigned for the return of women who left for family obligations. This shift was due, in part, to a shortage of teachers and a growth in state reforms for public entitlements.[1] In larger part, the newfound authority of the "marrying-kind" of woman teacher was a strategy of "domestic containment" in Canada after the Second World War. Franca Iacovetta defines "domestic containment" as state-sanctioned efforts "to police not only the political but also the social, personal, moral, and sexual lives of its citizens – a process, which ironically involved the repression of liberal Western democracies of individual rights and freedoms in the name of demographic rights and freedoms."[2]

Within the context of postwar uncertainties, the nuclear family model, and more specifically the male breadwinner model, became synonymous with a strong consumer economy, peaceful relations, and a defence against Communism.[3] The school, as a symbol of hope for the nation's democratic future, had a critical role to teach the "moral authority" of heterosexual citizenship. The example of an increasing number of women teachers, in particular, their bodily performance for students of "democratic" ideals, was a central part of lessons in containment. "Spinster" teachers became unacceptable ambassadors to the public just as teachers of the "marrying-kind" became "better teachers, biologically speaking."[4]

This chapter examines postwar campaigns that glorified married women teachers in Canada's two largest English school boards, Toronto and Vancouver, based on school board reports, teacher federation records, and newspapers.[5] Oral histories of twenty women teachers, completed between 2002 and 2005, and including single, married, and lesbian women, are analysed to demonstrate the scrutiny of their performance in the name of moral educational "democracy." For the most part, interviewees were in their early to mid-twenties when they entered teaching and the period soon after the war marked the beginning of their careers. The majority of interviewees identified themselves as middle class, White, heterosexual, and Anglo-Saxon. Only two identified with a further marginalized group, one as a lesbian and the other, Chinese Canadian. As a group, these profiles represent the typical teacher hired to work in postwar schools.

Judith Butler's concept of gender as performative is helpful for understanding women teachers' physicality in schools as symbolic sites of nationalist rhetoric. Butler argues that gender roles are social identities developed within specific historical contexts and learned through the "stylized repetition of acts": "the gendered body acts its part in culturally restricted corporeal spaces and enacts interpretations within the confines of already existing directives."[6] The script for gendered performances is thus written in some form before the individual body is needed to publically enact it. Gender roles are, as Butler states, "put on, invariably, under constraint, daily and incessantly, with anxiety and pleasure."[7] This chapter demonstrates that the new "democratic freedom" of married women to teach was contained within a repressive conception of national togetherness defined by a hegemonic "normality"; school officials advertised pretty new teachers, inspected for motherly behaviour, and pathologized single women.[8] For women who were White, middle class, and married, becoming sentinels for domestic virtue was much easier than for women whose bodies betrayed that possibility for performance.

"Motherly" Guardians of Postwar Liberal Democracy

In the 1940s and 1950s, Canada's secondary schools embraced democracy as their primary goal. Canadians sought to avoid totalitarianism in the wake of the Holocaust and ensure participatory citizenship at a time of growing civil rights and decolonization movements. Democratic measures included the signing of the United Nations Charter in 1945, accompanied by the 1948 Universal Declaration of Human Rights (drafted by Canadian John Humphrey), the establishment of the Canadian Citizenship Act in 1949, and numerous renewed social security initiatives.[9] Democracy was more than a political arrangement, it was a social contract based on common citizenship meant to provide a stable order following the trauma of war. Carole Pateman's influential work demonstrates that the democratic social contract was founded on a sexual contract based on the distinction between public and private spheres. Within liberal democratic thought, women as sexual, weak, and irrational, decreed by nature itself, can play only supportive roles beyond the private sphere.[10] Women's "inherent" concern for family, and thus women's agency itself, is a sideshow, albeit always critical, to public debates and the determination of national citizenship. As Anne Phillips argues, masculinist citizenship does not simply exclude women from the state, but rather results in their "secondary" inclusion.[11] Women are the critical "Other" in substantiating the basis for ideal citizenship, namely, the rational, objective, politically autonomous individual, or the alpha male.

Several feminist educators have explored the public/private split for schooling "democratic" identities, particularly in the British context, and the woman teacher's role in that process. Valerie Walkerdine and Helen Lucey argue that children learn fictions of their free will, a non-coercive technique to manage a citizenry, from mothers and women teachers.[12] As "naturally" non-authoritarian nurturers, mothers and women teachers are responsible for safeguarding masculine models of democracy that subordinate female powers. Women then serve, in effect, to uphold democratic citizenship and the state itself. As Madeleine Arnot and Jo-Anne Dillabough describe, women are the keepers, cultivators, and symbols of democracy.[13] In theory, women are reproductive, benevolent actors or virtuous beings.[14] Nira Yuval-Davis summarizes the position of women in liberal "democratic" nations: "Girls did not need to act; they had to become the national embodiment."[15] Their actions are set within educational parameters that constrict their authority in terms of "correct" and "incorrect" mothering, and serve to reconstitute the legitimacy of a masculine version of the "right citizen."

This was the role for women teachers in postwar Toronto and Vancouver. As Canadian historians Shirley Tillotson, Mona Gleason, and Mary Louise Adams have demonstrated, educational campaigns offering national egalitarianism contained those qualities and practices that lay outside desired postwar norms.[16] Spurred by fears of social deviance in the atomic age, educators mandated that students gain an appreciation of "democratic" values best expressed in the White, Judeo-Christian, middle-class, heterosexual, nuclear family. Teachers were responsible for implementing new social services and character education courses towards this goal. Officials agreed, however, that it was the teacher, more than instruction, that formed citizen habits among youth. A 1951 article for the *Bulletin*, the newsletter of the Ontario Secondary School Teachers' Federation (OSSTF), "In Praise of Teachers," vividly described teachers' responsibility as a patriotic duty. The author described each school as a "miniature nation, where the young citizens are forming habits, acquiring attitudes towards the world they live in and towards their fellow-citizens ... The teachers – it is almost too awful a responsibility to put down in black and white – are the statesmen in those miniature nations."[17] The exemplar of the teacher played the most critical role in ensuring "normative" citizenship through lessons in "conformity."

While male teachers certainly bore responsibility as school statesman, it was women teachers who shouldered the primary burden for students' moral development. Norman McLeod, past president of the OSSTF, insisted that teachers had to emulate community standards. He wrote, "Any teacher who feels secure and satisfied in the complete privacy of his own class-room and his own home is living a strange paradise."[18] It becomes clear that McLeod is directing his comments to women teachers when he goes on to specify that it is mandatory for a good and happy teacher to have a soft voice, elegant language, and "avoid nagging."[19] The equivalent federation newsletter on the Pacific coast, the *B.C. Teacher*, published similar imperatives. In a 1946 issue, the editors reprinted a report by Toronto principals, which they argued, was equally applicable to men and women teachers. This assertion is highly suspect as the authors referred in detail to the housewife-like duties as critical, silent influences on the character of students. In this description, each teacher reproduces, rather than produces, a constructive learning environment by "dressing modestly and tastefully; keeping her desk and the window-sills neat; having a few good large pictures, if possible, and having them well placed; and arranging displays of work in an artistic manner."[20]

Women teachers were the moral guardians of the democratic state and liable for normative femininity. Their dress and deportment were used to shape the boundaries of national embodiment for masculinist citizenship. Although women's nurturing and motherly "instinct" had been praised in teaching for almost half a century by this point, if married, they were to remain within the confines of the private sphere. Alternatively, it was critical in the postwar years that marriage and even motherhood be on public display. Paradoxically, married or marriageable women working in schools were wanted to ensure that the male bread-winner model of family was a clear choice for students seeking a stable democratic future. To the extent that the woman teacher embraced her "inherent" private sphere capabilities, her professional body served to uphold the biological foundation of postwar moral democracy. Teaching bodies that lay outside a correct motherhood model threatened national stability. Young women teachers were cautioned against unbridled femininity, with its display of emotional and sexual wiles, which undermined masculine authority. "Spinster" teachers, with their rejection of heterosexuality, were unsightly, even dangerous, citizenship representatives. Too much or too little embodiment of "womanhood" was problematic for women teachers. It was the "marrying-kind" of women who exhibiting the right degree of heterosexuality and fertility became attractive for the school and the nation.

"Pretty, New Teachers"

A movement was underfoot across Canada for the "marrying-kind" of woman to enter teaching. Teacher supply represented a national emergency. F. Henry Johnson, coordinator for teacher education in British Columbia, told newspapers that the province would be short 750 teachers by 1956.[21] The postwar baby boom occupied elementary classes, while secondary school increases were spurred by immigration and a general demand for higher education. School officials relied on women's flexible labour and introduced programs to entice them into the workforce. Departments of Education in both provinces adopted emergency measures to address the shortage, issuing temporary certificates or Letters of Permission, providing crash summer courses, and reducing practice teaching.[22]

Both the Toronto and Vancouver boards targeted women who had left the profession due to marriage. Z.S. Phimister, superintendent and chief inspector of schools, reported to the *Globe and Mail* that the Toronto board would lessen mandatory maternity leave for those "young women teachers supporting their husbands who are attending medical school or theological college."[23] Officials in British Columbia extolled the virtues of married women by announcing that without bringing them "back to the profession, even though they have been absent of years ... there is no doubt that chaos would have existed."[24] Broader policies supported endeavours to attract the "marrying-kind." In 1944, Vancouver women who married after placement in a school gained "security of tenure," and for Toronto women, an official bar to married women was lifted in 1946.[25] Furthermore, in 1951, the Ontario Teachers' Federation created single salary schedules to base pay on qualifications, not gender.[26] The BCTF adopted this policy in 1954.[27] Wage discrimination in practice continued, as the majority of women teachers could not secure higher-paying administrative positions in these cities.[28]

These policy changes complemented media pronouncements, in radio broadcasts, newspaper columns, booklets, and posters, that extolled the virtues of the "marrying-kind" of woman for the nation's schools. For example, at the beginning of the 1952 school year, C.C. Goldring, Director of the Toronto Board of Education, spoke to the newspaper with pride about high marriage rates among their women teachers. He reported to the *Globe and Mail*, "Men like the motherly qualities of the kindergarten teacher, the rim lines of the physical education teachers, and the home economics teachers' skill with the skillet."[29] In Vancouver, newspapers regularly advertised the sexually attractive women who were joining the board at the beginning of each new school year. One such picture in the *Vancouver Sun* in 1950 proclaimed, "Pretty, New Teachers," accompanied by the caption that these teachers were "enough to send dad to school with junior."[30]

Women answered calls for more teachers. Their rates of participation in the profession reached near wartime levels of 70 per cent by the mid-1950s.[31] Toronto Board of Education *Year Book* statistics in 1954 show that 271 of the 754 secondary school teachers were women, and 51 of that number were married.[32] Vancouver produced similar statistics: 246 of 755 secondary teachers, 68 married.[33] J.D. Aikenhead, professor of education at the University of Alberta in Calgary, undertook national research on teacher recruitment, acknowledging that "more women than men had returned" to teaching.[34] He asserted, however, that women's reasons reflected simply a public extension of their propensity for private nurturing. They entered the system, he contended, not for a steady wage, but due to their "fondness for children, a liking for colleagues, and a desire to serve society."[35]

Over half of the women interviewed for this study were married during their teaching days, at which point they were usually in their mid- to late twenties. Of those who married, some spoke of financial necessity.[36] All the interviewees viewed teaching as one of the only accessible avenues for women to have a career, because they could continue to work while married. Melanie Kilburn justified entering teaching, instead of medicine in which she was most interested, knowing, "It was either you had a career that would fit in with marriage and children or you were going to go through this long training to always be full time [as a mother]. Now how did that fit?"[37] Four married interviewees recalled specific postwar inducements enticing them back into teaching. Abigail Sears remembered that originally after getting married "you knew you were out." She continued teaching because of "an order in council in Victoria for me to be permitted to teach … the principal went to bat for me."[38] While most women did not refer to explicit policies, they did remember pressure-filled requests from local administrators to return to the teaching force. Sadie Chow was adamant that after the birth of each child she was not going to teach. Each time, however, she recalled a "phone campaign" from the Vancouver Board's home economics coordinator insisting that she come back to school. Sadie was convinced by this coordinator, who stated, "With your mind, you'd just sit home and vegetate … you know your children don't have the quantity of time with you but I am sure they have the quality."

Sadie's recollection indicates that while the barrier to married women working may have lifted, mothers still needed to justify their presence. In explaining her decision, Sadie insisted she was a reluctant participant, always found good child care, and did not seek out the position. Her desire to rationalize returning to work is understandable given that five of the seven teachers with offspring in this study described tensions in the workplace despite changes to policy. For example, after Alma Erickson returned to teaching, she remembered that male teachers assumed that she was inexperienced and treated her like a beginner. Although teachers' federation representatives, political officials, and educational administrators in both Toronto and Vancouver encouraged the "marrying-kind" to participate in schools, the women's stories indicate that they encountered intense scrutiny of their performance on arrival.

"Correct Mothering"

Officials wanted to ensure that despite women's physical presence in the school, which symbolized a disruption of the nuclear family, they would still be examples of "correct" mothering. Feminist historians have noted that women teachers have long been specific targets for surveillance by the public. North American studies have examined nineteenth-century and early twentieth-century women teachers who, placed on a pedestal as moral guardians, republican mothers, and Protestant missionaries, were scrutinized for private and public appearances and behaviour that did not fit within the bounds of femininity.[39] By mid-century, psychologists assumed the role of community overseers for mothers, their children, and, in this case, women teachers.[40]

Male psychologists, who had an unprecedented place in postwar schools, asserted that women teachers should carry gendered roles originating in the home into classrooms. They urged women teachers, as they did mothers in general, to temper their tendencies to smother children. The University of Saskatchewan's Samuel Laycock, lauded professor of educational psychology, warned women teachers against cultivating reclusive and needy adolescents.[41] Based on a survey of classrooms across Canadian provinces, Laycock charged the "dithery" and "tense" teacher, "who sees all her Johnnies as individuals whom she can boss or dominate," with thwarting children's psychological fulfilment.[42] In one contribution for the *B.C. Teacher*, he was unambiguous about his gendered perceptions of teachers' mental stability. Poor mental health in teachers revealed itself with "emotional problems," "malicious gossip," "over-sensitive" personalities, and "nagging."[43] Psychologists affirmed that women's embodied selves were sites for the differentiation and medicalization of what was "normal" or "abnormal," "right" or "wrong" gender behaviour in classrooms as elsewhere.[44]

Laycock's assertions on the national scene permeated educational discourses in both British Columbia and Ontario. In a Toronto address, J.G. Althouse, the chief director of education for Ontario, advised student teachers and their inspectors to search for the "danger of overteaching," which he characterized as teachers who "talk too much."[45] Vancouver School Board officials responded directly, claiming that "talking too much" was a problem for their new teachers (who were primarily women) and was being addressed.[46] A contributor to the *B.C. Teacher* noted that psychologists' allegations against women were circulating across North America. She warned fellow women teachers: "Some recent studies have found teachers as a group more neurotic than other groups of women ... we tend to be an emotionally immature group."[47] Psychologists provided scientific justification for educational authorities who sought exhibition of heterosocial behaviour from their female staff.

In her research on women's work in the military during the Second World War, Ruth Roach Pierson argues that public fear over the destruction of "proper" femininity rose as women joined the "masculine" world.[48] Such fears were exacerbated in the postwar period as women's employment rose again. A visual advocacy of heterosexual values was critical for women undertaking professional lives during this time.[49] Kathryn McPherson, in her work on nursing, demonstrates that health-care administrators believed a more youthful and less constrictive feminine figure would increase the attractiveness of nursing and deter entry into other growing employment options.[50] Administrators invoked a heterosocial youth culture by persuading women to attend residence dances and wear a more tailored uniform.[51] This created a more "normative" connection between heterosexuality than in the past; nurses' prescribed uniform signified their official subservience to male doctors.

Although teachers would not wear a uniform, school officials did provide edicts for women's dress that signified heterosexuality or status as marriageable material. This is evident in the regular controversies that emerged in British Columbia newspapers regarding female attire. For example, a principal reportedly suspended three girls for wearing slacks, with Stan Evans, the assistant secretary of the British Columbia Teachers' Federation (BCTF), affirming the legal right of schools to ensure that "skirts really make ladies."[52] At the same time, women were encouraged not to take femininity too far. Controversy surrounded the new modern woman's look of tight sweaters and sheer nylon blouses, which were "disturbing for male students trying to focus on their work." Such dress was actually banned for female employees.[53] Women teachers legitimated their position in the workplace by exhibiting "proper" feminine appearances that included the assertion of sexual difference.

The dress and deportment of women served to reproduce the nuclear family in the school, with men as the legitimate breadwinners – a central character lesson for postwar "democratic" citizenship. When asked about their regular workday routines, interviewees gave detailed descriptions of their distinct personas in the mixed-sex environment. Beth Merle of Toronto forcefully explained that she always wore: "a skirt or blouse. Certainly not pants."[54] Vancouverite Abigail Sears was equally clear: "No pants!" Melanie Kilburn recalled in her Toronto collegiate institute making the appropriate clothing shift from gym tunic to classroom skirt: "I had a wrap-around skirt and as I whizzed down the hall, I would be wrapping it around ... so that it would cover the bare legs." Melanie hid any hint of unladylike bare legs and shorts after she left the gym. These interviewees were ensuring that as working women they were not perceived to be taking on masculine appearances or the authority of male teachers.

Women in both Ontario and British Columbia noted this lesson started in teacher training and carried throughout their careers. Melanie Kilburn learned the expectations of "looking and acting like a teacher" during her time at the Ontario College of Education from 1951 to 1952: "you had white running shoes ... your posture had to be just right and your uniform had to be just so. We needed that to get into the schools." Donna Weber, another physical education teacher, identified a University of British Columbia professor who said she would not succeed "because I had poor posture, I smoked and my running shoes weren't clean."[55] Proper posture and abstinence from smoking had long been associated with reproductive health and thus women's ability to fulfil their biological imperative for motherhood. Interactions with male administrators further ingrained women's "virtuous" manner in the classroom. On the west coast, Grace Logan commented that she had a school board inspector speak to her after class and "he had just one complaint, that my voice was too loud." She said, "I wasn't aware it was loud, I tried to lower the tone of my voice."[56] In the east, Karen Phillips recalled an inspector "told the French teacher that she hadn't powdered her nose, her nose was shiny. She should pay more attention to her appearance."[57] Although Phillips did not imply she learned to powder her nose, the memory lingered of school boards' efforts to differentiate and discipline the bodies of their female staff.

Interviews illustrate that women understood the imperative of portraying happy participation in the school's visual replication of the White, middle-class, nuclear family model. Women's ability to exhibit these values, which was easier for teachers who shared those characteristics, garnered them respectability within their schools and communities. Phillips recalled a woman colleague from the English department who "came from a wealthy family and used to dress up in all her finery for the class, so that these poor working class children would know what it was like." Catharine Darby spoke of "a lot of immigrants coming in … they wanted to do better for their children when they came to Canada." Her part, as she described, was to show these students techniques in home economics that were "as useful as possible, so it meant that we didn't do ethnic stuff … the clothing we made was Western."[58] Catharine's narrative, as with others possessing racial and class privilege, suggests that some women found authority in the conventions of the "marrying-kind" of teacher.

In contrast, Sadie Chow, a second-generation Chinese Canadian and home economist, struggled to look Caucasian in order to garner authority as the right kind of married woman. She asserted her ability to dress in a finer way and teach her female students how to "effectively" present themselves in the world. She described an elaborate dressing scheme each week that would make her the epitome of students' aspirations: "every week I wore a different colour and the object of the game was to teach kids how to colour co-ordinate and to accessorize." She describes this and other lessons as necessary attempts to "White" her self in cooking and dress in order to be an exemplar for the future homemakers that made up her class. Although largely accepting the imperative to reproduce postwar nationalist, "democratic" values, her body betrayed other histories and possibilities. She offered the following story in illustration: "I was teaching a lesson on less tender cuts of meat ... all of a sudden I heard a chair snap and this girl stood up ... she said 'I'm not gonna take anything from a God damn Chinaman anymore!'" Sadie starkly revealed the social sanctions that could accompany a woman's failure to fully symbolize postwar "normativity."

"Deviant Spinster"

Although all women faced sanctions of "correct" mothering in the classroom, it was single women who suffered chastisement for not being of the "marrying-mind." Public trepidation surrounded the ever-increasing number of women in the male-dominated public sphere, and in this case, the male-dominated secondary school. Women's greater access to higher education and paid labour provided new opportunities to opt out of heterosexual relationships. Teaching, in particular, afforded White, middle-class, educated women a socially acceptable means to be removed from traditional family structures. This, however, was not without consequence. With increasing tolerance for married women, because of their bodily portrayal of heteronormativity, came a heightened intolerance of independent women living outside marital relationships. Where once such women had been the admired backbone of Canadian education, they were increasingly suspect, dismissed as inadequate spinsters.

Sheila L. Cavanagh argues that the nuclear family model was as much about compulsory heterosexuality as fears of growing lesbianism.[59] Single women teachers, who "refused to organize their private lives and sexuality around a man," were treading on dangerous ground, potentially understood as "emotionally maladjusted, sexually inverted, celibate and/or queer."[60] Madiha Didi Khayatt, in her work on lesbian teachers, demonstrates that sexologists and psychologists of the period imposed a medicalized model of sexuality that connected the lack of a stable nuclear family background with spinsterhood, mental illness, and subsequently lesbianism.[61] Fears and accusations of instability were particularly pronounced for young, fertile women in expanding cities who chose independence with a career.[62] Many single teachers of this period, and particularly of this study, fit that mould. They were not the "old spinster," but, rather, the young, fertile, urban, single woman.

Cavanagh suggests that postwar discussion of the "unmarried teacher" assumed a eugenics cast, despite Holocaust atrocities. She quotes an excerpt from an article entitled "Better Teachers, Biologically Speaking," published in *Education Digest*, a popular magazine: "the married are, on the whole, biologically superior to the unmarried (... longevity, keeping out of jail, and freedom from mental disease) so are the fertile superior to the sterile. It is desirable not merely that teachers should marry, but also that they should have children."[63] When young, eligible, White women refused to marry, they challenged their obligations as future mothers and reproducers of "democratic" citizenship.[64] As professionals, they also failed to communicate the nature of proper citizenship.

Spinsters, who were neither reproductive outside the school nor productive inside the classroom, appeared unattractive at best, and at times, even monstrous to educational authorities. Cartoons in the papers used the spinster teacher image to police teachers and, in contrast, celebrate young, attractive, marrying women. The threat of the spinster teacher loomed large and was characterized by spindly bodies covered by oversized skirts and jackets, glasses hanging from sharp noses, and hair tight in a bun; all in all, far from the attractive vessel for the national embodiment of "democratic" stability. One such cartoon mocked Education Week, an annual campaign to encourage the community to learn more about schools. It depicted a spinster teacher surrounded by dead plants, bored children, and falling pictures of apples (in other situations a recognizable sign of students' affections for their teacher).[65] The spinster teacher, with her rejection or inability to fulfil the role of wife or mother, was an objectionable envoy to the public.

School officials' support of this view could very well have been a public relations exercise to swell the ranks of marriageable women teachers. In 1955, the report of the West Coast conference of the Canadian Education Association (CEA), in the context of its efforts to enhance public understanding of education, noted, "It was hoped that some mass medium process could be devised to parallel 'Medic' for the medical profession, and 'Dragnet' and 'Mr. D.A.' for the police departments. At present, all we have is 'Our Miss Brooks,' which is worse than useless."[66]

Our Miss Brooks may have been "useless," albeit a successful radio and television personality in the late 1940s and 1950s, because she was yet another spinster woman teacher. Even her attractiveness could not counterbalance her sharp wit, tough talk, and failure to win Mr. Boynton, the school's biology teacher. We can only speculate whether the CEA would have referred to Miss Brooks as a meaningless media darling when upon the show's cancellation, in 1956, she finally married Mr. Boynton and supposedly lived happily ever after.

Women teachers were positioned between the virtuous, loving mother and the deviant, single spinster teacher, who rejected her "natural" purpose. Fran Thompson's memories of her teaching days as a single woman are representative of many of the women's narratives. She struggled to identify herself as a "respectable" woman and a "proper" teacher within available discourses. When Fran, a single woman, began teaching in a Toronto school, she clearly did not want to emulate the social character of her unmarried mentors. She stated:

> I had a rather prejudiced opinion myself. I bought the stereotype that these unmarried women would be old spinsters ... she dressed in long black skirts, thick stockings and funny looking coats.

Fran depicted the spinster as the typical older teacher who was alone, rough, and oddly dressed. She characterized her own appearance when she began teaching in the 1950s as having been "well-dressed ... always a skirt or something like that."[67]

Physical education teacher Jessie Russell of Vancouver, who was married, referred to scepticism of her femininity due to her subject area. She alluded to societal misgivings about potential associations with a masculine muscular physique and stereotypical "butch" lesbian exterior. She remembered a university professor bringing students to watch her teach a physical education class for the explicit reason that

> you keep looking feminine, you're not a jock, you dress nicely and you, you know you're careful about your appearance and you do a good job at the lesson.

Jessie highlighted her ability to be an "effective" physical education teacher while simultaneously exhibiting her "womanliness." She went on to describe her work as having a profound influence on the presentation of her students' sense of self. Jessie explained that she

> just wanted to look like a nice PE teacher ... like my hair was always in a ponytail ... I met one [student] at a reunion and she said every morning she would try and do her hair the way I had it.[68]

She, like most of the women interviewed, made concerted efforts to steer through the pitfalls for women's embodiment of postwar norms.

The pitfalls were more treacherous for lesbian teachers of the period. Sophie Canning, a lesbian, although not out during those days, claimed the ability to "dress the part" demanded by the times. She depicted her dress, however, less in terms of expressing a non-spinster or "new woman" identity, than covering-up her "demonized" sexuality. When discussing the issue of character lessons for her students, she commented that she never felt comfortable addressing personal issues because she lived her "life in the closet." Canning's attire provided a protective second skin. Unlike the other interviewees, she only wore pants: "long blue pants, fairly tight, and one time I had to do something and I was dressed up and this person came up [to me and said], 'My god your legs aren't blue!'" Sophie concluded, "See I had a dress problem." Her "problem," as she defined it, was the need to play a part, not revealing herself too much, at the same time as rejecting the binary of the postwar model of femininity. Canning took the next moment to recall her favourite lesson. It was a dance lesson to a mixed class of boys and girls: "God it was fun and I started them out exactly [letting them] dance with whoever they want."[69] Sophie refused to impose the same heterosocial programming on her students that she felt urged to portray.

"Democracy" in postwar schools personified a highly gendered social contract. The "democratic" nation, recovering from the traumas of war, employed women teachers' bodies in its efforts for "domestic containment" or the repression of social, moral, and sexual freedoms in the name of demographic freedoms.[70] Women teachers, whether single, married, or lesbian, were accountable for the embodiment, performance, and reproduction of the nuclear family as exemplars for students as the future citizens of the nation. Penina M. Glazer and Miriam Slater write, "Women had to be sensitive to an ever present scrutiny of their performance, personal style and presentation of self."[71] The educational community demanded that women teachers advertise their propensity for marriage and motherhood and embody rigid standards of morality as mothers or future mothers. Rejection of heterosocial deportment equated to a rejection of professional and personal respectability and, more alarmingly, the core values of Canada's postwar democracy. But as Emma Rich reflects from her work on women in England's teacher training programs, "There is no simple materiality, no correct behaviour which these women can unequivocally achieve." She remarks, "Their inclusion in their profession is contradictory, by mere virtue of the fact that as women they remain subordinates in a dominant Gender Order which underpins the dominant educational discourses."[72] The "marrying-kind" of teacher gained new entry into the profession, assuming responsibility for conveying a separate spheres ideology based on her inferiority. She was asked to work in the name of a liberal democracy that safeguarded masculine models of citizenship and, ultimately, subordinated her authority.

Notes

Funding support for this research came from the Social Sciences and Humanities Research Council of Canada. I wish to thank the women teachers who shared their life stories for this research. I also extend thanks to Jane Nicholas and Patrizia Gentile, and the other contributors to this collection, for their feedback on drafts of this chapter.

1 Alison Prentice et al., *Canadian Women: A History* (Toronto: Harcourt Brace Jovanovich, 1988), 351; Ann Porter, "Women and Income Security in the Post-War Period: The Case of Unemployment Insurance, 1945–1962," *Labour/Le Travail* 31 (1993), 111–44; Shirley Tillotson, "Human Rights Law as Prism: Women's Organizations, Unions and Ontario's Female Employees Fair Remuneration Act, 1951," *Canadian Historical Review* 72 (1991), 532–57.

2 Franca Iacovetta, "Recipes for Democracy? Gender, Family and Making Female Citizens in Cold War Canada," in *Rethinking Canada: The Promise of Women's History*, ed. Veronica Strong-Boag et al. (Don Mills, ON: Oxford University Press, 2002), 301.

3 Joy Parr, Introduction, in *A Diversity of Women: Ontario, 1945–1980*, ed. Joy Parr (Toronto: University of Toronto Press, 1995), 5.

4 Paul Popenoe, "Better Teachers, Biologically Speaking," *Education Digest* 2, no. 8 (1937), 5, as quoted in Sheila L. Cavanaugh, "The Heterosexualization of the Ontario Woman Teacher in the Postwar Period," *Canadian Women's Studies* 18, no. 1 (1999), 67.

5 Secondary school teachers are the focus of this research because this level was and continues to be considered primarily responsible for the production of "good" citizens. Few education officials and commentators in the postwar era, however, made a significant distinction between elementary and secondary school when discussing the role of women teachers. Both elementary and secondary women teachers were liable for the embodiment and performance of patriarchal citizenship.

6 Judith Butler, "Performative Acts and Gender Constitution: An Essay in Phenomenology and Feminist Theory," in *Performing Feminisms: Femin-*

ist Critical Theory and Theatre, ed. S. Case (Baltimore, MD: Johns Hopkins University Press, 1990), 277. Butler's concept of gendered performance is also used in Kathryn McPherson's work on nursing in Canada. See Kathryn McPherson, "'The Case of the Kissing Nurse': Femininity, Sexuality, and Canadian Nursing, 1900–1970," in *Gendered Pasts: Historical Essays in Femininity and Masculinity in Canada*, ed. K. McPherson, C. Morgan, and N. Forestell (Don Mills, ON: Oxford University Press, 1999), 181.

7 Butler, "Performative Acts and Gender Constitution," 282.

8 This chapter derives from my larger study on democracy and women teachers. See Kristina R. Llewellyn, "In the Name of Democracy: The World of Women Teachers in Toronto and Vancouver, 1945–1960," doctoral dissertation, University of British Columbia, 2006.

9 See Alvin Finkel, *Social Policy and Practice in Canada: A History* (Waterloo: Wilfrid Laurier University Press, 2006).

10 Carole Pateman, *The Sexual Contract* (Cambridge: Polity, 1988); Carole Pateman, *The Disorder of Women: Democracy, Feminism, and Political Theory* (Stanford, CA: Stanford University Press, 1989).

11 Anne Phillips, *Engendering Democracy* (University Park, PA: Pennsylvania State University Press, 1991).

12 Valerie Walkerdine and Helen Lucey, *Democracy in the Kitchen: Regulating Mothers and Socialising Daughters* (London: Virago, 1989).

13 Madeleine Arnot and Jo-Anne Dillabough, "Feminist Politics and Democratic Values in Education," *Curriculum Inquiry* 29, no. 2 (1999), 164.

14 Jane Roland Martin, "Excluding Women from the Educational Realm," as cited by Arnot and Dillabough, ibid., 165.

15 Nira Yuval-Davis, "Women, Citizenship and Difference," *Feminist Review* 57 (1997), 45.

16 Shirley Tillotson, *The Public at Play: Gender and Politics of Recreation in Post-War Ontario* (Toronto: University of Toronto Press, 2000); Mona Gleason, *Normalizing the Ideal: Psychology, Schooling, and the Family in Postwar Canada* (Toronto: Toronto University Press, 1999); Mary Louise Adams, *The Trouble with Normal: Postwar Youth and the Construction of Heterosexuality* (Toronto: University of Toronto Press, 1994).

17 H.L. Tracy, "In Praise of Teachers," *Bulletin*, Oct. (1951), 162.

18 Norman McLeod, "Taking Stock," *Bulletin*, 15 Dec. (1957), 358.

19 Ibid., 359–60.

20 "Are You a Weak Teacher?" *B.C. Teacher*, Feb. (1946), 186–8.

21 F.S. Rivers and R.W.B. Jackson, "Teacher Supply in Canada," *Canadian Education* 8 (June 1953), 20. See also W.G. Fleming, *Estimates of Teacher Supply and Demand in Ontario Secondary Schools for 1957–1972*, Education Research

Series, No. 3, Department of Educational Research, Ontario College of Education (Toronto: University of Toronto Press, 1956).

22 Herbert Edgar Smith, "Teacher Training," in *Canadian Education Today: A Symposium*, ed. Joseph Katz (Toronto: McGraw-Hill, 1956), 168; Doris French, *High Button Bootstraps: Federation of Women's Teachers' Associations of Ontario, 1918–1968* (Toronto: Ryerson Press, 1968), 142; Robert M Stamp, *The Schools of Ontario, 1876–1976* (Toronto: University of Toronto Press, 1982), 199. Recruitment was even aimed at high schools, with B.C.'s Department of Education beginning Future Teachers' Clubs in 1954. Although policy did not allocate these clubs by gender, Vancouver secondary schools' yearbooks show all-female clubs. See F. Henry Johnson, *A Brief History of Canadian Education* (Toronto: McGraw-Hill, 1968), 219.

23 *Globe and Mail*, 23 Jan. 1959.

24 "What We Said," *B.C. Teacher* (Sept.–Oct. 1959), 14.

25 Patricia Anne Staton and Beth Light, *Speak with Their Own Voices: A Documentary History of the Teachers of Ontario and the Women Elementary Public School Teachers in Ontario* (Toronto: FWTAO, 1987), 143–4; CVA, Public School Records, *Vancouver Personnel and Research Subject Files*, Loc. 59-A-1, File 18, *Report to Personnel Committee, February 7th 1955: Status of Married Women as Teachers*, 1955.

26 This policy was enacted in conjunction with the province's 1952 Female Employees' Fair Remuneration Act.

27 Punham Khosla, Laura King, and Linda Read, *The Unrecognized Majority: A History of Women Teachers in British Columbia* (Vancouver: BCTF, Status of Women Committee in British Columbia, 1979), 40. The BCTF had encouraged boards as early as the mid-1940s to remove overt sex differences, with Vancouver reported as one of the last to hold out. Gender equity policies within the BCTF were due, in part, to the leadership of Hilda Cryderman and Mollie Cunningham.

28 Gaskell, *Problems and Professionalism*, 31–2.

29 "Cupid So Busy Can't Get Enough P.T. Teachers" and "See Kindergarten Spot to Choose Motherly Wife," *Globe and Mail*, 9 Jan. 1952.

30 "Pretty, New Teachers," *Vancouver Sun*, 15 Sept. 1950.

31 The employment of women teachers was similar to national trends in which women's participation in paid labour reached over 30%, with over half married. This percentage was higher than any previous during peacetime. See Strong-Boag, "Canada's Wage-Earning Wives," 7.

32 Toronto District School Board Sesquicentennial Museum and Archives (TDSBA.), Toronto Board of Education, *Year Book* (Toronto: Noble Scott, 1954), 12.

33 City of Vancouver Archives (CVA), Public School Records, *Vancouver Personnel and Research Subject Files*, Loc. 59-A-1, File 18, "Calculations of Married Women on Staff, School Term 1956–1957," 1957. These statistics are not exact as many women did not denote themselves as Miss or Mrs. and instead used initials. Furthermore, it is believed that many women did not reveal to the board that they were married because it would affect their employment status. Thus, the records are low estimates of the number of women. For more on the position of married women teachers in British Columbia, see, Stella Shopland, *Status of Married Women Teachers in the Province of British Columbia*, M.A. thesis, University of Washington, 1957.

34 J.D. Aikenhead, "Research on the Teacher Shortage," *Education: A Collection of Essays on Canadian Education*, vol. 2, *1956–1958* (Toronto: Gage, 1959), 38. Cecilia Reynolds argues that teaching became an increasingly acceptable job for a man due to the increasing credentials of the profession. Men in the teaching labour force steadily increased after 1921. Reynolds notes, however, that an increase mostly took place in the expanding administration level. See Reynolds, "Hierarchy and Hegemony," 98–9.

35 Aikenhead, "Research on Teacher Shortage," 38.

36 See, e.g., Interview with Sadie Chow (pseudonym), conducted on 16 Sept. 2005, in Vancouver; Interview with Alma Erickson (pseudonym), conducted on 15 Sept. 2005, in Vancouver.

37 Interview with Melanie Kilburn (pseudonym), conducted on 21 Jan. 2002, in Toronto.

38 Interview with Abigail Sears (pseudonym), conducted on 17 May 2005, in Vancouver.

39 Marjorie Theobald, "Teachers, Memory and Oral History," in *Telling Women's Lives: Narrative Inquiries in the History of Women's Education*, ed. Kathleen Weiler and Sue Middleton (Philadelphia, PA: Open University Press, 1999), 17–18.

40 See also Wendy Mitchinson, this volume. Mitchinson notes that during this period male psychologists associated childhood obesity with weak gender identity.

41 Gleason, *Normalizing the Ideal*, 124–5.

42 S.R. Laycock, "You Can't Get Away from Discipline," *Educational Review of the New Brunswick Teachers' Federation* 60 (1946), 7, quoted in Gleason, *Normalizing the Ideal*, 124–5. See also S.R. Laycock, "Teaching – A Job in Human Relations," *Education: A Collection of Essays on Canadian Education*, vol. 2, *1956–1958* (Toronto: Gage, 1959), 77–80.

43 S.R. Laycock, "Professional Ethics and Mental Health," *B.C. Teacher* (May–

June 1957), 397–8. See also S.R. Laycock, "Your Job in Public Relations," *B.C. Teacher* (Jan. 1955), 152–4; S.R. Laycock, "Invest in Good Teachers," *B.C. Teacher* (Jan. 1957), 210–11.

44 Gleason, *Normalizing the Ideal*, 3–18. For information on the medicalization of women's bodies as a site for restricting gender roles, see Wendy Mitchinson, *The Nature of Their Bodies: Women and Their Doctors in Victorian Canada* (Toronto: University of Toronto Press, 1991).

45 J.G. Althouse, *Addresses: A Selection of Addresses by the Late Chief Director of Education for Ontario, Covering the Years 1936–1956* (Toronto: Gage, 1958), 146 and 205.

46 "City's Experienced Teachers Not Guilty of Talking Too Much," *Province*, 9 April 1955.

47 May Hill Arbuthnot, "Teachers Are People," *B.C. Teacher* (May–June 1946), 325.

48 Ruth Roach Pierson, *"They're Still Women after All": The Second World War and Canadian Womanhood* (Toronto: McClelland and Stewart, 1986).

49 See also Bonnie Schmidt, this volume. Schmidt demonstrates that when women disrupted the male preserve of national policing in the 1960s, femininity rather than functionality determined their uniforms and mitigated concerns for male civic authority.

50 McPherson, "The Case of the Kissing Nurse," 190.

51 Ibid., 191–3.

52 "Girls in Slacks Spark a Furore," *Province*, 22 Dec. 1956.

53 "Tight Clothes in Dirty Thirties Never Raised Teachers' Eyebrows," *Province*, 9 Sept. 1958; "'Naughty Nylon' Problem Invades City Schools," *Province*, 28 May 1952. For information on the look of the new "woman" in Toronto schools, see Adams, *The Trouble with Normal.*

54 Interview with Beth Merle (pseudonym), conducted on 23 Nov. 2001, in Toronto.

55 Interview with Donna Weber (pseudonym), conducted on 22 May 2005, in Vancouver.

56 Interview with Grace Logan (pseudonym), conducted on 19 Sept. 2005, in Vancouver.

57 Interview with Karen Phillips (pseudonym), conducted on 26 Nov. 2001, in Toronto.

58 Interview with Catharine Darby (pseudonym), conducted on 19 May 2005, in Vancouver.

59 Cavanagh, "The Heterosexualization of the Ontario Woman Teacher." See also Cecilia Reynolds, "Too Limiting a Liberation: Discourse and Actuality

in the Case of Married Women Teachers," in *Feminism and Education: A Canadian Perspective*, ed. F. Forman, M. O'Brien, J. Haddad, D. Hallman, and P. Masters (Toronto: Centre for Women's Studies in Education, 1990); Alison Oram, "Embittered, Sexless or Homosexual: Attacks on Spinster Teachers in 1918–1939," in *Not a Passing Phase: Reclaiming Lesbians in History 1840–1985*, ed. Lesbian History Group (London: Women's Press, 1989).

60 Cavanagh, "Heterosexualization of the Ontario Woman Teacher," 66.

61 Madiha Didi Khayatt, *Lesbian Teachers: An Invisible Presence* (Albany, NY: SUNY Press, 1992), 21–6.

62 Carolyn Strange discusses public fears during the industrial revolution of young women finding jobs in cities that offered less supervision and more pleasurable leisure options. See Carolyn Strange, *Toronto's Girl Problem: The Perils and Pleasures of the City, 1880–1930* (Toronto: University of Toronto Press, 1995).

63 Popenoe, "Better Teachers, Biologically Speaking," as quoted in Cavanaugh, "Heterosexualization of the Ontario Woman Teacher," 67.

64 Ibid.

65 "It's still Education Week," *Vancouver Sun*, 6 March 1952. See also Helen Smith and Pamela Wakewich, this volume. They illustrate that cartoons served to articulate the frightening possibility that malleable female bodies, at worst masculinized, could permanently unsettle the gender order and produce an unhealthy nation.

66 CVA, Public School Records, *Vancouver Personnel and Research Subject Files*, Loc. 58-F-1, File 18, "Proceedings of the CEA – Kellogg Vancouver Metropolitan Zone Conference held at the University of British Columbia," Thursday, 3 Nov. 1955. For more on cultural representations of teaching, see Sari Knopp Biklen, *School Work: Gender and the Cultural Construction of Teaching* (New York: Teachers College Press, 1995), and Sandra Weber and Claudia Mitchell, *"That's Funny, You Don't Look like a Teacher": Interrogating Images and Identity in Popular Culture* (Washington, DC: Falmer, 1995).

67 Interview with Fran Thompson (pseudonym), conducted on 20 Nov. 2001, in Toronto.

68 Interview with Jessie Russell (pseudonym), conducted on 16 Sept. 2005, in Vancouver.

69 Interview with Sophie Canning (pseudonym), conducted on 17 Sept. 2005, on Vancouver Island.

70 Iacovetta, "Recipes for Democracy?" 301.

71 Penina M. Glazer and Miriam Slater, *Unequal Colleagues: The Entrance of Women into the Professions, 1890–1940* (New Brunswick, NJ: Rutgers University

Press, 1987), 232, as quoted by Cavanaugh, "The Gender of Professionalism and Occupational Closure," 55.

72 Emma Rich, "Gender Positioning in Teacher Education in England: New Rhetoric, Old Realities," *International Studies in Sociology of Education* 11, no. 2 (2001), 145.

17 Contesting a Canadian Icon: Female Police Bodies and the Challenge to the Masculine Foundations of the Royal Canadian Mounted Police in the 1970s

BONNIE REILLY SCHMIDT

In the early morning of 23 January 1978, Royal Canadian Mounted Police (RCMP)[1] Constable Candace Smith lay on the pavement outside of room 20 at the Countryside Inn in Virden, Manitoba. Smith had just been shot by Herbert Archer who, moments earlier, had fatally shot her partner Constable Dennis Onofrey. Smith was injured in the thigh by a blast from Archer's shotgun before being hit a second time by a .308 rifle bullet that also struck her thigh before entering her abdomen.[2] After Archer fled the scene, Smith regained consciousness and crawled along the sidewalk towards the safety of the motel's registration office before being found by a fellow police officer.[3]

The shootout at the Countryside Inn was the subject of national headlines for months following the incident.[4] Much of the media coverage not only focused on the shootout, but drew attention to Smith as the first female RCMP officer to be shot in the line of duty. Smith also became the focus of attention within the RCMP, where a number of her colleagues criticized her failure to shoot Archer, who at one point during their exchange of gunfire exited the hotel room with his back to her. Instead of firing, Smith ordered Archer to drop his weapon, affording him time to dart back into the room and continue shooting. Although the actions of the male officers at the scene who failed to shoot Archer were also called into question, references to their decisions during the shooting were indirect, subtle, and gender neutral.[5]

Smith's perceived inability to shoot a suspect while under fire reinforced assumptions about women as the weaker sex and too emotional for police work.[6] For some critics of female police officers, women's reproductive capacities governed their emotions, rendering them irrational and more passive than male police officers. Their bodies were perceived to be unruly and uncontrollable, secreting fluids that made them unsuitable as figures of civic authority. In contrast, men were perceived to be free from the type of body that governed women and were endowed with physical strength, reason, aggression, and rationality. While the near-fatal shooting of Smith appeared to validate critiques of female police officers as unequal to the job, Smith's physical rehabilitation and eventual return to active duty challenged conventional perceptions of women as the weaker sex.[7] Her example represents just one of the many ways women contested and renegotiated understandings of their role as capable law enforcement officers. More importantly for this essay, Smith's experience illustrates the importance of studying the corporeality of the female police body in historical analyses of police forces.

This chapter explores the ways the hiring of women as police officers and the female police body contested the masculine foundations of the RCMP and its long-standing connection to the Canadian nation. For more than one hundred years, the RCMP served as an image of Canadian manhood and ideal citizenship that was representative of the state and its authority. Although the arrival of a new police body called into question idealized representations of masculine citizenry, the hiring of women as Mounties, in 1974, did little to dismantle gendered notions of biological difference and its connection to ideal citizenship and the nation. Indeed, male and female bodies continued to be perceived in binary opposition, operating in an unequal power relationship despite the RCMP's official employment equity policies. This becomes evident when the specificity of the female police body is studied. In particular, how the female police body was clothed and trained reveals the ways in which the RCMP grappled with incorporating women into its ranks without compromising its highly masculinized image. Throughout this chapter the female police body emerges as a site of contestation – one that disturbed prevailing notions of masculinity and femininity in the nation in general, and the RCMP in particular.

The Nation and the Male Police Body

The origins of the heroic image of the RCMP and the male police body as representative of nation are deeply rooted in the history of the police force. Historian Michael Dawson argues that there are, in fact, two histories of the RCMP: the "classic" story and the "unofficial" history, in which the "myth of the heroic Mountie conceals the actual history of a Force that repressed Native peoples, spied on and crushed working-class organizations, discriminated against women, and persecuted homosexuals."[8] Classic versions were highly favourable accounts that positioned the North-West Mounted Police (NWMP) as a central actor in restoring law and order in the west and in facilitating the safe and orderly settlement of the region.[9] Prime Minister John A. Macdonald is generally credited to be the visionary behind the formation of a paramilitary mounted force that also fulfilled a civilian police function. As early as 1869, Macdonald viewed the maintenance of law and order in the newly acquired western territories as crucial to populating the region and attracting economic investment. Future settlers needed protection from Native violence, and the Indigenous population needed protection from ruthless American whisky traders. However, it was not until the Cypress Hills Massacre in 1873 that Macdonald's government acted and the NWMP was hastily formed.

By the turn of the new century, the image of the hero on horseback who "always gets his man" was so popular that men from across the Empire enlisted in response to the promise of adventure.[10] These highly masculinized narratives followed a heroic storyline that seldom, if ever, mentioned women. When women were mentioned, they were the wives of commanding officers who were most often portrayed as civilizing influences and exemplars of White, British womanhood.[11] The marginalization of women in historical narratives of the police force rendered them invisible as actors in the history of the RCMP and, by corollary, the nation.

In the first decades of the twentieth century, the mythic image of the Mountie was reinforced through numerous memoirs and histories written by former police officers. Following the classic storyline, these narratives did little to discourage heroic representations of the police force and cast it in a positive light, suggesting that members of the RCMP actively contributed to the making of the Mountie myth.[12] Popular literature further enhanced these representations with more than 150 dime novels about the police force published between 1890 and 1940.[13] Comics, postcards, songs, poems, and radio programs about Mounties proliferated throughout the first half of the twentieth century.

Innovations such as the motion picture camera intensified the RCMP's romanticized image with the production of 256 Mountie films by Hollywood.[14] In these films, the masculine police body was idealized: the Mountie hero was always portrayed as handsome, strong, physically fit, and of Anglo-Saxon descent.[15] He was also a gentleman, well-bred, morally upright, gallant, courageous, and possessed of an inner strength that demanded respect for his authority. The Mountie represented true Canadian manhood. His ideal physical appearance represented his superiority over other men, and his body mirrored his "standing and respectability" in society.[16] As Holliday and Hassard suggest, representation is key to the processes by which some bodies are excluded and not recognized as worthy of belonging to the hegemonic group.[17] In classic representations, the figure of the Mountie embodied elite definitions of masculine authority to legitimate the power of a state interested in being perceived as civilized, economically viable, predominantly White, and, above all, infused with masculine virility.

In the closing decades of the twentieth century, what Dawson has termed as "unofficial" versions of RCMP history emerged as professional historians revisited classic interpretations from a more critical perspective.[18] In these revisionist accounts, the Mountie is positioned as a gendered, racialized, and mythic representation of Canada that reinforced the hegemonic control of White, middle-class men over the emerging nation. Daniel Francis explains that myths idealize events or institutions that embody the cultural values of a specific group; but they also marginalize anyone posing a threat to the dominant cultural project.[19] The body of the hero on horseback was invested with a distinct cultural meaning that marginalized First Nations peoples, women, ethnic and cultural minorities, and those who posed a threat to dominant cultural narratives. Anne Phillips argues in *Engendering Democracy* that adherents of liberal democracies have insinuated "the male body and male identity into their definitions of the norm," resulting in the exclusion of women and minority groups from definitions of ideal citizenship.[20] Definitions that privileged White males of Anglo-Saxon descent not only concealed the presence of women as participants in building the nation, but positioned the idea of female police officers as contrary to the Canadian ideal and masculinity as the only legitimate representation of state authority.

The Nation and the Contested Male Police Body

The masculine RCMP body and its close association with representations of the nation remained largely uncontested for 101 years. Complicit in perpetuating the Mountie myth were a number of RCMP commissioners who recognized the value of connecting the Mountie image with the nation's history. Although not all commissioners specifically worked to this end, many were at least cognizant of the importance of portraying the police force as a national asset. In 1970, Commissioner W.L. Higgitt was thinking of an earlier time when he wrote that "it is important that we restore rather than further erode our image."[21] Higgitt, responding to changes in dress regulations made in 1965 by a previous commissioner,[22] turned his attention to the Mountie body to remind the public of the connection between the RCMP and the history of the nation. Higgitt issued Standing Orders that stated the "felt hat, shirt, tie, breeches, leather belt and long boots with spurs will be worn by all operational members which includes those performing duties on Detachments, Municipal Details, Highway Patrols, Sub-Division Traffic Supervisors and Section NCO's."[23] The commissioner's orders made dressing the police body a site of contestation for many police officers. Wearing breeches and boots with spurs while driving a police cruiser, chasing suspects on foot, or in the summer heat, became a contentious issue among the rank and file.

Despite these objections, the Mountie body was viewed as a valuable tool in communicating specific ideals about manliness, citizenship, and the traditions of the dominant cultural group. Marcel Mauss observed, in 1935, that techniques of the body were "*of a mechanical, physical or physiochemical order,*" and that there was no technique in the absence of tradition.[24] Similarly, Jennifer Craik suggests that rules about uniforms are a "technique" of the biological, sociological, and psychological body. The rules "are highly detailed and fastidious. Wearing a uniform properly – understanding and obeying rules about the uniform-in-practice – turning the garments into communicative statements – is more important than the items of clothing and decoration themselves."[25] For the commissioner, reinstating the classic RCMP uniform into everyday policing activities was a mechanical, physical, and easily recognizable technique that conveyed messages about tradition, state authority, and the nation to Canadians.

While the RCMP was reinstating an image from an earlier era, the male police body as representative of the nation became a site of contestation for a number of individuals and groups interested in improving women's rights.[26] The operation of unequal power relations between men and women in Canadian society was evident in the continued dominance of the male police body in Canada's federal police force. This dominance was called into question in 1970 by the commissioners of the Royal Commission on the Status of Women in Canada (RCSWC).[27] In their final report, the commissioners challenged the RCMP for its exclusionary hiring practices, noting that although policewomen were common in municipal forces in Canada,[28] the RCMP had "remained strictly a male preserve." The commissioners recommended that "enlistment in the

Royal Canadian Mounted Police be open to women."[29] The importance of the RCSWC findings cannot be underestimated. Oral history accounts revealed that male and female officers, in hindsight, viewed the RCSWC's recommendations as influential in changing RCMP hiring policies. One female officer commented, "Left on its own, I don't believe the RCMP would have acted" to hire women, and there was "no question" that the RCSWC was the impetus.[30] Indeed, the RCMP later acknowledged that the recommendations of the RCSWC were a factor in motivating commanding officers to consider changing the force's policy.[31]

It is noteworthy that the media seized on the image of the Mountie to contest the findings of the RCSWC. The commission's final report discussed thirty briefs that specifically protested "the degrading, moronic picture of woman" as solely obsessed with a desire to please "masculine hero-figures" in representations produced by the media.[32] It was not surprising, then, that some members of the media chose to contest demands for increased rights for women through a reworking of the image of the hero on horseback, particularly since this masculine image represented the larger nation, something demands for women's rights were perceived as disrupting.

Kristina Llewellyn, in her chapter in this volume, discusses how cartoonists during the period after the Second World War frequently responded to fears about independent women by lampooning the spinster schoolteacher. The spinster was often depicted as unattractive, spindly, with a sharp nose, and hair in a tight bun, unsuitable as a "vessel for reproduction" with her rejection of the more socially acceptable role of wife and mother. Similarly, editorial cartoonists frequently speculated on what female Mounties would look like, but, in contrast to the spinster, offered highly sexualized interpretations of the female body in uniform that contrasted significantly with images of the masculine Mountie body.

In 1970, Edd Uluschak, editorial cartoonist for the *Edmonton Journal*, depicted three buxom female Mounties, dressed in mini-skirted uniforms with Stetson hats and Strathcona boots, standing at attention and reporting for duty to a desk sergeant. Their tight-fitting tunics cannot contain their breasts and a button pops off of one jacket. The caption below reads, "With a motto like 'We always get our man' recruiting is no problem!"[33] In this portrayal, Uluschak twists the original meaning of the motto to confine women to biological formulations of sexual difference. He works on a deeply social level when he depicts women as primarily biological and sexual entities or the "other sex," and therefore subject to a hierarchical social relationship with men. For Gisela Bock, biology is a "modern metaphor for the old assumption that men are ungendered and women are gendered beings, that men are the 'one' and women the 'other sex.'"[34] Uluschak situates the female body as occupying the wrong space, using humour to suggest the absurdity of women's claims to equality in a conventionally masculine space. The female Mountie body is depicted as unruly and uncontainable in the classic RCMP uniform, a sexual distraction and therefore inappropriate as a figure of civic authority.

Further, Uluschak relies on the gender stereotype of woman as a moral threat, linking female Mounties to the disruption of morality, respectability, and social order in Canadian society. Several scholars have demonstrated how, throughout the twentieth century, the liberal state defined and controlled women through legislation to prevent abortion, govern rape, dispense maternity benefits, and regulate marriage.[35] Uluschak's cartoon caption not only suggests that female police officers were a moral and sexual threat to men, but that female Mounties represented sexual competition with other women, including Mountie wives.[36] Constructed images such as Uluschak's positioned them as temptresses and seductresses and, by implication, a threat to heterosexual monogamy. They were "somehow different to other women," but at the same time they were like all other women[37] and therefore a threat to social order in general and to police culture in particular.

The Nation and the Arrival of a New Police Body

As a result of pressure exerted on the RCMP by politicians and women's groups, the recommendations of the RCSWC were finally implemented. When Commissioner Maurice Nadon announced, on 24 May 1974, that the RCMP would be hiring women for the first time, 292 women from across Canada applied for a position in the first all-female troop, Troop 17. Thirty-two women, between the ages of nineteen and twenty-nine, and representing every province except Prince Edward Island, were chosen. They were sworn in simultaneously, on 16 September 1974, so that no one woman would be able to say that she was the "first" female Mountie to be engaged.[38] It was a precedent that has never been duplicated. The RCMP emphasized that its intention was to transfer the pressure of being the "first" onto a group of women rather than an individual.[39] This precedent suggests, however, that although the police force was hiring women in response to outside pressures, it was intent on defining the terms of women's inclusion as police officers.

At the training academy, training officers had less than six months to prepare for the arrival of the first female recruits. One senior officer involved in the preparations recalled that consideration was briefly given to erecting a fence around the women's barracks, so concerned were the officers over how male recruits would respond to the presence of women. Conventional notions about the uncontrollable female body and women as the weaker sex contributed to the idea that the female police body was in need of containment but also, ironically, in need of protection from male recruits. Commanding officers were also charged with converting one of the men's barracks into accommodations deemed suitable for women. The media took a keen interest in these preparations, and several reporters commented on the fact that urinals had to be removed, bathtubs installed, and a common shower refitted with individual stalls. This interest in the renovation of washroom facilities was one way the media drew attention to the biological differences between men and women, a significant indicator of how women were disrupting one of the nation's iconic institutions.[40]

Apart from changing structural facilities at the academy, training procedures were developed to accommodate the female police body. At the time, RCMP training was characterized as one of the "most demanding police-training programmes in the world, a grueling hybrid of military boot camp and modern police college."[41] Darryl Butler, an instructor at the academy in 1974, recalled that RCMP staff was unsure of how the women were going to "react to the type of training we did in those days."[42] Assumptions about the female body, grounded in formulations of sexual difference, created uncertainty for the commanding officers. How do you make a body uniform when it does not fit the established model? Did women have sufficient strength to meet the rigorous demands of the RCMP's training program? How would women respond to foot drill? Would they be able to handle a firearm? Accordingly, instructors were charged with modifying course objectives to physical standards that were "equivalent" rather than "equal" to those required of men. For example, while men were expected to lift at least 125 pounds in weights by the time they graduated, weight training was optional for Troop 17.[43]

Foot drill, however, was one area where the women were expected to meet male requirements. Foot drill had a long tradition in the training of members of the RCMP and was afforded significant amounts of time during recruits' six months of training. It was viewed as a conditioning process that instilled self-discipline and developed quick responses among recruits. Drill instructors were expected to "transform the troops into smoothly moving units that can change direction without losing a beat the instant" a command is given.[44] As Amy Shaw has shown in this collection, military drills informed the discourses surrounding the Anglo-South Africa War and Canadian nationhood. Drills were viewed as "appropriate masculine behaviour" and were closely associated with manly adventure, endurance, and patriotism. Marcel Mauss argues that marching was a technique of the body that revealed the specificities, forms, and special habits of a culture and a nation. The body was "man's first and most natural technical object," and marching was an effective reflection of the existence of a nation's traditional rites.[45] Michel Foucault also noticed techniques of the body in the "ideal figure of the soldier" whose body was subjected, broken down, rearranged, and ultimately rendered docile by the minute details of military discipline and "general formulas of domination." For Foucault, discipline increased "the forces of the body (in economic terms of utility) and diminishe[d] these same forces (in political terms of obedience)."[46] This dissociation of power from the body, especially when engaged in precision drill, breaks down the natural gestures and movements of the body by imposing on it a new set of restraints.[47] The close connection between military drill with codes of masculinity, citizenship, and representations of the nation called into question the ability of women to adequately perform the rites and techniques of the body so important to the image of the RCMP and its training program.

Socially constructed ideas about the unruly and unpredictable nature of the female body rendered it inappropriate as a docile mechanism for the control and use of the commanding officers of the RCMP. It was an unlikely conduit of state authority and power. Indeed, Constable Barbara Woods, a member of the first troop of women, remembered that "adjusting to the semi-military ways of the Force was not easy and the Drill Staff took pains to teach us to march without a wiggle!"[48] Assumptions about the female body and the potential for its failure to perform drill exercises threatened to disrupt the RCMP's tradition of paramilitary discipline. One instructor recalled, however, being pleasantly surprised to learn that "women could march nicely, they could swing their arms, whereas men are bulky and can't swing in unison; women could always swing their arms straight up and it looked good."[49] The visual impact of women conducting drill manoeuvres overtly challenged the masculine space of the police academy, weakening perceptions of it as a space where the female body did not belong.

While the success of female Mounties in the drill hall contested perceptions about disciplining the unruly female body, their achievement was undermined by the footwear they were issued. The Strathcona boots issued to male RCMP officers were originally created for both walking and riding, and they had a lace instep and gusset that allowed for greater flexibility when marching.[50] Strathconas also created a stomping sound that conveyed authority, precision, and strength when worn during drill manoeuvres. In contrast, female Mounties had, as one instructor noticed, "those little shoes that clicked," black pumps with heels that could not duplicate the sound of the Strathconas.[51] The clicking noise made by the women's shoes not only suggested the improbability of the female body to meet male standards for paramilitary service, but situated femininity as an implausible substitute for masculinity and ideal Canadian manhood.

In addition to structural changes to the barracks at the academy, how to dress the female police body was a subject of concern for the RCMP. As far as can be ascertained, dressing the first female police officers in the famous Review Order of Dress, the red serge tunic, Stetson hat, riding breeches, and Strathcona boots worn by male officers was never considered, suggesting reluctance on the part of the police force to compromise its masculine image and its close association with the nation. Amy Shaw points out that the distinctive clothing worn by Canadians and members of the NWMP fighting in the Anglo-South Africa War, particularly the Stetson hat and Strathcona boots, became symbols of Canadian manhood that linked soldiers to Canada's self-imagining. The insistence on the feminization of the classic Mountie uniform for female police officers was evidence that such national imaginings continued to enjoy considerable cachet in Canadian society.

The specificity of dressing the female police body in uniform is an important factor for understanding the ways dichotomous distinctions between men and women operated in the RCMP and Canadian society. Kathleen Canning argues that the term "the body," when used in a broad sense, blurs differences among distinct bodies, and she advocates for specificity, which allows for a "more conceptually conscious and historically grounded use of the term."[52] Attention to the specificity of the female body allows for the emergence of gendered meanings in historical analysis, an approach evident in the work of Ruth Roach Pierson. In *"They're still Women after All": The Second World War and Canadian Womanhood*, Pierson explores how the Canadian military embarked on a recruitment campaign that positioned women's work in the armed forces as "not incompatible with femininity." How to dress the female body in a service uniform received particular attention from the military, who hired a fashion designer to create a suitable uniform. Based on the assumption that women were concerned with their appearance, the design, fit, and fashionable style of the women's uniform featured prominently in recruitment literature.[53] Following the Second World War, appropriate working attire for professional women was closely scrutinized. Kristina Llewellyn illustrates how female nurses and teachers were expected to convey gender difference and subordination through their dress and deportment. Llewellyn argues that the regulation of women's dress at work not only positioned heterosexuality as normative, but reproduced the nuclear family in the school and signified the subservience of nurses to doctors.

In contrast to Llewellyn's examples, the red-serge dress uniform worn by male members of the RCMP was credited with contributing to a "high degree of loyalty and 'esprit de corps' among its members."[54] It is not surprising, then, that the RCMP negotiated tensions over incorporating women into the rank-and-file through the design of a new uniform deemed more suitable for women. The men of the RCMP's tailor shop were instructed to design "stylish, feminine uniforms which were at the same time functional and reflected the traditional uniform of the Force."[55] The idea that the women's uniform was only meant to *reflect* the traditional male uniform illustrates the gendered approach to the subordinate female body taken by the RCMP, who like the Canadian military during the Second World War, apparently considered a feminine appearance essential to women's work as police officers.

Surprisingly, the RCMP did not consult with the Canadian military regarding the development of the new uniform. Instead, they turned to the executive director of Fashion Canada, "one of the best known Canadian designers"[56] to meet the requirements of a stylish but feminine design. Designing working uniforms for women changed dramatically in the postwar period, notably in the airline industry, where female flight attendants began to "wear stylish designer suits, genteelly accessorized with hats and white gloves" as opposed to earlier versions that were more militaristic in appearance.[57] Airlines, in the 1970s, routinely hired fashion designers to clothe their flight attendants, and the RCMP appears to have followed that industry's cue. As a result of consultations with the fashion industry, "womanly lines" were "accentuated by eliminating pockets from the red serge jacket" for the women's dress uniform.[58] White gloves and a pillbox hat rounded out the design. Apart from the colour, the dress uniform worn by female Mounties had little connection to the image of Canada that was commonly associated with the red-serge uniform worn by the men. For operational wear, a triangular necktie was designed, an accoutrement that reinforced conventional notions of femininity and distinguished the women as different from their male peers. Pockets, an operational necessity for police officers, were also eliminated from the slacks and blouses of the operational uniform worn by the first women.

The feminization of the Mountie uniform presented significant operational problems for female officers. One key flaw was that the original design did not allow for the wearing of a holster and service revolver. Instead, a square brown handbag with shoulder straps, fitted with a holster and bullet holders, was designed to carry a firearm and handcuffs. The handbag was more than a symbol of femininity; it also represented a significant safety hazard in the field for both male and female officers. A purse with shoulder straps was easily accessible to a suspect during an altercation, and quick access to a handgun was almost impossible with a purse clasp.

Oral histories also revealed that all of the women, when asked about their uniform, remembered the unworkability of the pillbox hat which invariably flew off during pursuits or on windy days. Kate Morton disliked the hat so much that a fellow officer acquired a forage cap (worn by the men) for her to wear on patrol, although she had to be careful not to let her commanding officer see her wearing it. Morton recalled wanting the same uniform as the men because it was more practical, while the women's uniform "set me up as being different, especially the hat."[59] Wearing the forage cap was one way Morton (and her male colleague) contested gendered notions regarding the uniformed police body by transgressing boundaries and renegotiating the tension between functionality and "stylish femininity."

The design of the women's uniform illustrates how masculinity and femininity continued to be perceived in binary opposition within the RCMP. While the sexualized female body dressed in a classic Mountie uniform did not materialize in quite the same way editorial cartoonists had predicted, the female uniform did reinforce femininity and emphasized the differences between male and female police bodies, allowing the figure of the male Mountie in red serge to remain the dominant image of civic authority and the nation. Indeed, the male uniform was such an integral part of the masculine image of the RCMP that it was not until 1990 that women were issued the same uniform as men. The eventual inclusion of women in the image conveyed by the Mountie dress uniform reveals that it was possible for the female police body to be equally representative of civic and state authority.

Conclusion

Examining the specificity of the female police body and how it disrupted the masculine foundations of the RCMP uncovers the place of gender and corporeality in the history of Canada's federal police force. As a methodological strategy, the female body dismantled, blurred, and contested conceptualizations of masculinity and femininity in the RCMP and the nation. Although the police force officially supported employment equity legislation, the incorporation of women into RCMP ranks was negotiated by feminizing the women's uniform and renovating their accommodations at the training academy. As a result, the female Mountie was more closely associated with femininity rather than civic authority. This association allowed the masculinized image of the RCMP to remain a dominant trope in representations of the nation, one that, although disrupted, would remain firmly established for many years to come.

Notes

1 The RCMP has undergone three name changes since its inception. The North-West Mounted Police (NWMP) was founded in 1873, and its name reflected the police force's original mandate to police the North-West Territories. In 1904, the status "Royal" was conferred on the NWMP (RNWMP) by King Edward VII in recognition of the military contributions made by members of the police force during the Anglo-South Africa War. The police force's present name, the Royal Canadian Mounted Police, originated with the reorganization of the RNWMP in 1918 and its amalgamation with a smaller federal police force, the Dominion Police. The term "Mountie" is a colloquialism used by Canadians when referring to members of the RCMP (or, earlier, the NWMP or RNWMP).

2 Brian Cole, "Virden Gun Battle Sounded Like War," *Winnipeg Free Press*, 16 Nov. 1978.

3 Brian Cole, "I Knew I Had to Shoot, Policewoman Testifies," *Winnipeg Free Press*, 15 Nov. 1978.

4 So extensive was the media coverage that jury selection for Archer's trial was difficult. Potential jurors openly admitted that their "impartiality had been compromised by news reports." Ted Allan, "Search for Unbiased Jurors: Archer Trial for Murder Opens with Legal Challenge," *Winnipeg Free Press*, 7 Nov. 1978.

5 The material for this essay is drawn from a larger research project undertaken as part of my doctoral dissertation entitled "Women in Red Serge: Female Police Bodies and the Disruption of the Image of the Royal Canadian Mounted Police," at Simon Fraser University, in progress.

6 For further discussion on the idea of women as the weaker sex, see Patricia Vertinsky, *The Eternally Wounded Woman: Women, Doctors and Exercise in the Late Nineteenth Century* (Manchester: Manchester University Press, 1990); Cynthia Eagle Russett, *Sexual Science: The Victorian Construction of Womanhood* (Cambridge, MA: Harvard University Press, 1989); Carol Smart, ed. *Regulating Womanhood: Historical Essays on Marriage, Motherhood and Sexuality* (London: Routledge, 1992).

7 Smith's injuries were life-threatening and she underwent eight hours of surgery followed by three months of recovery in the hospital. Canadian Press, "Injured RCMP Officer Leaves Hospital," *Globe and Mail*, 28 April 1978.

8 Michael Dawson, *The Mountie: From Dime Novel to Disney* (Toronto: Between the Lines, 1998), 13.

9 See A.L. Haydon, *The Riders of the Plains: Record of the Royal North-West Mounted Police of Canada, 1873–1918* (Toronto: Copp Clark, 1919); John Peter Turner, *The North-West Mounted Police, 1873–1893* (Ottawa: E. Cloutier, King's Printer, 1950); S.W. Horrall, "Sir John A. Macdonald and the Mounted Police Force for the Northwest Territories," *Canadian Historical Review* 53, no. 2 (1972), 179–200; David Cruise and Alison Griffiths, *The Great Adventure: How the Mounties Conquered the West* (Toronto: Viking, 1996).

10 The saying that Mounties "always get their man" has generally been credited to American journalist John Healey who reported in 1877 that Mounties, who had crossed the border into Montana looking for whisky traders, were "worse than bloodhounds when they scent the track of a smuggler, and they fetch their men every time." Paul Palango, *The Last Guardians: The Crisis in the RCMP – and Canada* (Toronto: McClelland and Stewart, 1998), 287n1. Also Robert Thacker, "Canada's Mounted: The Evolution of a Legend," *Journal of Popular Culture* 14, no. 2 (1980), 304.

11 In September 1877, Mary Macleod, the wife of NWMP Commissioner James Macleod, along with the wives of two other NWMP officers, travelled with the commissioner and 108 of his men to participate in the signing of Treaty 7 with the Blackfoot Confederacy. Although Mary and the other women present were witnesses who also signed the treaty, their participation is omitted from classic histories. For more on imperial womanhood and women as colonizers, see Katie Pickles and Myra Rutherdale, eds., *Contact Zones: Aboriginal and Settler Women in Canada's Colonial Past* (Vancouver: UBC Press, 2005); Katie Pickles, *Female Imperialism and National Identity: Imperial Order Daughters of the Empire* (New York: Palgrave, 2002); Sarah Carter, *The Import-*

ance of Being Monogamous: Marriage and Nation Building in Western Canada to 1915 (Edmonton: University of Alberta Press, 2008), and *Capturing Women: The Manipulation of Cultural Imagery in Canada's Prairie West* (Montreal and Kingston: McGill-Queen's University Press, 1997).

12 For early histories and memoirs, see John G. Donkin, *Trooper and Redskin in the Far North West* (London: Sampson, Low, Marston, Searle and Rivington, 1889); Charles P. Dwight, *Life in the North West Mounted Police and Other Sketches* (Toronto: National Publishing, 1892); Murray Hayne, *The Pioneers of the Klondyke* (London: Sampson, Low, Marson, and Co., 1898); Samuel B. Steele, *Forty Years in Canada* (Toronto: McClelland, Goodchild and Stewart, 1915).

13 Andrew R. Graybill, *Policing the Great Plains: Rangers, Mounties, and the North American Frontier, 1875–1910* (Lincoln, NE: University of Nebraska Press, 2007), 16–22.

14 Pierre Berton, *Hollywood's Canada: The Americanization of Our National Image* (Toronto: McClelland and Stewart, 1975), 111.

15 Michael Dawson, "'That Nice Red Coat Goes to My Head Like Champagne': Gender, Antimodernism and the Mountie Image, 1880–1960," *Journal of Canadian Studies* 32, no. 3 (1997), 123. The ideal male body figured prominently in RCMP recruitment advertisements. In 1919, applicants had to be between the ages of twenty-two and forty, active, and able-bodied with a "thoroughly sound constitution," be a minimum height of five feet eight inches, a maximum weight of 175 pounds, and have a chest measurement of at least thirty-five inches. Haydon, *Riders of the Plains*, 403–4. These requirements remained largely unchanged until 1974.

16 Dawson, "'That Nice Red Coat,'" 123–4.

17 Ruth Holliday and John Hassard, eds., Introduction, *Contested Bodies* (London: Routledge, 2001), 3.

18 See Dawson, *The Mountie*; Steve Hewitt, "Spying 101: The RCMP's Activities at the University of Saskatchewan, 1920–71," and Gary Kinsman "Constructing Gay Men and Lesbians as National Security Risks, 1950–1970," in *Whose National Security? Canadian State Surveillance and the Creation of Enemies*, ed. Gary Kinsman, Dieter K. Buse, and Mercedes Steedman (Toronto: Between the Lines, 2000), 91–109, 143–53; Steve Hewitt, *Riding to the Rescue: The Transformation of the RCMP in Alberta and Saskatchewan, 1914–1939* (Toronto: University of Toronto Press, 2006).

19 Daniel Francis, *National Dreams: Myth, Memory, and Canadian History* (Vancouver: Arsenal Pulp Press, 1997), 11.

20 Anne Phillips, *Engendering Democracy* (Cambridge: Polity, 1991), 149.

21 Commissioner W.L. Higgitt, "Dress Regulations," RCMP internal memo, 30

Sept. 1970, reprinted in Jack Ramsay, "My Case against the RCMP," *Maclean's*, July 1972, 23.

22 In 1965, Commissioner George McLellan changed the uniform for general police duties from the Stetson hat, Strathcona boots, and riding breeches to the wearing of the more modern forage cap, blue trousers, and brown jacket. Higgitt believed McLellan's changes tarnished the image of the RCMP. Darryl Butler, email message to author, 8 April 2010.

23 "Dress Regulations," *Maclean's*, July 1972, 23.

24 Marcel Mauss, *Techniques, Technology and Civilisation*, ed. Nathan Schlanger (New York: Berghahn, 2006), 83; original emphasis.

25 Jennifer Craik, "The Cultural Politics of the Uniform," *Fashion Theory* 7, no. 2 (2003), 128.

26 Inspector G.R. Crosse stated that one of the reasons women were being "allowed" into the force was "increasing pressure from women's groups." Ruth Warwick, "Women Join Ranks," *Regina Leader-Post*, 20 Sept. 1974.

27 Right Hon. L.B. Pearson, "Announcement of Establishment of Royal Commission to Study Status," House of Commons *Debates*, 3 Feb. 1967, 12613.

28 Vancouver was the first to hire policewomen, in 1912. Chloe Owings, *Women Police: A Study of the Development and Status of the Women Police Movement* (Montclair, NJ: Patterson Smith, 1969 [1925]), 62.

29 *Report of the Royal Commission on the Status of Women in Canada* (Ottawa: Information Canada, 1970), 133–4. Hereinafter referred to as "Final Report."

30 Joyce Bennett, interview by author, 10 Oct. 2008. Interview subjects quoted throughout the remainder of this text have been assigned a pseudonym to protect their identity and the identity of their peers. The exceptions are cases where names are a matter of public record, are recorded in published memoirs or RCMP studies, appear in open-access archival material, or have been identified in the media. The interviews quoted here took place during a four-year period, between 2006 and 2010, and were audio recorded.

31 Staff Sergeant S.E. Stark, *The Role of Female Constables in "E" Division* (Vancouver: RCMP "E" Division Staffing and Personnel Branch, 1986), 3.

32 "Final Report," RCSWC, 15.

33 Reprinted as Figure 9.2 in Barbara M. Freeman, *The Satellite Sex: The Media and Women's Issues in English Canada, 1966–1971* (Waterloo: Wilfrid Laurier University Press, 2001), 231.

34 Gisela Bock, "Women's History and Gender History: Aspects of an International Debate," *Gender and History* 1, no. 1 (1989), 12.

35 Mariana Valverde, *The Age of Light, Soap and Water: Moral Reform in English Canada, 1885–1920* (Toronto: McClelland and Stewart, 1991); Margaret Little, "'A Fit and Proper Person': The Moral Regulation of Single Moth-

ers in Ontario, 1920–1940," in *Gendered Pasts: Historical Essays in Femininity and Masculinity in Canada*, ed. K. McPherson, C. Morgan, and N. Forestell (Toronto: University of Toronto Press, 2003), 123–38; Ann Porter, *Gendered States: Women, Unemployment Insurance and the Political Economy of the Welfare State in Canada, 1945–1997* (Toronto: University of Toronto Press, 2003); Franca Iacovetta, "Recipes for Democracy: Gender, Family, and Making Female Citizens in Cold War Canada," *Canadian Woman Studies* 20 (Summer 2000), 12–21.

36 For more on the idea of sexual competition between single and married women, see Marlene Epp, *Women without Men: Mennonite Refugees of the Second World War* (Toronto: University of Toronto Press, 2002), 147.

37 Jennifer Brown and Frances Heidensohn, *Gender and Policing: Comparative Perspectives* (London: Macmillan, 2000), 162.

38 Royal Canadian Mounted Police, press release, Ottawa, Ontario, 11 Sept. 1974.

39 "Women RCMP Officers Inevitable: MacRae," *Saskatoon Star-Phoenix*, 8 Nov. 1974.

40 For example, see Martin O'Malley, "Women Mounties Fitting In," *The Toronto Globe and Mail*, 5 Dec. 1974, W7; Ruth Warwick, "Basic Training Program Same for Fairer Sex," *Regina Leader-Post*, 20 Sept. 1974; "Mounties Get Their First Women," *Toronto Star*, 28 Dec. 1974.

41 Tony Leighton, "Red Serge and High Spirits: Blood, Sweat and Fears – Life in the RCMP Training Depot," *Equinox* 22 (1985), 40.

42 Darryl Butler, interview by author, 11 Sept. 2008.

43 Martin O'Malley, "Women Mounties Fitting In." Weight training was the only area where the women were not required to meet the same standards as men in 1974. The women who chose to lift weights set goals that were based on their weight and height. Cameron Montgomery, interview with author, 24 May 2007.

44 Leighton, "Red Serge and High Spirits," 46.

45 Mauss, *Techniques, Technology and Civilisation*, 79.

46 Michel Foucault, *Discipline and Punish: The Birth of the Prison*, 2nd ed., trans. Alan Sheridan (New York: Random House, 1995), 138.

47 Ibid., 151.

48 B.J. Woods, "History Has Been Made," *RCMP Quarterly* 40, no. 2 (1975), 4.

49 Darryl Butler, interview.

50 For general information on the development of the Strathcona boot during the Anglo-South Africa War, see the Canada War Museum website at http://www.warmuseum.ca/cwm/exhibitions/boer/strathconaboot_e.shtml.//.

51 Darryl Butler, interview.

52 Kathleen Canning, *Gender History in Practice: Historical Perspectives on Bodies, Class and Citizenship* (Ithaca, NY: Cornell University Press, 2006), 169.

53 Ruth Roach Pierson, *"They're Still Women after All": The Second World War and Canadian Womanhood* (Toronto: McClelland and Stewart, 1986), 139.

54 James J. Boulton, *Uniforms of the Canadian Mounted Police* (North Battleford, SK: Turner-Warwick, 1990), 2.

55 Ibid., 504.

56 Marsha Erb, "New Uniform Neat, Plain and Functional," *Saskatoon Star-Phoenix*, 8 Nov. 1974.

57 Kathleen M. Barry, *Femininity in Flight: A History of Flight Attendants* (Durham, NC: Duke University Press, 2007), 51.

58 O'Malley, "Women Mounties Fitting In."

59 Kate Morton, interview by author, 26 Feb. 2008.

Bibliography

Adams, Annmarie. *Architecture in the Family Way: Doctors, Houses and Women, 1870–1900.* Montreal and Kingston: McGill-Queen's University Press, 1996.

Adams, Mary Louise. *The Trouble with Normal: Postwar Youth and the Construction of Heterosexuality.* Toronto: University of Toronto Press, 1994.

Adams, Mary Louise. "To Be an Ordinary Hero: Male Figure Skaters and the Ideology of Gender." *Avante* 3, no. 3 (1997). Online at http://www.plover.com/rainbowice/mla1.html.

Adams, Mary Louise. "'Death to the Prancing Prince': Effeminacy, Sport Discourses and the Salvation of Men's Dancing." *Body and Society* 11, no. 4 (2005): 63–86. http://dx.doi.org/10.1177/1357034X05058020.

Alexander, Edward P. *Museums in Motion.* Nashville, TN: Alta Mira Press, 1979.

Anderson, Benedict. *Imagined Communities: Reflections on the Origin and Spread of Nationalism.* London: Verso, 1991.

Arnot, Madeleine, and Jo-Anne Dillabough. "Feminist Politics and Democratic Values in Education." *Curriculum Inquiry* 29, no. 2 (1999): 159–89. http://dx.doi.org/10.1111/0362-6784.00120.

Arnup, Katharine. *Education for Motherhood: Advice for Mothers in Twentieth-Century Canada.* Toronto: University of Toronto Press, 1994.

Babor, Thomas, et al. *Alcohol: No Ordinary Commodity.* Toronto: Oxford Medical Publications, 2003.

Bachelard, Gaston. *The Poetics of Space.* Boston, MA: Beacon Press, 1969.

Backhouse, Constance. *Colour Coded: A Legal History of Racism in Canada, 1900–1950.* Toronto: Osgoode Society for Canadian Legal History, 1999.

Baillargeon, Denyse. *Babies for the Nation: The Medicalization of Motherhood in Quebec 1910–1970.* Waterloo: Wilfrid Laurier University Press, 2009.

Ballantyne, Tony, and Antoinette Burton, eds. *Bodies in Contact: Rethinking Colonial Encounters in World History.* Chapel Hill, NC: Duke University Press, 2005.

Banet-Weiser, Sarah. *The Most Beautiful Girl in the World: Beauty Pageants and National Identity*. Berkeley, CA: University of California Press, 1999.

Barcan, Ruth. "'Regaining What Mankind Has Lost through Civilization': Early Nudism and Ambivalent Moderns." *Fashion Theory* 8, no. 1 (2004): 63–82. http://dx.doi.org/10.2752/136270404778051870.

Barringer, Tim. "The South Kensington Museum and the Colonial Project." In *Colonialism and the Object: Empire, Material Culture and the Museum*, ed. Tim Barringer and Tom Flynn, 11–27. London: Routledge, 1998.

Barry, Kathleen M. *Femininity in Flight: A History of Flight Attendants*. Durham, NC: Duke University Press, 2007.

Barthel, Diane. *Putting on Appearances: Gender and Advertising*. Philadelphia, PA: Temple University Press, 1988.

Bashford, Alison. "Quarantine and the Imagining of the Australian Nation." *Health* 2, no. 4 (1998): 387–402.

Bates, Christina. "Shop and Factory: The Ontario Millinery Trade in Transition, 1870–1930." In *Fashion: A Canadian Identity*, ed. Alexandra Palmer, 113–38. Toronto: University of Toronto Press, 2004.

Beauvais, Johnny. *Kahnawake: A Mohawk Look at Canada and Adventures of Big John Canadian, 1840–1919*. Montreal: N.P., 1985.

Bederman, Gail. *Manliness and Civilization: A Cultural History of Gender and Race in the United States, 1880–1917*. Chicago, IL: University of Chicago Press, 1995.

Béland, Mario, ed. *Painting in Quebec, 1820–1850*. Quebec City: Musée du Québec, 1992.

Belisle, Donica. "Negotiating Paternalism: Women and Canada's Largest Department Stores, 1890–1960." *Journal of Women's History* 19, no. 1 (2007): 58–81. http://dx.doi.org/10.1353/jowh.2007.0004.

Belisle, Donica. *Retail Nation: Department Stores and the Making of Modern Canada*. Vancouver: UBC Press, 2011.

Bennett, John, and Susan Rowley. *Uqalurait: An Oral History of Nunavut*. Montreal and Kingston: McGill-Queen's University Press, 2004.

Bennett, Tony. "The Exhibitionary Complex." In *Culture/Power/History: A Reader in Contemporary Social Theory*, ed. Nicholas B. Dirks, et al., 123–54. Princeton, NJ: Princeton University Press, 1994.

Bently, Amy. *Eating for Victory: Food Rationing and the Politics of Domesticity*. Chicago: University of Chicago Press, 1998.

Berger, Carl. "The True North Strong and Free." In *Nationalism in Canada*, ed. Peter Russell, 3–26. Toronto: McGraw-Hill, 1966.

Berger, Carl. *The Sense of Power: Studies in the Ideas of Canadian Imperialism, 1867–1914*. Toronto: University of Toronto Press, 1970.

Berger, Carl. *The Writing of Canadian History.* Toronto: University of Toronto Press, 1986.

Berman, Morris. *Coming to Our Senses: Body and Spirit in the Hidden History of the West.* New York: Bantam, 1989.

Bernstein, Susan David. "Designs after Nature: Evolutionary Fashions, Animals, and Gender." In *Victorian Animal Dreams: Representations of Animals in Victorian Literature and Culture,* ed. Deborah Morse and Martin Danahay, 65–80. Burlington, VT: Ashgate, 2007.

Berton, Pierre. *Hollywood's Canada: The Americanization of Our National Image.* Toronto: McClelland and Stewart, 1975.

Bhabha, Homi K. "Introduction: Narrating the Nation." In *Nation and Narration,* ed. Homi K. Bhabha, 1–7. London: Routledge, 1990.

Blanchot, Maurice. *The Writing of the Disaster.* Lincoln, NE: University of Nebraska Press, 1995.

Bliss, Michael. "Privatizing the Mind: The Sundering of Canadian History, the Sundering of Canada." *Journal of Canadian Studies/Revue d'études canadiennes* 26, no. 4 (1992): 5–17.

Bock, Gisela. "Women's History and Gender History: Aspects of an International Debate." *Gender and History* 1, no. 1 (1989): 7–30. http://dx.doi. org/10.1111/j.1468-0424.1989.tb00232.x.

Bordo, Susan. "The Body and the Reproduction of Femininity." In *Writing on the Body: Female Embodiment and Feminist Theory,* ed. Kate Conboy, et al., 90–112. New York: Columbia University Press, 1997.

Boulton, James J. *Uniforms of the Canadian Mounted Police.* North Battleford, SK: Turner-Warwick, 1990.

Bourdieu, Pierre. "Sport and Social Class." *Social Sciences Information/Information sur les Sciences Sociales* 17, no. 6 (1978): 819–40. http://dx.doi.org/10.1177/053901847801700603.

Bourke, Joanna. *Dismembering the Male: Men's Bodies, Britain and the Great War.* Chicago, IL: University of Chicago Press, 1996.

Braidotti, Rosi. "Mothers, Monsters, and Machines." In *Writing on the Body: Female Embodiment and Feminist Theory,* ed. Katie Conboy, Nadia Medina, and Sarah Stanbury, 59–79. New York: Columbia University Press, 1997.

Braidotti, Rosi. "Signs of Wonder and Traces of Doubt: On Teratology and Embodied Differences." In *Feminist Theory and the Body: A Reader,* ed. Janet Price and Margrit Shildrick, 290–301. New York: Oxford University Press, 1999.

Brooker, Bertram. "Nudes and Prudes." In *Documents in Canadian Art,* ed. Douglas Fetherling, 66–75. Peterborough: Broadview, 1987.

Brown, David. "Canadian Imperialism and Sporting Exchanges: The Nineteenth-Century Cultural Experience of Cricket and Lacrosse." *Canadian Journal of History of Sport* 18, no. 1 (1987): 55–66.

Brown, Jennifer, and Frances Heidensohn. *Gender and Policing: Comparative Perspectives*. London: Macmillan, 2000.

Bryant, Mark. *World War II in Cartoons*. London: Grub Street, 1989.

Buckner, Phillip, ed. *Canada and the British Empire*. Oxford: Oxford University Press, 2008.

Buckner, Phillip, and R. Douglas Francis, eds. *Canada and the British World: Culture, Migration, and Identity*. Vancouver: UBC Press, 2006.

Bunford, Sheila. *One Woman's Arctic*. Toronto: McClelland and Stewart, 1973.

Burnett, Kristin. *Taking Medicine: Women's Healing Work and Contact in Southern Alberta, 1880–1930*. Vancouver: UBC Press, 2010.

Burr, Christina. "Gender, Sexuality, and Nationalism in J.W. Bengough's Verses and Political Cartoons." *Canadian Historical Review* 83, no. 1 (2002): 247–74.

Burt, Ramsay. *The Male Dancer: Bodies, Spectacle, Sexualities*. 2nd ed. London: Taylor and Francis, 2007.

Butler, Judith. "Performative Arts and Gender Constitution: An Essay in Phenomenology and Feminist Theory." In *Performing Feminisms: Feminist Critical Theory and Theatre*, ed. Sue-Ellen Case, 270–82. Baltimore, MD: Johns Hopkins University Press, 1990.

Butler, Judith. *Bodies that Matter: On the Discursive Limits of Sex*. London: Routledge, 1993.

Butler, Judith. *Gender Trouble: Feminism and the Subversion of Identity*. London: Routledge, 1999 [1990].

Bynum, Caroline Walker. "Why All the Fuss about the Body? A Medievalist's Perspective." *Critical Inquiry* 22, no. 1 (1995): 1–33. http://dx.doi.org/10.1086/448780.

Cahn, Susan K. "From the 'Muscle Moll' to the 'Butch' Ballplayer: Mannishness, Lesbianism and Homophobia in U.S. Women's Sports." In *The Politics of Women's Bodies: Sexuality, Appearance, and Behavior*, ed. Rose Weitz, 67–81. New York: Oxford University Press, 1998.

Caldwell, Theodore C., ed. *The Anglo-Boer War: Why Was It Fought? Who Was Responsible?* Boston, MA: D.C. Health, 1965.

Campion-Vincent, Véronique. "Organ Theft Narratives as Medical and Social Critique." *Journal of Folklore Research* 39, no. 1 (2002): 33–50.

Camporesi, Piero. *Juice of Life: The Symbolic and Magic Significance of Blood*. Robert R. Barr (trans.). New York: Continuum, 1995.

Canning, Kathleen. "The Body as Method? Reflections on the Place of the Body in Gender History." *Gender and History* 11, no. 3 (1999): 499–513. http://dx.doi.org/10.1111/1468-0424.00159.

Canning, Kathleen. *Gender History in Practice: Historical Perspectives on Bodies, Class and Citizenship.* Ithaca, NY: Cornell University Press, 2006.

Carr, E.H. *What Is History?* Harmondsworth: University of Cambridge Press and Penguin, 1961.

Carroll, Michael K. *Pearson's Peacekeepers: Canada and the United Nations Emergency Force, 1956–67.* Vancouver: UBC Press, 2009.

Carter, Alexandra, and Janet O'Shea, eds. *The Routledge Dance Studies Reader.* 2nd ed. London: Routledge, 2010.

Carter, Sarah. *Capturing Women: The Manipulation of Cultural Imagery in Canada's Prairie West.* Montreal and Kingston: McGill-Queen's University Press, 1997.

Carter, Sarah. *The Importance of Being Monogamous: Marriage and Nation Building in Western Canada to 1915.* Edmonton: University of Alberta Press, 2008.

Cartwright, Lisa. "A Cultural Anatomy of the Visible Human Project." In *The Visible Woman: Imaging Technologies, Gender and Science,* ed. Paula A. Treichler, Lisa Cartwright, and Constance Penley, 21–43. New York: New York University Press, 1998.

Cavanaugh, Sheila L. "The Heterosexualization of the Ontario Woman Teacher in the Postwar Period." *Canadian Women's Studies* 18, no. 1 (1999): 55–69.

Chapnick, Adam. *The Middle Power Project: Canada and the Founding of the United Nations.* Vancouver: UBC Press, 2005.

Christie, Nancy, and Michael Gauvreau, eds. *Cultures of Citizenship in Postwar Canada.* Montreal and Kingston: McGill-Queen's University Press, 2003.

Clark, Kenneth. *The Nude: A Study in Ideal Form.* Harmondsworth: Penguin, 1960.

Clark Hine, Darlene, et al., eds. *The African-American Odyssey: Combined Volume, Special Edition.* 4th ed. Upper Saddle River, NJ: Pearson/Prentice-Hall, 2010.

Cohen, Colleen Ballerino, Richard Wilk, and Beverly Stoeltje, eds. *Beauty Queens and the Global Stage: Gender, Contests, and Power.* London: Routledge, 1996.

Cole, Douglas. "Canada's 'Nationalistic' Imperialists." *Journal of Canadian Studies/Revue d'études canadiennes* 5, no. 3 (1970): 44–9.

Coleman, Daniel. *White Civility: The White Literary Project of English Canada.* Toronto: University of Toronto Press, 2006.

Collingwood, R.G. *The Idea of History.* London: Oxford University Press, 1956.

Colpitts, George. "Conservation, Science, and Canada's Fur Farming industry, 1913–1945" *Social History* 30, no. 59 (1997): 77–107.

Comacchio, Cynthia. *"Nations Are Built of Babies": Saving Ontario Mothers and Children, 1900–1940.* Montreal and Kingston: McGill-Queen's University Press, 1993.

Comacchio, Cynthia. "Mechanomorphosis: Science, Management, and 'Human

Machinery' in Industrial Canada, 1900–45." *Labour/Le Travail* 41 (1998): 35–67. http://dx.doi.org/10.2307/25144226.

Comacchio, Cynthia. "'The Rising Generation': Laying Claim to the Health of Adolescents in English Canada, 1920–1970." *Canadian Bulletin of Medical History* 19, no. 1 (2002): 139–78.

Connerton, Paul. *How Societies Remember.* Cambridge: Cambridge University Press, 1989. http://dx.doi.org/10.1017/CBO9780511628061.

Cooper, Afua P. "Black Women and Work in Nineteenth-Century Canada West: Black Woman Teacher Mary Bibb." In *"We're Rooted Here and They Can't Pull Us Up": Essays in African Canadian Women's History,* ed. Peggy Bristow, et al., 143–70. Toronto: University of Toronto Press, 1994.

Cooper Albright, Ann. "Techno Bodies or, Muscling with Gender in Contemporary Dance." *Choreography and Dance* 5, no. 1 (1998): 79–86.

Copp, Terry. *The Anatomy of Poverty: The Condition of the Working Class in Montreal, 1897–1929.* Toronto: McClelland and Stewart, 1974.

Corbin, A., J.J. Courtine, and G. Vigarello, eds. *Histoire du corps: De la Renaissance aux Lumières.* 3 vols. Paris: Seuil, 2005.

Courtine, Jean-Jacques. Introduction. In *Histoire du corps: Les mutations du regard, le XXe siècle,* vol. 3, ed. Alain Corbin, Jean-Jacques Courtine, and Georges Vigarello, 7–12.Paris: Seuil, 2006.

Craik, Jennifer. "The Cultural Politics of the Uniform." *Fashion Theory* 7, no. 2 (2003): 127–47. http://dx.doi.org/10.2752/136270403778052140.

Crais, Clifton, and Pamela Scully. *Sara Baartman and the Hottentot Venus: A Ghost Story and a Biography.* Princeton, NJ: Princeton University Press, 2009.

Cranfield, John, and Kris Inwood. "The Great Transformation: A Long-Run Perspective on Physical Well-Being in Canada." *Economics and Human Biology* 5, no. 2 (2007): 204–28. http://dx.doi.org/10.1016/j.ehb.2007.02.001.

Critser, Greg. *Fat Land: How Americans Became the Fattest People in the World.* Boston, MA: Mariner Books, 2004.

Cronon, William. *Changes in the Land: Indians, Colonists, and the Ecology of New England.* New York: Hill and Wang, 1983.

Cruise, David, and Alison Griffiths. *The Great Adventure: How the Mounties Conquered the West.* Toronto: Viking, 1996.

Daley, Caroline. *Leisure and Pleasure: Reshaping and Revealing the New Zealand Body, 1900–1960.* Auckland: Auckland University Press, 2003.

Davies Cordova, Sarah. "Romantic Ballet in France, 1830–1850." In *The Cambridge Companion to Ballet,* ed. Marion Kant, 113–25. Cambridge: Cambridge University Press, 2007.

Dawson, Michael. "'That Nice Red Coat Goes to My Head Like Champagne': Gender, Antimodernism and the Mountie Image, 1880–1960." *Journal of Canadian Studies/Revue d'études canadiennes* 32, no. 3 (1997): 119–39.

Dawson, Michael. *The Mountie: From Dime Novel to Disney*. Toronto: Between the Lines, 1998.

de Certeau, Michel. *The Practice of Everyday Life*. Steven Rendall (trans.). Berkeley, CA: University of California Press, 1984.

Desjardins, Gaston. *L'amour en patience: La sexualité adolescente au Québec, 1940–1960*. Sainte-Foy: Presses de l'Université du Québec, 1995.

Desmond, Jane, ed. *Meaning in Motion: New Cultural Studies of Dance*. Durham, NC: Duke University Press, 1997. ·

Desmond, Jane, ed. *Dance Desires: Choreographing Sexualities on and off the Stage*. Madison, WI: University of Wisconsin Press, 2001.

Desser, David. *Hollywood Goes Shopping*. Minneapolis, MN: University of Minnesota Press, 2000.

Dils, Ann, and Ann Cooper Albright, eds. *Moving History/Dancing Cultures: A Dance History Reader*. Middletown, CT: Wesleyan University Press, 2001.

Doolittle, Lisa. "The Trianon and On: Reading Mass Social Dancing in the 1930s and 1940s in Alberta, Canada." In *Ballroom, Boogie, Shimmy Sham, Shake: A Social and Popular Dance Reader*, ed. Julie Malnig, 11–25. Urbana, IL: University of Illinois Press, 2001. http://dx.doi.org/10.2307/1477801.

Douglas, Mary. *Purity and Danger: An Analysis of Concepts of Pollution and Taboo*. London: Routledge, 1966. http://dx.doi.org/10.4324/9780203361832

Dow, Bonnie J. "Feminism, Miss America and Media Mythology." *Rhetoric and Public Affairs* 6, no. 1 (2003): 127–49. http://dx.doi.org/10.1353/rap.2003.0028.

Driver, Tom F. *The Magic of Ritual: Our Need for Liberating Rites that Transform Our Lives and Our Communities*. San Francisco, CA: Harper, 1991.

Dufresne, Sylvie. "Le Carnaval d'hiver de Montréal (1883–1889)." M.A. thesis, Université du Québec à Montréal, 1980.

Duncan, Carol. "MoMA's Hot Mamas." In *The Expanding Discourse: Feminism and Art History*, ed. Norma Broude and Mary D. Gerrard, 346–57. New York: Westview, 1992.

Dyer, Richard. *White*. London: Routledge, 1997.

Eliot, Karen. *Dancing Lives: Five Female Dancers from the Ballet d'Action to Merce Cunningham*. Urbana, IL: University of Illinois Press, 2007.

Ellison, Jenny. "'Stop Postponing Your Life until You Lose Weight and Start Living Now': Vancouver's Large as Life Action Group, 1979–1985." *Journal of the Canadian Historical Association* 18, no. 1 (2007): 241–65. http://dx.doi.org/10.7202/018261ar.

Emberley, Julia V. *Venus and Furs: The Cultural Politics of Fur*. London: I.B. Tauris, 1998.

Epp, Marlene. *Women without Men: Mennonite Refugees of the Second World War*. Toronto: University of Toronto Press, 2002.

Evans Braziel, Jana, and Kathleen LeBesco, eds. *Bodies Out of Bounds: Fatness and Transgression.* Berkeley, CA: University of California Press, 2001.

Ewing, Elizabeth. *Fur in Dress.* London: B.T. Batsford, 1981.

Fahrni, Magda. *Household Politics: Montreal Families and Postwar Reconstruction.* Toronto: University of Toronto Press, 2005.

Fahy, Thomas Richard. *Freak Shows and the Modern American Imagination: Constructing the Damaged Body from Willa Cather to Truman Capote.* New York: Palgrave Macmillan, 2006.

Faue, Elizabeth. *Community of Suffering and Struggle: Women, Men, and the Labor Movement in Minneapolis, 1915–1945.* Chapel Hill, NC: University of North Carolina Press, 1991.

Fausto-Sterling, Anne. *Sexing the Body: Gender Politics and the Construction of Sexuality.* New York: Basic Books, 2000.

Felman, Shoshana, and Dori Laub. *Testimony: Crises of Witnessing in Literature, Psychoanalysis and Theory.* London: Routledge, 1992.

Finkel, Alvin. *Social Policy and Practice in Canada: A History.* Waterloo: Wilfrid Laurier University Press, 2006.

Fisher, Jennifer, and Anthony Shay, eds. *When Men Dance: Choreographing Masculinities across Borders.* Oxford: Oxford University Press, 2009.

Flaherty, Marth. "I Fought to Keep My Hair." In *Northern Voices: Inuit Writing in English,* ed. Penny Petrone, 274–89. Toronto: University of Toronto Press, 1988.

Foss, Brian. "Living Landscape." In *Edwin Holgate.* Exh. Cat, ed. Rosalind Pepall and Brian Foss, 38–54. Montreal: Montreal Museum of Fine Arts, 2005.

Foster, Susan Leigh, ed. *Choreographing History.* Bloomington, IN: Indiana University Press, 1995.

Foucault, Michel. *An Introduction,* vol. 1, *The History of Sexuality.* Robert Hurley (trans.). New York: Penguin, 1990.

Foucault, Michel. *Discipline and Punish: The Birth of the Prison.* 2nd ed., Alan Sheridan (trans.). New York: Random House, 1995.

Foucault, Michel. *Society Must Be Defended: Lectures at the College de France, 1975–1976.* David Macey (trans.). New York: Picador, 1997.

Foucault, Michel. *The Birth of the Clinic: An Archaeology of Medical Perception.* A.M. Sheridan (trans.). London: Routledge, 2003.

Foulkes, Julia L. *Modern Bodies: Dance and American Modernism from Martha Graham to Alvin Ailey.* Chapel Hill, NC: University of North Carolina Press, 2002.

Francis, Daniel. *National Dreams: Myth, Memory, and Canadian History.* Vancouver: Arsenal Pulp Press, 1997.

Freeman, Barbara M. *The Satellite Sex: The Media and Women's Issues in English Canada, 1966–1971.* Waterloo: Wilfrid Laurier University Press, 2001.

French, Doris. *High Button Bootstraps: Federation of Women's Teachers' Associations of Ontario, 1918–1968.* Toronto: Ryerson Press, 1968.

Freud, Sigmund. "The Sexual Aberrations." In *On Sexuality: Three Essays on the Theory of Sexuality and Other Works,* ed. Angela Richards, James Strachey (trans.), 1–38. London: Penguin, 1991.

Fuchs, Victor R. *The Economics of the Fur Industry.* New York: Columbia University Press, 1957.

Gallagher, Catherine, and Thomas Laqueur, eds. *The Making of the Modern Body: Sexuality and Society in the Nineteenth Century.* Berkeley, CA: University of California Press, 1987.

Garafola, Lynn. "Reconfiguring the Sexes." In *The Ballets Russes and Its World,* ed. Lynn Garafola and Nancy Van Norman Baer, 245–68. New Haven, CT: Yale University Press, 1999.

Garafola, Lynn. "The Sexual Iconography of the Ballets Russes." *Ballet Review* 28, no. 3 (2000): 70–7.

Garland Thomson, Rosemarie. *Extraordinary Bodies: Figuring Physical Disability in American Culture and Literature.* New York: Columbia University Press, 1996.

Garland Thomson, Rosemarie, ed. *Freakery: Cultural Spectacles of the Extraordinary Body.* New York: New York University Press, 1996.

Garroutte, Eva Marie. *Real Indians: Identity and the Survival of Native America.* Berkeley, CA: University of California Press, 2003.

Gentile, Patrizia. "Queen of the Maple Leaf: A History of Beauty Contests in Twentieth-Century Canada." Doctoral dissertation, Queen's University, 2006.

Gere, David. *How to Make Dances in an Epidemic: Tracking Choreography in the Age of AIDS.* Madison, WI: University of Wisconsin Press, 2004.

Gilman, Sander. *Picturing Health and Illness: Images of Identity and Difference.* Baltimore, MD: Johns Hopkins University Press, 1995.

Gimlin, Debra. "What Is Body Work?" *Social Compass* 1, no. 1 (2007): 353–70. http://dx.doi.org/10.1111/j.1751-9020.2007.00015.x.

Glazer, Penina M., and Miriam Slater. *Unequal Colleagues: The Entrance of Women into the Professions, 1890–1940.* New Brunswick, NJ: Rutgers University Press, 1987.

Gleason, Mona. "Embodied Negotiations: Children's Bodies and Historical Change in Canada, 1930–1960." *Journal of Canadian Studies/Revue d'études canadiennes* 32, no. 1 (1999): 112–38.

Gleason, Mona. *Normalizing the Ideal: Psychology, Schooling, and the Family in Postwar Canada.* Toronto: Toronto University Press, 1999.

Gleason, Mona. "Disciplining the Student Body: Schooling and the Construction of Canadian Children's Bodies, 1930 to 1960." *History of Education Quar-*

terly 41, no. 2 (2001): 189–215. http://dx.doi.org/10.1111/j.1748-5959.2001
.tb00084.x.

Gleason, Mona. "Race, Class, and Health: School Medical Inspection and 'Healthy' Children in British Columbia, 1890–1930." *Canadian Bulletin of Medical History* 19 (2002): 95–112.

Gleason, Mona. "From 'Disgraceful Carelessness' to 'Intelligent Precaution': Accidents and the Public Child in English Canada, 1900–1950." *Journal of Family History* 30, no. 2 (2005): 230–41. http://dx.doi.org/10.1177/0363199004270785.

Gleason, Mona. "Between Education and Memory: Health and Childhood in English Canada, 1900–1950." *Scientia Canadensis* 29, no. 1 (2006): 49–72. http://dx.doi.org/10.7202/800503ar.

Gleason, Mona. "Size Matters: Medical Experts, Educators, and the Provision of Health Services to Children in Early to Mid-Twentieth-Century English Canada." In *Healing the World's Children: Interdisciplinary Perspectives on Child Health in the Twentieth Century*, ed. Cynthia Comacchio, Janet Golden, and George Weisz, 176–204. Montreal and Kingston: McGill-Queen's University Press, 2008.

Gleason, Mona. "Lost Voices, Lost Bodies? Doctors and the Embodiment of Children and Youth in English Canada from 1900 to 1940." In *Lost Kids: Vulnerable Children and Youth in Twentieth-Century Canada and the United States*, ed. Mona Gleason, Tamara Myers, Leslie Paris, and Veronica Strong-Boag, 136–54. Vancouver: UBC Press, 2009.

Gordon, Linda. *Women's Bodies, Women's Lives*. New York: Viking, 1976.

Gosse, Van. "'To Organize in Every Neighborhood, in Every Home': The Gender Politics of American Communists between the Wars." *Radical History Review*, no. 50 (1991): 109–41. http://dx.doi.org/10.1215/01636545-1991-50-109.

Gould, Stephen J. *The Mismeasure of Man*. New York: W.W. Norton, 1981.

Gowing, Laura. *Women, Touch and Power in Seventeenth-Century England*. New Haven, CT: Yale University Press, 2003.

Grace, Sherrill. *Canada and the Idea of North*. Montreal and Kingston: McGill-Queen's University Press, 2001.

Granatstein, Jack. *Who Killed Canadian History?* Toronto: HarperCollins, 1998.

Granatstein, J.L., and David Bercuson. *War and Peacekeeping: From South Africa to the Gulf – Canada's Limited Wars*. Toronto: Key Porter Books, 1991.

Grandbois, Michèle. "The Challenge of the Nude," In *The Nude in Modern Canadian Art, 1920–1950*. Exh. Cat., ed. Michèle Grandbois et al., 21–2. Quebec City: Musée national des beaux-arts du Québec, 2009.

Grandbois, Michèle, et al., eds. *The Nude in Modern Canadian Art, 1920–1950*. Exh. Cat. Quebec City: Musée national des beaux-arts du Québec, 2009.

Graybill, Andrew R. *Policing the Great Plains: Rangers, Mounties, and the North American Frontier, 1875–1910.* Lincoln, NE: University of Nebraska Press, 2007.

Greig, Christopher J. "The Idea of Boyhood in Postwar Ontario, 1945–1960." Doctoral dissertation, University of Western Ontario, 2008.

Grosz, Elizabeth. *Volatile Bodies: Towards a Corporeal Feminism.* Indianapolis, IN: Indiana University Press, 1994.

Guay, Donald. *La Conquête du sport: Le sport et la société québecoise au XIXe siècle.* Montreal: Lanctot, 1997.

Hall, Robert, Gordon Dodds, and Stanley Triggs, eds. *The World of William Notman: The Nineteenth Century through a Master Lens.* Toronto: McClelland and Stewart, 1993.

Hamilton, Carolyn, Verne Harris, and Graeme Reid. Introduction. In *Refiguring the Archive*, ed. Carolyn Hamilton, Verne Harris, Jane Taylor, Michele Pickover, Graeme Reid, and Razia Saleh, 7–18. Dordrecht: Kluwer Academic, 2002. http://dx.doi.org/10.1007/978-94-010-0570-8_1.

Haraway, Donna. *When Species Meet.* Minneapolis, MN: University of Minnesota Press, 2008.

Hau, Michael. *The Cult of Health and Beauty in Germany: A Social History, 1890–1930.* Chicago, IL: University of Chicago Press, 2003.

Hayday, Matthew. "Fireworks, Folk-Dancing, and Fostering a National Identity: The Politics of Canada Day." *Canadian Historical Review* 91, no. 2 (2010): 287–314. http://dx.doi.org/10.3138/chr.91.2.287.

Heath, Gordon L. *A War with a Silver Lining: Canadian Protestant Churches and the South African War, 1899–1902.* Montreal and Kingston: McGill-Queen's University Press, 2009.

Helps, Lisa. "Body, Power, Desire: Mapping Canadian Body History." *Journal of Canadian Studies/ Revue d'études Canadiennes* 41, no. 1 (2007): 126–50.

Heron, Craig. *Booze: A Distilled History.* Toronto: Between the Lines, 2003.

Heron, Craig. "The Boys and Their Booze: Masculinities and Public Drinking in Working-Class Hamilton, 1890–1946." *Canadian Historical Review* 86, no. 3 (2005): 411–52.

Herrnstien, Richard, and Charles Murray. *The Bell Curve: Intelligence and Class Structure in American Life.* New York: Free Press, 1994.

Hewitt, Steve. "Spying 101: The RCMP's Activities at the University of Saskatchewan, 1920–71." In *Whose National Security? Canadian State Surveillance and the Creation of Enemies*, ed. Gary Kinsman, Dieter K. Buse, and Mercedes Steedman, 91–109. Toronto: Between the Lines, 2000.

Hewitt, Steve. *Riding to the Rescue: The Transformation of the RCMP in Alberta and Saskatchewan, 1914–1939.* Toronto: University of Toronto Press, 2006.

Hill, Charles. *Canadian Painting in the 1930s.* Exh. Cat. Ottawa: National Gallery of Canada, 1975.

Hoganson, Kristin L. *Fighting for American Manhood: How Gender Politics Provoked the Spanish-American and Philippine-American Wars.* New Haven, CT: Yale University Press, 1998.

Holliday, Ruth, and John Hassard. "Contested Bodies: An Introduction." In *Contested Bodies*, ed. Ruth Holliday and John Hassard, 1–18. London: Routledge, 2001.

Holman, Valerie, and Debra Kelly. "War in the Twentieth Century: The Functioning of Humour in Cultural Representation." *Journal of European Studies* 31, no. 123 (2001): 247–63. http://dx.doi.org/10.1177/004724410103112301.

Holmes, Rachel. *The Hottentot Venus: The Life and Death of Saartjie Baartman.* London: Bloomsbury, 2007.

Holtzmann-Kevels, Bettyann. *Naked to the Bone: Medical Imaging in the Twentieth Century.* New Brunswick, NJ: Rutgers University Press, 1997.

Horrall, S.W. "Sir John A. Macdonald and the Mounted Police Force for the Northwest Territories." *Canadian Historical Review* 53, no. 2 (1972).

Houlihan, Patrick. "Poetic Image." In *Exhibiting Cultures: The Poetics and Politics of Museum Display*, ed. Ivan Karp and Steven D. Lavine, 205–11. Washington, DC: Smithsonian Books, 1990.

Howell, Colin D. *Blood, Sweat and Cheers: Sport and the Making of Modern Canada.* Toronto: University of Toronto Press, 2001.

Howson, Alexandra. *The Body in Society: An Introduction.* Cambridge: Polity, 2004.

Huckenpahler, Victoria. "Confessions of an Opera Director: Chapters from the Mémoires of Dr. Louis Véron, Pt. 1." *Dance Chronicle* 7, no. 1 (1983): 50–106. http://dx.doi.org/10.1080/01472528308568877.

Hudson, Anna. "Art and Social Progress: The Toronto Community of Painters, 1933–1950." Doctoral dissertation, University of Toronto, 1997.

Hudson, Anna. "Disarming Conventions of Nudity in Canadian Art." In *The Nude in Modern Canadian Art, 1920–1950.* Exh. Cat., ed. Michèle Grandbois et al. Quebec City: Musée national des beaux-arts du Québec, 2009.

Hyam, Roland. *Empire and Sexuality.* Manchester: Manchester University Press, 1991.

Iacovetta, Franca. "Recipes for Democracy? Gender, Family and Making Female Citizens in Cold War Canada." In *Rethinking Canada: The Promise of Women's History*, ed. Veronica Strong-Boag, et al., 299–312. Don Mills, ON: Oxford University Press, 2002.

Iacovetta, Franca. *Gatekeepers: Reshaping Immigrant Lives in Cold War Canada.* Toronto: Between the Lines, 2006.

Iacovetta, Franca, and Valerie J. Korinek. "Jell-O Salads, One Stop Shopping and Maria the Homemaker: The Gender Politics of Food." In *Sisters or Strangers? Immigrant, Ethnic and Racialized Women in Canadian History*, ed. Marlene

Epp, Franca Iacovetta, and Frances Swyripa, 190–230. Toronto: University of Toronto Press, 2004.

Idlout d'Argencourt, Leah. "C.D. Howe." In *Northern Voices: Inuit Writing in English*, ed. Penny Petrone. Toronto: University of Toronto Press, 1988.

Innis, Harold. *The Fur-Trade of Canada*. Toronto: Oxford University Press, 1927.

Irving, Dan. "Normalized Transgressions: Legitimizing the Transsexual Body as Productive." *Radical History Review*, no. 100 (Winter 2008): 38–59. http://dx.doi.org/10.1215/01636545-2007-021.

Jacobs Brumberg, Joan. *The Body Project: An Intimate History of American Girls*. New York: Vintage, 1998.

Jasen, Patricia. *Wild Things: Nature, Culture, and Tourism in Ontario, 1790–1914*. Toronto: University of Toronto Press, 1995.

Jasen, Patricia. "Race, Culture and the Colonization of Childbirth in Northern Canada." *Social History of Medicine* 10, no. 3 (1997): 383–400. http://dx.doi.org/10.1093/shm/10.3.383.

Johnson, F. Henry. *A Brief History of Canadian Education*. Toronto: McGraw-Hill, 1968.

Jordanova, Ludmilla. *Sexual Visions: Images of Gender in Science and Medicine between the Eighteenth and Twentieth Centuries*. Madison, WI: University of Wisconsin Press, 1989.

Joseph, Nathan. *Uniforms and Nonuniforms: Communication through Clothing*. New York: Greenwood, 1986.

Karayanni, Stavros Stavrou. *Dancing Fear and Desire: Race, Sexuality and Imperial Politics in Middle Eastern Dance*. Waterloo: Wilfrid Laurier University Press, 2004.

Kealey, Gregory. "Class in English Canadian History Writing: Neither Privatizing, Nor Sundering." *Journal of Canadian Studies/Revue d'études canadiennes* 26, no. 1 (1992): 123–9.

Kealey, Linda, et al. "Teaching Canadian History in the 1990s: What 'National History' Are We Lamenting?" *Journal of Canadian Studies/Revue d'études canadiennes* 27, no. 2 (1992): 130–1.

Kelcey, Barbara E. "What to Wear to the Klondike: Outfitting Women for the Gold Rush." *Material History Review* 37 (Spring 1993): 20–9.

Kelm, Mary-Ellen. *Colonizing Bodies: Aboriginal Health and Healing in British Columbia, 1900–1950*. Vancouver: UBC Press, 1998.

Kersh, Roger, and James A. Morone. "Obesity, Courts and the New Politics of Public Health." *Journal of Health Politics, Policy and Law* 30, no. 5 (2005): 839–68. http://dx.doi.org/10.1215/03616878-30-5-839.

Khayatt, Madiha Didi. *Lesbian Teachers: An Invisible Presence*. Albany, NY: State University of New York Press, 1992.

Khosla, Punam, Laura King, and Linda Read. *The Unrecognized Majority: A History of Women Teachers in British Columbia.* Vancouver: B.C. Teachers' Federation, 1981.

Kidd, Bruce. "In Defense of Tom Longboat." *Canadian Journal of History of Sport* 14, no. 1 (1983): 34–63.

Kinsman, Gary. "Constructing Gay Men and Lesbians as National Security Risks, 1950–1970." In *Whose National Security? Canadian State Surveillance and the Creation of Enemies*, ed. Gary Kinsman, Dieter K. Buse, and Mercedes Steedman, 143–53. Toronto: Between the Lines, 2000.

Knopp Biklen, Sari. *School Work: Gender and the Cultural Construction of Teaching.* New York: Teachers College Press, 1995.

Kopelson, Kevin. *The Queer Afterlife of Vaslav Nijinsky.* Stanford, CA: Stanford University Press, 1997.

Krasnick Warsh, Cheryl. "Smoke and Mirrors: Gender Representation in North American Tobacco and Alcohol Advertisements before 1950." *Histoire sociale/ Social History* 31, no. 62 (1998): 183–222.

Krasnick Warsh, Cheryl. "Advertising Regulations (Canada)." In *Alcohol and Temperance in Modern History: An International Encyclopedia*, vol. 1, ed. Jack S. Blocker, Jr., David M. Fahey, and Ian Tyrell, 6. Santa Barbara, CA: ABC-CLIO, 2003.

Krasnick Warsh, Cheryl, and Veronica Strong-Boag, eds. *Children's Health Issues in Historical Perspective.* Waterloo: Wilfrid Laurier University Press 2005.

La Blanc, Barbara. "Changing Places: Dance, Society, and Gender in Cheticamp." In *Undisciplined Women: Tradition and Culture in Canada*, ed. Pauline Green Hill and Diane Tye, 101–12. Montreal and Kingston: McGill-Queen's University Press, 1997.

Laqueur, Thomas. *Making Sex: Body and Gender from the Greeks to Freud.* Cambridge, MA: Harvard University Press, 1992.

LaRocque, Emma. "My Hometown Northern Canada South Africa." In *Making Space for Indigenous Feminism*, ed. Joyce Green, 216–20. Black Point, NS: Fernwood, 2007.

Le Goff, Jacques, and Nicolas Truong. *Une histoire du corps au Moyen-Âge.* Paris: Liana Lévi, 2003.

LeBel, Alyne. "Une vitrine populaire: Les Grands Magasins Paquet." *Cap-Aux-Diamants: La revue d'histoire du Québec* 4, no. 2 (1988): 45–8.

Levenstein, Harvey A. *Revolution at the Table: The Transformation of the American Diet.* Berkeley, CA: University of California Press, 2003.

Lévesque, Andrée. *Red Travellers: Jeanne Corbin and Her Comrades.* Yvonne M. Klein (trans.). Montreal and Kingston: McGill-Queen's University Press, 2006.

Levine, Philippa, ed. *Gender and Empire*. Oxford: Oxford University Press, 2004.

Lingis, Alphonso. "Animal Body, Inhuman Face." In *Zoontologies: The Question of the Animal*, ed. Cary Wolfe, 165–82. Minneapolis, MN: University of Minnesota Press, 2003.

Little, Margaret. "'A Fit and Proper Person': The Moral Regulation of Single Mothers in Ontario, 1920–1940." In *Gendered Pasts: Historical Essays in Femininity and Masculinity in Canada*, ed. Kathryn McPherson, Cecilia Morgan, and Nancy Forestell, 123–38. Toronto: University of Toronto Press, 2003.

Llewellyn, Kristina R. "In the Name of Democracy: The World of Women Teachers in Toronto and Vancouver, 1945–1960." Doctoral dissertation, University of British Columbia, 2006.

Lobstein, Timothy. "What are the Factors Contributing to the Obesity Epidemic among Children and Youth?" Presentation Abstracts, International Conference on Physical Activity and Obesity in Children, Toronto, 24–7 June 2007.

Lorber, Judith, and Lisa Jean Moore, eds. *Gendered Bodies: Feminist Perspectives*. 2nd ed. New York: Oxford University, Press, 2010.

Lorell, Stephen. "Soviet Socialism and the Construction of Old Age." *Jahrbucher fur Geschichte Osteuropas, Neue Folge* 51, no. 4 (2003): 564–85.

Lovett, Laura. "The Popeye Principle: Selling Child Health in the First Nutrition Crisis." *Journal of Health Politics, Policy and Law* 30, no. 5 (2005): 803–38. http://dx.doi.org/10.1215/03616878-30-5-803.

Loy, John W., David L. Andrews, and Robert E. Rinehart. "The Body in Culture and Sport." *Sport Science Review* 2, no. 1 (1993): 69–91.

Lubinski, Christine. "Are We Addicted to Alcohol Advertising?" *Health* 20, no. 20 (2000). http://health20-20.org/article.php?id=23.

Luckyj, Natalie. *Expressions of Will: The Art of Prudence Heward*. Montreal and Kingston: McGill-Queen's University Press, 1986.

Lux, Maureen. *Medicine that Walks: Disease, Medicine, and Canadian Plains Native People, 1880–1940*. Toronto: University of Toronto Press, 2001.

Lynn, Richard. *The Global Bell Curve: Race, IQ, and Inequality Worldwide*. Augusta, GA: Washington Summit Publishers, 2008.

MacGregor, James G. *Edmonton: A History*. 2nd ed. Edmonton: Hurtig, 1975.

Mackey, Eva. *The House of Difference: Cultural Politics and National Identity in Canada*. Toronto: University of Toronto Press, 2002.

Malkki, Liisa. "Citizens of Humanity: Internationalism and Imagined Community of Nations." *Diaspora* 3, no. 1 (1994): 41–68. http://dx.doi.org/10.1353/dsp.1994.0013.

Mangan, J.A., and James Walvin, eds. *Manliness and Morality: Middle-Class Masculinity in Britain and America, 1800–1940*. Manchester: Manchester University Press, 1987.

Marotta, Jennifer Susan. "'Rejoicing that You Are a Subject of Her Gracious Queen Victoria': Race and Respectability within the Pages of *The Family Herald and Weekly Star*, 1873–1890." Paper presented at the Annual Conference of the Canadian Historical Association, Université de Laval, Quebec City, 15–27 May 2001.

Marrus, Michael R. *Samuel Bronfman: The Life and Times of Seagram's Mr. Sam*. London: Brandeis University Press, 1991.

Martin, Emily. *The Woman in the Body: A Cultural Analysis of Reproduction*. Boston, MA: Beacon Press, 2001.

Masquelier, Adeline, ed. *Dirt, Undress, and Difference: Critical Perspectives on the Body's Surface*. Bloomington, IN: Indiana University Press, 2005.

Masters, Jarvis Jay. "Scars." In *The Body Reader: Essential Social and Cultural Readings*, ed. Lisa Jean Moore and Mary Kosut, 329–31. New York: New York University Press, 2010.

Mauss, Marcel. *Techniques, Technology and Civilisation*, ed. Nathan Schlanger. New York: Berghahn, 2006.

Maynard, Steven. "'Horrible Temptations': Sex, Men, and Working-Class Male Youth in Urban Ontario, 1890–1935." *Canadian Historical Review* 78, no.2 (1987): 191–235.

McCaffrey, Moira. "Rononshonni – the Builder: McCord's Collection of Ethnographic Objects." In *The McCord Family: A Passionate Vision*, ed. Pamela Miller et al., Montreal and Kingston: McGill-Queen's University Press, 1992.

McClintock, Anne. *Imperial Leather: Race, Gender and Sexuality in the Colonial Contest*. London: Routledge, 1995.

McInnis, Edgar. *Canada: A Political and Social History*. Toronto: Holt, Rinehart and Winston, 1982.

McKay, Ian. *Reasoning Otherwise: Leftists and the People's Enlightenment in Canada, 1890–1920*. Toronto: Between the Lines, 2008.

McLaren, Angus. *Our Own Master Race: Eugenics in Canada, 1885–1945*. Toronto: McClelland and Stewart, 1990.

McLaren, Kristen. "'We Had No Desire to Be Set Apart': Forced Segregation of Black Students in Canada West Public Schools and Myths of British Egalitarianism." In *The History of Immigration and Racism in Canada: Essential Readings*, ed. Barrington Walker, 69–81. Toronto: Canadian Scholars' Press, 2008.

McLellan, David, ed. *Karl Marx: Selected Writing*. 2nd ed. Oxford: Oxford University Press, 2000.

McNally, David. *Bodies of Meaning: Studies on Language, Labor, and Liberation*. Albany, NY: SUNY Press, 2001.

McNally, David. *Monsters of the Market: Zombies, Vampires and Global Capitalism*. Leiden: Brill, 2010.

McPherson, Kathryn. "'The Case of the Kissing Nurse': Femininity, Sexuality, and Canadian Nursing, 1900–1970." In *Gendered Pasts: Historical Essays in Femininity and Masculinity in Canada*, ed. Kathryn McPherson, Cecilia Morgan, and Nancy Forestell, 179–98. Don Mills, ON: Oxford University Press, 1999.

McTavish, Lianne. "Learning to See in New Brunswick, 1867–1929." *Canadian Historical Review* 87, no. 4 (2006): 553–81.

Meadowcroft, Barbara. *Painting Friends: The Beaver Hall Women Painters*. Montreal: Vehicule, 1999.

Meglin, Joellen A. "Feminism or Fetishism? La Révolte des femmes and Women's Liberation in France in the 1830s." In *Rethinking the Sylph: New Perspectives on the Romantic Ballet*, ed. Lynn Garafola, 69–90. Hanover, NH: Wesleyan University Press, 1997.

Messner, Michael. *Out of Play: Critical Essays on Gender and Sport*. Albany, NY: SUNY Press, 2007.

Metcalfe, Alan. "The Evolution of Organized Physical Recreation in Montreal, 1840–1895." *Histoire sociale/Social History* 11 (May 1978): 144–66.

Metcalfe, Alan. *Canada Learns to Play: The Emergence of Organized Sport, 1807–1914*. Toronto: McClelland and Stewart, 1987.

Metzger, Deena. *Writing for Your Life*. New York: Random House, 1992.

Middleboe Christensen, Anne. "Deadly Sylphs and Decent Mermaids." In *The Cambridge Companion to Ballet*, ed. Marion Kant, 126–39. Cambridge: Cambridge University Press, 2007.

Miller, Carman. "A Preliminary Analysis of the Socio-Economic Composition of Canada's South Africa War Contingents." *Histoire sociale/Social History* 8, no. 5 (1975): 219–37.

Miller, Carman. *Painting the Map Red: Canada and the South African War, 1899–1902*. Montreal and Kingston: McGill-Queen's University Press, 1993.

Miller, J.R. *Skyscrapers Hide the Heavens: A History of Indian-White Relations in Canada*. Toronto: University of Toronto Press, 2000.

Mirzoeff, Nicholas. *Bodyscape: Art, Modernity and the Ideal Figure*. London: Routledge, 1995. http://dx.doi.org/10.4324/9780203393406

Mitchinson, Wendy. *The Nature of Their Bodies: Women and Their Doctors in Victorian Canada*. Toronto: University of Toronto Press, 1991.

Montagu, Ashley. Introduction. In *Race and I.Q.: Expanded Edition*, ed. Ashley Montagu, 1–18. New York: Oxford University Press, 1999.

Montgomery, Deborah. *The Women's War: New Zealand Women, 1939–1945*. Auckland: Auckland University Press, 2001.

Morris, Jerrold. *The Nude in Canadian Painting*. Toronto: New Press, 1972.

Morris, Nina J. "Naked in Nature: Naturism, Nature and the Senses in Early

20th Century Britain." *Cultural Geographies* 16, no. 3 (2009): 283–308. http://dx.doi.org/10.1177/1474474009105049.

Morrow, Don. "Sweetheart Sport, Barbara Ann Scott and the Post–World War II Image of the Female Athlete." *Canadian Journal of History of Sport* 18, no. 1 (1987): 36–54.

Morrow, Don. "The Knights of the Snowshoe: A Study of the Evolution of Sport in Nineteenth-Century Montreal." *Journal of Sport History* 15, no. 1 (1988): 5–40.

Morton, Desmond. *A Military History of Canada: From Champlain to Kosovo.* Toronto: McClelland and Stewart, 1999.

Moss, Mark. *Manliness and Militarism: Educating Young Boys in Ontario for War.* Don Mills, ON: Oxford University Press, 2001.

Mosse, George. *Nationalism and Sexuality: Respectability and Abnormal Sexuality in Modern Europe.* New York: Howard Furtig, 1985.

Motyer Raymond, Jocelyn. *The Nursery World of Dr. Blatz.* Toronto: University of Toronto Press, 1991.

Mulvey, Laura. "Visual Pleasures and Narrative Cinema." *Screen* 16 (Autumn 1975): 6–18.

Myers, Tamara. "Embodying Delinquency: Boys' Bodies, Sexuality, and Juvenile Justice History in Early-Twentieth-Century Quebec." *Journal of the History of Sexuality* 14, no. 4 (2005): 383–414. http://dx.doi.org/10.1353/sex.2006.0043.

Myers, Tamara. *Caught: Montreal's Modern Girls and the Law, 1869–1945.* Toronto: University of Toronto Press, 2006.

Myrone, Martin. "Prudery, Pornography and the Victorian Nude (Or, What Do We Think the Butler Saw?)." In *Exposed: The Victorian Nude.* Exh. Cat, ed. Alison Smith, 23–36. London: Tate Britain, 2000.

Nadeau, Chantal. *Fur Nation: From the Beaver to Brigitte Bardot.* London: Routledge, 2001.

Nathoo, Tasnim, and Aleck Ostry. *The One Best Way? Breastfeeding History, Politics, and Policy in Canada.* Waterloo: Wilfrid Laurier University Press, 2009.

Nead, Lynda. *The Female Nude: Art, Obscenity and Sexuality.* London: Routledge, 1992. http://dx.doi.org/10.4324/9780203328194.

Nelson, Charmaine. "Coloured Nude: Fetishization, Disguise, Dichotomy." M.A. thesis, Concordia University, 1995.

Nicholas, Jane. "'A Figure of a Nude Woman': Art, Popular Culture, and Modernity at the Canadian National Exhibition, 1927." *Histoire sociale/Social History* 41, no. 82 (2008): 313–44.

Nicholas, Jane. "Gendering the Jubilee: Gender and Modernity in the Diamond Jubilee of Confederation Celebrations, 1927." *Canadian Historical Review* 90, no. 2 (2009): 247–74. http://dx.doi.org/10.3138/chr.90.2.247.

Nicholson, Linda. "Interpreting Gender." *Sign* 20, no. 1 (1994): 79–105. http://dx.doi.org/10.1086/494955.

Novick, Peter. *That Noble Dream: The 'Objectivity Question' and the American Historical Profession.* Chicago, IL: University of Chicago Press, 1988. http://dx.doi.org/10.1017/CBO9780511816345.

O'Connor, Erin. *Raw Material: Producing Pathology in Victorian Culture.* Durham, NC: Duke University Press, 2000.

Ogborne, A.C., and R.G. Smart. "Will Restrictions on Advertising Reduce Alcohol Consumption?" *British Journal of Addiction* 75, no. 3 (1980): 293–96. http://dx.doi.org/10.1111/j.1360-0443.1980.tb01382.x.

Opp, James. *The Lord for the Body: Religion. Medicine, and Protestant Faith Healing in Canada, 1880–1930.* Montreal and Kingston: McGill-Queen's University Press, 2005.

Oram, Alison. "Embittered, Sexless or Homosexual: Attacks on Spinster Teachers in 1918–1939." In *Not a Passing Phase: Reclaiming Lesbians in History 1840–1985,* ed. Lesbian History Group, 99–118. London: Women's Press, 1989.

Orpana, Heather, et al. "BMI and Mortality: Results from a National Longitudinal Study of Canadian Adults." *Obesity* 18, no. 1 (2009): 214–18. http://www.nature.com/day/journal/v18/n1/full/oby2009191a.html.

Osborne, Brian S. "'Grounding' National Mythologies: The Case of Canada." In *Espace et culture,* ed. Serge Courville and Normand Séguin, 265–74. Sainte Foy, QC: Presses de l'Université Laval, 1995.

Ostry, Aleck. "The Early Development of Nutrition Policy in Canada." In *Children's Health Issues in Historical Perspective,* ed. Cheryl Krasnick Warsh and Veronica Strong-Boag, 191–207. Waterloo: Wilfrid Laurier University Press, 2003.

Ostry, Aleck. *Nutrition Policy in Canada, 1870–1939.* Vancouver: UBC Press, 2006.

Page, Robert. *Imperialism and Canada, 1895–1903.* Toronto: Holt, Rinehart, and Winston, 1972.

Palango, Paul. *The Last Guardians: The Crisis in the RCMP – and Canada.* Toronto: McClelland and Stewart, 1998.

Palmer, Alexandra. *Couture and Commerce: The Transatlantic Fashion Trade in the 1950s.* Vancouver: UBC Press, 2001.

Palmer, Alexandra, ed. *Fashion: A Canadian Perspective.* Toronto: University of Toronto, 2004.

Pantazzi, Sybille. "Foreign Art at the Canadian National Exhibition, 1905–1938." In *National Gallery of Canada Bulletin* 22 (1973): 21–41.

Parkin, Alan. *A History of Psychoanalysis in Canada.* Toronto: Toronto Psychoanalytic Society, 1987.

Parr, Joy. Introduction. In *A Diversity of Women: Ontario, 1945–1980*, ed. Joy Parr, 3–18. Toronto: University of Toronto Press, 1995.

Parr, Joy. *Sensing Changes: Technologies, Environments, and the Everyday, 1953–2003*. Vancouver: UBC Press, 2010.

Parr, Joy. "Our Bodies and Our Histories of Technology and the Environment." In *The Illusory Boundary: Environment and Technology in History*, ed. S. Cutcliffe and M. Reuss, 26–42. Charlottesville, VA: University of Virginia Press, 2010.

Pateman, Carole. *The Sexual Contract*. Cambridge: Polity, 1988.

Pateman, Carole. *The Disorder of Women: Democracy, Feminism, and Political Theory*. Stanford, CA: Stanford University Press, 1989.

Pearce, Susan. *Collecting in Contemporary Practice*. London: Sage, 1998.

Pease, Otis. *The Responsibilities of American Advertising: Private Control and Public Influence, 1920–1940*. New Haven, CT: Yale University Press, 1958.

Peeters, Evert. "Authenticity and Asceticism: Discourse and Performance in Nude Culture and Health Reform in Belgium, 1920–1940." *Journal of the History of Sexuality* 15, no. 3 (2006): 432–61. http://dx.doi.org/10.1353/sex.2007.0020.

Peiss, Kathy. *Hope in a Jar: The Making of America's Beauty Culture*. New York: Metropolitan Books, 1998.

Pendergast, Mark. *For God, Country and Coca-Cola: The Unauthorized History of the Great American Soft Drink and the Company that Makes It*. Toronto: Collier, 1994.

Peniston-Bird, Corinna. "Classifying the Body in the Second World War: British Men In and Out of Uniform." *Body and Society* 9, no. 4 (2003): 31–48. http://dx.doi.org/10.1177/135703403773684630.

Penlington, Norman. *Canada and Imperialism, 1896–1899*. Toronto: University of Toronto Press, 1965.

Perry, Adele. *On the Edge of Empire: Gender, Race, and the Making of British Columbia*. Toronto: University of Toronto Press, 2001.

Perry, Adele. "Nation, Empire and the Writing of History in Canada in English." In *Contesting Clio's Craft: New Directions and Debates in Canadian History*, ed. Christopher Dummitt and Michael Dawson, 123–40. Vancouver: UBC Press, 2008.

Petrone, Penny, ed. *Northern Voices: Inuit Writing in English*. Toronto: University of Toronto Press, 1988.

Phillips, Anne. *Engendering Democracy*. University Park, PA: Pennsylvania State University Press, 1991.

Phillips, Ruth. "Re-placing Objects: Historical Practices for the Second Museum Age." *Canadian Historical Review* 86, no. 1 (2005): 83–110.

Pickles, Katie. *Female Imperialism and National Identity: Imperial Order Daughters of the Empire*. New York: Palgrave, 2002. http://dx.doi.org/10.7228/manchester/9780719063909.001.0001.

Pickles, Katie, and Myra Rutherdale, eds. *Contact Zones: Aboriginal and Settler Women in Canada's Colonial Past.* Vancouver: UBC Press, 2005.

Pierson, Ruth Roach. *"They're Still Women After All": The Second World War and Canadian Womanhood.* Toronto: McClelland and Stewart, 1986.

Pine, Jason. "Embodied Capitalism and the Meth Economy." In *The Body Reader: Essential Social and Cultural Readings,* ed. Lisa Jean Moore and Mary Kosut, 164–83. New York: New York University Press, 2010.

Pinto, Barbara. "'Ain't Misbehavin': The Montreal Shamrock Lacrosse Club Fans, 1868–1884.'" In *Proceedings of the North American Society for Sport History.* Banff, AB: N.P. 1990.

Podruchny, Carolyn. "Festivals, Fortitude, and Fraternalism: Fur Trade Masculinity and the Beaver Club, 1785–1827." In *New Faces of the Fur Trade: Selected Papers of the Seventh North American Fur Trade Conference, Halifax, Nova Scotia, 1995,* ed. Jo-Anne Fiske, Susan Sleeper-Smith, and William Wicken, 31–52. East Lansing, MI: Michigan State University Press, 1998.

Pointon, Marcia. *Naked Authority: The Body in Western Painting, 1830–1908.* Cambridge: Cambridge University Press, 1990.

Porsild, Charlene. *Gamblers and Dreamers: Women, Men and Community in the Klondike.* Vancouver: UBC Press, 1999.

Porter, Ann. "Women and Income Security in the Post-War Period: The Case of Unemployment Insurance, 1945–1962." *Labour/Le Travail* 31 (1993): 111–44.

Porter, Ann. *Gendered States: Women, Unemployment Insurance and the Political Economy of the Welfare State in Canada, 1945–1997.* Toronto: University of Toronto Press, 2003.

Porter, Roy. "The History of the Body Reconsidered." In *New Perspectives on Historical Writing.* 2nd ed., ed. Peter Burke, 233–60. University Park, PA: Pennsylvania State University Press, 2001.

Potter, Evan. *Branding Canada: Projecting Canada's Soft Power through Public Diplomacy.* Montreal and Kingston: McGill-Queen's University Press, 2009.

Poulter, Gillian. "Snowshoeing and Lacrosse: Canada's Nineteenth-Century 'National Games.'" *Culture, Sport Society* 6, nos. 2/3 (2003): 293–320. Reprinted in *Ethnicity, Sport, Identity: Struggles for Status,* ed. J.A. Mangan and Andrew Ritchie, 293–320. London: Frank Cass, 2004.

Poulter, Gillian. "Montreal and Its Environs: Imagining a National Landscape, c. 1867–1885." *Journal of Canadian Studies/Revue d'études Canadiennes* 38, no. 3 (2004): 69–100.

Poulter, Gillian. "'Eminently Canadian': Indigenous Sports and Canadian Identity in Victorian Montreal." In *Hidden in Plain Sight: Contributions of Aboriginal Peoples to Canadian Identity and Culture,* ed. David R. Newhouse, Cora J. Voyageur, and Dan Beavon, 352–75. Toronto: University of Toronto Press, 2005.

Poulter, Gillian. *Becoming Native in a Foreign Land: Sport, Visual Culture, and Identity in Montreal, 1840–85.* Vancouver: UBC Press, 2009.

Prentice, Alison, et al. *Canadian Women: A History.* Toronto: Harcourt Brace Jovanovich, 1988.

Prevots, Naima. *Dance for Export: Cultural Diplomacy and the Cold War.* Hanover, NH: Wesleyan University Press, 1998.

Price, Janet, and Margrit Shildrick, eds. *Feminist Theory and the Body: A Reader.* New York: Oxford University Press, 1999.

Prince, Nicholette. "Influence of the Hudson's Bay Company on Carrier and Coast Salish Dress, 1830–1850." *Material History Review* 38 (Fall 1993): 15–26.

Radforth, Ian. *Royal Spectacle: The 1860 Visit of the Prince of Wales to Canada and the United States.* Toronto: University of Toronto Press, 2004.

Ralston Saul, John. *A Fair Country: Telling the Truths about Canada.* Toronto: Viking Canada, 2008.

Rangari, Ashole Dumodor. *Indian Caste System and Education.* Ann Arbor, MI: Deep Publications/University of Michigan Press, 1984.

Reynolds, Cecilia. "Hegemony and Hierarchy: Becoming a Teacher in Toronto, 1930–1980." *Historical Studies in Education/Revue d'histoire de l'éducation* 2, no. 1 (1990): 95–119.

Reynolds, Cecilia. "Too Limiting a Liberation: Discourse and Actuality in the Case of Married Women Teachers." In *Feminism and Education: A Canadian Perspective,* ed. F. Forman, M. O'Brien, J. Haddad, D. Hallman, and P. Masters, 145–65. Toronto: Centre for Women's Studies in Education, 1990.

Rich, Emma. "Gender Positioning in Teacher Education in England: New Rhetoric, Old Realities." *International Studies in Sociology of Education* 11, no. 2 (2001): 131–56. http://dx.doi.org/10.1080/09620210100200072.

Roper, Michael, and John Tosh, eds. *Manful Assertions: Masculinities in Britain since 1800.* London: Routledge, 1991.

Ross, Chad. *Naked Germany: Health, Race and the Nation.* Oxford: Berg, 2005.

Rothblum, Ester, and Sondra Solovay, eds. *Fat Studies Reader.* New York: New York University Press, 2009.

Rudin, Ronald. *Making History in Twentieth-Century Quebec.* Toronto: University of Toronto Press, 1997.

Rushton, J. Phillipe. "Race Differences in *g* and the 'Jensen Effect.'" In *The Scientific Study of General Intelligence: Tribute to Arthur R. Jensen,* ed. Helmuth Nyborg, 147–86. Boston, MA: Pergamon, 2003.

Rushton, J. Phillipe, and Arthur R. Jensen. "Thirty Years of Research on Race Difference and Cognitive Ability." *Psychology, Public Policy, and Law* 11, no. 2 (2005): 235–94. http://dx.doi.org/10.1037/1076-8971.11.2.235.

Russett, Cynthia Eagle. *Sexual Science: The Victorian Construction of Womanhood.* Cambridge, MA: Harvard University Press, 1989.

Russo, Mary. "Female Grotesques: Carnival and Theory." In *Writing on the Body: Female Embodiment and Feminist Theory*, ed. Kate Conboy et al., 318–36. New York: Columbia University Press, 1997.

Rutherdale, Myra. "'She Was a Ragged Little Thing': Missionaries, Embodiment, and Refashioning Aboriginal Womanhood in Northern Canada." In *Contact Zones: Aboriginal and Settler Women in Canada's Colonial Past*, ed. Katie Pickles and Myra Rutherdale, 148–73. Vancouver: UBC Press, 2005.

Rutherdale, Myra, and Jim Miller. "'It's Our Country': First Nations' Participation in the Indian Pavilion at Expo 67." *Journal of the Canadian Historical Association* 17, no. 2 (2006): 148–73. http://dx.doi.org/10.7202/016594ar.

Rutherdale, Myra, and Katie Pickles, eds. *Contact Zones: Aboriginal and Settler Women in Canada's Colonial Past*. Vancouver: UBC Press, 2005.

Rutherford, Jonathan. *Forever England: Reflections on Race, Masculinity and Empire*. London: Lawrence and Wishart, 1997.

Rutherford, Paul. *A World Made Sexy: From Freud to Madonna*. Toronto: University of Toronto Press, 2007.

Samuel, Raphael. *Theatres of Memory*. London: Verso, 1994.

Sangster, Joan. *Dreams of Equality: Women on the Canadian Left, 1920–1950*. Toronto: McClelland and Stewart, 1989.

Sangster, Joan. "*Robitnytsia*, Ukrainian Communists, and the 'Porcupinism' Debate: Reassessing Ethnicity, Gender, and Class in Early Canadian Communism, 1922–1930." *Labour/Le Travail* 56 (Fall 2005): 51–90.

Sangster, Joan. "The Beaver as Ideology: Constructing Images of Inuit and Native Life in Post–World War II Canada." *Anthropologica* 49, no. 2 (2007): 191–209.

Sangster, Joan. "Making a Fur Coat: Women, the Labouring Body, and Working-Class History." *International Review of Social History* 52, no. 2 (2007): 241–70. http://dx.doi.org/10.1017/S0020859007002933.

Sangster, Joan. "'Queen of the Picket Line': Beauty Contests in the Post–World War II Canadian Labor Movement, 1945–1970." *Labor: Studies in Working-Class History of the Americas* 5, no. 4 (2008): 83–106. http://dx.doi.org/10.1215/15476715-2008-029.

Scarry, Elaine. *The Body in Pain: The Making and Unmaking of the World*. Oxford: Oxford University Press, 1985.

Scheper-Hughes, Nancy, and Loïc Wacquant, eds. *Commodifying Bodies*. London: Sage, 2002.

Schiebinger, Londa. "Skeletons in the Closet: The First Illustrations of the Female Skeleton in Eigtheenth-Century Anatomy." In *The Making of the Modern Body: Sexuality and Society in the Nineteenth Century*, ed. Catherine Gallagher and Thomas Laqueur, 42–82. Berkeley, CA: University of California Press, 1987.

Schiebinger, Londa. *The Mind Has No Sex? Women in the Origins of Modern Science.* Cambridge, MA: Harvard University Press, 1991.

Schiebinger, Londa, ed. *Feminism and the Body.* New York: Oxford University Press, 2000.

Schwartz, Hillel. *Never Satisfied: A Cultural History of Diets, Fantasies and Fat.* London: Collier Macmillan, 1986.

Scott, Joan. "Gender: A Useful Category of Historical Analysis." *American Historical Review* 91, no. 5 (1986): 1053–75. http://dx.doi.org/10.2307/1864376.

Sekula, Allan. "The Body and the Archive." *October* 39 (1986): 3–64. http://dx.doi.org/10.2307/778312.

Shopland, Stella. "Status of Married Women Teachers in the Province of British Columbia." M.A. thesis, University of Washington, 1957.

Showalter, Elaine. *Sexual Anarchy: Gender and Culture at the Fin de Siècle.* New York: Bloomsbury, 1991.

Silverman, Jason. *Unwelcome Guests: Canada West's Response to American Fugitive Slaves, 1800–1865.* Milwood, NY: Associated Faculty Press, 1985.

Simpson, Donald G. *Under the North Star: Black Communities in Upper Canada.* Toronto: Africa New World Press, 2005.

Slavishak, Ed. "'Made by the Work': A Century of Labouring Bodies in the United States." In *The Body Reader: Essential Social and Cultural Readings*, ed. Lisa Jean Moore and Mary Kosut, 147–63. New York: New York University Press, 2010.

Smardz Frost, Karolyn. *I've Got a Home in Glory Land: A Lost Tale of the Underground Railroad.* Toronto: Thomas Allen, 2007.

Smardz Frost, Karolyn, et al., eds. *Ontario's African-Canadian Heritage: Collected Writings by Fred Landon, 1918–1967.* Toronto: Dundurn, 2009.

Smart, Carol, ed. *Regulating Womanhood: Historical Essays on Marriage, Motherhood and Sexuality.* London: Routledge, 1992.

Smart, Reginald G. "The New Drinkers – Teenage Use and Abuse of Alcohol." *Addictions* 23 (Spring 1971): 21.

Smith, Bonnie G. *The Gender of History: Men, Women and Historical Practice.* Cambridge, MA: Harvard University Press, 2000.

Smith, H., and P. Wakewich. "'I Was Not Afraid of Work': Female War Plant Employees and Their Work Environment." In *Canadian Environments: Essays in Culture, Politics and History*, ed. Robert C. Thomsen and Nanette L. Hale, 229–47. Brussels: P.I.E. Peter Lang, 2005.

Smith, H., and P. Wakewich. "Regulating Body Boundaries and Health during Wartime: Nationalist Discourses, Media Representations and the Experiences of Canadian Women War Workers." *Gender and History* 24, no. 1 (2012), 56–73.

Smith-Rosenberg, Carroll, and Charles Rosenberg. "The Female Animal: Medical and Biological Views of Women and Their Role in Nineteenth-Century America." In *From "Fair Sex" to Feminism: Sport and the Socialization of Women in the Industrial and Post-Industrial Eras*, ed. J.A. Mangan and Roberta J. Park, 13–37. London: Frank Cass, 1987.

Spencer, Emily. *Lipstick and High Heels: War, Gender and Popular Culture*. Kingston: Canadian Defence Academic Press, 2007.

Spurlock, John C. *New and Improved: The Transformation of American Women's Emotional Culture*. New York: New York University Press, 1998.

Stacey, C.P. *Canada and the Age of Conflict, 1867–1921*. Toronto: Macmillan, 1977.

Stack, Eileen. "The Significance of the Blanket Coat to Anglo-Canadian Identity." Paper presented at the 25th Annual Symposium of the Costume Society of America, Santa Fe, New Mexico, 22–5 May 1999.

Stack, Eileen. "Very Picturesque and Very Canadian: The Blanket Coat and Anglo-Canadian Identity in the Second Half of the Nineteenth Century." In *Fashion: A Canadian Perspective*, ed. Alexandra Palmer, 17–40. Toronto: University of Toronto Press, 2004.

Stamp, Robert M. *The Schools of Ontario, 1876–1976*. Toronto: University of Toronto Press, 1982.

Stamp, Robert M. "'Teaching the 'Children of Silence': Samuel Greene and the Hearing-Impaired." *Historical Studies in Education/Revue d'histoire de l'éducation* 17, no. 1 (2005): 165–8.

Stanley, Timothy J. *Contesting White Supremacy: School Segregation, Anti-Racism and the Making of Chinese Canadians*. Vancouver: UBC Press, 2011.

Starks, Tricia. *The Body Soviet: Propaganda, Hygiene, and the Revolutionary State*. Madison, WI: University of Wisconsin Press, 2008.

Starr, Michael E. "The Marlboro Man: Cigarette Smoking and Masculinity in America." *Journal of Popular Culture* 17, no. 4 (1984): 45–57. http://dx.doi.org/10.1111/j.0022-3840.1984.1704_45.x.

Staton, Patricia Anne, and Beth Light. *Speak with Their Own Voices: A Documentary History of the Teachers of Ontario and the Women Elementary Public School Teachers in Ontario*. Toronto: Federation of Women's Teachers Associations of Ontario, 1987.

Stearns, Peter. *Fat History: Bodies and Beauty in the Modern West*. New York: New York University Press, 2002.

Steedman, Carolyn. "*La théorie qui n'est pas une*, or Why Clio Doesn't Care." In *Feminists Revision History*, ed. Ann-Louise Shapiro, 73–93. New Brunswick, NJ: Rutgers University Press, 1994.

Steinem, Gloria. "Sex, Lies and Advertising." *Ms. Magazine*, July/August, 1990, 18–28.

Stempel, Carl William. "Towards a Historical Sociology of Sport in the United States: 1825–1875." Doctoral dissertation, University of Oregon, 1992.

Stephen, Jennifer. *Pick One Intelligent Girl: Employability, Domesticity and the Gendering of Canada's Welfare State.* Toronto: University of Toronto Press, 2007.

Stewart, Mary Lynn. *Dressing Modern Frenchwomen: Marketing Haute Couture, 1919–1939.* Baltimore, MD: Johns Hopkins University Press, 2008.

Stoler, Ann Laura. "Racial Histories and Their Regimes of Truth." In *Race Critical Theories: Text and Context,* ed. Philomena Essed and David Theo Goldberg, 369–70. Malden, MA: Blackwell, 2002.

Stoneley, Peter. *A Queer History of the Ballet.* London: Routledge, 2007.

Strange, Carolyn. *Toronto's Girl Problem: The Perils and Pleasures of the City, 1880–1930.* Toronto: University of Toronto Press, 1995.

Strange, Carolyn. "The Undercurrents of Penal Culture: Punishment of the Body in Mid-Twentieth-Century Canada." *Law and History Review* 19, no. 2 (2001): 343–85. http://dx.doi.org/10.2307/744133.

Strate, Grant. *Grant Strate: A Memoir.* Toronto: Dance Collection Danse Press/es, 2002.

Strong-Boag, Veronica. "Canada's Wage-Earning Wives and the Construction of the Middle Class, 1945–60." *Journal of Canadian Studies/Revue d'études Canadiennes* 29, no. 3 (1994): 5–25.

Sussman, Herbert. *Victorian Masculinities: Manhood and Masculine Poetics in Early Victorian Literature and Art.* Cambridge: Cambridge University Press, 1995.

Swart, Sandra. "A Boer and His Gun and His Wife Are Three Things Always Together: Republican Masculinity and the 1914 Rebellion." *Journal of Southern African Studies* 24, no. 4 (1998): 737–51. http://dx.doi.org/10.1080/03057079808708599.

Szasz, Thomas. *The Therapeutic State: Psychiatry in the Mirror of Current Events.* New York: Prometheus, 1984.

Tembeck, Iro Valaskakis. "Dance, the Church, and Repressive Morals in Catholic Quebec." In *Right to Dance: Dancing for Rights,* ed. Naomi M. Jackson. Banff: Banff Centre Press, 2004.

Terry, Jennifer, and Jacqueline L. Urla, eds. *Deviant Bodies: Critical Perspectives on Difference in Science and Popular Culture.* Indianapolis, IN: Indiana University Press, 1995.

Testi, Arnaldo. "The Gender of Reform Politics: Theodore Roosevelt and the Culture of Masculinity." *Journal of American History* 81, no. 4 (1995): 1509–33. http://dx.doi.org/10.2307/2081647.

Thacker, Robert. "Canada's Mounted: The Evolution of a Legend." *Journal of Popular Culture* 14, no. 2 (1980): 298–312. http://dx.doi.org/10.1111/j.0022-3840.1980.1402_298.x.

Theobald, Majorie. "Teachers, Memory and Oral History." In *Telling Women's*

Lives: Narrative Inquiries in the History of Women's Education, ed. Kathleen Weiler and Sue Middleton, 19–24. Philadelphia, PA: Open University Press, 1999.

Thobani, Sunera. *Exalted Subjects: Studies in the Making of Race and Nation in Canada.* Toronto: University of Toronto Press, 2007.

Tillotson, Shirley. "Human Rights Law as Prism: Women's Organizations, Unions and Ontario's Female Employees Fair Remuneration Act, 1951." *Canadian Historical Review* 72, no. 4 (1991): 532–57. http://dx.doi.org/10.3138/CHR-072-04-05.

Tillotson, Shirley. *The Public at Play: Gender and the Politics of Recreation in Post-War Ontario.* Toronto: University of Toronto Press, 2000.

Tinkler, Penny, and Cheryl Krasnick Warsh. "Feminine Modernity in Interwar Britain and North America: Corsets, Cars, and Cigarettes." *Journal of Women's History* 20, no. 3 (2008): 113–43. http://dx.doi.org/10.1353/jowh.0.0024.

Tosh, John. "What Should Historians Do with Masculinity? Reflections on Nineteenth-Century Britain." *History Workshop* 38, no. 1 (1994): 179–202. http://dx.doi.org/10.1093/hwj/38.1.179.

Trachtenberg, Alan. "The Group Portrait." In *Multiple Exposure: The Group Portrait in Photography.* Exh. Cat, ed. Leslie Tonkonow and Alan Trachtenberg, 11–23. New York: Independent Curators, 1995.

Treichler, Paula A., Lisa Cartwright, and Constance Penley, eds. *The Visible Woman: Imaging Technologies, Gender and Science.* New York: New York University Press, 1998.

Trépanier, Esther. "A Consideration of the Nude and Artistic Modernity in Canada." In *The Nude in Modern Canadian Art, 1920–1950.* Exh. Cat., ed. Michèle Grandbois et al. Quebec City: Musée national des beaux-arts du Québec, 2009.

Triggs, Stanley G. *The Composite Photographs of William Notman.* Montreal: McCord Museum, 1994.

Turner, Bryan S. *The Body and Society.* 2nd ed. London: Sage, 1996.

Turner, John Peter. *The North-West Mounted Police, 1873–1893.* Ottawa: E. Cloutier, King's Printer, 1950.

Turner, Terence C. "The Social Skin." In *Not Work Alone,* ed. J. Cherfas and R. Lewyn, 112–40. Beverly Hills, CA: Temple Smith, 1980.

Turner Wilcox, R. *The Mode in Furs: The History of Furred Costume of the World from the Earliest Times to the Present.* New York: Charles Scribner's Sons, 1951.

Valverde, Mariana. *The Age of Light, Soap and Water: Moral Reform in English Canada, 1885–1920.* Toronto: McClelland and Stewart, 1991.

Valverde, Mariana. *Diseases of the Will: Alcohol and the Dilemmas of Freedom.* Cambridge: Cambridge University Press, 1998.

van Dijck, José. *The Transparent Body: A Cultural Analysis of Medical Imaging.* Seattle, WA: University of Washington Press, 2005.

Varela, Francisco, Evan Thompson, and Eleanor Rosch. *The Embodied Mind: Cognitive Science and Human Experience.* Cambridge, MA: MIT Press, 1991.

Vellathottam, T. George, and Kevin G. Jones. "Highlights in the Development of Canadian Lacrosse to 1931." *Canadian Journal of History of Sport and Physical Education* 5, no. 2 (1974): 31–47

Vertinsky, Patricia. *The Eternally Wounded Woman: Women, Doctors and Exercise in the Late Nineteenth Century.* Manchester: Manchester University Press, 1990.

Vokey, Scott. "Inspiration for Insurrection or Harmless Humour? Class and Politics in the Editorial Cartoons of Three Toronto Newspapers during the Early 1930s." *Labour/Le Travail* 45 (2000): 141–70.

Wakewich, P. "Contours of Everyday Life: Women's Reflections on Embodiment and Health Over Time." In *The Gendered Society Reader.* Canadian Edition, ed. Michael S. Kimmel, Amy Aronson, and Amy Kaler, 321–8. Don Mills, ON: Oxford University Press, 2008.

Wakewich, P., and H. Smith. "The Politics of 'Selective' Memory: Revisioning Women's Wartime Work in the Canadian Public Record." *Oral History* 34, no. 2 (2006): 56–68.

Wakewich, P., H. Smith, and J. Lynes. "Women's Wartime Work and Identities: Women Workers at Canadian Car and Foundry Co. Limited, Fort William, Ontario, 1938–1945." In *Framing Our Past: Canadian Women's History in the Twentieth Century*, ed. S. Cook, L. McLean, and K. O'Rourke, 409–16. Montreal and Kingston: McGill-Queen's University Press, 2001.

Walden, Keith. "The Road to Fat City: An Interpretation of the Development of Weight Consciousness in Western Society." *Historical Reflections/Réflexions historiques* 12, no. 3 (1985): 331–73.

Walden, Keith. "Speaking Modern: Language, Culture, and Hegemony in Grocery Window Displays, 1887–1920." *Canadian Historical Review* 70, no. 3 (1989): 285–310. http://dx.doi.org/10.3138/CHR-070-03-01.

Walden, Keith. *Becoming Modern in Toronto: The Industrial Exhibition and the Shaping of a Late Victorian Culture.* Toronto: University of Toronto Press, 1997.

Walker, Barrington. "Killing the Black Female Body: Black Womanhood, Black Patriarchy, and Spousal Murder in Two Ontario Criminal Trials, 1892–1894." In *Sisters or Strangers? Immigrant, Ethnic, and Racialized Women in Canadian History*, ed. Marlene Epp, Franca Iacovetta, and Frances Swyripa, 89–107. Toronto: University of Toronto Press, 2004.

Walkerdine, Valerie, and Helen Lucey. *Democracy in the Kitchen: Regulating Mothers and Socialising Daughters.* London: Virago, 1989.

Wamsley, Kevin B. "The Public Importance of Men and the Importance of Public Men: Sport and Masculinities in 19th Century Canada." In *Sport and Gender in Canada*, ed. Philip White and Kevin Young, 75–92. New York: Oxford University Press, 1999.

Watson, Elwood, and Darcy Martin, eds. *"There She Is, Miss America": The Politics of Sex, Beauty, and Race in America's Most Famous Pageant.* New York: Palgrave Macmillan, 2004.

Weaver, John C. *The Great Land Rush and the Making of the Modern World, 1650–1900.* Montreal and Kingston: McGill-Queen's University Press, 2003.

Weber, Sandra, and Claudia Mitchell. *"That's Funny, You Don't Look like a Teacher": Interrogating Images and Identity in Popular Culture.* Washington, DC: Falmer, 1995. http://dx.doi.org/10.4324/9780203453568.

Whitaker, Reg, and Gary Marcuse. *Cold War Canada: The Making of a National Insecurity State, 1945–1957.* Toronto: University of Toronto Press, 1994.

White, Anne. "The *Persons* Case, 1929: A Legal Definition of Women as Persons." In *Framing Our Past: Canadian Women's History in the Twentieth Century,* ed. Sharon Anne Cook, Lorna R. McLean, and Kate O'Rourke, 216–21. Montreal and Kingston: McGill-Queen's University Press, 2001.

Williams, John. *Turning to Nature in Germany: Hiking, Nudism, and Nature Conservation, 1900–1940.* Stanford, CA: Stanford University Press, 2007.

Wilson, Diana Drake. "Realizing Memory, Transforming History." In *Museums and Memory,* ed. Susan Crane, 115–36. Stanford, CA: Stanford University Press, 2000.

Wilson, Shawn. *Research Is Ceremony.* Halifax: Fernwood, 2008.

Winks, Robin. *The Blacks in Canada: A History.* Montreal and Kingston: McGill-Queen's University Press, 1997.

Wolkowitz, Carol. "The Social Relations of Body Work." *Work, Employment and Society* 16, no. 3 (2002): 497–510. http://dx.doi.org/10.1177/095001702762217452.

Wolkowitz, Carol. *Bodies at Work.* London: Sage, 2006.

Woodcock, George. *The Monk and His Message: Undermining the Myth of History.* Vancouver: Douglas and McIntyre, 1992.

Woycke, James. *Au Naturel: The History of Nudism in Canada.* Etobicoke, ON: Federation of Canadian Naturists, 2003.

Wright, Cynthia. "'Feminine Trifles of Vast Importance': Writing Gender into the History of Consumption." In *Gender Conflicts: New Essays in Women's History,* ed. Franca Iacovetta and Mariana Valverde, 229–60. Toronto: University of Toronto Press, 1992.

Wright, Donald. "W.D. Lighthall and David Ross McCord: Antimodernism and English-Canadian Imperialism, 1880s–1918." *Journal of Canadian Studies/Revue d'études canadiennes* 32, no. 2 (1997): 134–53.

Wright, Don. *The Professionalization of History in English Canada.* Toronto: University of Toronto Press, 2005. http://dx.doi.org/10.3138/CHR.81.1.29.

Yuval-Davis, Nira. "Women, Citizenship and Difference." *Feminist Review* 57, no. 1 (1997): 4–27. http://dx.doi.org/10.1080/014177897339632.

Contributors

Tarah Brookfield is an assistant professor of history and youth and children's studies at Wilfrid Laurier University, Waterloo, Ontario. She is the author of *Cold War Comforts: Canadian Women, Child Safety, and Global Insecurity* (2012).

George Colpitts is an associate professor of history at the University of Calgary. He specializes in environmental history and researches human relationships with wild animals, the fur trade, and the social history of the Canadian fur industry. He is the author of *Game in the Garden: A Human History of Wildlife in Western Canada to 1940* (2002).

Patrizia Gentile is an associate professor at the Institute of Interdisciplinary Studies at Carleton University, Ottawa. She is co-author of *The Canadian War on Queers: National Security as Sexual Regulation* (2010). Her research interests include the history of beauty contests in Canada.

Kathryn Harvey is an historian (Ph.D., McGill University) and community activist. Having taught at McGill University, L'Université du Québec à Montréal (UQAM), and Carleton University, her most recent projects include creating an online course on the history of feminism for Athabasca University, in Alberta; oral history workshops with seniors; and mapping the cultural history of Montreal's southwest neighbourhoods. In 2008, she won the Canadian Historical Association award for best article.

Cheryl Krasnick Warsh is a professor of history at Vancouver Island University, Nanaimo, British Columbia, and past editor-in-chief of the *Canadian Bulletin of Medical History*. Her books include *Prescribed Norms:*

Women and Health in Canada and the United States since 1800 (2010), *Gender, Health and Popular Culture: Historical Perspectives* (2011), and *Moments of Unreason: The Practice of Canadian Psychiatry and the Homewood Retreat, 1883–1923* (1989).

Allana C. Lindgren is an associate professor of theatre at the University of Victoria, British Columbia. She is the author of *From Automatism to Modern Dance* (2003), the co-editor (with Kaija Pepper) of *Renegade Bodies: Canadian Dance in the 1970s,* and the dance editor for the *Routledge Encyclopedia of Modernism.* Her articles have appeared in a variety of journals, including *Dance Research Journal, Dance Chronicle, Circuit: Musiques contemporaines,* and *Theatre Research in Canada.*

Kristina R. Llewellyn is an assistant professor in social development studies at Renison University College, University of Waterloo. Her areas of teaching and research include history of education, sociology of education, citizenship education, gender and education, child/youth studies, qualitative methods, and social policy. Her current project is a SSHRC-funded study *Citizens of the World: Youth, Global Citizenship, and the Model United Nations.* She is the author of *Democracy's Angels: The Work of Women Teachers,* (2012).

Greg Marquis is a professor in the Department of History and Politics at the University of New Brunswick Saint John, where he teaches courses in Canadian and criminal justice history. His current research interests include the history of alcohol and drug regulation and Canadian popular culture.

Valerie Minnett is a Ph.D. candidate in the history department at Carleton University. She holds an M.Arch from McGill University. Her dissertation is tentatively titled "The Prescription and the Cure: Children's Bodies and Ideal Health in Canada, 1902–1940."

Wendy Mitchinson is a professor and Canada Research Chair in Gender and Medical History at the University of Waterloo. She has written widely on the history of women. Her most recent books are *Giving Birth in Canada, 1900–1950* and *Body Failure: Medical Views of Women, 1900–1950.* She is currently writing a book on the history of obesity, with the title "Fighting Fat in Canada, 1920–1980."

Jane Nicholas is an associate professor in the Department of Women's Studies at Lakehead University. Her book manuscript, "The Modern Girl: Feminine Modernities, the Body, and Commodities in the 1920s," is under contract with the University of Toronto Press. Her current SSHRC-funded project is on the history of the freak show in twentieth-century North America.

Gillian Poulter is an associate professor of Canadian history at Acadia University, in Nova Scotia, as well as coordinator of the Women's and Gender Studies Program there. She is interested in the ways in which ordinary people commemorate their lives, and her current project examines funeral rituals in rural Nova Scotia. She is the author of *Becoming Native in a Foreign Land: Sport, Visual Culture, and Identity in Montreal, 1840–1885*.

Myra Rutherdale is an associate professor in the Department of History at York University, Toronto. Her interests are in the area of colonial social formation, and she is currently at work on her second monograph, tentatively entitled "The Clean Igloo," which analyses the introduction of Westernized medicine into northern Canadian communities during the years from 1900 to 1970.

Bonnie Reilly Schmidt is a Ph.D. candidate at Simon Fraser University in British Columbia. From 1977 to 1987, she served as a police officer with the Royal Canadian Mounted Police. She is now in the final writing stages of her SSHRC-funded research entitled "Women in Red Serge: Female Police Bodies and the Disruption of the Image of the Royal Canadian Mounted Police." She has published articles in the *RCMP Quarterly* and the *Journal of the Canadian Historical Association*. Bonnie has also served as an adviser for an award-winning CBC Radio documentary titled, "First Ladies of the RCMP," which aired in 2011.

Mary-Ann Shantz holds a Ph.D. in history from Carleton University. She teaches at MacEwan University in Edmonton, Alberta, and is currently pursuing a research project on urban childhood in early twentieth-century Canada.

Amy Shaw is an associate professor of history at the University of Lethbridge. She is the author of *Crisis of Conscience: Conscientious Objection in*

Canada during the First World War, and the co-editor of *A Sisterhood of Suffering and Service: Women and Girls of Canada and Newfoundland during the First World War.*

Helen Smith (1956–2012). It is with great sadness that we report that Dr. Helen Smith passed away on 22 January 2012. Jointly appointed to the departments of history and women's studies at Lakehead University, in 1990, Helen Smith pioneered the study of women's and gender history at Lakehead and played a central role in the development of the Women's Studies Program. She was a passionate and engaging teacher and a generous mentor to her colleagues. Her previous work with collaborator Pamela Wakewich, on national ideals of gendered citizenship, cultural representations, and oral histories of Canadian women's wartime work, has appeared in *Gender & History, Oral History,* and *Labour/Le travail* as well as edited collections on Canadian women's and labour history. Dr. Smith will be greatly missed by students, colleagues, and members of the Canadian women's history community.

Pandora Syperek is completing doctoral studies in the history of art at University College London, where she teaches on modern and contemporary art and display practices. Funded by the Social Science and Humanities Research Council of Canada, her research focuses on the gendered aesthetics of jewel-like objects in the formation of London's Natural History Museum. Her essay, "'No Fancy So Wild': Slippery Gender Models in the Coral Gallery" is forthcoming in the anthology *Framing the Ocean, 1700 to the Present: The Sea as Social Space in Western Art* (Ashgate), edited by Tricia Cusack.

Anne Toews is a Ph.D. student in the history department at York University. She holds an M.A. in history from Simon Fraser University.

Pamela Wakewich is a professor of sociology and women's studies at Lakehead University, with a cross-appointment in human sciences at the Northern Ontario School of Medicine. Her contribution in this volume, with long-time and sadly missed collaborator, Helen Smith, is part of a larger research program on gender, place, health, and the body in historical and contemporary contexts. Her papers have been published in *Gender & History, Oral History, Labour/Le travail, Medical Anthropology,* and *Canadian Family Physician,* as well as in edited collections on Canadian women's health, gender and society, and women's labour history. Her current research explores the cultural environments shaping adolescent decision making regarding the HPV vaccine and culturally sensitive cervical cancer screening programs for Aboriginal women in Northern Ontario.

Barrington Walker is an sssociate professor of history at Queen's University, where he is also cross-appointed to the departments of cultural studies and gender studies. He is the author of *Race on Trial: Black Defendants in Ontario's Criminal Courts, 1858–1958*. His most recent publication is an edited collection entitled *The African Canadian Legal Odyssey: Historical Essays*.

Index

Aboriginal, 40–1, 44, 58, 71, 79, 99,
117–19, 121, 125–8, 258–9. *See also*
First Nations; Indigenous; Inuit
Adams, David, 184–6, 188, 195
adolescence, 270. *See also* teenagers
advertisements, 14, 141–2, 204, 210,
217, 270, 311, 321; alcohol, liquor,
16, 205, 209, 216–18; billboard,
205, 215; Canadian Banana Company Ltd, 277; drug, 278; and local
businesses, 313; *Mediscope*, 292;
newspaper, 137, 220; sexualized,
294. *See also* alcohol
alcohol, 16, 203–4, 207, 212; abuse,
39, 219; commercials, 217; companies, 211, consumption, 209–10,
216; industry, 205, 218; and provincial regulations, 210; women's access to, 211. *See also* drinking; drugs
Alkerton, Carl, 233, 235, 240
Anglo-Boer War, 14, 97–8, 104, 109
Archer, Herbert, 368
Armstrong, George, 193
Art Gallery of Toronto, 17, 155, 157,
160, 162–3, 165, 169–70, 174
Arctic, 117, 118, 121, 130. *See also*
northern Canada

authority, 33, 42, 347, 349, 356, 361,
372; administrative, 192; civic, 369,
374, 379–80; on fur cutting, 140;
male teachers, 355; masculine, 351,
371; medical, 299; moral, 347; patriarchal, 317; professional, 34, 300;
social, 228; state, 371–2, 376, 380

Baartman, Saartjie, 293, 302n19
Banfield, Beverly, 197
Barnett, Anita, 191
Beers, George, 80–2, 85–6
Bennett, R.B., 332
Bertin, Leonard, 294
biopolitics, 10, 12–13, 50–2
Black, 12–13, 51; body, 55; experience in Canada, 53; as inferior, 50;
longshoremen, 210; model, 162;
nude, 161, 171; schools, 56; students, 53, 57–8
Black Week, 98, 106
body: aging, 323; as a category of
historical inquiry, 8; colonizer's,
13; as cultural text, 118; deviant,
315; female, 14, 137, 148, 157,
172–4, 237–8, 305, 308, 311, 373–8;
as machine, 291; male, 14, 70, 79,

90, 311, 371–2; as metaphor, 331;
national, 60, 85; racialized, 13, 51;
in relation to health, 11; in relation
to nation, 4; sensual 35; as site of
social and cultural change, 290;
social, 306–7, 309; as surface, 17; as
tactical didactic tool, 329; transparent, 288, 290; type, 135, 137
body history, 5–6, 9, 12, 14, 134, 269
body image, 276
Boers, 98–9, 101–3, 104, 107
Bourne, Diane, 191
Bridle, Augustus, 159–60
Brooker, Bertram, 157, 160, 167–70,
173–4. See also censorship
Bruch, Hilde, 275. See also obesity
Buchanan, Donald, 155, 159, 167, 169,
171–2, 179n65. See also censorship
Buck, Tim, 340

Campbell, Walter R., 277
Canadian Group of Painters, 155,
159–60, 163, 171
Canadian National Exhibition
(CNE), 157, 160, 286
Canadian Nutrition Program, 274
Canadian soldiers, 14, 97, 100, 105–6,
109. See also Anglo-Boer War
Canadian Sunbathing Association
(CSA), 17, 228, 231–2
Cappon, Daniel, 275–6
Carr, Catherine, 197
Carter, Dyson, 338
Casselman, Cora Taylor Watt, 251
censorship, 16, 157, 160, 167, 174. See
also Brooker, Bertram; Buchanan,
Donald; nude
Chamberlain, Joseph, 98
children, 51, 87, 108, 118, 123–4, 127,
129, 170, 188, 233, 250, 294, 339;

Aboriginal, 117; in ads, 205, 208;
Black, 54, 61; bodies, 11, 18–19,
125, 271, 279–80, 335; healthy, 269,
271; Inuit, 274; marriage and, 352;
obese, obesity in, 269, 271, 273–4,
279; proper feeding of, 307; White
middle-class, 270; working-class,
356.
citizenship, 4–5, 13, 205, 262, 291,
336, 349, 369, 371; Canadian, 97;
cultural inscription of 16; embodied, 17, 230, 240–1; gendered, 290,
298, 300, 305; global, 259; healthy,
306; heterosexual, 347; imperialism
and, 14; masculinity and, 109, 350,
376; nationhood and, 7; participatory, 348; and representations of
beauty, 258. See also nationalism
Clark, Paraskeva, 159, 168, 172
clothing, 13–14, 81, 89–90, 117, 138,
149, 193, 227, 355, 372, 377; and
bodily hygiene, 118; Indigenous,
71, 79; infant, 123; lack of, 123; as
marker of colonial change, 119;
men's, 317, 356; nudism and, 237;
second-hand, 127; as uniform,
311; western-styled, 118, 126, 128;
winter, 71, 121–2; worn by soldiers,
109. See also fashion
Cold War, 197, 248, 250–1, 255, 330,
337–8
colonization, 4, 13, 15, 43–4, 118, 348
communism, 340, 347
concentration camps, 108
Connett, Ray, 230, 238–9
consumerism, 14–15, 129, 135, 269
corporeality, 7, 73, 100, 180, 195–6,
369, 380
cultural: hybridity, 127; narratives,
180, 371

D'Arcy McGee, Thomas, 70

Davis, William, 335

death, 5, 31, 39, 52, 62, 108–9, 332–3, 340; beaten to, 335; and capitalism, 337; premature, 339; rate, 108

democracy, 240, 250, 339, 348–9; and citizenship, 20, 355, 358; liberal, 361; postwar, 20, 351, 360; social, 171

Dempsey, Lotta, 294–5

dieting, 277–9

doctors, 18, 119, 126, 278, 286–7, 291, 294, 299, 307, 328, 331, 355, 378. *See also* health; medicine; nurses; physicians

drinking, 204, 207, 209–11, 217, 220; age, 214; mixed-gender, 211. *See also* alcohol; drugs

drugs, 277–8. *See also* alcohol; drinking

Duke of Edinburgh, 387

Duncan, Isadora, 189

dyeing, 135, 138, 140, 142, 145. *See also* clothing

eating habits, 270–1, 275, 277, 280, 309

educational psychology, 13, 50, 52, 62–3, 354

embodiment, 5–6, 19, 101, 180, 186, 230, 241, 321, 351; and body work, 306; concept of, 5; feminine, 322; of history, 4; of male power, 315; national, 349–50, 358; and performance of identity, 70; of postwar norms, 360; racialized, 13, 15; wartime, 320

eugenics, 358

Ewen, Tom, 335

exercise, 79, 85, 89, 157, 193, 276–7,

279, 334, 376; character building, 250; lack of, 376; mental, 57; patriotic, 105. *See also* fitness

exhibition, 19, 38, 73, 155, 162, 165, 258, 286–8, 291, 293–4, 298; art, 175; of First Nations, 41; of heterosexual behaviour, 354; of Lady X, 290; of nudes, 170

fashion, 14–15, 117–20, 128, 138, 140, 145, 148–9, 157, 160, 252–3; accessories, 134; celebrity, 135; designer, 378; infant, 123; magazines, 255; models, 209, 314; modern, 129; show, 117, 130, 139, 146. *See also* clothing

fat, 277; bodies; 18; boys, 337; cells, 274–5; children, 272, 274. *See also* obesity

femininity, 14, 118, 219, 226, 240–1, 298, 312–15, 317, 320–2, 350, 353–5, 359–60, 369, 377, 379, 380; beauty and, 261; loss of, 239, 313; stereotypical, 191–2, unbridled, 351. *See also* masculinity

feminism, 218, 262; second-wave, 9, 204

First Nations, 31–2, 36, 41–4, 70–1, 79, 258, 371. *See also* Aboriginal; Inuit

First World War, 5, 134, 135, 139, 207, 269, 271, 339. *See also* Second World War

fitness, 227, 230, 271, 273, 276–7, 297. *See also* exercise

Four Seasons Nature Park, 232, 234–6

Franca, Celia, 180, 181, 183, 184, 191–2, 193, 196. *See also* National Ballet of Canada

fur, 124, 125, 128, 129, 135, 171, 203,

253; garments, 139, 149; industry, 145, 149; processing, 15; retail-manufacturers, 142; trade, 71, 73; widespread use of, 138. *See also* fashion

gaze: of empirical science, 34; female, 174; of an imagined audience, 295; male, masculine, 137, 173, 174; medical, 19, 287, 290, 294, 300; of newcomers, 124; nude bodies and, 226; nudist, 230, 238; public's, 255; as voyeuristic, 165; women as object of, 239
Gotshalks, Jury, 186, 188
Great Depression, 159, 334, 337
Group of Seven, 155, 158–9, 160–1, 169, 170

Haig, G.T., 273
Haliburton, Robert Grant, 70
Harris, Mildred, 239
Hawirko, Leonore, 278
health, 4, 5, 10, 11, 18–19, 79, 101, 185, 287, 291, 297–9, 329, 331, 334, 336, 338, 340; alcohol, 203–4, 219; children's, 269–73, 277; experts, 279; gender, 89, 356, hygiene, 126 insurance, 339; mental, 227–8, 230, 238, 240–1, 354; nudism, 226–31, 240–1; public health, 51–2, 214, 288, 290, 292, 305–11; sport, 80. *See also* citizenship; doctors; medicine; nurses; obesity; physicians
Heeney, Arnold, 195
Heward, Prudence, 160–1, 170, 172–3
Holgate, Edwin, 160–2, 165–6, 170
homosexual, homosexuality, 183–4, 186, 370
Hughes, Thomas, 80

identity, 7, 44; Canadian, 9, 38, 71, 86, 89–90, 258; clothing and, 119, 126; construction of, 229; crisis, 257; cultural and social, 118; formation, 17; male, masculine, 105, 371; middle-class, 90; national, 70, 80, 90–1, 248; "new woman," 360; religious, 90; sexual, 231, 292, 293
immigrants, 17, 51, 227, 257, 261, 270, 235, 358
imperialism, 13, 14, 37, 39, 50, 97–8, 103–6, 110
Indigenous: bodies of, 13, 15, 44; clothing, 79; conceptions of bodies, 11; cultural genocide of, 43; objects, 39; in prison, 43; sports, 13. *See also* Aboriginal; First Nations; Inuit
internationalism, 247–9, 251–2, 255, 256, 260
Inuit, 118, 122–7, 129; children, 274. *See also* Aboriginal; First Nations
IQ, 50–1, 53–4; measurements, 58; race and, 62–3; testing, 13, 52, 57

Jackson, A.Y., 161

Kelly, Grace, 212
Kent County, 49, 53–6, 59, 61–2
Khrushchev, Nikita, 340
King, William Lyon Mackenzie, 207
Korean War, 248–9
Kruger, Paul, 99

labour, 138, 186, 330, 333–4, 336, 341n7, 342n13; labour and the body, 306–7, 309, 332; labour and health, 18; labourers, 39; women's labour 308–9, 351
labour history, 10

lacrosse, 13, 70, 71, 80–7, 90
Landon, Fred, 49, 53–4, 56
Lansdowne, (Lord) Henry Charles
    Keith Pett-Fitz Maurice, 76
LaRoque, Sharon, 258, 259, 260
Lindsay, Lionel M., 272, 274, 276–8
Lisiecki, Ted, 235–6
Lismer, Arthur, 169
Livingstone, Kay, 251
Lyman, John, 161

Macdonald, John A., 370
Maguire, Trevor, 332
Majuba Day, 106
malnutrition, 18, 270, 271, 275, 280,
    336. *See also* nutrition
Martel, Antonio, 278
Marx, Karl, 330, 331, 333
Marxism, 329–30
masculinity, 14, 15, 73,91, 98, 100,
    105–6, 118, 185, 195, 371; and
    alcohol, 204, 209, 212, 219; Black,
    12; citizenship, 97, 109, 376; in
    contrast with femininity, 377, 379,
    380; heterosexual, 186. *See also*
    femininity
McCord, David Ross, 31–6, 38–42, 44.
    See also museum
McCrimmon, Jean, 294
media, 181, 183, 189, 195, 203, 204,
    207, 210, 215, 216, 218, 220, 233–4,
    239, 253, 288, 290, 292, 294, 298,
    311, 352, 368, 373, 375
medicine, 18–19, 125, 129, 210, 214–
    15, 227, 269–71, 276, 288, 290–5,
    308, 331, 334, 339, 351; bodies of
    medical workers, 126; medical his-
    tory, 10–11; medical profession,
    120, 124, 279, 286, 299–301; medi-
    cal science, 274; medicalization, 18,

354, 357. *See also* doctors health;
    nurses; physicians
memory, 32, 34–6, 40–1, 44, 79, 108,
    320, 323, 356
Miss America, 231, 232, 262
Miss Canada, 16, 76, 231, 251, 252,
    258
Miss Edmonton, 252, 253
Miss Nude, 232–6, 237–40
missionaries, 102, 119–21, 123, 127–8,
    353
modernism, 145, 158, 160, 171, 173
mother blaming, 271
Muhlstock, Louis, 155, 157
multiculturalism, 247, 257, 258, 260,
    263
museum, 31–2, 34–44, 291, 292

National Ballet of Canada, 181–2,
    183, 185, 189, 191, 193–7
nationalism, 17, 20, 38–9, 98, 104,
    162, 182. *See also* citizenship
Newton, Lilias Torrance, 16, 155–8,
    160, 162–3, 165, 167, 169–75
North-West Mounted Police, 109,
    370
northern Canada, 119. *See also* Arctic
Notman, William, 71, 73, 76, 81, 90
nuclear family, 188, 347, 349, 353,
    355–6, 357, 360, 378
nurses, 119, 121, 126, 127, 286, 355,
    378. *See also* doctors; health; medi-
    cine
nutrition, 204, 270, 271–6, 279, 280,
    308–9, 333, 334. *See also* malnu-
    trition

Oak, Lorraine, 250, 254, 256
obesity, 11, 18, 269–80, 307, 336. *See
    also* fat

Onofrey, Dennis, 368
Ontario Society of Artists, 157, 160, 165, 169
organ theft, 328, 335

ParticipACTION, 277
Pavlov, Ivan, 331
Pearson, Lester B., 248, 250
physicians, 270–1, 272, 274–9, 290–2, 294–5, 299–300. *See also* doctors; health; medicine; nurses
pornography, 167, 174
Prince Philip, 277, 287
prudery, 165, 167
psychology, 13, 50, 52, 62–3, 228, 271, 276, 354
puritanism, 166–7

queer, 357. *See also* homosexual; homosexuality

Reims, Charles, 328, 330
Roberts, (Lord), Frederick Sleigh, 98, 106–7
Robertson, S.F., 292
Roosevelt, Eleanor, 248
Royal Commission on the Status of Women, 372
Ruehle, Karl, 235, 236–7
Russell, John Wentworth, 157, 167–70, 172–4
Ryerson, Stanley B., 339

Second World War, 16, 157, 203, 207, 226, 227, 248, 251, 270, 274, 275, 305, 330, 337, 347, 354, 373, 378. *See also* First World War
Smith, Candace, 368
snowshoeing, 13, 71, 73, 76, 79, 80, 81, 86, 89, 90

socialism, 20, 329, 330, 331, 336–8, 340
Soviet Union, 330–1, 337–40
spinster, 347, 351, 357–60, 373; teachers, 347, 351
Sprague, P.H., 278
St Laurent, Louis, 181, 339
Stalin, Josef, 337, 340
Stein, Lisa, 232, 234–5, 237
Steinem, Gloria, 218
Stevens, Dorothy, 161, 165–6, 172–3

Tanser, H.A. See educational psychology; IQ
teachers: lesbian, 357, 360; male, 350, 353, 355; mental health in, 354
teenagers, 117–18, 272–3, 277. See adolescence
Thompson, J. Walter, 205
Tidmarsh, F.W., 274–5
tobogganing, 13, 71, 76, 86, 89, 90
Trotsky, Leon, 331

Uitlanders, 99
Underground Railroad (UGGR), 13, 49–50, 53, 54, 55, 63. *See also* Blacks
United Nations (U.N.), 247–50, 252–3, 255, 257, 260–1
United Nations Association (UNA), 248–51, 252–3, 256, 259–60
United Nations Children Fund (UNICEF), 250, 262

von Hagens, Gunther, 301, 304n41

Whiteness: and the Canadian nation, 17; institutionalized, 13; as social norm, 182
White-settler, 37, 42
winter carnivals, 86, 89–90

STUDIES IN GENDER AND HISTORY

General Editors: Franca Iacovetta and Karen Dubinsky

1 Suzanne Morton, *Ideal Surroundings: Domestic Life in a Working-Class Suburb in the 1920s*

2 Joan Sangster, *Earning Respect: The Lives of Working Women in Small-Town* Ontario, *1920–1960*

3 Carolyn Strange, *Toronto's Girl Problem: The Perils and Pleasures of the City, 1880–1930*

4 Sara Z. Burke, *Seeking the Highest Good: Social Service and Gender at the University of Toronto, 1888–1937*

5 Lynne Marks, *Revivals and Roller Rinks: Religion, Leisure, and Identity in Late-Nineteenth-Century Small-Town Ontario*

6 Cecilia Morgan, *Public Men and Virtuous Women: The Gendered Languages of Religion and Politics in Upper Canada, 1791–1850*

7 Mary Louise Adams, *The Trouble with Normal: Postwar Youth and the Making of Heterosexuality*

8 Linda Kealey, *Enlisting Women for the Cause: Women, Labour, and the Left in Canada, 1890–1920*

9 Christina Burr, *Spreading the Light: Work and Labour Reform in Late-Nineteenth-Century Toronto*

10 Mona Gleason, *Normalizing the Ideal: Psychology, Schooling, and the Family in Postwar Canada*

11 Deborah Gorham, *Vera Brittain: A Feminist Life*

12 Marlene Epp, *Women without Men: Mennonite Refugees of the Second World War*

13 Shirley Tillotson, *The Public at Play: Gender and the Politics of Recreation in Postwar Ontario*

14 Veronica Strong-Boag and Carole Gerson, *Paddling Her Own Canoe: The Times and Texts of E. Pauline Johnson (Tekahionwake)*

15 Stephen Heathorn, *For Home, Country, and Race: Constructing Gender, Class, and Englishness in the Elementary School, 1880–1914*

16 Valerie J. Korinek, *Roughing It in the Suburbs: Reading* Chatelaine *Magazine in the Fifties and Sixties*

17 Adele Perry, *On the Edge of Empire: Gender, Race, and the Making of British Columbia, 1849–1871*

18 Robert A. Campbell, *Sit Down and Drink Your Beer: Regulating Vancouver's Beer Parlours, 1925–1954*

19 Wendy Mitchinson, *Giving Birth in Canada, 1900–1950*

20 Roberta Hamilton, *Setting the Agenda: Jean Royce and the Shaping of Queen's University*

21 Donna Gabaccia and Franca Iacovetta, eds, *Women, Gender, and Transnational Lives: Italian Workers of the World*

22 Linda Reeder, *Widows in White: Migration and the Transformation of Rural Women, Sicily, 1880–1920*

23 Terry Crowley, *Marriage of Minds: Isabel and Oscar Skelton Re-inventing Canada*

24 Marlene Epp, Franca Iacovetta, and Frances Swyripa, eds., *Sisters or Strangers? Immigrant, Ethnic, and Racialized Women in Canadian History*

25 John G. Reid, *Viola Florence Barnes, 1885–1979: A Historian's Biography*

26 Catherine Carstairs, *Jailed for Possession: Illegal Drug Use Regulation and Power in Canada, 1920–1961*

27 Magda Fahrni, *Household Politics: Montreal Families and Postwar Reconstruction*

28 Tamara Myers, *Caught: Montreal Girls and the Law, 1869–1945*

29 Jennifer A. Stephen, *Pick One Intelligent Girl: Employability, Domesticity, and the Gendering of Canada's Welfare State, 1939–1947*

30 Lisa Chilton, *Agents of Empire: British Female Migration to Canada and Australia, 1860s–1930*

31 Esyllt W. Jones, *Influenza 1918: Disease, Death, and Struggle in Winnipeg*

32 Elise Chenier, *Strangers in Our Midst: Sexual Deviancy in Postwar Ontario*

33 Lara Campbell, *Respectable Citizens: Gender, Family, and Unemployment in the Great Depression, Ontario, 1929–1939*

34 Katrina Srigley, *Breadwinning Daughters: Young Working Women in a Depression-era city, 1929–1939*

35 Maureen Moynagh with Nancy Forestell, eds., *Documenting First Wave Feminisms, Volume 1: Transnational Collaborations and Crosscurrents*

36 Mona Oikawa, *Cartographies of Violence: Women, Memory, and the Subject(s) of the "Internment"*

37 Karen Flynn, *Moving beyond Borders: A History of Black Canadian and Caribbean Women in the Diaspora*

38 Karen Balcom, *The Traffic in Babies: Cross Border Adoption and Baby-Selling Between the United States and Canada, 1930–1972*

39 Nancy M. Forestell and Maureen Moynagh, eds., *Documenting First Wave Feminisms, Volume II: Canada–National and Transnational Contexts*

40 Patrizia Gentile and Jane Nicholas, eds., *Contesting Bodies and Nation in Canadian History*